The
GENERAL
KNOWLEDGE
COMPENDIUM

For IAS Prelims General Studies (Paper1) & State PSC EXAM

- **Corporate Office :** 45, 2nd Floor, Maharishi Dayanand Marg, Corner Market, Malviya Nagar, New Delhi-110017

  Tel. : 011-49842349 / 49842350

Chief Editor : Satya Prakash
Compiled & Edited by : Satish Gupta

Typeset by Disha DTP Team

Printed at Repro Knowledgecast Limited, Thane

DISHA PUBLICATION

ALL RIGHTS RESERVED

For further information about the books from DISHA,

Log on to **www.dishapublication.com** or email to **info@dishapublication.com**

Contents

INTERNATIONAL & NATIONAL ORGANISATION

1
Chapter

UNITED NATIONS

Introduction

- The United Nations (UN) is an intergovernmental organization to promote international co-operation. A replacement for the ineffective **League of Nations**, the organization was established on **24 October 1945** after World War II in order to prevent another such conflict.

- In the century prior to the UN's creation, several international treaty organizations and conferences had been formed to regulate conflicts between nations, such as the **International Committee of the Red Cross** and the **Hague Conventions** of 1899 and 1907. Following the catastrophic loss of life in the First World War, **the Paris Peace Conference** established the League of Nations to maintain harmony between countries.

- The League lacked representation for colonial peoples (then half the world's population) and significant participation from several major powers, including the US, USSR, Germany, and Japan; it failed to act against the Japanese invasion of **Manchuria** in 1931, the Second Italo-Ethiopian War in 1935, the Japanese invasion of China in 1937, and German expansions under Adolf Hitler that culminated in the Second World War.

- The text of the "Declaration by United Nations" was drafted by President Franklin Roosevelt, British Prime Minister Winston Churchill, and Roosevelt aide Harry Hopkins, while meeting at the White House, 29 December 1941. **Roosevelt** first coined the term United Nations to describe the Allied countries. "On New Year's Day 1942, President Roosevelt, Prime Minister Churchill, Maxim Litvinov of the USSR, and T. V. Soong of China, signed a short document which later came to be known as the **United Nations Declaration** and the next day the representatives of twenty-two other nations added their signatures."

- The term **United Nations was first officially used when 26 governments signed this Declaration**. One major change from the Atlantic Charter was the addition of a provision for religious freedom, which Stalin approved after Roosevelt insisted. By 1 March 1945, 21 additional states had signed.

- The United Nations was formulated and negotiated among the delegations from the Soviet Union, the UK, the US and China at the Dumbarton Oaks Conference in 1944. After months of planning, the UN Conference on International Organization opened in San Francisco, 25 April 1945, attended by 50 governments and a number of non-governmental organizations involved in drafting the United Nations Charter. "

- The first meetings of the General Assembly, with 51 nations represented, and the Security Council took place in London beginning 6 January 1946. The General Assembly selected New York City as the site for the headquarters of the United Nations, and the facility was completed in 1952. Its site—like UN headquarters buildings in Geneva, Vienna, and Nairobi—is designated as international territory. The Norwegian Foreign Minister, Trygve Lie, was elected as the first UN Secretary-General.

The UN Flag and the Emblem

The UN General Assembly adopted the UN flag on 20 Oct. 1947. The white UN emblem is super-imposed on a light blue back ground. The emblem consists of the globe map projected from the North pole and embraced in twin olive branches (symbol of peace). The UN logo was approved on 7 Oct. 1946.

Aims and Objectives

The Main objectives of the UN are :
(1) To maintain peace and security in the world.
(2) To work together to remove poverty, disease and illiteracy and encourage respect for each other's rights of basic freedom.
(3) To develop friendly relations among nations.
(4) To be a centre to help nations achieve these common goals.

Membership

Chapter II, Article 4 of the UN Charter outlines the rules for membership:
1. Membership in the United Nations is open to all other peace-loving states that accept the obligations contained in the present Charter and, in the judgment of the Organization, are able and willing to carry out these obligations.
2. The admission of any such state to membership in the United Nations will be effected by a decision of the General Assembly upon the recommendation of the Security Council.

UN International Years/Decades/Weeks

The United Nations designates specific days, weeks, years and decades as occasions to mark particular events or topics in order to promote, through awareness and action, the objectives of the Organization. Usually, it is one or more Member States that propose these observances and the General Assembly establishes them with a resolution. On occasion, these celebrations are declared by the specialized agencies of the United Nations, such as UNESCO, UNICEF, FAO, etc., when they concern issues that fall within the scope of their competencies. Some of them may be later adopted by the General Assembly.

UN International Years

Year	
2000	International Year for the Culture of Peace; and International Year of Thanksgiving
2001	International Year of Volunteers; and United Nations Year of Dialogue among Civilizations; and International Year of Mobilization against Racism, Racial Discrimination, Xenophobia and Related Intolerance
2002	International Year of Mountains; and International Year of Culture Heritage; and International Year of Ecotourism
2003	International Year of Freshwater
2004	International Year to Commemorate the Struggle against Slavery and Its Abolition; and International Year of Rice
2005	International Year of Microcredit; and International Year for Sport and Physical Education
2006	International Year of Deserts and Desertification
2008	International Year of the Potato; and International Year of Planet Earth; and International Year of Sanitation; and International Year of Languages
2009	International Year of Human Rights Learning - from 10 December 2008 (Human Rights Day) to 10 December 2009 International Year of Reconciliation; and International Year of Natural Fibres; and International Year of Astronomy
2010	International Year of Biodiversity; and International Year for the Rapprochement of Cultures International Year of Youth: Dialogue and Mutual Understanding - from 12 August 2010 (International Youth Day) to 11 August 2011
2011	International Year of Forests; and International Year of Chemistry; and International Year for People of African Descent
2012	International Year of Cooperatives
2013	International Year of Water Cooperation.
2014	International Year of Family Farming & International Year of Crystallagraphy
2015	International Year of Light based Technologies International Year of soils.
2016	International Year of Pulses
2017	International Year of Sustainable Tourism for Development
2019	International Year of Indigenous Languages International Year of Moderation International Year of the Periodic Table of Chemical Elements
2022	International Year of Artisanal Fisheries and Aquaculture
2024	International Year of Camelids

UN International Decades

2021-2030	International Decade of Ocean Science for Sustainable Development
2019-2028	United Nations Decade of Family Farming
2018-2028	International Decade for Action "Water for Sustainable Development"
2016-2025	United Nations Decade of Action on Nutrition
2015-2024	International Decade for People of African Descent
2014-2024	United Nations Decade of Sustainable Energy for Art
2011–2020	Third International Decade for the Eradication of Colonialism. United Nations Decade on Biodiversity. Decade of Action for Road Safety.

2010–2020	United Nations Decade for Deserts and the Fight against Desertification.
2008–2017	Second United Nations Decade for the Eradication of Poverty.
2006–2016	Decade of Recovery and Sustainable Development of the Affected Regions (third decade after the Chernobyl disaster).
2005–2015	International Decade for Action, "Water for Life".
2005–2014	United Nations Decade of Education for Sustainable Development. Second International Decade of the World's Indigenous People.
2003–2012	United Nations Literacy Decade: Education for All.
2001–2010	International Decade for a Culture of Peace and Non-violence for the Children of the World. Decade to Roll Back Malaria in Developing Countries, Particularly in Africa. Second International Decade for the Eradication of Colonialism.

UN International Weeks

1–7 February	World Interfaith Harmony Week
21–27 March	Week of Solidarity with the Peoples Struggling against Racism and Racial Discrimination
24–30 April	World Immunization Week [WHO]
8–14 May 2017	UN Global Road Safety Week [WHO]
25–31 May	Week of Solidarity with the Peoples of Non-Self-Governing Territories
1–7 August	World Breastfeeding Week [WHO]
4–10 October	World Space Week
24–30 October	Disarmament Week
6–12 November	International Week of Science and Peace
13–19 November	World Antibiotic Awareness Week [WHO]

Quick Facts

Established	1945
Headquarters	New York
Member States	193
Official Language	Arabic, Chinese, English, French, Russian, and Spanish
United Nations Day	24 October
Six main bodies of the United Nations	The General Assembly, The Security Council, The Economic and Social Council, The Trusteeship Council, The International Court of Justice and The Secretariat

The Trusteeship Council, suspended operations in 1994, upon the independence of Palau, the last remaining UN trustee territory and now it has five Principal Organs.

Organs of the UN

General Assembly

The General Assembly is the main deliberative assembly of the United Nations. Composed of all United Nations member states, the assembly meets in regular yearly sessions under a president elected from among the member states.

The first session convened on 10 January 1946 in the Methodist Central Hall Westminster in London and included representatives of 51 nations.

When the General Assembly votes on important questions, a two-thirds majority of those present and voting is required. Each member country has one vote. Apart from approval of budgetary matters, resolutions are not binding on the members. The Assembly may make recommendations on any matters within the scope of the UN, except matters of peace and security that are under consideration by the Security Council.

Draft resolutions can be forwarded to the General Assembly by eight committees:

- **General Committee** – a supervisory committee consisting of the assembly's president, vice-president, and committee heads.
- **Credentials Committee** – responsible for determining the credentials of each member nation's UN representatives.
- **First Committee** (Disarmament and International Security).
- **Second Committee** (Economic and Financial).
- **Third Committee** (Social, Humanitarian, and Cultural).
- **Fourth Committee** (Special Political and Decolonization).
- **Fifth Committee** (Administrative and Budgetary).
- **Sixth Committee** (Legal).

Security Council

The Security Council is charged with maintaining peace and security among countries. While other organs of the United Nations can only make 'recommendations' to member governments, the Security Council has the power to make binding decisions that member governments have agreed to carry out, under the terms of Charter **Article 25**. The decisions of the Council are known as United Nations Security Council resolutions. The Security Council held its first session on 17 January 1946.

The Security Council is composed of 15 Members (Permanent and Non-Permanent Members)

5 Permanent Members	China, France, Russian Federation, The United Kingdom, and The United States.
10 Non-permanent Members	Ten non-permanent members elected for two-year terms by the General Assembly (with end of term date)

VETO POWER

The United Nations Security Council "power of veto" refers to the veto power wielded solely by the five permanent members of the United Nations Security Council (China, France, Russia, United Kingdom, and United States), enabling them to prevent the adoption of any "substantive" resolution, as well as decide which issues fall under "substantive" title.

The veto is exercised when any permanent member—the so-called "P5"—casts a "negative" vote on a "substantive" draft resolution. Abstention or absence from the vote by a permanent member does not prevent a draft resolution from being adopted.

Article 27 of the United Nations Charter states:

1. Each member of the Security Council shall have one vote.
2. Decisions of the Security Council on procedural matters shall be made by an affirmative vote of nine members.
3. Decisions of the Security Council on all other matters shall be made by an affirmative vote of nine members including the concurring votes of the permanent members; provided that, in decisions under Chapter VI, and under paragraph 3 of Article 52, a party to a dispute shall abstain from voting.

Secretariat

The United Nations Secretariat is headed by the Secretary-General, assisted by a staff of international civil servants worldwide. It provides studies, information, and facilities needed by United Nations bodies for their meetings. It also carries out tasks as directed by the UN Security Council, the UN General Assembly, the UN Economic and Social Council, and other UN bodies.

The Secretariat is headed by the Secretary-General, who acts as the spokesperson and leader of the UN. The current Secretary-General is Antonio Guterres, who took over from Ban K, Moon, in 2007, and will be eligible for reappointment his first term expires.

Secretaries-General of the United Nations

No.	Name	Country of origin	Took office	Left office
1	Trygve Lie	Norway	2-Feb-46	10-Nov-52
2	Dag Hammarskjold	Sweden	10-Apr-53	18-Sep-61
3	U Thant	Burma	30-Nov-61	1-Jan-71
4	Kurt Waldheim	Austria	1-Jan-72	1-Jan-81
5	Javier Pérez de Cuéllar	Peru	1-Jan-82	1-Jan-91
6	Boutros Boutros-Ghali	Egypt	1-Jan-92	1-Jan-96
7	Kofi Annan	Ghana	1-Jan-97	1-Jan-06
8	Ban Ki-moon	South Korea	1-Jan-07	31-Dec-16
9	Antonio Guterres	Portugal	1-Jan-17	Incumbent

International Court of Justice

The International Court of Justice (ICJ), located in The Hague, Netherlands, is the primary judicial organ of the United Nations. Established in 1945 by the United Nations Charter, the Court began work in 1946 as the successor to the Permanent Court of International Justice.

The ICJ is composed of fifteen judges elected to nine-year terms by the UN General Assembly and the UN Security Council from a list of people nominated by the national groups in the Permanent Court of Arbitration. The election process is set out in Articles 4–19 of the ICJ statute.

Current Members

Name	Nationality	Position	Term
Abdulqawi Ahmed Yusuf	Somalia	President	Member of the Court since 6 February 2009; re-elected as from 6 February 2018; Vice-President of the Court from 6 February 2015 to 5 February 2018; President of the Court since 6 February 2018
Xue Hanqin	China	Vice-President	Member of the Court since 29 June 2010; re-elected as from 6 February 2012; Vice-President of the Court since 6 February 2018
Peter Tomka	Slovakia	Member	Member of the Court since 6 February 2003; re-elected as from 6 February 2012; Vice-President of the Court from 6 February 2009 to 5 February 2012; President of the Court from 6 February 2012 to 5 February 2015
Ronny Abraham	France	Member	Member of the Court since 15 February 2005; re-elected as from 6 February 2009 and as from 6 February 2018; President of the Court from 6 February 2015 to 5 February 2018
Mohamed Bennouna	Morocco	Member	Member of the Court since 6 February 2006; re-elected as from 6 February 2015
Antônio Augusto Cançado Trindade	Brazil	Member	Member of the Court since 6 February 2009; re-elected as from 6 February 2018

Joan E. Donoghue	United States of America	Member	Member of the Court since 9 September 2010; re-elected as from 6 February 2015
Giorgio Gaja	Italy	Member	Member of the Court since 6 February 2012
Julia Sebutinde	Uganda	Member	Member of the Court since 6 February 2012
Dalveer Bhandari	**India**	**Member**	**Member of the Court since 27 April 2012, re-elected as from 6 February 2018**
Patrick Lipton Robinson	Jamaica	Member	Member of the Court since 6 February 2015
James Richard Crawford	Australia	Member	Member of the Court since 6 February 2015
Kirill Gevorgian	Russian Federation	Member	Member of the Court since 6 February 2015
Nawaf Salam	Lebanon	Member	Member of the Court since 6 February 2018
Yuji Iwasawa	Japan	Member	Member of the Court since 22 June 2018
Philippe Couvreur	Belgium	Member	Registrar since 10 February 2000, re-elected on 8th February 2007 and again on 3 February 2014

Economic and Social Council

Economic and Social Council (ECOSOC) assists the General Assembly in promoting international economic and social cooperation and development. ECOSOC has 54 members, all of which are elected by the General Assembly for a three-year term.

The president is elected for a one-year term and chosen from the small or mid-sized powers represented on the ECOSOC. The current president of the ECOSOC is Inga Marins Chatardenva Rhondaking. He was elected on 27 July 2018 and is the 74th President of ECOSOC.

Trusteeship Council

It is one of the principal organs of United Nations which armed at ensuring the fact that the trust territories were administered in the best interest of their inhabitant and of international peace and security. It was formed in 1945 to fulfilled its mission and collapsed on 1 November 1994.

SPECIALIZED AGENCIES OF THE UNITED NATIONS

United Nations Educational, Scientific and Cultural Organization (UNESCO)

Established : 16 November 1945
Headquarters : Place de Fontenoy, Paris, France
Head : Audrey Azoulay
Members : 195 member states and 11 associate members

Functions

- Mobilizing for education by providing every child, irrespective of its gender quality education as a fundamental human right
- Creation of World Heritage Sites to support cultural diversity and protect sites of outstanding universal value.
- Pursuing scientific cooperation
- Protecting freedom of expression

The United Nations Children's Fund (UNICEF)

Established : 11 December 1946
Headquarters: New York City
Head : Tore Hattrem
Members : 36 Member States

Functions

- Child protection from violence, exploitation and abuse along with social inclusion for disabled.
- Basic education and gender equality through programmes like girls education innovation for education learning for the peace out-of-school initiative.
- Policy advocacies and partnership through data analysis, leveraging resources and child participation.

International Labour Organization (ILO)

Established : 1919
Headquarters: Geneva, Switzerland
Head : Guy Ryder
Members : 187 member states

Functions

- Creation of international labour standards.
- Formulation of international policies.
- Technical assistance training.
- Education, research and publishing activities.

World Bank (WB)

Established : July 1944
Headquarters : Washington, DC, USA
Head : Jim Yong Kim
Members : 189 Countries

Functions

- The World Bank is an international financial institution that provides loans to countries of the world for capital projects. It comprises two institutions: the international bank for Reconstruction and Development (IBRD), and the international Development Association (IDA). The World Bank is a component of the World Bank Group.
- World Bank provides various technical services to the member countries.
- Bank can grant loans to a member country up to 20% of its share in the paid-up capital.
- Quantities of loans, interest rate and terms and conditions are determined by the Bank itself.
- Bank grants loans for a particular project duly submitted to the Bank by the member country.

The International Monetary Fund (IMF)

Established	: 27 December 1944
Headquarters	: Washington, D.C.
Head	: Christine Lagarde
Members	: 189 countries

Functions

- Surveillance over Members' Economic Policies.
- Financing Temporary Balance of Payments Needs.
- Combating Poverty in Low-Income Countries.
- Mobilizing External Financing.

The World Health Organization (WHO)

Established	: 7 April 1948
Headquarters	: Geneva, Switzerland
Head	: Dr. Tedros Adhamom Ghebreyerus
Members	: 194 member states

Functions

- Providing leadership on matters critical to health and engaging in partnerships where joint action is needed;
- Shaping the research agenda and stimulating the generation, dissemination of valuable knowledge.
- Providing technical support, catalyzing change, and building sustainable institutional capacity.
- Monitoring the health situation and assessing health trends.

International Fund for Agricultural Development Objective (IFAD)

Established	: 1977
Headquarters	: Rome, Italy
Head	: Gilbert F. Houngbo
Members	: 176 member states.

Functions

To ensure that poor rural mass have access to:

- Natural resources, especially secure access to land and water
- Improved agricultural technologies and effective production services.
- A broad range of financial services.

The Food and Agriculture Organization of the United Nations (FAO)

Established	: 16 October 1945, in Quebec City, Canada
Headquarters	: Palazzo, Rome, Italy
Head	: José Graziano da Silva
Members	: 194 Countries

Functions

- Help eliminate hunger, food insecurity and malnutrition.
- Make agriculture, forestry and fisheries more productive and sustainable.
- Reduce rural poverty.

International Atomic Energy Agency (IAEA)

Established	: 29 July, 1957
Headquarters	: Vienna, Austria
Head	: Yukiya Amano
Members	: 170 member states

Functions

- Peaceful uses: Promoting the peaceful uses of nuclear energy by its member states.
- Safeguards: Implementing safeguards to verify that nuclear energy is not used for military purposes.
- Nuclear safety: Promoting high standards for nuclear safety.

United Nations Industrial Development Organization (UNIDO)

Established	: 1966 (converted to a specialized agency in 1985)
Headquarters	: Vienna, Austria
Head	: Li Yong
Members	: 168 Nations

Functions

- Assists developing countries in the formulation of development, institutional, scientific and technological policies and programmes in the field of industrial development.
- Analyzes trends, disseminates information and coordinates activities in their industrial development.
- Acts as a forum for consultations and negotiations directed towards the industrialization of developing countries.

The United Nations World Tourism Organization (UNWTO)

Established	: 1975
Headquarters	: Madrid, Spain
Head	: Zurab Pololikashvili
Members	: 158 member states

Functions

- To promote and develop sustainable tourism so as to contribute to economic development, international understanding, peace, prosperity etc.

The World Food Programme (WFP)

Established	:	1961
Headquarters	:	Rome, Italy
Head	:	David Beasley (April, 2017 - Present)
Members	:	36 member states

Functions

- Save lives and protect livelihoods in emergencies.
- Support food security and nutrition and (re) build livelihoods in fragile settings.
- Reduce risk and enable people, communities and countries to meet their own food and nutrition needs.

The World Intellectual Property Organization (WIPO)

Established	:	July 14, 1967
Headquarters	:	Geneva, Switzerland
Head	:	Francis Gurry (Director-General)
Members	:	191 member states

Functions

- Promoting creative intellectual activity and for facilitating the transfer of technology related to industrial property to the developing countries.

The United Nations Development Programme (UNDP)

Established	:	1966
Headquarters	:	New York City
Head	:	Achinm Steiner (Administrator)
Members	:	193 countries

Functions

- Poverty reduction.
- Crisis prevention and recovery.
- Environment and Energy.

The United Nations High Commissioner for Refugees (UNHCR)

Established	:	14 December 1950
Headquarters	:	Geneva, Switzerland
Head	:	Filippo Grandi (High Commissioner)
Members	:	102 members, Standing committee observer States (10).

Functions

- To lead and co-ordinate international action to protect refugees and resolve refugee problems worldwide.
- To protect and providing humanitarian assistance to whom it describes as other persons "of concern," including internally displaced persons.

The United Nations Environment Programme (UNEP)

Established	:	5 June 1972
Headquarters	:	Nairobi, Kenya
Head	:	Erik Solheim (Executive Director)
Members	:	193 countries

Functions

- Assessing global, regional and national environmental conditions and trends.
- Developing international and national environmental instruments.
- Strengthening institutions for the wise management of the environment.

The United Nations Population Fund (UNFPA)

Established	:	1969
Headquarters	:	New York City
Head	:	Dr. Natalia Kanem (Executive Director)
Members	:	36 countries (Representives)

Functions

- Universal access to reproductive health services by 2015.
- Universal primary education and closing the gender gap in education by 2015.
- Reducing maternal mortality by 75 per cent by 2015.
- Reducing infant mortality.

United Nations Conference on Trade and Development (UNCTAD)

Established	:	1964
Headquarters	:	Geneva, Switzerland
Head	:	Mukhisa Kituyi (Secretary Genera)
Members	:	194 member states

Functions

- To formulate policies relating to all aspects of development including trade, aid, transport, finance and technology.

UN Women

Established	July 2010
Headquarters	New York
Head	Phumzile Mlambo-Ngcuka (Executive Director)
Members	41 Member States elected to three-year terms

UN Women is the UN organization dedicated to gender equality and the empowerment of women. A global champion for women and girls, UN Women was established to accelerate progress on meeting their needs worldwide.

UN Women supports UN Member States as they set global standards for achieving gender equality, and works with governments and civil society to design laws, policies, programmes and services needed to ensure that the standards are effectively implemented and truly benefit women and girls worldwide.

It works globally to make the vision of the Sustainable Development Goals a reality for women and girls and stands behind women's equal participation in all aspects of life, focusing on four strategic priorities:

- Women lead, participate in and benefit equally from governance systems
- Women have income security, decent work and economic autonomy
- All women and girls live a life free from all forms of violence
- Women and girls contribute to and have greater influence in building sustainable peace and resilience, and benefit equally from the prevention of natural disasters and conflicts and humanitarian action

INTERNATIONAL TELECOMMUNICATION UNION (ITU)

Headquarters	: Geneva, Switzerland
Established	: 1865
Head	: Houlin Zhao (Secretary General)
Members	: 193 Countries

- ITU was founded in Paris in 1865 as the International Telegraph Union. It took its present name in 1934, and in 1947 became a specialized agency of the United Nations.
- The ITU coordinates the shared global use of the radio spectrum, promotes international cooperation in assigning satellite orbits, works to improve telecommunication infrastructure in the developing world, and assists in the development and coordination of worldwide technical standards.
- The ITU is active in areas including broadband Internet, latest-generation wireless technologies, aeronautical and maritime navigation, radio astronomy, satellite-based meteorology, convergence in fixed-mobile phone, Internet access, data, voice, TV broadcasting, and next-generation networks.

UNIVERSAL POSTAL UNION (UPU)

Established	: 1874
Headquarters	: Bern, Switzerland
Head	: Bishar Abdirahman Hussein
Members	: 41 Countries

- It is a specialized agency of the United Nations that coordinates postal policies among member nations, in addition to the worldwide postal system.
- The UPU contains four bodies consisting of the Congress, the Council of Administration (CA), the Postal Operations Council (POC) and the International Bureau (IB).

ECONOMIC ORGANISATIONS

Group of 20

Established	: 1919
Head Quarters	: No Head Quarters
Head TT	: Rotational Basis
Members	: 19 Countries + European Union

- The Group of Twenty (G20) is a leading forum of the world's major economies that seeks to develop global policies to address today's most pressing challenges. The G20 is made up of 19 countries and the European Union. The 19 countries are Argentina, Australia, Brazil, Canada, China, Germany, France, India, Indonesia, Italy, Japan, Mexico, Russia, Saudi Arabia, South Africa, South Korea, Turkey, the United Kingdom and the United States.
- The G20 was born out of a meeting of G7 finance ministers and central bank governors in 1999 who saw a need for a more inclusive body with broader representation to have a stronger impact on addressing the world's financial challenges.
- Collectively, G20 members represent all inhabited continents, 85 percent of global economic output, two-thirds of the world's population, and 75 percent of international trade.
- G20 policy-making is enriched by the participation of key international organizations regularly invited to G20 meetings, guest countries invited at the president's discretion, and engagement groups composed of different sectors civil society.

Group of 15

Established	: 1989
Head Quarters	: Geneva (Technical support facility)
Head	: Rotational Basis
Members	: 17 Counties

- The Group of Fifteen (G-15) was established at a Summit Level Group of Developing Countries in September 1989, following the conclusion of the Ninth Non-Aligned Summit Meeting in Belgrade.
- The Group was originally founded by 15 developing countries. While there are now 17 member countries (Algeria, Argentina, Brazil, Chile, Egypt, India, Indonesia, Islamic Republic of Iran, Jamaica, Kenya Malaysia, Mexico, Nigeria, Senegal, Sri Lanka, Bolivarian Repubvlic of Venezuela and Zimbabwe.), the original name of the Group has been retained.
- The G-15 was established in the firm belief of the considerable potential for greater and mutually beneficial cooperation among developing countries, especially in the areas of investment, trade and technology.

Group of 8

Established	:	1975
Head Quarters	:	No Head Quarters
Head	:	Rotational Basis
Members	:	8 Countries

☞ **The G-8 reformatted as G-7 from 2014 due to suspension of Russia's participation.**

- The Group of Eight is a forum, created by France in 1975, for governments of six countries in the world: France, Germany, Italy, Japan, the United Kingdom, and the United States. In 1976, Canada joined the group (thus creating the G7).
- In 1997, the group added Russia thus becoming the G8. In addition, the European Union is represented within the G8, but cannot host or chair. "G8" can refer to the member states or to the annual summit meeting of the G8 heads of government.

Group of 7

The Group of Seven (G-7) is an informal bloc of industrialized democracies—the United States, Canada, France, Germany, Italy, Japan, and the United Kingdom—that meets annually to discuss issues such as global economic governance, international security, and energy policy.

- It started at Rambouillet in 1975 at the initiative of French President Valéry Giscard d'Estaing and German Chancellor Helmut Schmidt.
- France, West Germany, Italy, Japan, the United Kingdom, and the United States formed the Group of Six in 1975 (Canada joined the following year).
- At its beginnings, the G-7 was an informal gathering of heads of state and governments of the world's most advanced economies (Canada, France, Germany, Italy, Japan, the United Kingdom and the United States).
- Since 2005, the G-7 has been holding dialogues with the major emerging economies of Brazil, China, India, Mexico and South Africa.
- The G-7 deals with such issues as: global economic outlook and macroeconomic management, international trade, energy, climate change, and relations with developing countries.
- Russia belonged to the forum from 1998 through 2014—then the G8-but was suspended after its annexation of Crimea in March of that year.

Group of 77

Established	:	1964
Headquarters	:	Geneva (Liaison offices)
Head	:	Rotational Basis
Members	:	134 Countries

- The Group of 77 (G-77) was established on 15 June 1964 by seventy-seven developing countries signatories of the "Joint Declaration of the Seventy-Seven Countries" issued at the end of the first session of the United Nations Conference on Trade and Development (UNCTAD) in Geneva.
- Beginning with the first "Ministerial Meeting of the Group of 77 in Algiers (Algeria) on 10 - 25 October 1967, which adopted the Charter of Algiers", a permanent institutional structure gradually developed which led to the creation of Chapters of the Group of 77 with Liaison offices in Geneva (UNCTAD), Nairobi (UNEP), Paris (UNESCO), Rome (FAO/IFAD), Vienna (UNIDO), and the Group of 24 (G-24) in Washington, D.C. (IMF and World Bank). Although the members of the G-77 have increased to 134 member countries, the original name was retained because of its historic significance.

Group of 24

Established	:	1971
Headquarter	:	Belgrade(Serbia)
Head	:	Mangala Samaraweera **(Chair)**
Members	:	24 Countries

- The Intergovernmental Group of Twenty-Four on international Monetary Affairs and Development (G-24) coordinates the position of developing countries on monetary and development issues in the deliberations and decisions of the Bretton Woods Institutions (BWI).
- G-24 focuses on issues on the agendas of the International Monetary and financial committee (IMFC) and the Development Committee (DC) as well as in other relevant international fora.
- The G-24 operates at the political and operational level. The political level is comprised of Ministers, their Deputies, the Bureau, and other Washington-based representatives who participate in the Committee of the Whole and in any ad hoc meetings. The operational level is run by the G-24 Liaison Office, which includes the G-24 Secretariat.
- The governing body of the G-24 meets twice a year, preceding the Spring and Fall meetings of the International Monetary and Financial Committee and the Joint Development Committee of the World Bank and the International Monetary Fund.
- The plenary G-24 meetings are addressed by the heads of the IMF and the World Bank Group as well as by senior officials of the UN system. Issues are first discussed by the Deputies and culminate at the Ministerial level by the approval of a document that sets out the consensus views of member countries. The Ministerial document is released as a public Communique at a press conference held at the end of the meetings. Decision-making within the G-24 is by consensus.

Central Bank of West African States (BCEAO)

Established	: 1959
Headquarters	: Dakar, Senegal
Head	: Tiémoko Meyliet KONE
Member	: 8 Countries

- The Central Bank of West African States is a central bank serving the eight west African countries which share the common West African CFA franc currency and comprise the West African Economic and Monetary Union (UEMOA):
- The Bank is active in developing financial inclusion policy and is a member of the Alliance for Financial Inclusion.

South Centre

Established	: 31 June 1995
Headquarters	: Geneva, Switzerland
Head	: Dr Carlos Maria Correa (Executive Director)
Members	: 54 countries

- To analyze the development problems of the developing countries, encourage them to value and share their common experience and provide intellectual and policy support for them to act collectively and individually, particularly at the international level.

IBSA Dialogue Forum

Established	: 2003
Headquarters	: Stafford, st, Abbotsford Victoria
Head	: Rotational basis
Members	: 3 Countries

- To promote South-South cooperation and build consensus on issues of international importance.
- To increase the trade opportunities among the three countries, as well as facilitate the trilateral exchange of information, technologies and skills to complement each other strengths.
- To promote the international poverty alleviation and social development with main focus being on equitable development.
- To explore avenues to promote cooperation in broad range of areas, which include agriculture, climate change/global Warming, culture, defence, education, energy, health, information society, science and technology, social development, trade and investment, tourism and transport.

Common Market for Eastern and Southern Africa (COMESA)

Established	: 1994
Headquarter	: Lusaka, (Zambia)
Head	: H.E. Hery Rajonarimampianine
Members	: 19 Countries

- To facilitate the removals of the structural and insitutional weaknesses of Member States so that they are able to attain collective and sustained development.
- Promotion of peace and security in the region.

Organization of the Petroleum Exporting Countries (OPEC)

Established	: 1960
Headquarters	: Vienna (Austria)
Head	: Mohammad Sanusi Barkindo
Members	: 15 Countries

- The Organization of the Petroleum Exporting Countries (OPEC) was founded in Baghdad, Iraq, with the signing of an agreement in September 1960 by five countries namely Islamic Republic of Iran, Iraq, Kuwait, Saudi Arabia and Venezuela. They were to become the Founder Members of the Organization.
- These countries were later joined by Qatar (1961), Indonesia (1962), Libya (1962), the United Arab Emirates (1967), Algeria (1969), Nigeria (1971), Ecuador (1973), Gabon (1975), Angola (2007), Equatorial Guinea (2017) and Congo (2018).
- Ecuador suspended its membership in December 1992, but rejoined OPEC in October 2007. Indonesia suspended its membership in January 2009, reactivated it again in January 2016, but decided to suspend its membership once more at the 171st Meeting of the OPEC Conference on 30 November 2016. Gabon terminated its membership in January 1995. However, it rejoined the Organization in July 2016.Currently, the Organization has a total of 15 Member Countries.
- The Secretariat was originally established in 1961 in Geneva, Switzerland. In April 1965, the 8th (Extraordinary) OPEC Conference approved a Host Agreement with the Government of Austria, effectively moving the Organization's headquarters to the city of Vienna on September 1, 1965.

Asia-Pacific Economic Cooperation (APEC)

Established	: 1989
Headquarters	: Singapore
Head	: Alan BOLLARD (Executive Director)
Members	: 21 Countries

- The idea of APEC was firstly publicly broached by former Prime Minister of Australia Bob Hawke during a speech in Seoul, Korea, on 31 January 1989. Ten months later, 12 Asia-Pacific economies met in Canberra, Australia, to establish APEC. The founding members were Australia; Brunei Darussalam; Canada; Indonesia; Japan; Korea; Malaysia; New Zealand; the Philippines; Singapore; Thailand; and the United States.

- China; Hong Kong, China; and Chinese Taipei joined in 1991. Mexico and Papua New Guinea followed in 1993. Chile acceded in 1994. And in 1998, Peru; Russia; and Viet Nam joined, taking the full membership to 21.

- APEC ensures that goods, services, investment and people move easily across borders. Members facilitate this trade through faster customs procedures at borders; more favourable business climates behind the border; and aligning regulations and standards across the region. For example, APEC's initiatives to synchronize regulatory systems are a key step to integrating the Asia-Pacific economy. A product can be more easily exported with just one set of common standards across all economies

Organisation for European Economic Cooperation (OECD)

Established	: 1961
Headquarters	: Paris, France
Head	: Angel Gurría (Secretary-General)
Members	: 36 Countries

- The Organisation for European Economic Cooperation (OEEC) was established in 1948 to run the US-financed Marshall Plan for reconstruction of a continent ravaged by war. By making individual governments recognise the interdependence of their economies, it paved the way for a new era of cooperation that was to change the face of Europe. Encouraged by its success and the prospect of carrying its work forward on a global stage, Canada and the US joined OEEC members in signing the new OECD Convention on 14 December 1960.

- The Organisation for Economic Co-operation and Development (OECD) was officially born on 30 September 1961, when the Convention entered into force.

- The mission of the Organisation for Economic Co-operation and Development (OECD) is to promote policies that will improve the economic and social well-being of people around the world. The OECD provides a forum in which governments can work together to share experiences and seek solutions to common problems.

- OECD works with governments to understand what drives economic, social and environmental change. OECD measures productivity and global flows of trade and investment. It's analysed and compares data to predict future trends. OECD set international standards on a wide range of things, from agriculture and tax to the safety of chemicals.

BRICS

Established	: 2001
Headquarters	: Rotational Basis
Head	: Rotational Basis
Members	: 5 (South Africa join in 2010)

- BRICS is made up of China, Brazil, Russia, India and South Africa. The first BRIC Foreign Ministers' Meeting was held in 2006 among China, Brazil, Russia and India on the margins of the general debate of the 61st session of the United Nations General Assembly, which drew the prelude for BRIC cooperation. In 2009, the first BRIC Summit was held in Yekaterinburg, Russia. Since then, the Summit has become an annual event. To date, 8 Summits have been held.

- In December 2010, China, as the Chair, invited South Africa to join BRIC and attend the Summit in Sanya, China. BRIC officially enlarged to include 5 countries and the acronym changed into BRICS.

- In the 10 years since its inception, BRICS cooperation has continued to consolidate its foundation and expanded to more areas. It is now a multi-level process led by the Summit, buttressed by meetings of the national Security Advisors Foreign Ministers and other ministerial meetings, and enriched by pragmatic cooperation in dozens of areas such as economy, trade, finance, business, agriculture, education, health, science and technology, culture, think tanks, and friendship cities. Cooperation mechanisms such as the New Development Bank, Contingent Reserve Arrangement, Business Council and Think Tank Council have been established. Pragmatic cooperation has gone to greater depth to yield more fruitful results and exerted important influence globally.

- The NDB is a multilateral development bank established by Brazil, Russia, India, China and South Africa with the objective of financing infrastructure and sustainable development projects in BRICS and other emerging economies and developing countries, complementing the efforts of multilateral and regional financial institutions toward global growth and development.

- It was established during the sixth BRICS Summit in Fortaleza (Brazil-2014) by the 5 member countries. The Bank formally came into existence as a legal entity at the Ufa Summit (Russia) in July 2015. It is headquartered in Shanghai, China and Mr. K.V. Kamath is its current President.

- BRICS countries come from Asia, Africa, Europe and America and are all members of the G20. Together, they account for 26.46% of world land area, 42.58% of world population, 13.24% of World Bank voting power and 14.91% of IMF quota shares, according to IMF's estimates.

European Free Trade Association (EFTA)

Established	: 1960
Headquarters	: Geneva
Head	: Tormod Sveen (Director)
Members	: 4 Countries

- EFTA was founded by the Stockholm Convention in 1960. Relations with the EEC, later the European Community

(EC) and the European Union (EU), have been at the core of EFTA activities from the beginning. Since the beginning of the 1990s, EFTA has actively pursued trade relations with third countries in and beyond Europe.

- The European Free Trade Association (EFTA) is an intergovernmental organisation set up for the promotion of free trade and economic integration to the benefit of its four Member States – Iceland, Liechtenstein, Norway and Switzerland – and the benefit of their trading partners around the globe.

- The four EFTA States are all open, competitive economies committed to the progressive liberalization of trade in the multinational arena as well as in free trade agreements.

Bay of Bengal Initiative for Multi-Sectoral Technical and Economic Cooperation (BIMSTEC)

Established	: 1997
Headquarters	: Dhaka,Bangladesh
Head	: Shahidul Islam
Members	: 7 Countries

- It is a regional organization comprising seven Member States lying in the littoral and adjacent areas of the Bay of Bengal constituting a contiguous regional unity. This sub-regional organization came into being on 6 June 1997 through the Bangkok Declaration. It constitutes seven Member States: five deriving from South Asia, including Bangladesh, Bhutan, India, Nepal, Sri Lanka, and two from Southeast Asia, including Myanmar and Thailand. Initially, the economic bloc was formed with four Member States with the acronym 'BIST-EC' (Bangladesh, India, Sri Lanka and Thailand Economic Cooperation).

- Following the inclusion of Myanmar on 22 December 1997 during a special Ministerial Meeting in Bangkok, the Group was renamed 'BIMST-EC' (Bangladesh, India, Myanmar, Sri Lanka and Thailand Economic Cooperation). With the admission of Nepal and Bhutan at the 6th Ministerial Meeting (February 2004, Thailand), the name of the grouping was changed to 'Bay of Bengal Initiative for Multi-Sectoral Technical and Economic Cooperation' (BIMSTEC).

- The objective of building such an alliance was to harness shared and accelerated growth through mutual cooperation in different areas of common interests by mitigating the onslaught of globalization and by utilizing regional resources and geographical advantages. Unlike many other regional groupings, BIMSTEC is a sector-driven cooperative organization. Starting with six sectors— including trade, technology, energy, transport, tourism and fisheries—for sectoral cooperation in the late 1997, it expanded to embrace nine more sectors—including agriculture, public health, poverty alleviation, counter-terrorism, environment, culture, people to people contact and climate change—in 2008.

MERCOSUR

Established	: 1991
Headquarters	: Montevideo (Uruguay)
Head	: Ms. Linda Rabbaglietti
Members	: 4 Founding Member (Venezuela Suspended)

- MERCOSUR/MERCOSUL is a common market (Southern Common Market) established based on the Treaty of Asuncion signed by the four countries of Argentina, Brazil, Paraguay and Uruguay on March 26, 1991.Venezuela had joined Mercosur in 2012.

- Mercosur, an economic and political bloc comprising Argentina, Brazil, Paraguay, Uruguay and Venezuela suspended Venezuela in 2016. The Organization of the American States (OAS) recommended suspending Venezuela from the bloc unless the Maduro administration moved to hold elections.

- It aims at promoting free trade of goods, services, and production inputs. Mercosur functions as a customs union and free-trade area and has ambitions to become a common market along the lines of the European Union. However more than 20 years after its founding the group still struggles to achieve that goal.

Indian-Ocean Rim Association (IORA)

Established	: 1997
Headquarters	: Ebene Cyber City, Mauritius
Head	: Nomvuyo N. Nokwe (Secretary General)
Members	: 21 Notions

- To promote sustainable growth and balanced development of the region and member states
- To focus on those areas of economic cooperation which provide maximum opportunities for development, shared interest and mutual benefits
- To promote liberalisation, remove impediments and lower barriers towards a freer and enhanced flow of goods, services, investment, and technology within the Indian Ocean rim.

Bank for International Settlement (BIS)

Established	: 1930
Headquarters	: Basel, (Switzerland)
Head	: Jens Weidmann, Frankfurl ammain
Members	: 60 Central Banks

- To serve central banks in their pursuit of monetary and financial stability, to foster international cooperation in those areas and to act as a bank for central banks.
- acting as a prime counterparty for central banks in their financial transactions; and
- serving as an agent or trustee in connection with international financial operations.

International Finance Corporation (IFC)

Established	: 1956
Headquarters	: Washington, DC US
Head	: Philippe CELE Houerou
Members	: 184 countries

- It is an international financial institution that offers investment, advisory, and asset management services to encourage private sector development in developing countries.
- The IFC's stated aim is to create opportunities for people to escape poverty and achieve better living standards by mobilizing financial resources for private enterprise, promoting accessible and competitive markets, supporting businesses and other private sector entities, and creating jobs and delivering necessary services to those who are poverty-stricken or otherwise vulnerable.

European Bank for Reconstruction and Development(EBRD)

Established	: 1991
Headquarters	: London
Head	: Suma Chakrabarti (President)
Members	: 64 Countries

- To support countries of the former Eastern Bloc in the process of establishing their private sectors.
- The EBRD mandates to work only in countries that are "committed to democratic principles". It promotes "environmentally sound and sustainable development", and does not finance "defense-related activities, the tobacco industry, selected alcoholic products, substances banned by international law and stand-alone gambling facilities".

Economic Cooperation Organization (ECO)

Established	: 1985
Headquarters	: Tehran (Iran)
Head	: Halil Ibrahim (Secretary General)
Members	: 10 Countries

- Progressive removal of trade barriers and promotion of intra-regional trade; Greater role of ECO region in the growth of world trade; Gradual integration of the economies of the Member States with the world economy;
- Development of transport & communications infrastructure linking the Member States with each other and with the outside world;
- Economic liberalization and privatization.
- The ECO is an ad hoc organization under the United Nations Charter (Chapter VIII).

Colombo Plan (CP)

Established	: 1950
Headquarters	: Colombo (Sri Lanka)
Head	: Mohamed Hussain Shared (Council President)
Members	: 27

- To promote interest in and support for the economic and social development of Asia and the Pacific;
- To promote technical cooperation and assist in the sharing and transfer of technology among member countries;
- To keep under review relevant information on technical cooperation between the member governments, multilateral and other agencies with a view to accelerating development through cooperative effort;
- To facilitate the transfer and sharing of the developmental experiences among member countries within the region with emphasis on the concept of South-South cooperation.

World Trade Organization (WTO)

Established	: 1995
Headquarters	: Geneva, Switzerland
Head	: Roberto Azevêdo
Members	: 164 Countries

- The World Trade Organization is the international organization whose primary purpose is to open trade for the benefit of all. World Trade Organization (WTO) is the only international organization dealing with the global rules of trade between nations. Its main function is to ensure that trade flows as smoothly, predictably and freely as possible.
- The WTO also provides a legal and institutional framework for the implementation and monitoring of these agreements, as well as for settling disputes arising from their interpretation and application. The current body of trade agreements comprising the WTO consists of 16 different multilateral agreements (to which all WTO members are parties) and two different plurilateral agreements (to which only some WTO members are parties).
- WTO was established in 1995, and its predecessor organization the GATT has helped to create a strong and prosperous international trading system, thereby contributing to unprecedented global economic growth.

- The WTO currently has 164 members, of which 117 are developing countries or separate customs territories.
- WTO's main activities are (i) negotiating the reduction or elimination of obstacles to trade (import tariffs, other barriers to trade) and agreeing on rules governing the conduct of international trade (e.g. antidumping, subsidies, product standards, etc.),(ii) administering and monitoring the application of the WTO's agreed rules for trade in goods, trade in services, and trade-related intellectual property rights,(iii) monitoring and reviewing the trade policies of our members, as well as ensuring transparency of regional and bilateral trade agreements,(iv) settling disputes among our members regarding the interpretation and application of the agreements ,(v) building capacity of developing country government officials in international trade matters etc.

European Union-(EU)

Established	: 1993
Headquarters	: Brussels, Belgium
Head	: Antonio Tajani
	(European Parliament president)
Members	: 28 Countries

- The European Union is a unique economic and political union between 28 EU countries that together cover much of the continent. The predecessor of the EU was created in the aftermath of the Second World War. The first steps were to foster economic cooperation: the idea being that countries that trade with one another become economically interdependent and so more likely to avoid conflict.
- The result was the European Economic Community (EEC), created in 1958, and initially increasing economic cooperation between six countries: Belgium, Germany, France, Italy, Luxembourg and the Netherlands. Since then, 22 other members joined and a huge single market (also known as the 'internal' market) has been created and continues to develop towards its full potential.
- What began as a purely economic union has evolved into an organization spanning policy areas, from climate, environment and health to external relations and security, justice and migration. A name change from the European Economic Community (EEC) to the European Union (EU) in 1993 reflected this.
- The EU's main economic engine is the single market. It enables most goods, services, money and people to move freely. The EU aims to develop this huge resource to other areas like energy, knowledge and capital markets to ensure that Europeans can draw the maximum benefit from it.

Association of Southeast Asian Nations (ASEAN)

Established	: 1967
Headquarters	: Jakarta, Indonesia
Head	: Dato Lim Jock Hoi
Members	: 10 Countries

- The Association of Southeast Asian Nations, or ASEAN, was established on 8 August 1967 in Bangkok, Thailand, with the signing of the ASEAN Declaration (Bangkok Declaration) by the Founding Fathers of ASEAN, namely Indonesia, Malaysia, Philippines, Singapore and Thailand. Brunei Darussalam then joined on 7 January 1984, Viet Nam on 28 July 1995, Lao PDR and Myanmar on 23 July 1997, and Cambodia on 30 April 1999, making up what is today the ten Member States of ASEAN.
- The Association of Southeast Asian Nations is a regional intergovernmental organization comprising ten Southeast Asian countries that promotes intergovernmental cooperation and facilitates economic, political, security, military, educational, and sociocultural integration amongst its members and other Asian states.
- It also regularly engages other states in the Asia-Pacific region and beyond. Being a global powerhouse, the central platform for cooperation in Asia-Pacific, and one of the world's most prominent and influential organisations, ASEAN maintains a global network of alliances and is involved in numerous international affairs.

Arab League

Established	: 1945
Headquarters	: Cairo
Head	: Ahmad Aboul Gheit
Members	: 22 Countries

- The Arab League is an intergovernmental organization (IGO), a voluntary association of independent African and Middle East countries whose peoples are mainly Arabic speaking.
- The stated purposes of the Arab League are to strengthen ties among the member states, coordinate their policies, and promote their common interests. The league was founded in Cairo in 1945 by Egypt, Iraq, Jordan (originally Transjordan, Jordan, as of 1950), and Yemen.
- According to its charter, the founding members of the Arab League (Egypt, Syria, Transjordan, Iraq, Saudi Arabia, Lebanon, and Yemen) agreed to seek "close cooperation" on matters of economics, communication, culture, nationality, social welfare, and health.
- They renounced violence for the settlement of conflicts between members and empowered League offices to mediate in such disputes, as well as in those with non-members. Signatories agreed to collaborate in military affairs; this accord was strengthened with a 1950 pact committing members to treat acts of aggression on any member state as an act against all.

Gulf Cooperation Council (GCC)

Established	: 1981
Headquarters	: Saudi Arabia
Head	: Abdul Latif bin Rashid al Zayani
Members	: 6 Countries

- Gulf Cooperation Council (GCC), political and economic alliance of six Middle Eastern countries—Saudi Arabia, Kuwait, the United Arab Emirates, Qatar, Bahrain, and Oman. The GCC was established in Riyadh, Saudia Arabia, in May 1981. The purpose of the GCC is to achieve unity among its members based on their common objectives and their similar political and cultural identities, which are rooted in Islamic beliefs. Presidency of the council rotates annually.
- The GCC Charter states that the basic objectives are:
  (1) To effect co-ordination, integration and inter-connection between member states in all fields in order to achieve unity between them.
  (2) To deepen and strengthen relations, links and areas of cooperation now prevailing between their peoples in various fields.
  (3) To formulate similar regulations in various fields including the following: A. Economic and financial affairs. B. Commerce, customs and communications. C. Education and culture. D. Social and health affairs. E. Information and tourism. F. Legislative and administrative affairs.
  (4) To stimulate scientific and technological progress in the fields of industry , mining, agriculture , water and animal resources: to establish scientific research : to establish joint ventures and encourage cooperation by the private sector for the good of their peoples.

Shanghai Cooperation Organisation (SCO)

```
Established    : 2001
Headquarters   : Beijing, China
Head           : General Rashid Alimov
                 (SCO Secretary)
Members        : 8 Countries
```

- The Shanghai Cooperation Organisation (SCO) is a permanent intergovernmental international organisation, the creation of which was announced on 15 June 2001 in Shanghai (China) by the Republic of Kazakhstan, the People's Republic of China, the Kyrgyz Republic, the Russian Federation, the Republic of Tajikistan, and the Republic of Uzbekistan. It was preceded by the Shanghai Five mechanism.
- Currently the SCO comprises eight member states, namely the Republic of India, the Republic of Kazakhstan, the People's Republic of China, the Kyrgyz Republic, the Islamic Republic of Pakistan, the Russian Federation, the Republic of Tajikistan, and the Republic of Uzbekistan,
- The SCO counts four observer states, namely the Islamic Republic of Afghanistan, the Republic of Belarus, the Islamic Republic of Iran and the Republic of Mongolia, the SCO has six dialogue partners, namely the Republic of Azerbaijan, the Republic of Armenia, the Kingdom of Cambodia, the Federal Democratic Republic of Nepal, the Republic of Turkey, and the Democratic Socialist Republic of Sri Lanka

- The SCO's main goals are as follows: strengthening mutual trust and neighbourliness among the member states; promoting their effective cooperation in politics, trade, the economy, research, technology and culture, as well as in education, energy, transport, tourism, environmental protection, and other areas; making joint efforts to maintain and ensure peace, security and stability in the region; and moving towards the establishment of a democratic, fair and rational new international political and economic order.

COMMONWEALTH OF NATIONS

```
Established    : 1965
Headquarters   : London (U.K)
Head           : Queen Elizabeth II
Members        : 53 Nations
```

- The Commonwealth is a voluntary association of 53 independent and equal sovereign states. Member countries are supported by a network of more than 80 intergovernmental, civil societies, cultural and professional organisations. The last country to join the Commonwealth was Rwanda in 2009.
- The Commonwealth spans the globe and includes both advanced economies and developing countries. It encompasses Africa (19 countries), Asia (7), the Caribbean and Americas (13), Europe (3), and the Pacific (11).
- The Commonwealth Secretariat, established in 1965, supports Commonwealth member countries to achieve development, democracy and peace. We are a voice for small and vulnerable states and a champion for young people.
- The Pacific nation of Nauru is the smallest Commonwealth member country with a population of about 10,000. The most populous member country is India with over 1.2 billion people.

Non-Aligned Movement (NAM)

```
Established    : 1961
Headquarters   : Jakarta, Indonesia
Head           : Rotational Basis
Members        : 120 Countries
```

- The Non-Aligned Movement (NAM) is a group of states which are not formally aligned with or against any major power bloc. As of 2012, the movement has 120 members, 17 observer countries and 10 observer Organizations.
- The organization was founded in Belgrade in 1961, and was largely conceived by India's first prime minister, Jawaharlal Nehru; Indonesia's first president, Sukarno; Egypt's second president, Gamal Abdel Nasser; Ghana's first president Kwame Nkrumah; and Yugoslavia's President, Josip Broz Tito.

- J.L. Nehru has described the five pillars to be used as a guide for Sino-Indian relations called Panchsheel (five restraints), these principles would later serve as the basis of the Non-Aligned Movement. The five principles were: **1• Mutual respect for each other's territorial integrity and sovereignty 2• Mutual non-aggression 3• Mutual non-interference in domestic affairs 4• Equality and mutual benefit 5• Peaceful co-existence**
- NAM has sought to create an independent path in world politics that would not result in member States becoming pledges in the struggles between the major powers. It identifies the right of independent judgment, the struggle against imperialism and neo-colonialism, and the use of moderation in relations with all big powers as the three basic elements that have influenced its approach.
- From the beginning of the Movement, its work was an essential factor for the decolonization process, which then led to the achievement of freedom and independence of many countries and peoples, as well as the creation of new States. NAM has played an important role in the strengthening of international peace and security.

ENVIRONMENTAL CONSERVATIONS/ ORGANISATIONS

International Union for Conservation of Nature (IUCN)

Established	: 1948
Headquarters	: Gland, Switzerland
Head	: ZHANG Xinsheng (President)
Members	: 1300 Member organisations

- IUCN was founded in **October 1948** as the International Union for the Protection of Nature (or IUPN) following an international conference in Fontainebleau, France.
- The organisation changed its name to the International Union for Conservation of Nature and Natural Resources in 1956 with the acronym IUCN (or UICN in French and Spanish). This remains our full legal name to this day.
- The International Union for Conservation of Nature (IUCN) is a Union uniquely composed of both government and civil society organisations. It provides public, private and non-governmental organisations with the knowledge and tools that enable human progress, economic development and nature conservation to take place together.
- IUCN has evolved into the world's largest and most diverse environmental network. It harnesses the experience, resources and reach of its 1,300 Member organisations and the input of some 13,000 experts. IUCN is the global authority on the status of the natural world and the measures needed to safeguard it. Our experts are organised into six commissions dedicated to species survival, environmental law, protected areas, social and economic policy, ecosystem management, and education and communication.
- Much of IUCN's subsequent work in the 1960s and 1970s was devoted to the protection of species and the habitats necessary for their survival. In 1964, IUCN established the IUCN Red List of Threatened Species™, which has since evolved into the world's most comprehensive data source on the global extinction risk of species.
- The IUCN Red List of Threatened Species™ provides taxonomic, conservation status and distribution information on plants, fungi and animals that have been globally evaluated using the IUCN Red List Categories and Criteria.
- This system is designed to determine the relative risk of extinction, and the main purpose of the IUCN Red List is to catalogue and highlight those plants, fungi and animals that are facing a higher risk of global extinction (i.e. those listed as Critically Endangered, Endangered and Vulnerable).
- The IUCN Red List also includes information on plants, fungi and animals that are categorized as Extinct or Extinct in the Wild; on taxa that cannot be evaluated because of insufficient information (i.e., are Data Deficient); and on plants, fungi and animals that are either close to meeting the threatened thresholds or that would be threatened were it not for an ongoing taxon-specific conservation programme (i.e., are Near Threatened).
- The IUCN Red List of Threatened Species™ provides taxonomic, conservation status and distribution information on plants, fungi and animals that have been globally evaluated using the IUCN Red List Categories and Criteria. This system is designed to determine the relative risk of extinction, and the main purpose of the IUCN Red List is to catalogue and highlight those plants, fungi and animals that are facing a higher risk of global extinction (i.e. those listed as Critically Endangered, Endangered and Vulnerable).
- The IUCN Red List also includes information on plants, fungi and animals that are categorized as Extinct or Extinct in the Wild; on taxa that cannot be evaluated because of insufficient information (i.e., are Data Deficient); and on plants, fungi and animals that are either close to meeting the threatened thresholds or that would be threatened were it not for an ongoing taxon-specific conservation programme (i.e., are Near Threatened).
- IUCN also played a fundamental role in the creation of key international conventions, including the Ramsar Convention on Wetlands (1971), the World Heritage Convention (1972), the Convention on International Trade in Endangered Species, (1974) and the Convention on Biological Diversity (1992).
- IUCN also played a fundamental role in the creation of key international conventions, including the Ramsar Convention on Wetlands (1971), the World Heritage Convention (1972), the Convention on International Trade in Endangered Species, (1974) and the Convention on Biological Diversity (1992).

World Wildlife Fund (WWF)

Established	: 1961
Headquarters	: Gland, Switzerland
Head	: Carter Roberts (President & CEO)
Members	: –(Works in 100 countries)

- World Wildlife Fund was conceived in April, 1961, and set up shop in September, 1961, at IUCN's headquarters in Morges, Switzerland. World Wildlife Fund, Inc. (WWF)—the U.S. appeal—became the second national organization to be formed in 1961. The giant panda becomes the logo for WWF.

- The world's leading conservation organization, WWF works in 100 countries and is supported by more than one million members in the United States and close to five million globally. WWF's unique way of working combines global reach with a foundation in science, involves action at every level from local to global, and ensures the delivery of innovative solutions that meet the needs of both people and nature.

- The main functions of WWF are: 1) Protect and restore species and their habitats, 2) Strengthen local communities' ability to conserve the natural resources they depend upon, 3) Transform markets and policies to reduce the impact of the production and consumption of commodities, 4) Ensure that the value of nature is reflected in decisions made by individuals, communities, 5) governments and businesses, Mobilize hundreds of millions of people to support conservation.

United Nations Environment Programme (UNEP)

Established	: 1972
Headquarters	: Nairobi, Kenya
Head	: Erik Solheim
Members	: 58 countries (Governing council Comprises)

- The United Nations Environment Programme (UN Environment) is the leading global environmental authority that sets the global environmental agenda, promotes the coherent implementation of the environmental dimension of sustainable development within the United Nations system, and serves as an authoritative advocate for the global environment.

- UNEP mission is to provide leadership and encourage partnership in caring for the environment by inspiring, informing, and enabling nations and peoples to improve their quality of life without compromising that of future generations.

- UNEP categorize our work into seven broad thematic areas: climate change, disasters and conflicts, ecosystem management, environmental governance, chemicals and waste, resource efficiency, and environment under review. In all of our work, we maintain our overarching commitment to sustainability.

International Renewable Energy Agency (IREA)

Established	: 2009
Headquarters	: Masdar City (UAE)
Head	: Adnan Z. Amin (Director-General)
Members	: 158 Countries

- The International Renewable Energy Agency (IRENA) is an intergovernmental organisation that supports countries in their transition to a sustainable energy future, and serves as the principal platform for international cooperation, a centre of excellence, and a repository of policy, technology, resource and financial knowledge on renewable energy.

- IRENA promotes the widespread adoption and sustainable use of all forms of renewable energy, including bio energy, geothermal, hydropower, ocean, solar and wind energy in the pursuit of sustainable development, energy access, energy security and low-carbon economic growth and prosperity.

  IRENA provides a wide range of products and services, including:

  Annual reviews of renewable energy employment;

  (1) Renewable energy capacity statistics;

  (2) Renewable energy cost studies;

  (3) Renewable Readiness Assessments, conducted in partnership with governments and regional organisations, to help boost renewable energy development on a country by country basis;

  (4) The Global Atlas, which maps resource potential by source and by location;

  (5) Renewable energy benefits studies;

  (6) Remap, a roadmap to double renewable energy use worldwide by 2030;

  (7) Renewable energy technology briefs;

  (8) Facilitation of regional renewable energy planning;

  (9) Renewable energy project development tools like the Project Navigator, the Sustainable Energy Marketplace and the IRENA/ADFD Project Facility.

World Meteorological Organisation (WMO)

Established	: 1873
Headquarters	: Geneva (Switzerland)
Head	: Petteri Taalas (Secretary-General)
Members	: 191 (185 Member States and 6 Member Territories)

- WMO originated from the International Meteorological Organization (IMO), which was founded in 1873 to facilitate the exchange of weather information across national borders. Established in 1950, the WMO became a specialized agency of the United Nations in 1951.

- Its mandate is in the areas of meteorology (weather and climate), operational hydrology and related geophysical sciences. Since its establishment, WMO has played a unique and powerful role in contributing to the safety and welfare of humanity.
- It has fostered collaboration between the National Meteorological and Hydrological Services of its Members and furthered the application of meteorology in many areas.
- The Organization plays a leading role in international efforts to monitor and protect the environment through its Programmes. In collaboration with other United Nations agencies and National Meteorological and Hydrological Services, WMO supports the implementation of a number of environmental conventions and is instrumental in providing advice and assessments to governments on related matters. These activities contribute towards ensuring the sustainable development and well-being of nations.

International Atomic Energy Agency (IAEA)

Established	: 1957
Headquarters	: Vienna (Austria)
Head	: Yukiya Amano (General Director)
Members	: 170 Countries

- The International Atomic Energy Agency is the world's central intergovernmental forum for scientific and technical co-operation in the nuclear field.
- It works for the safe, secure and peaceful uses of nuclear science and technology, contributing to international peace and security and the United Nations' Sustainable Development Goals.
- The Statute of the IAEA was approved on 23 October 1956 by the Conference on the Statute of the International Atomic Energy Agency, which was held at the Headquarters of the United Nations. It came into force on 29 July 1957.

People for the Ethical Treatment of Animals (PETA)

Established	: 1980
Headquarters	: Norfolk, Virginia, United States
Head	: Ingrid Newkirk
Members	: – (6.5 million people member)

- People for the Ethical Treatment of Animals (PETA) is the largest animal rights organization in the world, with more than 6.5 million members and supporters.
- PETA focuses its attention on the four areas in which the largest numbers of animals suffer the most intensely for

the longest periods of time: in the food industry, in the clothing trade, in laboratories, and in the entertainment industry. PETA also work on a variety of other issues, including the cruel killing of rodents, birds, and other animals who are often considered "pests" as well as cruelty to domesticated animals.

- PETA works through public education, cruelty investigations, research, animal rescue, legislation, special events, celebrity involvement, and protest campaigns.

Environmental Justice Foundation (EJF)

Established	: 2001
Headquarters	: Cambridge
Head	: Princess Laurentien (President)
Members	: 30 Member staff in 8 countries

- Dynamic, nimble and effective, the **Environmental Justice Foundation** (EJF) is working to secure a world where natural habitats and environments can sustain, and be sustained by, the communities that depend upon them for their basic needs and livelihoods.
  - (i) To promote the non-violent resolution of human rights abuses and related environmental issues in the Global South.
  - (ii) To protect the environment and human rights.
- Resolve environmental and human rights abuses.
- Protect the local environment that sustains their basic human needs of a shelter, food and income.
- Its work covers five main campaigning areas: 'Illegal, Unreported and Unregulated' fishing (IUU); pesticide use; cotton production; shrimp farming; and climate refugees.
- Training and equipping affected environmental justice communities in producer countries to investigate record and expose abuses and then campaign effectively for an equitable resolution to the issues.
- It sees its role as a catalyst working to achieve long-term change, by alerting governments, international policy makers, consumers and businesses to the damaging human and environmental effects that western demand has on the natural environment and local communities, primarily in the global south.

Fauna and Flora International

Established	: 1903
Headquarters	: Cambridge
Head	: HRH Princess Laurentien (President)
Members	: Over 80 countries

- Objective of this organisation is to safeguard the future of southern Africa's large mammal populations that declined alarmingly due to over-hunting and habitat encroachment.
- Working in tandem with landowners, government and sport hunters, the Society helped pass legislation which

- controlled hunting in vast stretches of East Africa and South Africa.
- Establishing much of today's global conservation infrastructure – including the World Conservation Union (IUCN), the World Wide Fund for Nature (WWF), and the Convention on the International Trade in Endangered Species of Wild Flora and Fauna (CITES).
- Building local capacity for conservation.
- Integrating biodiversity and human needs.
- Direct protection of species and habitats.
- Securing land for conservation.
- Emergency response to conservation needs.
- Influencing policy and the practice of conservation.
- Bridging the gap between business and biodiversity.

Green Cross International (GCI)

Established	: 1993
Headquarters	: Geneva, Switzerland
Head	: Mikhail Gorbachev's
Heading Member	: Above 30 country.

- The objective of GCI is to address the inter-connected global challenges of security, poverty eradication and environmental degradation through a combination of advocacy and local projects.
- To provide training individuals on how to construct rainwater harvesting systems, Green Cross provides comprehensive programmes that further the values of cooperation among all stakeholders.
- GCI has various water related activities seeking to prevent and resolve conflicts over natural resources.
- To promote cooperation between countries that share river waters and sanitation needs of people for water.
- Green Cross supported the drive for safe-drinking water and sanitation to be recognized as a Human Right in 2010.
- Smart Water for Green Schools (SWGS) project is our flagship on-the-ground activity for providing sustainable access to safe drinking water and sanitation to tens of thousands of people in Asia, Africa, Latin America and Europe, with more countries coming online in the future.

International Federation of Organic Agriculture Movements (IFOAM - Organics International)

Established	: 1972
Headquarters	: Bonn, Germany
Head	: Louise Luttikholt (Executive Directo)
Members	: 800 affiliates in more than 100 countries.

- The objective of IFOAM is to lead, unite and assist the organic movement in its full diversity.
- Worldwide adoption of ecologically, socially and economically sound systems, based on the Principles of Organic Agriculture.
- Maintaining an organic farming standard, and an organic accreditation and certification service.
- Participating in international agricultural and environmental negotiations with the United Nations and multilateral institutions to further the interests of the organic agricultural movement worldwide.
- Establishment and spreading of organic standards and certification around the world.

Wildlife Conservation Network (WCN)

Established	: 2002
Headquarters	: San Francisco, USA
Head	: David Berger (Director)
Members	: 51-100 Staff (Saves endangered species in 37 countries)

- The objective of WCN is to launch developing community-based projects that help wildlife and people co-exist.
- Providing its partners with capital, strategic capacity-building services, training, and operational support.
- Forms partnerships with a select number of field-based conservation projects committed to protecting endangered wildlife.
- WCN began the Elephant Crisis Fund to address the current wave of elephant poaching that is devastating Africa's elephant population.

World Business Council for Sustainable Development (WBCSD)

Established	: 1992
Headquarters	: Geneva, Switzerland
Head	: Federico Merlo (CMD Member Relation)
Member	: 200 Member Countries

- The objective of WBCSD are:
  (i) Promote sustainable development.
  (ii) Participate in policy development to create the framework conditions for business to make an effective contribution to sustainable human progress.
  (iii) Develop and promote the business case for sustainable development.
  (iv) Demonstrate the business contribution to sustainable development solutions and share leading edge practices among members.
  (v) Contribute to a sustainable future for developing nations in transition.
- Providing a platform for companies to explore sustainable development, share knowledge, experiences and best practices, and to advocate business positions on these

issues in a variety of forums, working with governments, non-governmental and intergovernmental organizations.

- Working on a variety of issues related to sustainable areas such as Energy & Climate, Development, Ecosystems and the Role of Business in Society.
- Executing sector specific projects on cement, urban infrastructure initiative, tires, corporate reporting, water, energy efficiency in buildings, forest solutions, and electricity utilities.

European Environment Agency (EEA)

Established	:	1990
Headquarters	:	Copenhagen, Denmark
Head	:	Laura Burke (Director General)
Members	:	33 states

- It is providing independent information on the environment, helping those involved in developing, adopting, implementing and evaluating environmental policy, as well as informing the general public.
- Developing the network and coordinating its activities by working closely together with national environment agencies or environment ministries.
- Providing independent information on the environment.
- It is governed by a management board composed of representatives of the governments of its 33 member states, a European Commission representative and two scientists appointed by the European Parliament, assisted by a committee of scientists.

SCIENTIFIC ORGANISATIONS/ALLIANCES

World Federation of Engineering Organisations (WFEO)

Established	:	1968
Headquarters	:	Paris (France)
Head	:	Marlene Kanga (President)
Members	:	100 Nations

- On March, 4th 1968, representatives of 50 scientific and technical associations from all over the world met under the auspices of the United Nations Educational, Scientific and Cultural Organization (UNESCO) in Paris to establish the World Federation of Engineering Organizations (WFEO), whose charter as an international, non-governmental organization is to unite multidisciplinary engineering associations throughout the world.
- WFEO encourages all of its national and international members to contribute to global efforts to establish a sustainable, equitable and peaceful world by providing an international perspective and enabling mechanisms:

(i) To provide information and leadership to the engineering profession on issues of concern to the public or the profession.

(ii) To serve society and to be recognized, by national and international organizations and the public, as a respected and valuable source of advice and guidance on the policies, interests and concerns that relate engineering and technology to the human and natural environment.

(iii) To make information on engineering available to the countries of the world and to facilitate communication between its member nations.

(iv) To foster peace, socioeconomic security and sustainable development among all countries of the world, through the proper application of technology.

(v) To facilitate relationships between governments, business and people by adding engineering dimension to discussions on policies and investment.

National Space Society (NSS)

Established	:	1987
Headquarters	:	Washington, DC (USA)
Head	:	Alice Hoffman (chairman)
Members	:	72 different govt. Agencies

- The Mission of NSS is to promote social, economic, technological, and political change in order to expand civilization beyond Earth, to settle space and to use the resulting resources to build a hopeful and prosperous future for humanity.
- Accordingly, NSS support steps toward this goal, including human spaceflight, commercial space development, space exploration, space applications, space resource utilization, robotic precursors, defence against asteroids, relevant science, and space settlement oriented education.

International Union of Biochemistry and Molecular Biology (IUBMB)

Established	:	1955
Headquarters	:	–
Head	:	Andrew H.-J. Wang (President)
Members	:	75 Countries

- The International Union of Biochemistry and Molecular Biology founded in 1955 unites biochemists and molecular biologists in 75 countries that belong to the Union as an Adhering Body or Associate Adhering Body represented by a biochemical society, a national research council or an academy of sciences.
- The Union is devoted to promoting research and education in biochemistry and molecular biology throughout the world and gives particular attention to areas where the

subject is still in its early development. It achieves this in several ways.

- The IUBMB organizes or sponsors workshops, symposia and training sessions on biochemical and molecular biological education and provides free textbooks and journals to training institutions in developing nations.
- The Union also funds short-term fellowships for younger and mid-career biochemists and molecular biologists to travel to other institutions to perform research not possible in their own laboratories and provides Travel Fellowships for young scientists to attend its Congresses. Sponsorship of meetings and fellowships is restricted to regions that belong to the IUBMB.

IUBMB seeks to advance the international molecular life sciences community by:

- Promoting interactions across the diversity of endeavors in the molecular life sciences.
- Creating networks that transcend barriers of ethnicity, culture, gender and economic status.
- Creating pathways for young scientists to fulfill their potential.
- Providing evidence-based advice on public policy.
- Promoting the values, standards and ethics of science and the free and unhampered movement of scientists of all nations.

National Aeronautics and Space Administration (NASA)

Established	: July 29, 1958
Headquarters	: Washington D.C., USA
Head	: Jim Bridenstine (Administrator)
Members	: –

- The objective of NASA is to better understanding Earth through the Earth Observing system, advancing heliophysics through the efforts of the Science Mission Directorate's Heliophysics Research Program.
- Most US space exploration efforts have been led by NASA, including the Apollo Moon landing missions, the Skylab space station, and later the Space Shuttle.
- NASA is supporting the International Space Station and is overseeing the development of the Orion Multi-Purpose Crew Vehicle, the Space Launch System and Commercial Crew vehicles.
- The agency is also responsible for the Launch Services Program (LSP) which provides oversight of launch operations and countdown management for unmanned NASA launches.

National Informatics Centre (NIC)

Established	: 1976
Headquarters	: New Delhi
Head	: Neeta Verma (Director General)
Members	: Link with 36 States/UT and central govt.

- National Informatics Centre (NIC) was established in 1976 and has since emerged as a "prime builder" of e-Government / e-Governance applications up to the grassroots level as well as a promoter of digital opportunities for sustainable development. NIC, through its ICT Network, "NICNET", has institutional linkages with all the Ministries /Departments of the Central Government, 36 State Governments/ Union Territories, and about 708 District administrations of India.
- NIC has been instrumental in steering e-Government/e-Governance applications in government ministries/ departments at the Centre, States, Districts and Blocks, facilitating improvement in government services, wider transparency, promoting decentralized planning and Centre, States, Districts and Blocks, facilitating improvement in government services, wider transparency, promoting decentralized planning and management, resulting in better efficiency and accountability to the people of India. Informatics-led-development" programme of the government has been spearheaded by NIC to derive competitive advantage by implementing ICT applications in social & public administration.
- The following major activities are being undertaken: a) Setting up of ICT Infrastructure b)Implementation of National and State Level e-Governance Projects/Products c)Consultancy to the Government departments d)Research & Development and e)Capacity Building.
- NIC is implementing Information Technology Projects, in close collaboration with Central and State Governments. NIC endeavours to ensure that the latest technology in all areas of IT is available to its users.
- It is one of the total solution providers to the Government and is actively involved in most of the IT enabled applications and has changed the mindset of the working community in the Government to make use of the latest state of the art technology in their day to day activities to provide better services to the citizens.

International Science for council (ISC)

Established	: 2018
Headquarters	: Paris (France)
Head	: Daya Reddy
Members	: 40 International + 140 National & Regional Organisation

- The International Science Council (ISC) was created in 2018 from a merger of the International Council for Science (founded in 1931) and the International Social Science Council (founded in 1952).
- The International Science Council (ISC) is a non-governmental organization with a unique global membership that brings together 40 international scientific Unions and Associations and over 140 national and regional scientific organizations including Academies and Research Councils.

- The Council convenes the scientific expertise and resources needed to lead on catalysing, incubating and coordinating impactful international action on issues of major scientific and public importance.

  The Council's activities focus on three principle areas of work.

  (i) Science-for-policy to stimulate and support international scientific research and scholarship, and to communicate science that is relevant to international policy issues.

  (ii) Policy-for-science to promote developments that enable science to contribute more effectively to major issues in the international public domain.

  (iii) Scientific freedom and responsibility to defend the free and responsible practice of science.

- With a broad range of co-sponsored international research programmes, networks and committees, the Council's activities span a broad range of issues, from global sustainability, poverty, urban health and wellbeing and disaster risk reduction, to data, observing systems and science advice to governments.

World Academy of Science (WAS)

Established	: 1983
Headquarters	: Trieste (Italy)
Head	: Bai Chunli
Members	: Representing in 100 Countries

The objective of WAS is to promote scientific capacity and excellence for sustainable development in the South/developing countries.

- To provide funds for research often forces scientists in developing countries into intellectual isolation, jeopardizing their careers, their institutions and their nations.

- To recognize, support and promote excellence in scientific research in the South/developing countries.

- To provide promising scientists in the South with research facilities necessary for the advancement of their work.

- To facilitate contacts between individual scientists and institutions in the South or developing countries.

- To encourage South-North cooperation between individuals and centres of scholarship.

- To promote scientific research on major developing countries problems.

International Union of Pure and Applied Physics (IUPAP)

Established	: 1922
Headquarters	: Singapore
Head	: Kennedy Reed (President)
Members	: 60 Countries

- It is the only international physics organization that is organized and run by the physics community itself. Its members are communities of physicists in countries or regions around the world. Currently there are 60 members.

- The International Union of Pure and Applied Physics (IUPAP) was established in 1922 in Brussels with 13 Member countries and the first General Assembly was held in 1923 in Paris.

- The main objective of IUPAP are:

  (i) stimulate and facilitate international cooperation in physics and the worldwide development of science.

  (ii) To assist in the worldwide development of physics.

  (iii) To foster international cooperation in physics.

  (iv) To help in the application of physics toward solving problems of concern to humanity.

- Sponsoring international meetings; fostering communications and publications; and encouraging research and education.

- Fostering the free circulation of scientists; promoting international agreements on the use of symbols, units, nomenclature and standards.

- Cooperating with other organizations on disciplinary and interdisciplinary problems.

International Union of Pure and Applied Chemistry (IUPAC)

Established	: 1919
Headquarters	: USA
Head	: Qi-Feng Zhou (President)
Members	: More than 55 National Country

- IUPAC was formed in 1919 by chemists from industry and academia, who recognized the need for international standardization in chemistry.

- The standardization of weights, measures, names and symbols is essential to the well being and continued success of the scientific enterprise and to the smooth development and growth of international trade and commerce.

- This desire for international cooperation among chemists and facilitation of the work of the international, but fragmented, chemistry community were the earliest characteristics of the Union. Even before the creation of IUPAC (1919), a predecessor body, the International Association of Chemical Societies (IACS), had met in Paris in 1911 and produced a set of proposals for the work that the new Association should address. These included:

- Nomenclature of inorganic and organic chemistry;

- Standardization of atomic weights;

- Standardization of physical constants;

- Editing tables of properties of matter;

- Establishing a commission for the review of work;

- Standardization of the formats of publications;
- Measures required to prevent repetition of the same papers.

International Arctic Science Committee (IASC)

> **Established** : 1990
> **Headquarters**: Akureyri (Iceland)
> **Head** : Larry Hinzman (President)
> **Members** : 23 Nations

- IASC was founded in 1990 by representatives of national scientific organizations of the eight Arctic countries - Canada, Denmark, Finland, Iceland, Norway, Russia (at that time Union of Soviet Socialist Republics), Sweden and the United States of America. The Founding Articles of IASC were signed in Resolute Bay, Canada
- Over the years, IASC has evolved into the leading international science organization of the North and its membership today includes 23 countries involved in all aspects of Arctic research, including 15 non-Arctic countries (Austria, China, the Czech Republic, France, Germany, India, Italy, Japan, the Netherlands, Poland, Portugal, South Korea, Spain, Switzerland and the UK).
- The International Arctic Science Committee (IASC) is a non-governmental, international scientific organization. The Founding Articles committed IASC to pursue a mission of encouraging and facilitating cooperation in all aspects of Arctic research, in all countries engaged in Arctic research and in all areas of the Arctic region.
- Overall, IASC promotes and supports leading-edge multi-disciplinary research in order to foster a greater scientific understanding of the Arctic region and its role in the Earth system.

To achieve this mission IASC:

- Initiates, coordinates and promotes scientific activities at a circumarctic or international level;
- Provides mechanisms and instruments to support science development;
- Provides objective and independent scientific advice on issues of science in the Arctic and communicates scientific information to the public;
- Seeks to ensure that scientific data and information from the Arctic are safeguarded, freely exchangeable and accessible;
- Promotes international access to all geographic areas and the sharing of knowledge, logistics and other resources;
- Provides for the freedom and ethical conduct of science;
- Promotes and involves the next generation of scientists working in the Arctic; and
- Promotes polar cooperation through interaction with relevant science organizations.

International Union of Geological Sciences (IUGS)

> **Established** : 1961
> **Headquarters** : Beijing (China), secretariat
> **Head** : Qiuming CHENG (President)
> **Members** : 121 Countries

- It acts as the coordinating body for the international organization of science.
- It promotes and encourages the study of geological problems, especially those of worldwide significance, and supports and facilitates international and interdisciplinary cooperation in the earth sciences.
- It participates in the Global Network of National Geoparks (GGN).

DEFENCE ORGANISATIONS

North Atlantic Treaty Organization (NATO)

> **Established** : 1949
> **Headquarters** : (Brussels, Belgium)
> **Head** : Jens Stoltenberg (Secretary General)
> **Members** : 29 Countries

- At present, NATO has 29 members. In 1949, there were 12 founding members of the Alliance: Belgium, Canada, Denmark, France, Iceland, Italy, Luxembourg, the Netherlands, Norway, Portugal, the United Kingdom and the United States. The other member countries are: Greece and Turkey (1952), Germany (1955), Spain (1982), the Czech Republic, Hungary and Poland (1999), Bulgaria, Estonia, Latvia, Lithuania, Romania, Slovakia and Slovenia (2004), Albania and Croatia (2009), and Montenegro (2017).
  (i) Provision for enlargement is given by Article 10 of the North Atlantic Treaty.
  (ii) Article 10 states that membership is open to any "European State in a position to further the principles of this Treaty and to contribute to the security of the North Atlantic area".
  (iii) Any decision to invite a country to join the Alliance is taken by the North Atlantic Council, NATO's principal political decision-making body, on the basis of consensus among all Allies.
- NATO's purpose is to guarantee the freedom and security of its members through political and military means;

POLITICAL - NATO promotes democratic values and enables members to consult and cooperate on defence and security-related issues to solve problems, build trust and, in the long run, prevent conflict.

MILITARY - NATO is committed to the peaceful resolution of disputes. If diplomatic efforts fail, it has the military power to undertake crisis-management operations. These are carried out under the collective defence clause of NATO's founding treaty - Article 5 of the Washington Treaty or under a United Nations mandate, alone or in cooperation with other countries and international organisations.

Warsaw Treaty Organisation (Warsaw Pact)

Established	: 1955
Headquarters	: Moscow
Head	: Pyotr Lushev (Last)
Members	: 8 Nations

- The Warsaw Treaty Organization (WTO), also referred to as the Warsaw Pact, was created on May 14, 1955, by Albania, Bulgaria, Czechoslovakia, East Germany, Hungary, Poland, Romania, and the Soviet Union. Officially known as the Warsaw Treaty of Friendship, Cooperation, and Mutual Assistance, it was a Soviet-led political and military alliance intended to harness the potential of Eastern Europe to Soviet military strategy and to consolidate Soviet control of Eastern Europe during the Cold War.

- The organization was used to suppress dissent in Eastern Europe through military action. It never enlarged beyond its original membership, and was dissolved in 1991, prior to the disintegration of the Soviet Union itself.

- The Soviet and East European governments presented the WTO as their response to the creation of the Western European Union and the integration of West Germany into the North Atlantic Treaty Organization (NATO) in 1955. Though often described as an alliance, the facade of collective decision-making in WTO masked the reality of Soviet political and military domination.

- The 1955 treaty established the Joint Command of the armed forces (Article 5) and the Political Consultative Committee (Article 6), both headquartered in Moscow. In practice, however, the Joint Command, as well as the Joint Staff drawn from the general staffs of the signatories, was part of the Soviet General Staff. Both the Pact's commander in chief and its chief of staff were Soviet officers. The Joint Armed Forces had no command structure, logistics, directorate of operations, or air defence network separate from the Soviet defence ministry.

ARMS CONTROL

Nuclear Non-proliferation Treaty (NPT)

Established	: 1968
Headquarters	: Moscow (Russia)
Head	: Izumi Nakamitsu under-secretary General & High Representation
Members	: 191 Countries

- The Nuclear Non-proliferation Treaty (NPT) formally called the Treaty on the Non-proliferation of Nuclear Weapons.

- The NPT is a landmark international treaty whose objective is to prevent the spread of nuclear weapons and weapons technology, to promote cooperation in the peaceful uses of nuclear energy and to further the goal of achieving nuclear disarmament and general and complete disarmament.

- The Treaty represents the only binding commitment in a multilateral treaty to the goal of disarmament by the nuclear-weapon States. Opened for signature in 1968, the Treaty entered into force in 1970.

- On 11 May 1995, the Treaty was extended indefinitely. A total of 191 States have joined the Treaty, including the five nuclear-weapon States. More countries have ratified the NPT than any other arms limitation and disarmament agreement, a testament to the Treaty's significance.

Nuclear-Weapon-Free Zones (NWFZ)

- The establishment of Nuclear-Weapon-Free Zones (NWFZ) is a regional approach to strengthen global nuclear non-proliferation and disarmament norms and consolidate international efforts towards peace and security. Article VII of the Nuclear Non-Proliferation Treaty (NPT) states: "Nothing in this Treaty affects the right of any group of States to conclude regional treaties in order to assure the total absence of nuclear weapons in their respective territories".

- General Assembly resolution 3472 B (1975) defines a Nuclear-Weapon-Free Zone **as**

  ...any zone recognized as such by the General Assembly of the United Nations, which any group of States, in the free exercises of their sovereignty, has established by virtue of a treaty or convention whereby:

  (a) The statute of total absence of nuclear weapons, to which the zone shall be subject, including the procedure for the delimitation of the zone, is defined;

  (b) An international system of verification and control is established to guarantee compliance with the obligations deriving from that statute.

- There are five Treaties on regional Nuclear-Weapons-Free-Zones that require its parties to conclude a comprehensive safeguards agreement with the IAEA:

  1. Treaty for the Prohibition of Nuclear Weapons in Latin America and the Caribbean (Treaty of Tlatelolco, 1967)

  2. South Pacific Nuclear Free Zone Treaty (Treaty of Rarotonga, 1985)

  3. Treaty on the Southeast Asia Nuclear Weapon-Free Zone (Treaty of Bangkok, 1995)

  4. African Nuclear-Weapon-Free Zone Treaty (Treaty of Pelindaba, 1996)

  5. Treaty on a Nuclear-Weapon-Free Zone in Central Asia (Treaty of Semipalatinsk, 2006)

Strategic Arms Reduction Treaty (START)

Established	: 1991 (Signed)
Headquarters	: Washington, DC
Head	: Daryl Kimball (Executive Director)
Members	: 5 (United States, Russian Federation, Belarus, Kazakhstan and Ukraine)

- The Strategic Arms Reduction Treaty, now known as START I, was one of the key weapons agreements forged during the détente period of the late Cold War era. Negotiations for strategic weapon reductions of the United States and Soviet Union arsenals began in 1982, when both nations sought a lessening of Cold War tensions.
- The initial enthusiasm for the treaty waned when the Soviet Union withdrew from talks regarding weapons reduction after the United States deployed several immediate-range missiles in allied nations in Western Europe. Negotiations did not begin again until 1985, and then progressed slowly until the fall the Iron Curtain and Soviet-influenced communism in Eastern Europe.
- START I was finally signed by United States President George H. W. Bush and Soviet Premier Mikhel Gorbachev in Moscow on July 31, 1991.
- The START I treaty expired 5 December 2009. On 8 April 2010, the replacement New START treaty was signed in Prague by United States President Barack Obama and Russian President Dmitry Medvedev. Following ratification by the U.S. Senate and the Federal Assembly of Russia, it went into force on 26 January 2011. This Treaty was the first to provide tremendous reductions of American and Soviet/Russian strategic nuclear weapons.

Biological Weapons Convention (BWC)

Established	: 1972
Headquarters	: New York
Head	: Daryl Kimball, Executive Director
Members	: 182 States-Parties

- The Convention on the Prohibition of the Development, Production and Stockpiling of Bacteriological (Biological) and Toxin Weapons and on their Destruction (usually referred to as the Biological Weapons Convention or Biological and Toxin Weapons Convention, abbreviation: BTWC) was the first multilateral disarmament treaty banning the production of an entire category of weapons.
- The Convention was the result of prolonged efforts by the international community to establish a new instrument that would supplement the 1925 Geneva Protocol. The Geneva Protocol prohibits use but not possession or development of chemical and biological weapons.
- A draft of the BWC, submitted by the British was opened for signature on 10 April 1972 and entered into force 26 March 1975 when twenty-two governments had deposited their instruments of ratification. It commits the 181 states which are party to it as of July 2018 to prohibit the development, production, and stockpiling of biological and toxin weapons.
- However, the absence of any formal verification regime to monitor compliance has limited the effectiveness of the Convention. An additional six states have signed the BWC but have yet to ratify the treaty.

The Missile Technology Control Regime (MTCR)

Established	: 1987
Headquarters	: Washington, DC
Head	: Rotates on an ad hock basis (chairmanship)
Members	: 35 Countries

- The Missile Technology Control Regime (MTCR) is an informal political understanding among states that seek to limit the proliferation of missiles and missile technology. The regime was formed in 1987 by the G-7 industrialized countries (Canada, France, Germany, Italy, Japan, the UK, and the United States).

Argentina (1993)	Greece (1992)	Portugal (1992)
Australia (1990)	Hungary (1993)	Republic of Korea (2001)
Austria (1991)	Iceland (1993)	Russian Federation (1995)
Belgium (1990)	India (2016)	South Africa (1995)
Bulgaria (2004)	Ireland (1992)	Spain (1990)
Brazil (1995)	Italy (1987)	Sweden (1991)
Canada (1987)	Japan (1987)	Switzerland (1992)
Czech Republic (1998)	Luxembourg (1990)	Turkey (1997)
Denmark (1990)	Netherlands (1990)	Ukraine (1998)
Finland (1991)	New Zealand (1991)	United Kingdom (1987)
France (1987)	Norway (1990)	United States of America (1987)
Germany (1987)	Poland (1998)	

- It is a multilateral, consensus – based grouping of 35 member countries that are voluntarily committed to the non-proliferation of missiles capable of carrying chemical, biological and nuclear weapons of mass destruction (WMDs).
- It controls the export of the technologies and materials involved in ballistic missile systems and unmanned aerial vehicles particularly capable of carrying nuclear warheads of above 500kg payload for more than 300 km.
- This is a non–treaty association of member countries with certain guidelines about the information sharing, national control laws and export policies for missile systems and a rule-based regulation mechanism to limit the transfer of such critical technologies of these missile systems.

Important Facts

- It was established in April 1987 by G-7 countries – USA, UK, France, Germany, Canada, Italy, and Japan, to check the spread of unmanned delivery systems capable of carrying nuclear weapons of above 500kg for more than 300km. In 1992, it was extended for all types of weapons of mass destruction.
- Now, it has 35 full members including India and 4 "non-adherent members" – Israel, Macedonia, Romania, and Slovakia.
- China is not a member of this regime but it had verbally pledged to adhere to its original guidelines but not to the subsequent additions.
- These efforts of non-proliferation of ballistic missile systems had further been strengthened by "The International Code of Conduct against Ballistic Missile Proliferation", also known as the Hague Code of Conduct (HCOC), which was established on 25 November 2002 as an arrangement to prevent the proliferation of ballistic missiles with 136 UN member countries including India.

India's Journey to MTCR

2005: Prime Minister Manmohan Singh committed India's "harmonisation and adherence" to MTCR guidelines.

2008: US President Geogre W. Bush informed the US Congress that India was adhering to guidelines.

2010: After India-US civil nuclear deal, US announced to work towards opening the doors for India to ghe four arms control regimes–MTCR, NSG, Australia Group and Wassenaar Arrangement.

October 2015: India's membership application to MTCR not accepted in Rotterdam plenary because of objection by Italy.

May 2016: Italy removed it virtual veto after the second Italina marine returned home in the fishermen murder case.

June 2016: India adhered voluntarily to the Hague Code of Conduct against Ballistic Missile Proliferation.

October 2016: As a new member India will be entitled to "full participation" in organizational activities including the plenary of MTCR which will take place in South Korea.

MTCR achieve its objectives

- Export Controls The Regime rests on adherence to common export policy (the Guidelines) applied to an integral common list of items (the MTCR Equipment, Software, and Technology Annex.)
- Meetings MTCR Partners regularly exchange information about relevant missile non-proliferation issues in the context of the Regime's overall aims.
- Dialogue and Outreach The MTCR Chair and MTCR Partners undertake outreach activities to non-Partners in order to keep them informed about the group's activities and to provide practical assistance regarding efforts to prevent the proliferation of WMD delivery systems.

Achievements

- It has significantly contributed to curbing or slows down the nuclear programmes of some countries.
- Argentina dropped its joint ballistic missile programme" Condor II" with Egypt and Iraq.
- Poland and the Czech Republic vanished their ballistic missiles in an effort to join the regime.
- Brazil, South Africa, South Korea, and Taiwan also withdrew or curbed their missiles or space launch vehicle programs.
- Recently, it played a major role to hamper Libyan and Syrian missile efforts.

Nuclear Suppliers Group (NSG)

Established	: 1974
Headquarters	: –
Head	: Jānis Zlamets (Chairmanship)
Members	: 48 Countries

- The Nuclear Suppliers Group (NSG) is a group of nuclear supplier countries ("NSG Participating Governments") that seeks to contribute to the non-proliferation of nuclear weapons through the implementation of two sets of guidelines for their nuclear exports and nuclear-related exports.
- The Nuclear Suppliers Group (NSG) was created following the explosion in 1974 of a nuclear device by a non-nuclear-weapon State, which demonstrated that nuclear technology transferred for peaceful purposes could be misused.

There are currently 48 Participating Governments (PGs) of the NSG. The year of participation is in brackets.				
Argentina (1994)	Cyprus (2000)	Ireland (1984)	New Zealand (1994)	South Africa (1995)
Australia (1978)	Czech Republic (1978*)	Italy (1978)	Norway (1989)	Spain (1988)
Austria (1991)	Denmark (1984)	Japan (1974)	Poland (1978)	Sweden (1978)
Belarus (2000)	Estonia (2004)	Kazakhstan (2002)	Portugal (1986)	Switzerland (1978)
Belgium (1978)	Finland (1980)	Latvia (1997)	Romania (1990)	Turkey (2000)
Brazil (1996)	France (1974)	Lithuania (2004)	Rep. of Korea (1995)	Ukraine (1996)
Bulgaria (1984)	Germany (1974)	Luxembourg (1984)	Russia (1974)	U.K. (1974)
Canada (1974)	Greece (1984)	Malta (2004)	Serbia (2013)	U.S. (1974)
China (2004)	Hungary (1985)	Mexico (2012)	Slovakia (1978*)	
Croatia (2005)	Iceland (2009)	Netherlands (1978)	Slovenia (2000)	

(* Czechoslovakia separated into the Czech Republic and Slovakia – participation date 5 Mar 1993)

- The European Commission and the Chair of the Zangger Committee participate as observers.
- Shortly after entry into force of the Treaty on the Non-Proliferation of Nuclear Weapons (NPT) in 1970, multilateral consultations on nuclear export controls to reach common understandings on how to implement Article III.2 of the NPT led to the establishment of two separate mechanisms for dealing with nuclear exports: the Zangger Committee in 1971 and what has become known as the Nuclear Suppliers Group in 1975.
- The Zangger Committee established the original Trigger List and three conditions of supply: (1) a non-explosive use assurance, (2) an International Atomic Energy Agency (IAEA) safeguards requirement, and (3) a re-transfer provision that requires the receiving state to apply the same conditions when re-exporting these items.
- The NSG, known originally as the "London Club," convened a series of meetings to facilitate a consistent interpretation of the obligations arising from that Article among major suppliers in and outside of the NPT, following the explosion in 1974 of a nuclear device by a non-nuclear-weapon State, an event which demonstrated that nuclear technology transferred for peaceful purposes could be misused.
- The NSG elaborated on the three original conditions of supply with the Part 1 Guidelines and adopted the original Zangger Committee's Trigger List as an annex to the Guidelines.
- As a part of NSG outreach, the group maintains a public document entitled "The Nuclear Suppliers Group: Its Origins, Role, and Activities", which it updates periodically for publication by the IAEA as INFCIRC 539.

India and NSG

- The NSG was established in 1975 in response to India's nuclear test in 1974. Though NSG is admitting new countries but it is allowing only those countries which are signatory of Non-Proliferation Treaty (NPT) or Comprehensive Test Ban Treaty (CTBT). India has signed neither the NPT nor is it a member of CTBT.

- Since long time India is trying to get NSG membership. It was civil nuclear deal with US, concluded in 2008, that paved the way for India's application as a member of NSG. Considering India's commitment to separate its civilian and military nuclear programmes and its non proliferation record in nuclear weapons India has got support from various NSG members.

Importance of NSG membership-

- It will pave the way to access technology for a range of uses from medicine to building nuclear power plants for India.
- By accessing latest technology, India can commercialize the production of nuclear power equipment. This, in turn will boost innovation and high tech manufacturing in India.
- Having the ability to offer its own nuclear power plants to the world means spawning of an entire nuclear industry and related technology development. This could give the Make in India programme a big boost.
- An NSG membership will make indigenous nuclear industry companies comply with international norms and make it easier for them to trade in international market.
- There is pressing need to scale up nuclear power production to realise India's commitment to reduce dependence on fossil fuels and to ensure 40% of its energy is sourced from renewable and clean sources. It will possible only if India gains access to NSG.

The Australia Group (AG)

Established	: 1985
Headquarters	: Paris (Regular Meeting)
Head	: Michael Gregory (Head of the Secretariat)
Members	: 43 Nations

- The Australia Group is an informal arrangement which aims to allow exporting or transshipping countries to reduce the risk of assisting **chemical and biological weapon (CBW)** proliferation.

- Participants in the Australia Group do not undertake any legally binding obligations: the effectiveness of their cooperation depends solely on a shared commitment to CBW non-proliferation goals and the strength of their respective national measures. Key considerations in the formulation of participants' export licensing measures are:
  (i)   they should be effective in impeding the production of chemical and biological weapons;
  (ii) they should be practical, and reasonably easy to implement, and
  (iii) they should not impede the normal trade of materials and equipment used for legitimate purposes.
- All states participating in the Australia Group are parties to the Chemical Weapons Convention (CWC) and the Biological Weapons Convention (BWC), and strongly support efforts under those Conventions to rid the world of CBW.
- In April 1984, following the findings of a special mission dispatched by the UN Secretary General to Iran to investigate the use of chemical weapons (CW) by Iraq in the Iran-Iraq War, a number of governments introduced licensing measures on the export of certain chemicals used in the manufacture of CW. They took this action in order to meet the political requirement for a response to Iraq's violation of the **1925 Geneva Protocol** through the use of chemical weapons against Iran in the Iran-Iraq War and the very clear evidence that Iraq had obtained much of the materials for its CW program from the international chemical industry.
- As a result, Australia Group was established in Brussels in June **1985**. All participating countries agreed there was benefit in continuing the process, and meetings of the AG are now held in Paris on an annual basis.
- **There are 43 Members** — Argentina, Australia, Austria, Belgium, Bulgaria, Canada, Croatia, Cyprus, Czech Republic, Denmark, Estonia, European Union, Finland, France, Germany, Greece, Hungary, Iceland, India, Ireland, Italy, Japan, Republic of Korea, Latvia, Lithuania, Luxembourg, Malta, Mexico, Netherlands, New Zealand, Norway, Poland, Portugal, Romania, Slovakia, Slovenia, Spain, Sweden, Switzerland, Turkey, Ukraine, United Kingdom, and United States.

India's Membership: On 19 January 2018 India formally became the 43rd member of the Australia Group (AG).

- The main objective of AG participants' is to use licensing measures to ensure that exports of certain chemicals, biological agents, and dual-use chemical and biological manufacturing facilities and equipment, do not contribute to the spread of CBW.
- Participants have recognised from the outset that export licensing measures are not a substitute for the strict and universal observance of the **1925 Geneva Protocol**, the **1972 Biological and Toxin Weapons Convention (BWC)** and the Chemical Weapons Convention (CWC). All participants in the Australia Group are States Parties to both the BWC and the CWC.

- The six Common Control Lists cover:
  (i)   CW precursors;
  (ii) dual-use chemical manufacturing facilities and equipment and related technology;
  (iii) dual-use biological equipment;
  (iv) biological agents;
  (v)   plant pathogens; and
  (vi) animal pathogens.

The Wassenaar Arrangement

Established	: 1995
Headquarters	: Vienna (Austria),Secretariat
Head	: Philip Griffiths
Members	: 42 Nations

- The Wassenaar Arrangement has been established in order to contribute to regional and international security and stability, by promoting transparency and greater responsibility in transfers of conventional arms and dual-use goods and technologies, thus preventing destabilising accumulations.
- Participating States seek, through their national policies, to ensure that transfers of these items do not contribute to the development or enhancement of military capabilities which undermine these goals, and are not diverted to support such capabilities. The aim is also to prevent the acquisition of these items by terrorists.
- Agreement to establish the "Wassenaar Arrangement" was reached at the HLM held on 19 December 1995, in Wassenaar Netherlands, near The Hague and this was announced with a declaration issued at the Peace Palace in The Hague. At this time there was also agreement to locate the Secretariat in Vienna and establish a Preparatory Committee of the Whole to prepare for the first plenary meeting.
- The inaugural Plenary Meeting of the Wassenaar Arrangement was held 2-3 April 1996 in Vienna, Austria but consensus could not be reached on all issues. On 11-12 July 1996, the Plenary Meeting resumed, with Bulgaria and Ukraine participating, to make a total of 33 founding members. Final consensus on the "Initial Elements", the basic document of the WA, was reached and it was established that the new Control Lists and Information Exchange would be implemented from 1 November 1996.
- The first Plenary Meeting of the now operational Wassenaar Arrangement was held on 12-13 December 1996 in Vienna.

Member Nations of WA are: Argentina, Australia, Austria, Belgium, Bulgaria, Canada, Croatia, Czech Republic, Denmark, Estonia, Finland, France, Germany, Greece, Hungary, India, Ireland, Italy, Japan, Latvia, Lithuania, Luxembourg, Malta, Mexico, Netherlands, New Zealand, Norway, Poland, Portugal, Republic of Korea, Romania,

Russian Federation, Slovakia, Slovenia, South Africa, Spain, Sweden, Switzerland, Turkey, Ukraine, United Kingdom and United States.

The Member Nations:

(i) have agreed to maintain national export controls on items included in the WA Control Lists. These controls are implemented via national legislation;

(ii) are guided by agreed Best Practices, Guidelines or Elements;

(iii) have agreed to report on transfers and denials of specified controlled items to destinations outside the Arrangement;

(iv) exchange information on sensitive dual-use goods and technologies.

- It contains 22 main entries on items designed for military use, including certain items within the categories such as (but not limited to):

  (i) Small Arms & Light Weapons (and related ammunition);

  (ii) Tanks and other Military Armed Vehicles;

  (iii) Armoured/Protective Equipment,

  (iv) Aircraft & Unmanned Airborne Vehicles, Aero Engines & related equipment (for comprehensive details please refer to the 'Munitions List' on the Wassenaar Arrangement Website).

The Zangger Committee/ NPT Exporters Committee

Established	: 1971
Headquarters	: Vienna (Austria)
Head	: Shawn Caza
Members	: 39 Nations

- Between 1971 and 1974, a group of 15 States - some already parties to the Nuclear Non-Proliferation-Treaty (NPT), others prospective parties - held a series of informal meetings in Vienna chaired by Professor Claude Zangger of Switzerland. As suppliers or potential suppliers of nuclear material and equipment, their objective was to reach a common understanding on:

  (a) the definition of what constituted "equipment or material especially designed or prepared for the processing, use or production of special fissionable material" (as it was not defined anywhere in the Treaty);

  (b) the conditions and procedures that would govern exports of such equipment or material in order to meet the obligations of article III, paragraph 2 of the NPT, on a basis of fair commercial competition.

- The group, which came to be known as the **Zangger Committee**, decided that its status was informal and that its decisions would in themselves not be legally binding upon its members. Decisions of the Committee are taken by consensus.

- Thus, The Zangger Committee, also known as the **"NPT Exporters Committee"**, essentially contributes to the interpretation of article III, paragraph 2, of the Nuclear Non-Proliferation Treaty (NPT) and thereby offers guidance to all parties to the Treaty.

- Article III, paragraph 2, of the NPT performs a vital function in helping to ensure the peaceful use of nuclear material and equipment. Specifically, it provides:

  "Each State Party to the Treaty undertakes not to provide:

  (a) source or special fissionable material, or

  (b) equipment or material especially designed or prepared for the processing, use, or production of special fissionable material, to any non-nuclear-weapon State for peaceful purposes, unless the source or special fissionable material shall be subject to the safeguards required by this article."

- The main objective is that parties to the Treaty should not export, directly or indirectly, nuclear material and equipment to non-nuclear-weapon States unless the export is subject to International Atomic Energy Agency (IAEA) safeguards. By interpreting and implementing article III, paragraph 2, the Zangger Committee helps to prevent the diversion of exported nuclear items from peaceful purposes to nuclear weapons or other nuclear explosive devices, and thereby furthers the objectives of the Treaty and enhances the security of all States.

- As circumstances are changing with respect to the use of nuclear technology, it is the Zangger Committee's mission within the framework of the NPT to take account of changing security aspects and to adapt export control conditions and criteria from time to time according to the needs.

- The Zangger Committee understandings reflect the requirements laid down in article III, paragraph 2. There are three conditions of supply:

  (a) For exports to non-nuclear-weapon States, source or special fissionable material either directly transferred, or produced, processed, or used in the facility for which the transferred item is intended, shall not be diverted to nuclear weapons or other nuclear explosive devices;

  (b) For exports to non-nuclear-weapon States, such source or special fissionable material, as well as transferred equipment and non-nuclear material, shall be subject to safeguards under an agreement with the **International Atomic Energy Agency (IAEA);**

  (c) Source or special fissionable material, and equipment and non-nuclear material shall not be re-exported to a non-nuclear-weapon State unless the recipient State accepts safeguards on the re-exported item.

- These understandings were formally accepted by individual States members of the Committee in an exchange of notes among themselves.

The 39 - Member States are:

Argentina, Australia, Austria, Belarus, Belgium, Bulgaria, Canada, China, Croatia, Czech Republic, Denmark, Finland, France, Germany, Greece, Hungary, Ireland, Italy, Japan, Kazakhstan, Republic of Korea, Luxemburg, The Netherlands, New Zealand, Norway, Poland, Portugal, Romania, Russian Federation, Slovakia, Slovenia, South Africa, Spain, Sweden, Switzerland, Turkey, Ukraine, United Kingdom and United States of America.

The European Union is permanent observer.

Note: India is not a member of the Zangger Committee

SOCIAL & CULTURAL ORGANISATIONS

International Committee of the Red Cross–(ICRC)

Established	: 1863
Headquarters	: Geneva (Switzerland)
Head	: Peter Maurer (President)
Members	: 190 (National Red Cross and Red Crescent Societies)

- The International Committee of the Red Cross is established in 1863, the ICRC operates worldwide, helping people affected by conflict and armed violence and promoting the laws that protect victims of war. An independent and neutral organization, its mandate stems essentially from the Geneva Conventions of 1949. It is based in Geneva, Switzerland, and employ some 16,000 people in more than 80 countries.
- The ICRC is funded mainly by voluntary donations from governments and from National Red Cross and Red Crescent Societies.
- The work of the ICRC is based on the Geneva Conventions of 1949, their Additional Protocols, its Statutes those of the International Red Cross and Red Crescent Movement and the resolutions of the International Conferences of the Red Cross and Red Crescent.
- The ICRC is an independent, neutral organization ensuring humanitarian protection and assistance for victims of war and armed violence. It takes action in response to emergencies and promotes respect for international humanitarian law and its implementation in national law.
- National Red Cross and Red Crescent Societies in 190 countries who are members of the International Federation, and for those Societies who are in formation and invited as observers to the International Federation's General Assembly.

International Organization for Migration (IMO)

Established	: 1951
Headquarters	: Switzerland
Head	: William Lacy Swing
Members	: 172 Member States + 8 Observer States

- International Organization for Migration was established in 1951; IOM is the leading inter-governmental organization in the field of migration and works closely with governmental, intergovernmental and non-governmental partners.
- With 172 member states, a further 8 states holding observer status and offices in over 100 countries, IOM is dedicated to promoting humane and orderly migration for the benefit of all. It does so by providing services and advice to governments and migrants.
- IOM works to help ensure the orderly and humane management of migration, to promote international cooperation on migration issues, to assist in the search for practical solutions to migration problems and to provide humanitarian assistance to migrants in need, including refugees and internally displaced people.

The IOM Constitution recognizes the link between migration and economic, social and cultural development, as well as to the right of freedom of movement.

- IOM works in the four broad areas of migration management:
  (i)   Migration and development
  (ii)   Facilitating migration
  (iii) Regulating migration
  (iv)   Forced migration.
- IOM activities that cut across these areas include the promotion of international migration law, policy debate and guidance, protection of migrants' rights, migration health and the gender dimension of migration.

Amnesty International–(AI)

Established	: 1961
Headquarters	: London (UK)
Head	: Kumi Naidoo (Secretary General)
Members	: 159 Countries

- Amnesty International (AI) is a non-profit, independent international organization that works zealously to protect human rights around the world. Since its inception in 1961, Amnesty International has coordinated research, information, and education campaigns in order to focus world attention on such issues as freedom of conscience and expression, freedom from discrimination, and the cessation of physical and mental abuse and torture suffered by the victims of human rights violations.
- Amnesty International is a global movement of more than 7 million people who take injustice personally. We are campaigning for a world where human rights are enjoyed by all.
- In 1961, British lawyer Peter Benenson was outraged when two Portuguese students were jailed just for raising a toast to freedom. He wrote an article in The Observer newspaper and launched a campaign that provoked an incredible response. Reprinted in newspapers across the world, his call to action sparked the idea that people everywhere can unite in solidarity for justice and freedom.

- Amnesty has grown from seeking the release of political prisoners to upholding the whole spectrum of human rights. Our work protects and empowers people - from abolishing the death penalty to protecting sexual and reproductive rights, and from combating discrimination to defending refugees and migrants' rights. We speak out for anyone and everyone whose freedom and dignity are under threat.

Human Rights Campaign (HRC)

Established	: 1980
Headquarters	: Washington, D.C. (USA)
Head	: Chad Griffin (President)
Members	: More than 3 Million Members & Supporters nationwide

- The Human Rights Campaign Fund was founded by Steve Endean in 1980 as one of the first gay and lesbian political action committee in the United States. The Fund's mission was to provide financial support on behalf of the gay and lesbian community to political candidates who supported gay civil rights legislation. Vic Basile served as the Fund's first executive director.
- The Human Rights Campaign represents a force of more than 3 million members and supporters nationwide. As the largest national lesbian, gay, bisexual, transgender and queer civil rights organization, HRC envisions a world where LGBTQ people are ensured of their basic equal rights, and can be open, honest and safe at home, at work and in the community.
- The Human Rights Campaign Foundation improves the lives of lesbian, bisexual, transgender and queer (LGBTQ) people by working to increase understanding and encourage the adoption of LGBTQ-inclusive policies and practices.

World Food Programme (WFP)

Established	: 1961
Headquarters	: Rome (Italy)
Head	: David Beasley (President)
Members	: 36 Nations

- The World Food Programme's long experience in humanitarian and development contexts has positioned the organization well to support resilience building in order to improve food security and nutrition. WFP helps the most vulnerable people strengthen their capacities to absorb, adapt, and transform in the face of shocks and long-term stressors.
- Assisting 80 million people in around 80 countries each year, the World Food Programme (WFP) is the leading humanitarian organization saving lives and changing lives, delivering food assistance in emergencies and working with communities to improve nutrition and build resilience.
- As the international community has committed to end hunger, achieve food security and improved nutrition by 2030, one in nine people worldwide still do not have enough to eat. Food and food-related assistance lie at the heart of the struggle to break the cycle of hunger and poverty.
- At WFP, we are committed to providing a safe and respectful work environment for all our employees. We adopt a zero-tolerance approach to sexual harassment, harassment, abuse of authority and discrimination in the workplace. WFP has a clear and robust framework (HSHAPD Policy) to address and deter such behaviour.
- The World Food Programme created an Ethics Office in 2008 to ensure that all staff members observe and perform their functions with the highest standards of integrity, as required by the Charter of the United Nations, and in accordance with the Standards of Conduct for the International Civil Service.
- At the same time, WFP adopted a Whistleblower Protection Policy to guard against retaliation for individuals who report misconduct, provide information in good faith on wrongdoing by one or more employees, or cooperate with a duly authorized audit or investigation.

International Federation of Film Archives (FIAF)

Established	: 1938
Headquarters	: Brussels (Secretariat)
Head	: Frédéric Maire (President)
Members	: 89 Nations

- FIAF's official date of birth is generally recognized as 17 June 1938, as confirmed by the date of the "Agreement for the International Federation of Film Archives" signed in Paris by its four founder-members – the Cinémathèque française, Germany's Reichsfilmarchiv, the British Film Institute, and the Museum of Modern Art Film Library. However, the seeds of this project of international co-operation had been planted several months, if not years, before, and the Federation did not become a fully operational organization for many more months.
- FIAF, the International Federation of Film Archives, has been dedicated to the preservation of, and access to, the world's film heritage since 1938. It brings together the world's leading non-profit institutions in this field.
- Its affiliates are committed to the rescue, collection, preservation, screening, and promotion of films, which are valued both as works of art and culture and as historical documents. When FIAF was founded in June 1938, it had four members. As of May 2018, it comprises more than 166 institutions in 75 countries – a reflection of the extent

to which film heritage has become a world-wide concern. After 80 years of experience in this field, FIAF has grown to be the most important global network of cinematheques and film archives.

- **FIAF's missions are:**
  (i) To uphold a code of ethics for film preservation and practical standards for all areas of film archive work;
  (ii) To promote the creation of moving image archives in countries which lack them;
  (iii) To seek the improvement of the legal context within which film archives carry out their work;
  (iv) To promote film culture and facilitate historical research on both a national and international level;
  (v) To foster training and expertise in preservation and other archive techniques;
  (vi) To ensure the permanent availability of material from the collections for study and research by the wider community;
  (vii) To encourage the collection and preservation of documents and materials relating to the cinema;
  (viii) To develop co-operation between members and to ensure the international availability of films and documents.

International Music Council (IMC)

Established	: 1949
Headquarters	: Paris
Head	: Silja Fischer (General Secretariat)
Members	: 65 National Music Councils, over 50 international and regional music organizations

- The International Music Council (IMC) is the world's leading membership-based professional organisation dedicated to the promotion of the value of music in the lives of all peoples. IMC's mission is to develop sustainable music sectors worldwide, to create awareness about the value of music, to make music matter throughout the fabric of society, and to uphold basic music rights in all countries.
- IMC was founded in 1949 at the request of the Director-General of UNESCO as a non-governmental advisory body to the agency on musical matters. It is based at UNESCO headquarters in Paris and functions today independently as an international NGO official partner of UNESCO.

International Dance Organization (IDO)

Established	: 1981
Headquarters	: Slagelse (Denmark)
Head	: Michael Wendt (President)
Members	: 60 Countries

- The International Dance Organization (IDO) was founded as a non-profit organization on September 18, 1981 by Mr. Moreno Polidori, in Florence, Italy. The original founding member nations were Italy, France, Switzerland and Gibraltar. Mr. Polidori was appointed General Secretary and drew up the original statutes, by-laws and rules that governed the organization.
- The IDO is now not only involved with the granting of Continental and International Competitions and Championships, but is deeply involved with many aspects of our dance industry.
- It is constantly striving to improve the quality of its dancers, through participation, its adjudicators through education, and national member images by being involved with the largest dance organization in the world. The various disciplines, through their committees, are convened on a regular basis to ensure that the IDO rules are always current and up to date with its membership wishes.

CHILDREN/WOMEN WELFARE ORGANISATIONS/AGENCIES

International Alliance of Women (IAW)

Established	: 1904
Headquarters	: Geneva (Switzerland)
Head	: Joanna Manganara (President)
Members	: 41 member organizations

- Founded in 1904 and based in Geneva, the International Alliance of Women (IAW) is an international NGO comprising 41 member organizations involved in the promotion of the human rights of women and girls globally.
- The IAW has general consultative status with the UN Economic and Social Council and is accredited to many specialized UN agencies, has participatory status with the Council of Europe and is represented at the Arab League, the African Union and other international organizations. To promote women's human rights around the world, focusing particularly on empowerment of women and development issues and more broadly on gender equality.
- It has had general consultative status to the United Nations Economic and Social Council.
- Universal ratification and implementation without reservation of the Convention on the Elimination of All Forms of Discrimination Against Women (CEDAW) and its Optional Protocol.

International Forum for Child Welfare (IFCW)

Established	: 1989
Headquarters	: –
Head	: Heresa Costello (President)
Members	: 43 Nations

- The International Forum for Child Welfare is an international non-government organisation chartered under the laws of Switzerland, and in consultative status Category 11 with the Economic and Social Council of the United Nations.

- The IFCW was founded in 1989 after four years of development as part of a Congress on the Rights of the Child, "to strengthen national non-governmental child welfare organisations worldwide, to share concerns and to collaborate on new initiatives on behalf of this planet's most valuable resource - children."

- The mission of IFCW is to work for children worldwide to improve the quality of their lives and to enhance opportunities for the development of their full potential. This mission represents a commitment by IFCW's Members to work for the fulfilment of the Convention on the Rights of the Child in every nation and is to be achieved through the strengthening of nongovernmental child welfare organisations (NGOs) worldwide in their direct and indirect service to children and families by:

  (i) Organising and improving information exchange and cooperation among members.

  (ii) Educating world opinion on the interest and well-being of children.

  (iii) Promoting and organising conferences, seminars and study groups.

  (iv) Cooperating with other recognised bodies having similar objectives.

- Every year the IFCW - International Forum for Child Welfare- organizes the Executive Institute for directors and managers of the organizations members. The specific topic of each Executive Institute is related in each occasion with a contemporary critical challenge, for example, in leadership, management and development of human and financial resources.

- The Executive Institute uses the experience of managers, leaders, academic and consultants. The IFCW also help to build the capacity of their organizations members by means of regional seminars, prizes to social media to promote the use of professional and effective communication materials, improving the exchange and the cooperation among the members and building to the creation of nets of collaboration.

SPORTS ORGANISATIONS

International Association of Athlete Federation (IAAF)

Established	: 1912
Headquarters	: Monaco
Head	: SEBASTIAN COE
Members	: 200+ national member federations

- International Association of Athletics Federations (IAAF) formerly International Amateur Athletic Federation, track-and-field organization of national associations of more than 200 countries.

- It was founded as the International Amateur Athletic Association at Stockholm in 1912. In 1936 the IAAF took over regulation of women's international track-and-field competition from the Federation Sportive Feminine International, which had been founded in 1921.

- The major aims of the IAAF are to establish friendly cooperation among members; eliminate hindrance to participation in international meets on racial, religious, or political grounds; and compile rules and regulations governing competition. The IAAF is the ratifying body for all official world records in track-and-field events.

- It is recognized by the International Olympic Committee (IOC) and is financed by members' fees, publication sales, and the promotion of championships. Because of a shift toward professionalism in international athletic competitions, the organization changed its name to International Association of Athletics Federations in 2001. Headquarters, originally in Stockholm (1912–46) and London (1946–93), are now in Monaco.

Association of Summer Olympic International Federations (ASOIF)

Established	: 1983
Headquarters	: Lausanne Switzerland
Head	: Francesco Ricci Bitti (President)
Members	: 28 member International Federations Sports

- ASOIF was formed, as stated in the first article of its constitution 'to co-ordinate and to defend the common interests of its members' and to 'ensure close co-operation between its members, and members of the Olympic Movement and other organisations'. These needs were identified in order to preserve the unity of the Olympic movement while maintaining 'the authority, independence and autonomy of the member International Federations'. The members of ASOIF have since grown to 28 International Federations.

- ASOIF's mission is to unite, promote and support the International Summer Olympic Federations; to preserve their autonomy, while co-ordinating their common interests and goals.

- ASOIF's role is to serve and represent the Summer Olympic International Federations in the most competent, articulate and professional manner on issues of common interest in the Summer Olympic Games and the Olympic Movement, and on any other matter deemed necessary by the IFs.

- The International Federations have the responsibility and duty to manage and to monitor the everyday running of the world's various sports disciplines, including the practical organisation of events during the Games, and the supervision of the development of athletes practising these sports at every level.

- Each IF governs its sport at world level and ensures its promotion and development. They monitor the everyday administration of their sports and guarantee the regular organisation of competitions as well as respect for the rules of fair play.

Badminton World Federation (BWF)

Established : 1934
Headquarters : Kuala Lumpur (Malaysia)
Head : Poul-Erik Høyer (President)
Members : 188 Countries

- The Badminton World Federation (BWF) is recognised by the International Olympic Committee (IOC) and the International Paralympic Committee (IPC) as the world governing body for badminton.
- The International Badminton Federation (IBF), as it was originally called, was established in London, on 5 July 1934 with nine founding member associations. The BWF is a federation of 188 members globally.
- The Badminton World Federation (BWF) is the world governing body for badminton recognised by the International Olympic Committee (IOC) and International Paralympic Committee (IPC).
- The BWF regulates, promotes, develops and popularises the sport globally and organises inspiring world events. BWF has a vision of "giving every child a chance to play for life".

International Weightlifting Federation (IWF)

Established : 1905
Headquarters : Budapest (Hungary)
Head : Tamas AJAN (President)
Members : 192 affiliated National Federations worldwide

- The International Weightlifting Federation (IWF) is a permanent non-profit organization composed of 192 affiliated National Federations worldwide, from all five Continents. Weightlifting was one of the first sports included already in the first Modern Olympic Games 1896.
- The IWF was founded in 1905, being one of the oldest International Sport Federations. The IWF is the world controlling body for weightlifting.
- The IWF is recognized by the International Olympic Committee (IOC) as the sole controlling body for international weightlifting. The IWF is a member of

Sport Accord and the Association of Summer Olympic International Federations (ASOIF).

- Promote Weightlifting as a core sport & support the development, health and unity for the benefit of all its stakeholders.

Federation International de Football Association (FIFA)

Established : 1904
Headquarters : Zürich, Switzerland
Head : Gianni Infantino (President)
Members : 209 Member Association

- The Federation international de football association (FIFA, French for *International Federation of Association Football*) is the international sport governing body of association football, also known as soccer.
- It is the oldest and largest organization of its kind. Its headquarters are in Zürich, Switzerland. FIFA is responsible for the organization and governance of football's major international tournaments, most notably the FIFA World Cup, held since 1930.
- FIFA was founded in Paris on May 21, 1904—the French name and acronym persist to this day, even outside French-speaking countries. It is the oldest and largest organization of its kind. Robert Guérin was its first president.
- To oversee international competition among the national associations of Belgium, Denmark, France, Germany, the Netherlands, Spain, Sweden, and Switzerland.
- It is responsible for both the organization of a number of tournaments and their promotion, which generate revenue from sponsorship.
- Takes active roles in the running of the sport and developing the game around the world.

International Golf Federation (IGF)

Established : 1958
Headquarters : Lausanne, Switzerland
Head : Peter Dawson (President)
Members : 146 countries

- The International Golf Federation (IGF) was founded in 1958 and is recognised by the International Olympic Committee (IOC) and the International Paralympic Committee (IPC) as the International Federation for Golf.

IGF Vision; To ignite global excitement about golf and to grow the game.

IGF Mission;

(i) Promote Golf as an Olympic and Paralympic Sport
(ii) Encourage the international development of golf
(iii) Administer the statutes, practice and activities of golf as the recognized International Federation within the Olympic and Paralympic Movement

(iv) Organise the golf competitions at the Olympic Games, Youth Olympic Games and the World Amateur Team Championships

International Hockey Federation (IHF)

Established	: 1924
Headquarters	: Lausanne, Switzerland
Head	: Narinder Batra
Members	: 132 National Associations

- The formation of the International Hockey Federation in 1924 was not soon enough for the Paris Olympics but it did grant hockey re-entry in Amsterdam in 1928. Hockey has been on the programme ever since, with women's hockey included for the first time in Moscow in 1980.

- Motivated by hockey's omission from the 1924 Paris Games, the Federation International de Hockey sur Gazon (FIH) was founded by Paul Léautey. M. Léautey, who would later become the first president of the FIH, called together seven National Federations to form the sport's international governing body.

- These founding members, which represented both men's and women's hockey in their countries, were Austria, Belgium, Czechoslovakia, France, Hungary, Spain and Switzerland. Popularised in the late 19th century, the women's game developed quickly in many countries.

- In 1927, the International Federation of Women's Hockey Associations (IFWHA) was formed. After celebrating their respective Golden Jubilees - the FIH in 1974 and the IFWHA in 1980 - the two organisations came together in 1982 to form the current FIH.

- By 1964, there were already 50 countries affiliated with the FIH, as well as three Continental Associations - Africa, Pan America and Asia - and in 1974, there were 71 members. Today, the International Hockey Federation consists of five Continental Associations, 132 National Associations and is still growing.

International Tennis Federation (ITF)

Established	: 1913
Headquarters	: London (UK)
Head	: D. Haggerty (President)
Members	: 210 National Associations, together with six Regional Associations

- The need to establish a world governing body for tennis became obvious in 1911. By that time lawn tennis was beginning to develop rapidly worldwide and it seemed natural that National Associations already established should come together to form a liaison whereby the universal game would be uniformly structured.

- Credit for this concept is given to Duane Williams, who sadly died on board *Titanic* before seeing his idea come to fruition, Charles Barde and Henry Wallet. Representatives from 12 National Associations attended a General Conference in Paris on 1 March 1913 at which the International Lawn Tennis Federation (ILTF) was founded. A further three members were not present but had asked to join.

- The 15 inaugural members were:- Australasia (Australia and New Zealand), Austria, Belgium, Denmark, France, Germany, Great Britain, Hungary, Italy, Netherlands, Russia, South Africa, Spain, Sweden, Switzerland

Objectives are;

(i) Maintaining and enforcing the rules of tennis.

(ii) Regulating international team competitions.

(iii) Promoting the game and preserving the sport's integrity via anti-doping and anti-corruption programs.

- Partners with the Women's Tennis Association (WTA) and the Association of Tennis Professionals (ATP) to govern professional tennis.

- Organizes annual team competitions for men (Davis Cup), women (Fed Cup), and mixed teams (Hopman Cup), as well as tennis and wheelchair tennis events at the Summer Olympic and Paralympic Games.

- Maintains rankings for juniors, seniors, wheelchair and beach tennis.

International Cricket Council (ICC)

Established	: 1909
Headquarters	: Dubai (United Arab Emirates)
Head	: Shashank Manohar (President)
Members	: 104 Countries

- The ICC is the global governing body for cricket. Representing 105 members, the ICC governs and administrates the game and works with our members to grow the sport. The ICC is also responsible for the staging of all ICC Events.

- The ICC presides over the ICC Code of Conduct, playing conditions, the Decision Review System and other ICC regulations. The ICC also appoints all match officials that officiate at all sanctioned international matches. Through the Anti-Corruption Unit it coordinates action against corruption and match fixing.

(i) It appoints the umpires and referees that officiate at all sanctioned Test matches, One Day International and Twenty20 Internationals.

(ii) It promulgates the ICC Code of Conduct, which sets professional standards of discipline for international cricket.

(iii) It co-ordinates action against corruption and match-fixing through its Anti-Corruption and Security Unit (ACSU).

(iv) It does not govern domestic cricket in member countries, and it does not make the laws of the game.

International Olympic Committee (IOC)

Established	: 1894
Headquarters	: Lausanne, Switzerland
Head	: Thomas Bach
Members	: 115 Countries

- The IOC was created on 23 June 1894; the 1st Olympic Games of the modern era opened in Athens on 6 April 1896; and the Olympic Movement has not stopped growing ever since. The Olympic Movement encompasses organisations, athletes and other persons who agree to be guided by the principles of the Olympic Charter.

- The main objective is IOC;
  - (i) To encourage and support the organisation, development and coordination of sport and sports competitions;
  - (ii) To ensure the regular celebration of the Olympic Games;
  - (iii) To cooperate with the competent public or private organisations and authorities in the endeavour to place sport at the service of humanity and thereby to promote peace;
  - (iv) To act against any form of discrimination affecting the Olympic Movement;
  - (v) To encourage and support the promotion of women in sport at all levels and in all structures with a view to implementing the principle of equality of men and women.

- In 2009, the UN General Assembly granted the IOC Permanent Observer status. This decision enables the IOC to be directly involved in the UN Agenda and to attend UN General Assembly meetings where it can take the floor.

- To adopt or amend the Olympic Charter.

- The IOC uses these four major approaches in an attempt to minimize the negative environmental health concerns of a host city.

SAARC

South Asian Association for Regional Cooperation (SAARC)

Established	: 1985
Headquarters	: Kathmandu
Head	: Amjad Hussain B. Sial
Members	: 8 Countries

- The South Asian Association for Regional Cooperation (SAARC) was established with the signing of the SAARC Charter in Dhaka on 8 December 1985. SAARC comprises of eight Member States: Afghanistan, Bangladesh, Bhutan, India, Maldives, Nepal, Pakistan and Sri Lanka. The Secretariat of the Association was set up in Kathmandu on 17 January 1987.

- The objectives of the Association as outlined in the SAARC Charter are: to promote the welfare of the peoples of South Asia and to improve their quality of life; to accelerate economic growth, social progress and cultural development in the region and to provide all individuals the opportunity to live in dignity and to realize their full potentials; to promote and strengthen collective self-reliance among the countries of South Asia; to contribute to mutual trust, understanding and appreciation of one another's problems; to promote active collaboration and mutual assistance in the economic, social, cultural, technical and scientific fields; to strengthen cooperation with other developing countries; to strengthen cooperation among themselves in international forums on matters of common interests; and to cooperate with international and regional organizations with similar aims and purposes.

- Decisions at all levels are to be taken on the basis of unanimity; and bilateral and contentious issues are excluded from the deliberations of the Association.

Areas of SAARC Cooperation;
  - (i) Human Resource Development and Tourism
  - (ii) Agriculture and Rural Development
  - (iii) Environment, Natural Disasters and Biotechnology
  - (iv) Economic, Trade and Finance
  - (v) Social Affairs
  - (vi) Information and Poverty Alleviation
  - (vii) Energy, Transport, Science and Technology
  - (viii) Education, Security and Culture Other Important Organisations

International Organization for Standardization (ISO)

Established	: 1947
Headquarters	: Geneva, Switzerland
Head	: Pamela Tarif
Members	: 161 Countries

- It is an international standard-setting body composed of representatives from various national standards organizations.

- The organization promotes worldwide proprietary, industrial and commercial standards. It is the world's largest developer of voluntary international standards and facilitates world trade by providing common standards between nations.

- Nearly twenty thousand standards have been set covering everything from manufactured products and technology to food safety, agriculture and healthcare.

- ISO has formed joint committees with the International Electrotechnical Commission (IEC) to develop standards and terminology in the areas of electrical, electronic and related technologies.

- International Classification for Standards (ICS), maintained by ISO is an international classification system for technical standards. It is designed to cover every economic sector and virtually every activity of the humankind where technical standards may be used. The ICS uses an hierarchical classification, which consists of three nested levels called fields (Level 1), groups (Level 2) andsub-groups (Level 3).

- The ISO 9000 family of quality management systems standards is designed to help organizations ensure that they meet the needs of customers and other stakeholders while meeting statutory and regulatory requirements related to a product.

- ISO 9000 deals with the fundamentals of quality management systems, including the eight management principles upon which the family of standards is based. ISO 9001 deals with the requirements that organizations wishing to meet the standard must fulfill.

International Civil Aviation Organization (ICAO)

Established	: 1944
Headquarters	: Montreal, Quebec (Canada)
Head	: Dr. Fang Liu (Secretary General)
Members	: 192 Countries

- The International Civil Aviation Organization (ICAO) is a UN specialized agency, established by States in 1944 to manage the administration and governance of the Convention on International Civil Aviation (Chicago Convention).

- ICAO works with the Convention's 192 Member States and industry groups to reach consensus on international civil aviation Standards and Recommended Practices (SARPs) and policies in support of a safe, efficient, secure, economically sustainable and environmentally responsible civil aviation sector.

- These SARPs and policies are used by ICAO Member States to ensure that their local civil aviation operations and regulations conform to global norms, which in turn permits more than 100,000 daily flights in aviation's global network to operate safely and reliably in every region of the world.

- In addition to its core work resolving consensus-driven international SARPs and policies among its Member States and industry, and among many other priorities and programmes, ICAO also coordinates assistance and capacity building for States in support of numerous aviation development objectives; produces global plans to coordinate multilateral strategic progress for safety

and air navigation; monitors and reports on numerous air transport sector performance metrics; and audits States' civil aviation oversight capabilities in the areas of safety and security.

- Mission: To serve as the global forum of States for international civil aviation. ICAO develops policies and Standards, undertakes compliance audits, performs studies and analyses, provides assistance and builds aviation capacity through many other activities and the cooperation of its Member States and stakeholders.

- To adopt standards and recommended practices concerning air navigation, its infrastructure, flight inspection, prevention of unlawful interference, and facilitation of border-crossing procedures for international civil aviation.

- It defines the protocols for air accident investigation followed by transport safety authorities in countries signatory to the Convention on International Civil Aviation.

International Tribunal for the Law of the Sea (ITLOS)

Established	: 1982
Headquarters	: Hamburg (Germany)
Head	: Jin-Hyun Paik (President)
Members	: 168 (167 States and 1 international organization, EU)

- The United Nations Convention on the Law of the Sea was opened for signature at Montego Bay, Jamaica, on 10 December 1982. It entered into force 12 years later, on 16 November 1994.

- A subsequent Agreement relating to the implementation of Part XI of the Convention was adopted on 28 July 1994 and entered into force on 28 July 1996. This Agreement and Part XI of the Convention are to be interpreted and applied together as a single instrument.

- Establishes the International Seabed Authority, with responsibility for the regulation of seabed mining beyond the limits of national jurisdiction that is beyond the limits of the territorial sea, the contiguous zone and the continental shelf.

International Food Policy Research Institute (IFPRI)

Established	: 1975
Headquarters	: Washington, DC (USA)
Head	: Shenggen Fan (Director General)
Members	: more than 600 employees working in over 50 countries

- To improve the understanding of national agricultural and food policies to promote the adoption of innovations in agricultural technology.

- To focus on the role of agricultural and rural development in the broader development pathway of a country.

- To provide research-based policy solutions that sustainably reduces poverty and end hunger and malnutrition.
- It carries out food policy research and disseminates it through hundreds of publications, bulletins, conferences, and other initiatives.
- It is part of a network of international research institutes funded in part by the CGIAR, which in turn is funded by governments, private businesses and foundations, and the World Bank.
- Its institutional strategy depends on three pillars: research, capacity strengthening, and policy communication.
- It has conducted studies to model the effects of climate change on developing populations.
- It has done extensive research into areas related to malnutrition. It has conducted research all over the world on various issues that arise from malnutrition. It has looked at HIV and Malaria and how malnutrition affects the epidemiology of these diseases.

Financial Action Task Force (FATF) (on Money Laundering)

Established	: 1989
Headquarters	: Paris (France)
Head	: Marshall Billingslea (President)
Members	: 37 Countries

- The Financial Action Task Force (FATF) is an inter-governmental body established in 1989 by the Ministers of its Member jurisdictions.
- The objectives of the FATF are to set standards and promote effective implementation of legal, regulatory and operational measures for combating money laundering, terrorist financing and other related threats to the integrity of the international financial system.
- The FATF is therefore a "policy-making body" which works to generate the necessary political will to bring about national legislative and regulatory reforms in these areas.
- It monitors countries' progress in implementing the FATF Recommendations by 'peer reviews' ('mutual evaluations') of member countries.
- It studies money laundering trends, monitoring legislative, financial and law enforcement activities taken at the national and international level, reporting on compliance, and issuing recommendations and standards to combat money laundering.

- In addition to FATF's "Forty plus Nine" Recommendations, in 2000 FATF issued a list of "Non-Cooperative Countries or Territories" (NCCTs), commonly called the FATF Blacklist.
- It set out the principles for action and allows countries a measure of flexibility in implementing these principles according to their particular circumstances and constitutional frameworks. Both sets of FATF Recommendations are intended to be implemented at the national level through legislation and other legally binding measures.

International Fund for Agricultural Development (IFAD)

Established	: 1977
Headquarters	: Rome (Italy)
Head	: Gilbert F. Houngbo (President)
Members	: 176 Countries

- The objectives of the IFAD are;
  (i) To empower poor rural men and women in developing countries to achieve higher incomes and improve food security.
  (ii) Improve agricultural technologies and effective production services.
  (iii) Provide broad range of financial services.
  (iv) Ensure transparent and competitive markets for agricultural inputs and produce.
  (v) Create opportunities for rural off-farm employment and enterprise development.
  (vi) Participate in local and national policy and programming.
- Achieving the Millennium Development Goals, in particular the target to halve the proportion of hungry and extremely poor people by 2015.
- Through loans and grants, IFAD works with governments to finance programmes and projects that enable rural poor people to overcome poverty themselves.
- Its multilateral base provides a global platform to discuss important policy issues that influence the lives of rural poor people, as well as to draw attention to the centrality of rural development to meeting the Millennium Development Goals.
- IFAD is a partner in Compact 2025, a partnership that develops and disseminates evidence-based advice to politicians and other decision-makers aimed at ending hunger and malnutrition.

Exercise -1

1. Which of the following is not associated with the UNO?
   (a) ILO
   (b) WHO
   (c) ASEAN
   (d) All of the above

2. Which of the following is not a chief organ of the United Nations Organisations ?
   (a) International Labour Organisation
   (b) Security Council
   (c) International Court of Justice
   (d) General Assembly

3. In which year 'Human Rights resolution' was adopted by the U.N.?
   (a) 1948
   (b) 1945
   (c) 1946
   (d) 1947

4. Which of the following organizations brings out the publication known as 'World Economic Outlook'?
   (a) The International Monetary Fund
   (b) The United Nations Development Programme
   (c) The World Economic Forum
   (d) The World Bank

5. Which UN body deals with population problem?
   (a) UNFPA
   (b) UNDP
   (c) UNICEF
   (d) UNESCO

6. The headquarters of World Intellectual Property Organisation (WIPO) is located in
   (a) Paris
   (b) Madrid
   (c) New York
   (d) Geneva

7. Which of the following describe correctly the Group of Seven Countries (G-7)?
   (a) They are developing countries
   (b) They are industrialised countries
   (c) They are holding Atomic Bomb technology
   (d) They are countries who can launch their own satellites

8. Which of the following countries is not a member of the G-7 group?
   (a) Germany
   (b) France
   (c) Italy
   (d) Spain

9. Which of the following countries is not a member of SAARC?
   (a) Nepal
   (b) Bangladesh
   (c) Afghanistan
   (d) Myanmar

10. The main aim of SAARC is
    (a) Regional Cooperation
    (b) Internal affairs
    (c) Non-alignity
    (d) Peaceful Coexistence

11. The five permanent members of UN security council are
    (a) Japan, West Germany, USSR, UK and USA
    (b) Canada, China, France, USSR and USA
    (c) Germany, China, USSR, UK and USA
    (d) China, France, USSR, UK and USA

12. When was the South Asian Association for Regional Co-operation (SAARC) formed?
    (a) 1985
    (b) 1982
    (c) 1986
    (d) 1987

13. The international township built near Pondicherry in India in coloration with UNESCO is called
    (a) Elbaville
    (b) Auroville
    (c) Gayaville
    (d) Broadway

14. Which of the following is a cultural organisation?
    (a) UNESCO
    (b) ILO
    (c) WHO
    (d) FAO

15. What is the target of the Millennium Development Goal of the United Nations whit respect to Universal Primary Education?
    (a) All children both boys and girls would complete a full course primary schooling by 2025
    (b) All children both boys and girls are to be literate by 2050
    (c) All boys should go to school to complete a full course of primary schooling by 2025
    (d) All girls should be enrolled in primary school by 2015

16. Which of the following pair is **not** correct ?
    (a) SAARC — New Delhi
    (b) ASEAN — Jakarta
    (c) International Committee of the Red Cross — Geneva
    (d) INTERPOL — Leon

17. The International Court of Justice is located at
    (a) Geneva
    (b) Hague
    (c) Amsterdam
    (d) Vienna

18. Which is the Official Language of Islamic Development Bank ?
    (a) Arabic
    (b) English
    (c) Persian
    (d) All the above

19. Which of the following pairs of country and the purpose for which U.N. Peace Keeping Force is maintained is correctly is correctly matched?
    (a) Cyprus – to maintain peace between the two dominant ethnic groups in the country
    (b) Mozambique – To supervise a referendum
    (c) El Salvador – to deliver humanitarian aid
    (d) Lebanon – For supervising a 1992 accord

20. Which of the following is Human Rights Organisation?
    (a) The French Community
    (b) The Organisation of African Unity

(c)   The Arab League

(d)   Amnesty International

21.   The head quarters of the International Red Cross is situated in

(a)   Vienna   (b)   Paris

(c)   Hague   (d)   Geneva

22.   On which subjects, individuals get accused by the International Criminal Court:

(a)   Genocide

(b)   War-crime

(c)   Crime against individual

(d)   All the above

23.   Which organ of the United Nations has ceased to be operational?

(a)   Economic and Social Council

(b)   International Court of Justice

(c)   Trusteeship Council

(d)   Secretariat

24.   Which of the following awarded Noble Peace Prize for three times?

(a)   Human Rights Council

(b)   World Bank

(c)   International Committee of the Red Cross

(d)   UN Peacekeeping forces

25.   Which is the first specialised agency of the UN ?

(a)   UNCTAD   (b)   ILO

(c)   UNESCO   (d)   UNDP

26.   Which UN body shall exercise all functions of the UN relating to strategic areas, including the approval of the terms of the trusteeship agreements and also their alteration or amendment ?

(a)   UN General Assembly (b)   Security Council

(c)   UN body   (d)   Developed countries

27.   In the subject of independence of which country, UN General Assembly took initiative and secured independence from South Africa ?

(a)   India   (b)   Ethiopia

(c)   Namibia   (d)   None of the above

28.   Which is not a correct statement ?

(a)   Peacekeeping operations are established by the Security Council.

(b)   Peacekeepers are identified only by a United Nations red helmet

(c)   UN has no military forces of its own.

(d)   Peacekeepers wear their country's uniform.

29.   Which is recently created UN institution as part of the Human Rights Machinery :

(a)   High Commissioner for Human Rights

(b)   Commission on Human Rights

(c)   Human Rights Council

(d)   Human Rights Institute

30.   Who is the Secretary General of the UN ?

(a)   Kofi Annan   (b)   Ban Ki Moon

(c)   Antonio Guterres   (d)   None of the above

31.   Which one of the following is not related to disarmament ?

(a)   SALT   (b)   NPT

(c)   CTBT   (d)   NATO

32.   What is the function of the UN Population Fund for developing nation ?

(a)   Special emphasis on in-creasing the quality of reproductive health service

(b)   Ending the gender discrimination and violence, formulation of effective population policies

(c)   Reducing the spread of HIV/AIDS

(d)   All the above

33.   Which UN Organization is called as the World Bank ?

(a)   International Bank for Reconstruction and Development (IBRD)

(b)   International Banking System

(c)   International Banking Management System

(d)   All the above

34.   Amnesty International is an organisation associated with which of the following fields?

(a)   Protection of Cruelty to animals

(b)   Environment protection

(c)   Protection of human rights

(d)   Protection of historic monuments

35.   Other than Venezuela, which one among the following from South America is a member of OPEC?

(a)   Argentina   (b)   Brazil

(c)   Ecuador   (d)   Bolivia

36.   Which of the following is not a member of SAARC?

(a)   Bhutan   (b)   Bangladesh

(c)   Burma   (d)   Maldives

37.   Which one among the following statements about United Nations organs is correct?

(a)   Decisions of the General Assembly are binding on all members

(b)   The terms of the non permanent members of the Security Council is for three year

(c)   International Court of justice has 20 judges elected for a period of five years

(d)   The Trusteeship Council has been suspended since November, 1994

38.   Which of the following pair is **not** correct ?

(a)   World Conference against Racism — Durban

(b)   World Summit for Sustainable Development — Johannesburg

(c)   World Food Summit — Havana

(d)   World Education Forum — Dakar

39. Who was the first Indian to be President of UN General Assembly?
    (a) Mrs. Vijay Lakshmi Pandit
    (b) Ramesh Bhandari
    (c) Natwar Singh
    (d) Krishna Menon
40. Which of the following pair is **not** correct ?
    (a) Human Development Report — UNCTAD
    (b) World Health Report — WHO
    (c) World Development Report — World Bank
    (d) World Economic Outlook — IMF
41. Which of the following pair is **not** correct ?
    (a) World Summit for Children — New York
    (b) World Food Summit — Rome
    (c) World Conference in Human Rights — Geneva
    (d) World Summit for Social Development — Copenhagen
42. Where is the headquarters of World Intellectual Property Organization ?
    (a) Geneva   (b) Colombo
    (c) New Delhi   (d) Paris
43. What is the main work regarding education by the UNESCO ?
    (a) To provide basic education for all, expand access to basic education
    (b) Improve the quality of basic education
    (c) Education for the 21st century
    (d) All the above
44. What are the aims of the UN Industrial Development Organization ?
    (a) Helps developing countries on the issue of fight against marginalization and poverty
    (b) Helps developing countries
    (c) Mobilizes knowledge, skills, information and technology to promote productive employment, a competitive economy and sound environment
    (d) All the above
45. What are the functions of the World Health Organization:
    (a) To assist government to strengthen their health services
    (b) To assist advance work to eradicate diseases
    (c) To promote maternal and child health
    (d) All the above
46. What is Medecins Sans Frantieres (MSF) ?
    (a) An agency formed by the International Olympic Committee (IOC) to check misuse of drugs by sportspersons.
    (b) A non-governmental organization which specialized in international humanitarian aid and emergency medical assistance.
    (c) An organization to develop applications of nanotechnology in medicine.
    (d) An organization of medical practioners funded by the European Union which carries out research against spread of AIDS.
47. India has recently signed Safeguard agreement with IAEA. What does the 'IAEA' stand for ?
    (a) International Atomic Energy Agency
    (b) International Automobile Energy Agency
    (c) India Atomic Energy Agency
    (d) India Atomic Emergency Agency
48. Which of the following awards is given by UNESCO to those who popularize use of science in life?
    (a) Booker Prize   (b) Magsaysay Award
    (c) Kalinga Award   (d) Kalidas Samman
49. The three members of BRICS grouping aspiring for the membership of United Nations Security Council does not include-
    (a) South Africa   (b) Egypt
    (c) Brazil   (d) India
50. OPEC is a group of countries which:
    (a) Export oil   (b) produce cotton
    (c) are rich and developed (d) developing and poor
51. Which organisation passed a resolution asking all nations to sign the Nuclear Non Proliferation Treaty (NPT) without delay?
    (a) UN General Assembly
    (b) International Atomic Energy Agency (IAEA)
    (c) North Atlantic Treaty Organization (NATO)
    (d) South Asian Association of Regional Cooperation (SAARC)
52. Who among the following is not a member of G7?
    (a) France   (b) Germany
    (c) Russia   (d) Japan
53. UNESCO is an organisation working in the field of ____.
    (a) Social welfare
    (b) Protecting interest of prisoners of war
    (c) Framing international laws
    (d) International \ collaboration through education, culture and science.
54. The United Nations Framework Convention on Climate Change (UNFCCC) is an international treaty drawn at
    (a) United Nations Conference on the Human Environment, Stockholm, 1972
    (b) UN 'Conference on Environment and Development, Rio de Janeiro, 1992
    (c) World Summit on Sustainable Development, Johannesburg, 2002
    (d) UN Climate' Change Conference, Copenhagen, 2009
55. In the United Nations, who decides the quantum of contribution of each member to the income resources of the UN?

    (a) Trusteeship Council
    (b) Economic and Social Council
    (c) Security Council
    (d) General Assembly

56. Which one among the following administers the International Development Association?
    (a) UNDP   (b) UNIDO
    (c) IFAD   (d) IBRD

57. WTO came into existence at the conclusion of which Round of GATT?
    (a) Singapore   (b) Uruguay
    (c) Tokyo   (d) Merrakash

58. Where was the Sixth WTO Ministerial Conference (MC6) held?
    (a) Singapore   (b) Bangkok
    (c) Hong Kong   (d) Kuala Lumpur

59. Which one of the following is not a member of ASEAN?
    (a) Cambodia   (b) Malaysia
    (c) Singapore   (d) South Korea

60. Which one of the following countries is not a founder member of OPEC?
    (a) Algeria   (b) Kuwait
    (c) Iraq   (d) Iran

61. Which one of the following countries is not a member of ASEAN?
    (a) Brunei Darussalam   (b) Cambodia
    (c) Vietnam   (d) India

62. Which one of the following pairs is not correctly matched?

	Organisation	Headquarters
A	International Labour Organisation	Geneva
B.	International Maritime Organisation	London
C	International Monetary Fund	Washington D.C.
D.	International Atomic Energy Agency	New York

63. International Bank for Reconstruction and Development is also known as
    (a) Credit Bank   (b) Exim Bank
    (c) World Bank   (d) Asian Bank

64. In which of the following years was General Agreement on Tariffs and Trade (GATT) absorbed into the World Trade Organisation (WTO)?
    (a) 1991   (b) 1995
    (c) 2000   (d) 2005

65. Which one among the following statements about South Asia is not correct?
    (a) All the countries in South Asia are currently democracies
    (b) SAFTA was signed at the 12th SAARC Summit in Islamabad

    (c) The US and China play an influential role in the politics of some South Asian States
    (d) Bangladesh and India have agreements on river water sharing and boundary disputes

66. Which one among the following statements about United Nations organs is correct?
    (a) Decisions of the General Assembly are binding on all members
    (b) The term of the non-permanent members of the Security Council is for three years
    (c) International Court of justice has 20 Judges elected for a period of five years
    (d) The Trusteeship Council has been suspended since 1 November, 1994

67. The basis of European Union began with the signing of
    (a) Maastricht Treaty   (b) Treaty of Paris
    (c) Treaty of Rome   (d) Treaty of Lisbon

68. Which one among the following is not a clause of World Trade Organisation?
    (a) Most favoured nation treatment
    (b) Lowering trade barriers with negotiations
    (c) Providing financial support to the countries having deficit balance of payments
    (d) Discouraging unfair trade practices such as antidumping and export subsidies

69. Special Drawing Rights [SDRs] relate to
    (a) the World Bank
    (b) the Reserve Bank of India
    (c) the World Trade Organisation
    (d) the International Monetary Fund

70. Which one among the following is not a Millennium Development Goal of the United Nations ?
    (a) Eradicate extreme poverty
    (b) Reduce birth rate and death rate
    (c) Improve maternal health
    (d) Promote gender equality

71. Which among the following is not an aspect of Gender Mainstreaming (GM) ?
    (a) GM was established as a global strategy for achieving gender equality by the United Nations.
    (b) It was adopted in 1995 in the Beijing Platform of Action.
    (c) It requires a review of government policy in all sectors for eliminating gender disparity.
    (d) GM was followed by the Convention on the Elimination of all forms of Discrimination Against Women (CEDAW).

72. Which of the following statements is not true ?
    (a) The General Agreement on Tariffs and Trade (GATT) had regulated global trade since 1947.
    (b) GATT was replaced by the World Trade Organisation (WTO) in 1995.
    (c) The Most Favoured Nation principle under GATT provided that preferential trading agreements reached with one country should be extended to other countries.
    (d) The WTO has been able to cover in it agreements the agriculture and textile sectors which are the principal concerned for the Least Developed Countries (LDCs).

73. Which of the following is not true for SAFTA (South Asian Free Trade Area) ?
    (a) It is a step towards a South Asian customs union and common market.
    (b) The agreement came into effect in 2006.
    (c) The SAFTA is a trade liberalisation regime.
    (d) SAFTA agreement takes precedence over any other agreement a member country may have with states outside SAFTA.

74. Which of the following is not true about the Convention on the Elimination of all forms of Discrimination Against Women (CEDAW) ?
    (a) It defines what constitutes discrimination aganist women and sets up an agenda for national action
    (b) It was adopted in 1979 by the United Nations
    (c) It commits States to undertake measures to end discrimination in their legal system
    (d) India is not a ratifying country and is therefore not legally bound to put its provisions into practice

75. Who among the following is the founder of World Economic Forum ?
    (a) Klaus Schwab
    (b) John Kenneth Galbraith
    (c) Robert Zoellick
    (d) Paul Krugman

76. India became a member of which one of the following in 2016?
    (a) Non-Proliferation Treaty
    (b) Missile Technology Control Regime
    (c) Nuclear Suppliers Group
    (d) Wassenaar Arrangement

77. Which one of the following statements is not correct in respect of the South Asian Association for Regional Cooperation (SAARC)? **[2017-I]**
    (a) Its Headquarters is located in Kathmandu.
    (b) China is the only country with an Observer status in SAARC.
    (c) The First SAARC Summit was held in Dhaka.
    (d) The Eighteenth SAARC Summit was held in Nepal.

78. BRICS Summit, 2016 was held in **[2017-I]**
    (a) Brazil
    (b) China
    (c) India
    (d) South Africa

79. The Sustainable Development Goals (SDGs), which were adopted by the UNO in place of the Millennium Development Goals (MDGs), 2015, aim to achieve the 17 goals by the year
    (a) 2020
    (b) 2030
    (c) 2040
    (d) 2050

80. Which one of the following statements is **not** correct?
    (a) India joined MTCR in 2016. **[2018-I]**
    (b) India submitted a formal application for membership of the NSG in 2016.
    (c) India proposed the Comprehensive Convention on International Terrorism in 1996.
    (d) The Commonwealth Heads of Government Meeting (CHOGM) was held in 2016 at Malta.

81. The first BRICS Summit, after the inclusion of South Africa, was held at **[2018-I]**
    (a) Brasilia
    (b) Sanya
    (c) Yekaterinburg
    (d) Durban

82. 'European Stability Mechanism', sometimes seen in the news, is an
    (a) agency created by EU to deal with the impact of millions of refugees arriving from Middle East
    (b) agency of EU that provides financial assistance to eurozone countries
    (c) agency of EU to deal with all the bilateral and multilateral agreements on trade
    (d) agency of EU to deal with the conflicts arising among the member countries

83. The term 'Regional Comprehensive Economic Partnership' often appears in the news in the context of the affairs of a group of countries known as **[UPSC 2016]**
    (a) G20
    (b) ASEAN
    (c) SCO
    (d) SAARC

84. In the context of which of the following do you sometimes find the terms 'amber box, blue box and green box' in the news? **[UPSC 2016]**
    (a) WTO affairs
    (b) SAARC affairs
    (c) UNFCCC affairs
    (d) India-EU negotiations on FTA

85. Consider the following statements : **[UPSC 2016]**
    1. New Development Bank has been set up by APEC.
    2. The headquarters of New Development Bank is in Shanghai.
    Which of the statements given above is/are correct?
    (a) 1 only
    (b) 2 only
    (c) Both 1 and 2
    (d) Neither 1 nor 2

86. With reference to the International Monetary and Financial Committee (IMFC), consider the following statements : **[UPSC 2016]**
    1. IMFC discusses matters of concern affecting the global economy, and advises the International Monetary Fund (IMF) on the direction of its work.
    2. The World Bank participates as observer in IMFC's meetings.

    Which of the statements given above is/are correct?
    (a) 1 only   (b) 2 only
    (c) Both 1 and 2   (d) Neither 1 nor 2

87. Which of the following is not a member of 'Gulf Cooperation Council'? **[UPSC 2016]**
    (a) Iran   (b) Saudi Arabia
    (c) Oman   (d) Kuwait

88. With reference to 'Organization for the Prohibition of Chemical Weapons (OPCW)', consider the following statements : **[UPSC 2016]**
    1. It is an organization of European Union in working relation with NATO and WHO.
    2. It monitors chemical industry to prevent new weapons from emerging.
    3. It provides assistance and protection to States (Parties) against chemical weapons threats.

    Which of the statements given above is/are correct?
    (a) 1 only   (b) 2 and 3 only
    (c) 1 and 3 only   (d) 1, 2 and 3

89. With reference to 'Asia Pacific Ministerial Conference on Housing and Urban Development (APMCHUD)', consider the following statements: **[UPSC 2017]**
    1. The first APMCHUD was held in India in 2006 on the theme 'Emerging Urban Forms - Policy Responses and Governance Structure'.
    2. India hosts all the Annual Ministerial Conferences in partnership with ADB, APEC and ASEAN.

    Which of the statements given above is/are correct?
    (a) 1 only   (b) 2 only
    (c) Both 1 and 2   (d) Neither 1 nor 2

90. With reference to the role of UN-Habitat in the United Nations programme working towards a better urban future, which of the statements is/are correct? **[UPSC 2017]**
    1. UN-Habitat has been mandated by the United Nations General Assembly to promote socially and environmentally sustainable towns and cities to provide adequate shelter for all.
    2. Its partners are either governments or local urban authorities only.
    3. UN-Habitat contributes to the overall objective of the United Nations system to reduce poverty and to promote access to safe drinking water and basic sanitation.

Select the correct answer using the code given below:
    (a) 1, 2 and 3   (b) 1 and 3 only
    (c) 2 and 3 only   (d) 1 only

91. The Global Infrastructure Facility is a/an **[UPSC 2017]**
    (a) ASEAN initiative to upgrade infrastructure in Asia and financed by credit from the Asian Development Bank.
    (b) World Bank collaboration that facilitates the preparation and structuring of complex infrastructure Public-Private Partnerships (PPPs) to enable mobilization of private sector and institutional investor capital.
    (c) Collaboration among the major banks of the world working with the OECD and focused on expanding the set of infrastructure projects that have the potential to mobilize private investment.
    (d) UNCTAD funded initiative that seeks to finance and facilitate infrastructure development in the world.

92. Headquarters of the World Meteorological Organization is located in
    (a) Washington
    (b) Geneva
    (c) Moscow
    (d) London

93. Which one of the following was the venue of 2nd BRICS Youth Summit of the Ministers, Officials and Youth Delegations?
    (a) New Delhi   (b) Mumbai
    (c) Shillong   (d) Guwahati

94. Which one of the following is NOT one of the objectives of Act East Policy?
    (a) To promote economic cooperation, cultural ties and develop strategic relationship with countries in the Asia-Pacific region
    (b) To promote peace and amity with the neighbouring countries of Asia
    (c) To place emphasis on India- ASEAN cooperation in India's domestic agenda
    (d) To provide enhanced connectivity to the North East of India

95. Which one of the following is the theme of the World Health Day, 2017 celebrated by the World Health Organization?
    (a) Diabetes   (b) Food Safety
    (c) Depression: Let's Talk   (d) Ageing and Health

96. Justice Dalveer Bhandari of India was recently re-elected to the International Court of Justice after Christopher Greenwood pulled out before 12th round of voting. Christopher Greenwood was a nominee of
    (a) Canada   (b) Russia
    (c) Britain   (d) USA

Exercise -2

1. Which are the autonomous institutions for training and research within the UN ?
   1. UN Institute for Training and Research (UNITAR), UN Institute for Disarmament Research (UNDIR)
   2. UN Research Institute for Social Development, UN International Research and Training Institute for the Advancement of Women
   3. UN University, University for Peace

   Which of the statements given above is/are correct ?
   (a) 1 only   (b) 1 and 2
   (c) 2 and 3   (d) 1, 2 and 3

2. What are the functions of World Meteorological Organization ?
   1. To facilitate worldwide co-operation in the establishment of networks of stations for the making of meteorological observations as well as hydrological or other geophysical observations
   2. To promote standardization of meteorological and related observations and ensure the uniform publication of observations and statistics
   3. To promote activities in operational hydrology and to further enhance co-operation between meteorological and the hydrological services

   Which of the statements given above is/are correct?
   (a) 1 only   (b) 2 only
   (c) 3 only   (d) All of the above

3. Consider the following statements :
   1. UN agency associated with children's work is UNICEF
   2. UN International Drug Control Programme headquarters is located in Vienna

   Which of the statements given above is/are correct ?
   (a) 1 only   (b) 2 only
   (c) Both 1 and 2   (d) Neither 1 nor 2

4. Consider the following statements :
   1. The head-office of UN High Commissioner for Refugees is in Rome
   2. Peter Benson founded Amnesty International

   Which of the statements given above is/are correct ?
   (a) 1 only   (b) 2 only
   (c) Both 1 and 2   (d) Neither 1 nor 2

5. What functions are performed by the UN Secretary General ?
   1. The Secretary-General is the chief administrative officer of the Organization.
   2. The Secretary-General acts in the capacity of the chief administrative officer of the organization in all meetings of the General Assembly, the Security Council, The Economic and Social Council and of the Trusteeship Council.
   3. Secretary-General makes annual report to the UN General Assembly in the work of the Organization. The Secretary-General may bring to the notice of the Security Council any matter which in his opinion threatens the maintenance of international peace and security.

   Which of the statements given above is/are correct?
   (a) 1 only   (b) 1 and 2
   (c) 2 and 3   (d) All of the above

6. What is the general nature of the specialised agencies of the UN ?
   1. Most of the states are the members of these specialized agencies.
   2. All the specialised agencies have been brought in relationship with the UN through special agreements.
   3. Each specialised agency has a Constitution or Charter of its own which describes the duties, functions, constitution, etc. of the organisation.

   Whch of the statements given above is/are correct?
   (a) 1 and 2   (b) 3 only
   (c) 2 and 3   (d) All 1, 2 and 3

7. The aims and purposes of ASEAN is/are:
   1. To accelerate the economic growth, social progress and cultural development in the region through joint endeavours in the spirit of equality and partnership in order to strengthen the foundation for a prosperous and peaceful community of southeast asian nations.
   2. To promote regional peace and stability through abiding respect for justice and the rule of law in the relationship among countries of the region and adherence to the principles of the United Nations Charter.

   Choose from the codes given below:
   (a) 1 only   (b) 2 only
   (c) 1 and 2 only   (d) None

8. What is the main responsibility of the Organisation for the Prohibition of Chemical Weapons ?
   1. Maintain Chemical Weapons Warheads
   2. Implementation of the Chemical Weapons Convention

   Which of the statements given above is/are correct?
   (a) 1 only   (b) 2 only
   (c) Both 1 and 2   (d) None of these

9. What are the ad-hoc bodies of the UN General Assembly ?
   1. Special Committee on Peace Keeping Operation, Human Rights Committee, Committee on the Peaceful Use of Outer Space
   2. Special Committee on the Implementation of the Declaration on the Granting of Independent Countries and Peoples Commission on International Trade Law

Which of the statements given above is/are correct?
(a) 1 only   (b) 2 only
(c) 1 and 2   (c) None of these

10. What are the standing Committees of the Security Council ?
1. The Committee of Experts on Rules of Procedure
2. The Committee on the Admission of New Members
Which of the statements given above is/are correct?
(a) 1 only   (b) 2 only
(c) Both 1 and 2   (d) None of these

11. Consider the following statements :
1. North Atlantic Co-operation Council (NACC) is the name of the new organization which has replaced the North Atlantic Treaty Organisation (NATO)
2. The United States of America and the United Kingdom became the members of the NATO when it was formed in the year 1949.
Which of the statements given above is/are correct ?
(a) 1 only   (b) 2 only
(c) Both 1 and 2   (d) Neither 1 nor 2

12. Consider the following statements.
UNESCO's World Heritage mission is to
1. take over the management, maintenance and preservation of World Heritage sites.
2. encourage state parties to the Convention concerning the Protection of the World Cultural and Natural Heritage to nominate sites within their national territory for inclusion on the World Heritage List.
3. Provide emergency assistance for World Heritage sites in immediate danger.
Which of the statements given above are correct?
(a) 1, 2 and 3   (b) 1 and 3
(c) 1 and 2   (d) 2 and 3

13. Which of the following statements regarding the United Nations Peacekeeping Force is/are Correct?
1. The first peacekeeping force was sent to Egypt.
2. Peacekeeping force is accountable to the Security Council.
3. First women peacekeeping force was sent by India to Liberia.
Select the correct answer using the code given below
(a) 1, 2 and 3   (b) 1 and 2
(c) 3 only   (d) 1 and 3

14. Consider the following statements
1. BIMSTEC (Bay of Bengal Initiative for Multi-Sectoral Technical and Economic Cooperation) is visualized as a bridging link between ASEAN and SAARC
2. It was formerly known as the Bangkok Agreement.
Which of the statements given above is/ are correct?
(a) 1 only   (b) 2 only
(c) Both 1 and 2   (d) Neither 1 nor 2

15. Consider the following statements with reference to the United Nations Organization :
1. The General Assembly meets once in two years.
2. The Security Council has 15 members.
3. The non-permanent members of the Security Council are elected for a two-year term.
Which of the statements given above is/are correct?
(a) 1 and 2   (b) 2 and 3
(c) 3 only   (d) 1, 2 and 3

16. Which of the following statements with regard to New Development Bank BRICS, formerly referred to as the BRICS Development Bank, is/are correct?
1. The Headquarters of the Bank is situated at Moscow, Russia.
2. K. V. Kamath is the first President of the Bank.
Select the correct answer using the code given below.
(a) 1 only   (b) 2 only
(c) Both 1 and 2   (d) Neither 1 nor 2

17. Which of the following statements are correct with regard to the Transparency International?
1. It is a non-profit, non-governmental organisation.
2. It is dedicated to fighting corruption.
3. It is best known for its Corruption Perceptions Index.
4. Its secretariat is located in London, UK.
Select the answer from the codes given below:
(a) 1, 2 and 3   (b) 2, 3, and 4
(c) 1, 3 and 4   (d) 1, 2, 3 and 4

18. Consider the following statements about IAEA
1. It was set up as the world's Atoms of Peace organisation in 1957.
2. The IAEA Secretariat is headquartered at the Vienna international Centre in Vienna. Austria.
3. In terms of its statute, the IAEA reports annually to the UN General Assembly.
Which of the statements given above is/ are correct?
(a) 1, 2 and 3   (b) 1 only
(c) 2 and 3   (d) 3 only

19. Consider the following statements regarding India's advocacy for a permanent seat in the United Nations Security Council.
1. India is the largest democracy in the world.
2. India is among the top five largest growing economies in the world.
3. India has been the largest contributor to the United Nations peacekeeping Forces.
4. India is one of the top ten contributors of the United Nations Budget
Which of the statements given above is/are correct?
(a) 1, 2, 3 and 4   (b) Both 1 and 2
(c) 2 only   (d) 1, 3 and 4

20. Which of the following statements are correct with regard to the International Food Policy Research Institute (IFPRI)?
1. IFPRI's vision is 'Cheap Food to All'.

2. It seeks sustainable solutions for ending hunger and poverty.

3. IFPRI was established to identify and analyze alternative national and international strategies and policies for meeting the food needs of the developing world.

Which of the above statements are correct?

(a) 1 and 2   (b) 2 and 3

(c) 1 and 3   (d) 1, 2, and 3

21. With reference to 'Global Climate Change Alliance', which of the following statements is/are correct?

1. It is an initiative of the European Union.

2. It provides technical and financial support to targeted developing countries to integrate climate change into their development policies and budgets.

3. It is coordinated by World Resources Institute (WRI) and World Business Council for Sustainable Development (WBCSD).

Select the correct answer using the code given below:

(a) 1 and 2 only   (b) 3 only

(c) 2 and 3 only   (d) 1, 2 and 3

22. Consider the following statements about the European Union:

1. The European Union was known earlier as the European Community

2. The Single European Act (1986) and the Maastricht Treaty were milestones in its formation

3. Citizens of European Union countries enjoy dual citizenship

4. Switzerland is a member of the European Union

Which of the above statements is/are correct ?

(a) 2 and 4   (b) 1 and 3

(c) 3 and 4   (d) 1, 2 and 3

23. With reference to the United Nations, consider the following statements:

1. The Economic and Social Council (ECOSOC) of UN consists of 24 member States.

2. It is elected by a $2/3^{rd}$ majority of the General Assembly for a 3-year term.

Which of the statements given above is/are correct?

(a) 1 only   (b) 2 only

(c) Both 1 and 2   (d) Neither 1 nor 2

24. Consider the following statements

1. The five permanent members of the Security Council are the only countries recognized as nuclear-weapon states under the Nuclear Non-Proliferation Treaty.

2. The term of non-permanent members of the council is five years.

Which of the statements given above is/ are correct?

(a) 1 only   (b) 2 only

(c) Both 1 and 2   (d) Neither 1 nor 2

25. Consider the following statements:

1. The Commonwealth has no charter, treaty or constitution.

2. AU the territories/countries once under the British empire (jurisdiction/ rule/mandate) automatically joined the Commonwealth as its members.

Which of the statements given above is/are correct?

(a) 1 only   (b) 2 only

(c) Both 1 and 2   (d) Neither 1 nor 2

26. Consider the following statements:

1. North Atlantic Co-operation Council (NACC) is the name of the new organization which has replaced the North Atlantic Treaty Organization (NATO).

2. The United States of America and the United Kingdom became the members of the NATO when it was formed in the year 1949.

Which of the statements given above is/are correct?

(a) 1 only   (b) 2 only

(c) Both 1 and 2   (d) Neither 1 nor 2

27. Which among the following statements about European Union (EU) are correct?

1. The EU is the world's largest economy.

2. The EU has its own flag, anthem and currency.

3. The EU's combined armed forces are the second largest in the world.

4. The EU has its own Constitution.

Select the correct answer using the code given below

(a) 1, 2 and 3   (b) 1 and 4

(c) 2 and 3   (d) 3 and 4

28. The United Nations Frame Work classification for the reserves/resources of Minerals gives information regarding-

1. Economics Viability

2. Environment Viability

3. Social Viability

4. Geological Assessment

(a) 1 and 4   (b) 2 and 3

(c) 2 and 4   (d) 1, 2, 3 and 4

29. Consider the following countries :

1. Denmark

2. Japan

3. Russian Federation

4. United Kingdom

5. United States of America

Which of the above are the members of the 'Arctic Council'?

(a) 1, 2 and 3   (b) 2, 3 and 4

(c) 1, 4 and 5   (d) 1, 3 and 5

30. Consider the following statements :

1. BIMSTEC (Bay of Bengal Initiative for Multi-Sectoral Technical and Economic Cooperation) is visualised as a bridging link between ASEAN and SAARC.

2. It was formerly known as the Bangkok Agreement.

Which of the statements given above is/are correct?

(a) Only 1   (b) Only 2

(c) Both 1 and 2   (d) Neither 1 nor 2

31. Consider the following statements regarding India's advocacy for a permanent seat in the United Nations Security Council.

1. India is the largest democracy in the world.
2. India is among the top five largest growing economies in the world
3. India has been the largest contributor to the United Nations Peace keeping Forces.
4. India is one of the top ten contributors of the United Nations Budget.

Which of the statements given above is / are correct?
(a) 1, 2 and 4   (b) Both 1 and 2
(c) Only 2   (d) 1, 3 and 4

32. Consider the following statements about SAARC :
    1. The SAARC Secretariat is located at Kathmandu.
    2. The Secretariat is headed by the Secretary General, who is appointed by the Council of Ministers from Member States in alphabetical order for a three year term.
    3. The Secretary General is assisted by eight Directors on deputation from the Member States.

    Select the correct answer using the code given below:
    (a) 1 only   (b) 2 and 3 only
    (c) 1, 2 and 3   (d) 1 and 3 only

33. Consider the following statements on SAFTA:
    1. SAFTA is a trade liberalisation programme among the South-Eastern countries of Asia.
    2. According to SAFTA, the Ministerial Council shall meet at least once every year or more often as and when considered necessary by the Contracting States.

    Select the correct answer using the code given below :
    (a) 1 only   (b) 2 only
    (c) Both 1 and 2   (d) Neither 1 nor 2

34. Recently, the USA decided to support India's membership in multi-lateral export control regimes called the "Australia group" and the "Wassenaar arrangement". What is the difference between them ?

1. The Australia group is an informal arrangement which aims to allow exporting countries to minimize the risk of assisting chemical and biological weapons proliferation, whereas the Wassenaar arrangement is a formal group under the OECD holding identical objectives.
2. The Australia group comprises predominantly of Asian, African and north American countries, whereas the member countries of Wassenaar arrangement are predominantly from the European union and American continents.

Which of the statements given above is/are correct ?
(a) 1 only   (b) 2 only
(c) Both 1 and 2   (d) Neither 1 nor 2

35. With reference to a grouping of countries known as BRICS, consider the following statements:

[UPSC 2014]
1. The First Summit of BRICS was held in Rio de Janeiro in 2009.
2. South Africa was the last to join the BRICS grouping.

Which of the statements given above is/are correct?
(a) 1 only   (b) 2 only
(c) Both 1 and 2   (d) Neither 1 nor 2

36. Consider the following countries   **[UPSC 2015]**
    1. China   2. France
    3. India   4. Israel
    5. Pakistan

    Which among the above are Nuclear Weapons States as recognized by the Treaty on the Non-Proliferation of Nuclear Weapons, commonly known as Nuclear Non-Proliferation Treaty (NPT)?
    (a) 1 and 2 only   (b) 1, 3, 4 and 5 only
    (c) 2, 4 and 5 only   (d) 1, 2, 3, 4 and 5

Hints and Explanations

EXERCISE-1

1. (c)   2. (a)   3. (b)

4. (a) The World Economic Outlook (WEO) database contains selected macroeconomic data series from the statistical appendix of the World Economic Outlook report prepared by IMF.

5. (a)

6. (d)   7. (b)   8. (d)   9. (d)   10. (a)

11. (d)   12. (a)   13. (b)   14. (a)

15. (a) The target of Millennium Development Goal of the United Nations is

    "All children both boys and girls would complete a full course Primary schooling by 2015"

    Universal Primary education answer that by 2015 children everywhere answer that by 2015 children everywhere, boys and girls alike, complete a full course of primary education. Success is measured based on the number of children enrolled in primary education, the proportion who reach the last grade of primary school and literacy rates for those aged 15-24.

16. (a)   17. (b)   18. (a)   19. (a)   20. (d)

21. (d)   22. (d)   23. (c)   24. (c)   25. (b)

26. (b)   27. (c)   28. (b)   29. (c)   30. (b)

31. (d)   32. (d)   33. (a)   34. (c)

35. (c) The Organization of the Petroleum Exporting Countries (OPEC) is a cartel of twelve developing countries made up of Algeria, Angola, Ecuador, Iran, Iraq, Kuwait, Libya, Nigeria, Qatar, Saudi Arabia, the United Arab Emirates, and Venezuela.

36. (c)

37. (d) The United Nations Organisation was established in 1945, with the mission to maintain international peace and security and to promote friendly relationship between countries. It has 192 members. The General Assembly consists of the representatives of all member states. According to its charter, it has 5-permanent members and 10 non-permanent members, elected for 2-year term. International court of justice in principle organ of UN, It has 15 judges and are elected for 9-year term.

The Trusteeship Council is also a principle organ of UN, has established to safeguard the interest of the inhabitants of territories which are not yet fully self-governed. Now, its mission fulfilled and its operation is suspended since 1 November, 1944.

38. (c)	39. (a)	40. (a)	41. (c)	42. (a)
43. (d)	44. (d)	45. (d)	46. (b)	47. (a)
48. (c)	49. (b)	50. (a)	51. (b)	52. (c)
53. (d)				

54. (b) The United Nations framework convention on climate change is an international treaty drawn at UN conference on Environment and development, Rio de Janeiro, 1992.

55. (d)

56. (d) The International Development Association (IDA) is an international financial institution which is administered by International Bank for Reconstruction and Development (IBRD).

57. (d) The Marrakesh Agreement, manifested by the Marrakesh Declaration, was an agreement signed in Marrakesh, Morocco, on 15 April 1994, marking the culmination of the 12-year-long Uruguay Round and establishing the World Trade Organization.

58. (c) The Sixth WTO Ministerial Conference was held in Hong Kong, China, 13-18 December 2005.

59. (d) The Association of Southeast Asian Nations (ASEAN) was formed on 8 August 1967. It is a political and economic organization of ten Southeast Asian countries. Indonesia, Malaysia, Philippines, Singapore, Thailand, Brunei, Cambodia, Laos, Myanmar (Burma), and Vietnam. South Korea is not a member of ASEAN.

60. (a) The Organization of Petroleum Exporting Countries (OPEC) is an organization consisting of the world's major oil-exporting nations. The OPEC was founded in 1960 to coordinate the petroleum policies of its members, and to provide member states with technical and economic aid. Iraq, Kuwait, Iran, Saudi Arabia and Venezuela were the OPEC founding member nations in 1960. Algeria joined it later in 1969.

61. (d) The Association of Southeast Asian Nations (ASEAN) encompasses ten South East Asian countries: Brunei Darussalam, Cambodia, Indonesia, Lao PDR, Malaysia, Myanmar (Burma), Philippines, Singapore, Thailand, and Vietnam. East Asia Summit (EAS) includes ASEAN plus three countries as well as India, Australia, New Zealand, United States, and Russia. India is not the full member of ASEAN.

62. (d) The IAEA has its headquarters in Vienna, Austria. The IAEA was established as an autonomous organization on 29 July 1957 to the peaceful use of nuclear energy.

63. (c) The World Bank comprises two institutions: the International Bank for Reconstruction and Development (IBRD) and the International Development Association (IDA).

64. (b) The WTO officially commenced on 1 January 1995 under the Marrakech Agreement, signed by 123 nations on 15 April 1994, replacing the General Agreement on Tariffs and Trade (GATT), which commenced in 1948.

65. (a)

66. (d) The Trusteeship Council suspended operation on 1 November 1994, with the independence of Palau, the last remaining United Nations trust territory, on 1 October 1994. The aims of the Trusteeship System have been fulfilled to such an extent that all Trust Territories have attained self-government or independence, either as separate States or by joining neighbouring independent countries. It is made up of the five permanent members of the Security Council-China, France, Russian Federation, United Kingdom and United States.

67. (a) The Maastricht Treaty was signed on February 7, 1992 by the leaders of 12 member nations, and it reflected the serious intentions of all countries to create a common economic and monetary union. It is responsible for the creation of the European Union, signed in Maastricht (Netherlands).

68. (c) Countries facing balance-of-payment difficulty may apply import restrictions under provisions in the GATT 1994 agreement and under the General Agreement on Trade in Services (GATS).

69. (d) Special Drawing Rights (SDRs) are an international type of monetary reserve currency, created by the International Monetary Fund (IMF) in 1969, which operate as a supplement to the existing reserves of member countries.

70. (b) The Millennium Development Goals (MDGs) are eight international development goals that were established following the Millennium Summit of the United Nations in 2000. The goals are as follows:

1. To eradicate extreme poverty and hunger

2. To achieve universal primary education

3. To promote gender equality

4. To reduce child mortality

5. To improve maternal health

6. To combat HIV/AIDS, malaria, and other diseases

7. To ensure environmental sustainability

8. To develop a global partnership for development

71. (d) The Convention on the Elimination of All Forms of Discrimination against Women (CEDAW), adopted in 1979 by the UN General Assembly and is often described as an international bill of rights for women and GM was adopted in 1995.

72. (a) GATT was signed by 23 nations in Geneva on October 30, 1947 and took effect on January 1, 1948. It lasted until the signature by 123 nations in Marrakesh on April 14, 1994 of the Uruguay Round Agreements, which established the World Trade Organization (WTO) on January 1, 1995. The members of the World Trade Organization (WTO) agree to accord MFN status to each other. Exceptions allow for preferential treatment of developing countries, regional free trade areas and customs unions.

73. (d)

74. (c) In 1993, India ratified the Convention. It was adopted by the United Nations on 18 December 1979. The CEDAW entered into force on 3rd of September, 1981. It defines what constitutes discrimination against women and sets up an agenda for national action to end such discrimination. By accepting the Convention, States commit themselves to undertake a series of measures to end discrimination against women in all forms.

75. (a) The foundation was founded in 1971 by Klaus Schwab, a German-born business professor at the University of Geneva. Originally named the European Management Forum, it changed its name to the World Economic Forum in 1987.

76. (b) India joined Missile Technology Control Regime (MTCR) in 2016 with an aim to strengthen MTCR's objective of restricting the proliferation of missiles, complete rocket systems, and unmanned air vehicles.

77. (b) South Asian Association for Regional Cooperation (SAARC) is the regional intergovernmental organization and geopolitical group of nations in South Asia. Its members include Afghanistan, Bangladesh, Bhutan, India, Nepal, the Maldives, Pakistan, and Sri Lanka. Observer states include Australia, China, the European Union, Iran, Japan, Mauritius, Myanmar, South Korea, and United States.

78. (c) The 8th BRICS summit was held from October 15-16, 2016, in Benaulim, Goa, India. The witnessed summit participation of five member countries Brazil, Russia, India, China and South Africa. Several topics were discussed such as, fighting terrorism, setting up credit rating agency and research centres in agriculture and railways sectors.

79. (b) The Sustainable Development Goals (SDGs), otherwise known as the Global Goals, are a universal call to action to end poverty, protect the planet and ensure that all people enjoy peace and prosperity. The 17 Goals build on the successes of the Millennium Development Goals, while including new areas such as climate change, economic inequality, innovation, sustainable consumption, peace and justice, among other priorities. The SDGs came into effect in January 2016, and they will continue to guide UNDP policy and funding until 2030.

80. (d) India officially joined the Missile Technology Control Regime (MTCR) as a full member on 27th June 2016. India submitted its formal membership application to the NSG in May 2016. India proposed the Comprehensive Convention on International Terrorism in 1996. The Commonwealth Heads of Government Meeting 2015, also known as CHOGM 2015 was the 24th meeting of the heads of government of the Commonwealth of Nations. It was held in Malta from 27 to 29 November. It's a biennial summit meeting.

81. (b) In 2010, South Africa began efforts to join the BRIC grouping, and the process for its formal admission began in August of that year. South Africa officially became a member nation on 24 December 2010, after being formally invited by the BRIC countries to join the group. The group was renamed BRICS - with the "S" standing for South Africa - to reflect the group's expanded membership. In April 2011, the President of South Africa, Jacob Zuma, attended the 2011 BRICS summit in Sanya, China, as a full member.

82. (b) The European Stability Mechanism is a European Union agency that provides financial assistance, in the form of loans, to eurozone countries or as new capital to banks in difficulty.

83. (b) Regional Comprehensive Economic Partnership (RCEP) is a proposed free trade agreement (FTA) between the ten member states of the Association of Southeast Asian Nations (ASEAN) (Brunei, Burma (Myanmar), Cambodia, Indonesia, Laos, Malaysia, the Philippines, Singapore, Thailand, Vietnam) and the six states with which ASEAN has existing FTAs (Australia, China, India, Japan, South Korea and New Zealand).

84. (a) In WTO terminology, subsidies in general are identified by "Boxes" which are given the colours of traffic lights: green (permitted), amber (slow down — i.e. be reduced), red (forbidden).

85. (b) (i) The New Development Bank (NDB), formerly referred to as the BRICS Development Bank, is a Multilateral Development Bank established by the BRICS states (Brazil, Russia, India, China and

South Africa). Its headquarter is in Shanghai, China.

(ii) First statement is wrong- its BRICS nations. 2nd is right - HQ is Shanghai.

86. (c) (i) The IMFC advises and reports to the IMF Board of Governors on the supervision and management of the International Monetary and Financial System. It also considers proposals by the Executive Board to amend the Articles of Agreement and advises on any other matters that may be referred to it by the Board of Governors. A number of international institutions, including the World Bank, participate as observers in the IMFC's meetings.

(ii) Both statements are right as per the official IMF page: April 5, 2016.

87. (a) Iran is not the member of this middle eastern organization.
Gulf Cooperation Council (GCC) is a political and economic alliance of six Middle Eastern countries—Saudi Arabia, Kuwait, the United Arab Emirates, Qatar, Bahrain, and Oman.

88. (b) (i) The OPCW Member States share the collective goal of monitoring chemical industry to prevent new weapons from re-emerging; providing assistance and protection to States Parties against chemical threats; and fostering international cooperation to strengthen implementation of the Convention and promote the peaceful use of chemistry.

(ii) It won Nobel Peace prize in 2013. There is no specific mention of its association with EU, NATO or WTO on the official website of OPCW. Therefore, statement 1 is wrong. By elimination of all options with statement 1, we are left with answer (b).

89. (d) First statement is wrong because Official website says 2006's theme was "A Vision for Sustainable Urbanization in the Asia-Pacific by 2020". Besides, since 2016's summit's theme was emerging urban forms and it's a biennial event as per PTI, so both statements are wrong.

90. (b) From the official organization's website: UN-Habitat also partners with private organizations and civil society so second statement wrong. While Statement 1 and 3 are correct. Hence answer "B" only 1 and 3.

91. (b) World Bank had launched it in 2014.

92. (a)   93. (a)   94. (b)

95. (c)   96. (c)

EXERCISE-2

1. (a)   2. (d)   3. (c)

4. (b) The head-office of UN High Commissioner for Refugees is in Geneva.
Peter Benson founded Amnesty International

5. (d)   6. (d)

7. (c) ASEAN also aims to promote active collaboration and mutual assistance on matters of common interest in the economic, social, cultural, technical, scientific and administrative fields; provide assistance to each other in the form of training and research facilities in the educational, professional, technical and administrative spheres.

8. (c)   9. (c) 10. (c)

11. (b) The North Atlantic Co-operation Council (NACC) was founded in 1991. In 1997, it was replaced by the Euro-Atlantic Partnership Council. (EAPC).

12. (c) UNESCO's World Heritage mission is to catalogues names, and conserve sites of outstanding cultural of natural importance to the common heritage of humanity.
As of 2011, 936 sites are listed in 153 countries.

13. (c) Peackeeping, as defined by the UN, is a way to help countries torn by conflict and create conditions for sustainable peace 1948's United Nations Supervision Organization was the first UN keeping mission, it was to monitor Arab-Israeli ceasefire. Egypt was the second peace keeping mission. In 2007, the first women peacekeeping force was sent by India to Liberia.

14. (a) BIMSTEC was established on 6 June 1997. It is an international organization involving a group of countries of South Asia and South East Asia. The members of Bangladesh. India Myanmar, Srilanka, Thailand, Bhutan and Nepal.
ASEAN was established under the Bangkok Agreement.

15. (b)

16. (b) Kundapur Vaman Kamath, the first President of the New Development Bank of BRICS countries. He also took the charge as the chairman of Infosys.

17. (a) Its secretariat is located in Berlin, Germany. The organization is present in more than 100 countries. It came into existence in 1993.

18. (a) IAEA (International Atomic Energy Agency), is an international organization that seeks to promote the peaceful use of nuclear energy. It was established on 29 July, 1957. It has its headquarters in Vienna. Austria. The IAEA and its former Director General Mohamed Elbaradei were jointly awarded the Nobel Peace Prize on October 7, 2005. The IAEA's Current Director general is Yukio Amano.

19. (a) India is largest democracy in the world. With China, Brazil. India is among the largest growing economies in the world. India is second largest contributor to the United Nations peace keeping Forces.

20. (d) IFPRI's vision is 'A World Free of Hunger and Malnutrition.' IFPRI's mission is to provide research-based policy solutions that sustainably reduce poverty and end hunger and malnutrition.

21. (b)

22. (d) All the statement given in the question is correct, without '4' because Switzerland is not a member of European Union.

23. (d)

24. (a) United Nations organizations was established on 1945. It has 5 permanent member and 10-nonpermanent member. The term of no. permanent member is 2 years.

25. (d) 26. (b)

27. (a) The European Union was established in March 1957 as a result of Rome Treaty. It has 28- member countries, comprising world's largest economy. The Euro is a common currency of European Union. It was introduced in January 1, 1999. The Eu has its own Constitution. European Union doesn't have any unified armed forces.

28. (b) As per their organizations' "About us" page:
EuropeAid (DG for International Cooperation and Development) drives and oversees the overall implementation of the GCCA. So third statement is wrong.

29. (d) The Arctic Council is a high-level intergovernmental forum that addresses issues faced by the Arctic governments and the indigenous people of the Arctic. It has eight member countries: Canada, Denmark, Finland, Iceland, Norway, Russia, Sweden, and the United States.

30. (a) The Bay of Bengal Initiative for Multi-sectoral Technical and Economic Cooperation (BIMSTEC) is an international organisation involving a group of countries in South Asia and South East Asia. These are: Bangladesh, India, Myanmar, Sri Lanka, Thailand, Bhutan and Nepal. The Asia-Pacific Trade Agreement (APTA) is previously known as the Bangkok Agreement. It is the oldest preferential trade agreement between countries in the Asia-Pacific region.

31. (a) Pakistan has been the largest contributor to the United Nations peace keeping Force. India comes second.

32. (c) The SAARC Secretariat is based in Kathmandu, Nepal. The Secretariat is headed by the Secretary General, who is appointed by the Council of Ministers from Member States in alphabetical order for a three year term. The Secretary General is assisted by eight Directors on deputation from the Member States.
The South Asian Association for Regional Cooperation (SAARC) is an economic andgeopolitical organisation of eight countries that are primarily located in South Asia or theIndian subcontinent. The first summit was held inDhaka on 8 December 1985 when the organisation was established by the governments of Bangladesh, Bhutan, India, Maldives, Nepal, Pakistan, and Sri Lanka.

33. (b) SAFTA is a trade liberalization programme among the South Asian countries.

34. (d) Wassenar arrangement : Export Controls for Conventional Arms and Dual-Use Goods and Technologies.
Australia Group : It was formed to help member countries to identify exprot of Chemical and biological weapons. There are not many Asian / African countries in the Australia Group. Only Asian country is Japan and NOT a single African country is there. Wassenar agreement has South Africa, Japan, from Asia but yes, the countries from EU and Americas are there. But, both the statement are incorrect and the correct option is (d).

35. (b) BRICS is the acronym for an association of five major emerging national economies: Brazil, Russia, India, China, and South Africa. The grouping was originally known as "BRIC" before the inclusion of South Africa in 2010. The BRIC first formal summit held in Yekaterinburg, commenced on 16 June, 2009.

36. (a) NPT designated nuclear weapon states are China, France, Russia, United Kingdom and the United States. The NPT is a landmark international treaty whose objective is to prevent the spread of nuclear weapons and weapons technology and to promote cooperation in the peaceful uses of nuclear energy and to further the goal of achieving nuclear disarmament and complete disarmament. It is opened for signature in 1968 and the Treaty entered into force in 1970.

WORLD-PANORAMA

World Countries, Capital, Languages & their Currencies

Country	Capital	Main Language	Currency
Afghanistan	Kabul	Pushtu Dari	Afghani
Algeria	Algiers	Arabic, French	Algerian Dinar
Argentina	Buenos Aires	Spanish	Argentine Peso
Australia	Canberra	English	Australian Dollar
Azerbaijan	Baku	Azeri	Manat
Bahrain	Manama	Arabic, English	Bahraini Dinar
Bangladesh	Dhaka	Bangla	Taka
Belgium	Brussels	Flemish (Dutch), French, German	Euro
Bhutan	Thimphu	Dzongkha	Ngultrum
Bolivia	La Paz; Sucre	Aymara Spanish, Quechua	Boliviano
Bosnia and Herzegovina	Sarajevo	Serbo-Croatian	Conv.Mark
Brazil	Brazilia	Portuguese	Real
Bulgaria	Sofia	Bulgarian	Lev
Burkina Faso	Ouagadougou	French	Franc
Cambodia	Phnom-Penh	Khmer	Riel
Canada	Ottawa	French, English	Canadian Dollar
Chile	Santiago	Spanish	Peso
China	Beijing	Chinese (Mandarin)	Yuan
Colombia	Bogota	Spanish	Peso
Congo Formerly Zaire	Kinshasa	French	Congolese Franc
Costa Rica	San Jose	Spanish	Colon
Croatia	Zagreb	Croatian	Kuna
Cuba	Havana	Spanish	Peso
Czech Republic	Prague	Czech	Koruna
Denmark	Copenhagen	Danish	Krone

Country	Capital	Main Language	Currency
Ecuador	Quito	Spanish	United States dollar
Egypt	Cairo	Arabic	Egyptian Pound
Ethiopia	Addis Ababa	Amharic	Birr
Fiji	Suva	English	Fijian Dollar
Finland	Helsinki	Finnish, Swedish	Euro
France	Paris	French	Euro
French Guiana	Caine	French	Euro
Georgia	Tbilisi	Georgian	Lari
Germany	Berlin	German	Euro
Ghana	Accra	English	Ghana Cedi
Greece	Athens	Greek	Euro
Guatemala	Guatemala City	Spanish	Quetzal
Guyana	Georgetown	English	Guyana Dollar
Haiti	Port-au-Prince	French	Gourde
Honduras	Tegucigalpa	Spanish	Lempira
Hong Kong	Victoria	English, Chinese	Hong Kong Dollar
Hungary	Budapest	Hungarian	Forint
India	New Delhi	Hindi (official), English and 22 officially recognised regional languages	Rupee
Indonesia	Jakarta	Bahasa Indonesian, Dutch, English Javanese	Rupiah
Iran	Teheran	Persian (Farsi), Turk, Kurdish, Arabic	Rial
Iraq	Baghdad	Arabic, Kurdish	Iraqi Dinar
Ireland	Dublin	Irish, English	Euro
Israel	Jerusalem	Hebrew, Arabic	Shekel
Italy	Rome	Italian	Euro
Japan	Tokyo	Japanese	Yen
Jordan	Amman	Arabic, English	Jordan Dinar
Kazakhstan	Astana	Kazakh, Russian, German	Tenge
Kenya	Nairobi	Kiswahili, English, Kikuyu	Shilling
Korea, North	Pyongyang	Korean	Won
Korea, South	Seoul	Korean	Won
Kuwait	Kuwait city	Arabic, English	Kuwait Dinar
Lebanon	Beriut	Arabic, French, English	Pound
Libya	Tripoli	Arabic	Libyan Dinar
Luxembourg	Luxembourg	French, German, English, Luxembourgish	Euro
Malaysia	Putrajaya (formerly Kuala Lumpur)	Malay, English, Chinese, Tamil	Ringgit
Mauritius	Port Louis	English, French, Creole, Hindustani	Rupee Mauritian
Mexico	Mexico city	Spanish, Amerindian languages	Mexico Peso

Country	Capital	Main Language	Currency
Mongolia	Ulan Bator	Mangolian	Togrog
Myanmar	Naypyidar or Pyinmana (formerly Yangon)	Burmeses and tribal languages	Kyat
Netherlands	Amsterdam	Dutch	Euro
New Zealand	Wellington	English and Maori dialect	New Zealand Dollar
Nigeria	Abuja	English, Hansa, Ibo, Yoruba	Naira
Norway	Oslo	Norwegian	Krone
Oman	Muscat	Arabic	Omani Rial
Pakistan	Islamabad	Urdu, Punjabi, Sindhi, Pusthu, Baluchi, Brahvi, English	Pakistani Rupee
Peru	Lima	Spanish, Quechua, Aymara	Nuero Sol
Philippines	Manila	Filipino, English, Spanish	Peso
Poland	Wrsaw	Polish	Zloty
Portugal	Lisbon	Portuguese	Euro
Qatar	Doha	Arabic, English	Riyal (QAR)
Russia	Moscow	Russian	Russian ruble
Saudi Arabia	Riyadh	Arabic	Rial (SAR)
Serbia	Belgrade	Serbo-Croatian (official), Albanian	Dinar
Singapore	Singapore city	Malay, Chinese, Tamil, English	Singapore Dollar
Somalia	Mogadishu	Arabic, English, Italian	Somali Shilling
South Africa	Capetown	Afrikaans, English	Rand
Spain	Madrid	Spanish, Catalan, Basque, Galician	Euro
Sri Lanka	Colombo	Sinhala, Tamil, English	Sri Lankan Rupee
Sudan	Khartoum	Arabic, English, Dinka, Nubian	Sudanese Pound
Sweden	Stockholm	Swedish	Krona
Switzerland	Berne	German, French, Italian, Romansch	Swiss Franc
Syria	Damascus	Arabic, Kurdish, Armenian	Syrian Pound
Taiwan	Taipei	Mandarian Chinese, Taiwan, Hakka dialects	New Taiwan Dollar
Thailand	Bangkok	Thai, Chinese, English, Malay	Thai Baht
Tunisia	Tunis	Arabic, French	Dinar
Turkey	Ankara	Turkish, Kurdish, Arabic	Turkish Lira
Uganda	Kampala	English, Luganda, Swahili	Ugandan Shilling
United Arab Emirates	Abu Dhabi	Arabic	Dirham
United Kingdom	London	English, Welsh, Scots, Gaelic	Pound Sterling
United States of America	Washington D.C.	English	Dollar
Venezuela	Caracas	Spanish	Bolivar
Vietnam	Hanoi	Vietnamese, French, English, Chinese	Dong
Yemen	Sana'a	Arabic	Rial
Zimbabwe	Harare	English, Shona, Ndebela	Dollar (ZWD)

World Tallest Buildings

No.	Building	City	Country	Height	Built
1	Burj Khalifa	Dubai	UAE	2717 ft	2010
2	Shanghai Tower	Shanghai	China	2073 ft	2015
3	Abraj Al-Bait Clock Tower	Mecca	Saudi Arabia	1971 ft	2012
4	Ping An Finance Centre	Shenzhen	China	1965 ft	2017
5	Lotte World Tower	Seoul	South Korea	1819 ft	2016
6	One World Trade Center	New York City	USA	1776 ft	2014
7	Guangzhou CTF Finance Centre	Guangzhou	China	1739 ft	2016
8	Taipei 101	Taipei	Taiwan	1667 ft	2004
9	Shanghai World Financial Center	Shanghai	China	1614 ft	2008
10	International Commerce Centre	Hong Kong	China	1588 ft	2010
11	Changsha IFS Tower T1	Changsha	China	1483 ft	2017

Country with Longest Costline

Sl. No.	Countries	Coast Lines (km.)
1	Canada	202,080
2	Indonesia	54,716
3	Greenland	44,087
4	Russia	37,653
5	Philippines	36,289
6	Japan	29,751
7	Australia	25,760
8	Norway	25,148
9	United States	19,924
10	Antarctica	17,968

Country with Largest Aquatic Area

Sl. No.	Country	Aquatic Area (km^2)
1	Canada	8,91,163
2	Russia	7,20,580
3	USA	4,70,131
4	India	3,14,070
5	China	1,37,060
6	Iran	1,16,600
7	Ethiopia	1,04,300
8	Columbia	1,00,210
9	Indonesia	93,000
10	Congo	77,810

Largest and Smallest Countries

Largest Country (Area wise km^2)	Largest Country (Population wise)	Smallest Country (Area wise km^2)	Smallest Country (Population wise)
Russia (17,098,242)	China	Vatican city (0.44)	Vatican city
Canada (9,984,670)	India	Monaco (2)	Tuvalu
United States (9,833,517)	USA	Nauru (21)	Nauru
China (9,596,960)	Indonesia	Tuvalu (26)	Palau
Brazil (8,515,770)	Brazil	San Marino (61)	San Marino
Australia (7,741,220)	Nigeria	Liechtenstein (160)	Monaco
India (3,287,263)	Pakistan	Saint Kitts and Nevis (261)	Liechtenstein

Longest Rivers

River	Nation/Continent	Length in kms	Basin Area km^2
Nile	Africa	6693	3.25
Amazon	South America	6436	6.14
Yangtze Kiang	China	6380	1.72
Mississippi Missouri	USA	5959	3.20
Ob Irtysh	Russia	5568	2.97
Yenisey Angari a Selenga	Asia	5550	2.55
Yellow (Hwang Ho)	China	5464	–
Congo (Zaire)	Africa	4667	–
Parana Rio de la Plata	S. America	4500	2.58
Irtysh	Asia	4440	–
Mekong	Asia	4425	–

India's Rivers

Indus	Asia	3180
Brahmaputra	Asia	2948
Ganga-Hooghly-Padma	India	2620
Godawari	India	1465
Sutlej	India	1372
Krishna	India	1300
Narmada	India	1289
Chenab	India	1086
Ghaghara	India	1080

Shortest Rivers

Europe Ombia river, Croatia	30
North America, Roe River, Montana, USA	61
South America – Azvis River, Brazil	147

Deepest Rivers

Baikal, Russian Fedn	1637 m
Tanganyika, Africa	1463 m
Caspian Sea, Asia-Europe	1025 m
Malawi of Nyasa, Africa	706 m
Issyk-Kul, Kyrgyzstan	702 m

List of Important Geographical Discoveries Around the World

- **Amundsen (Norwegian)-**Discovered South Pole in 1912.
- **Byrd-American aviator and polar explorer.** Flew over the North Pole in 1926 and made the first flight over the South Pole in 1929. Discovered Edsel Ford mountains and Morei Byrd land.
- **Cabot (Venetian)-**Discovered New Foundland in 1494.
- **Captain Cook (English)-**Discovered Sandwich (now Hawaiian) Isles in 1770.
- **Columbus-**Discovered West Indies in 1492 and South America in 1498.
- **Copernicus-**Discovered Solar System in 1540. Propounded the astronomical system which bears his name.
- **David Livingstone-**Discovered course of the Zambesi, the Victoria Falls and Lake Nyasa in Africa.
- **Edmund Hillary-**Joint conqueror of Mount Everest with Tenzing. He also led a Trans-Atlantic expedition and reached South Pole on January 3, 1958.
- **Ferdinand de Lesseps-**Conceived the plan of the Suez Canal on which work was completed in 1869 through his efforts.
- **Francis Younghusband-**Explored the frontier regions of India, China and Tibet.
- **Kepler-**Discovered the Laws of Planetary Motion in 1609.
- **Lindbergh-**Performed the first solo-flight across the Atlantic in 1927 from New York to Paris.
- **Magellan-**Commanded the first expedition in 1519 to sail round the world. Discovered passage to the Pacific from the Atlantic through Straits afterwards named after him.
- **Marco Polo-**Venetian traveller who explored China, India, South Eastern countries and published the record of his various explorations. He was the first European to visit China.
- **Nansen-**Norwegian explorer who explored across Greenland and reached the highest altitude in the North Polar Region, till then attained.
- **Peary, Robert-**First to reach the North Pole in 1909.
- **Pedro Alvares Cabral (Portuguese) -** Discovered Brazil in 1500.

- **Shackleton-**Arctic explorer, reached within 160 km of the South Pole.
- **Sven Hedin-**Swedish explorer. Made great contribution to the geographic and archaeological knowledge of large areas of Central Asia.
- **Iksman-**Dutch navigator, discovered the Tasmania Island and New Zealand in 1642.
- **Tenzing (Indian)-**First to reach Mount Everest on 29th May, 1953 along with Edmund Hillary. The expedition was led by Col. Sir John Hunt.
- **Vasco da Gama (Portuguese)-**Rounded the Cape of Good Hope and discovered the sea route to India in 1498.

Countries and their National Emblems

Country	Emblem	Country	Emblem
Australia	Kangaroo	Bangladesh	Water Lily
Barbados	Head of a Trident	Belgium	Lion
Canada	White Lily	Chile	Candor & Huemul
Denmark	Beach	Dominica	Sisserou Parrot
France	Lily	Germany	Corn Flower
Guyana	Canje Pheasant	Hong Kong	Bauhinia (Orchid Tree)
India	Lioned Capital	Iran	Rose
Ireland	Shamrock	Israel	Candelabrum
Italy	White Lily	Ivory Coast	Elephant
Japan	Chrysanthemum	Lebanon	Cedar Tree
Luxembourg	Lion with Crown	Mongolia	The Soyombo
Netherlands	Lion	New Zealand	Southern Cross, Kiwi, Fern
Norway	Lion	Pakistan	Crescent
Papua New Guinea	Bird of paradise	Spain	Eagle
		Sierra Leone	Lion
Sri Lanka	Lion	Sudan	Secretary Bird
Syria	Eagle	Turkey	Crescent & Star
U.K.	Rose		

Main News Agencies of the World

Agency	Country	Agency	Country
Bernama	Malaysia	RIA Novasti	Russia
Bangladesh Sangbad Sangstha	Bangladesh	Islamic Republic News Agency	Iran
China News Service	China	JNS. org	Israel
Antara	Indonesia	Kenya News Agency	Kenya
Associated Press (AP)	USA	Kyodo News	Japan
Agence France presse	France	Middle East News Agency	Egypt
Associated Press of Pakistan	Pakistan	Press Trust of India (PTI)	India
Australia Associated Press	Australia	United News of India (UNI)	India
Algemean Nederlands Persbureau	Netherland	Samachar Bharti	India
Agenzia Nazionale Stampa Associate (ANSA)	Italy	Reuters	UK
Deutsche presse Agentur	Germany		

Press Trust of India (PTI)

It was incorporated in Madras on, 27th August, 1947 but started providing full-fledged news and information both in Hindi and English medium from 1st February, 1949. It's a non-profit sharing cooperative organization and known for its unbiased news coverage.

United News of India (UNI)

was founded on December 1961under the company acts. However its commercial application started on 21st March 1961.

Samachar Bharti

It came into being in 1967. It was supported by states like Bihar, Gujarat, Rajasthan and Karnataka. Samchar Bharti is well known for its services of news, sports, entertainment image stories and many more. It merged with other three agencies to form a nationalized news agency Samachar inFebruary 1976.

Prasar Bharti

It is an autonomous body set up by an Act of Parliament on 23 Nov, 1997. It has two major divisions Doordarshan Television Network and All India Radio. It is known to be the largest broadcasting agency in India.

All India Radio (AIR) or Akashwani

It was formed in 1930 as a part of Prasar Bharti. It is considered to be one of the nation's premier Public Service Broadcasters which truly lives up to its motto of 'Bahujan Hitaya: Bahujan Sukhaya'.At the beginning AIR started broadcasting in 23 languages and 146 dialects.

Doordarshan

It was launched on 15 September, 1959 as a part of Prasar Bharti with the motto Satyam Shivam Sundaram. It provides television, radio, online and mobile services throughout metropolitan and regional India with more than 60 channels which broadcast programmes in almost all regional languages along with Hindi and English. It has also a wide spread network in the overseas also.

Reuters

It is an English news service opened in London by Julius Reuter in 1851, and now the most important institution of its kind in the British Empire. It has correspondents in all the great news centres of the world and furnishes telegraph and other news features throughout the eastern hemisphere and, to some extent, to Latin America, the United States and Canada.

A F P Agence France-Presse (AFP)

It is an international news agency. The head-quarter of AFP is located in Paris. It was founded in 1944. It is the third largest in the world (after Associated Press and Reuters). AFP has regional offices in Nicosia, Montevideo, Hong Kong, and Washington, D.C., and bureaus in 150 countries. It transmits news in French, English, Arabic, Portuguese, Spanishand German.

Associated Press (AP)

It is one of the largest and most trusted sources of independent newsgathering. It is neither privately owned nor government-funded; instead, as a not-for-profit news cooperative owned by its American newspaper and broadcast members. Founded in 1846, AP has covered all the major news events of the past 165 years, providing high-quality, informed reporting of everything from wars and elections to championship games and royal weddings.Since the Pulitzer Prize was established, in 1917, AP has received 51 Pulitzers, including 31 photo Pulitzers.AP headquartered in New York, operates in more than 280 locations worldwide.

The British Broadcasting Corporation (BBC)

It is the public service broadcaster of the United Kingdom, head-quartered at Broadcasting House in London. It is the world's oldest national broadcasting organisation and the largest broadcaster in the world. The BBC is established under a Royal Charter and operates under its Agreement with the Secretary of State for Culture, Media and Sport. The history goes back to June 1920 when Britain's first live public broadcast from the Marconi factory in Chelms ford took place.

Al Jazeera

It is a Doha-based state funded broadcaster owned by the Al Jazeera Media Network, Partly funded by the house of Thani, the ruling family of Qatar. It is one of the largest news organizations with 80 bureaus around the world. The channel was launched on 1st November 1996 following the closure of the BBC's Arabic language telivision station.

Top International Daily Newspapers

Name of the Newspaper	Country of Publication
The New York Times	United States
The Daily Mail	United Kingdom
The People's Daily	China
The Washington Post	United States
The Daily Telegraph	United Kingdom
The Guardian	United Kingdom
USA Today	United States
The Wall Street Journal	United States
China Daily	China
Los Angeles Times	United States
The Independent	United Kingdom
The Times of India	India
The Examiner	United States
Daily News	United States
Financial Times	United Kingdom

National Animals : Some Major Countries

Country	Animal	Country	Animal
Afghanistan	Snow Leopard	Nepal	Cow
Australia	Black Eagle	New Zealand	Kiwi
Australia	Kangaroo	Pakistan	Markhor
Bangladesh	Royal Bengal tiger	South Africa	Springbok

Country	Animal	Country	Animal
Brazil	Macaw	Spain	Bull
Canada	North American Beaver	United Kingdom	Barbary Lion
China	Panda, Red Crowned Crane	United States	Bald Eagle
Denmark	Mute Swan	India	Bengal Tiger
Japan	Green Pheasant	Kuwait	Camel
Myanmar	Tiger	Belgium	Lion

Some Official Books

Blue Book : An official report of the British Government

Green Book : An official publication of italy and iran

Grey Book : An official reports of the Government of japan and Belgium

Orange Book : An official Publications of the Government of Netherlands

White Book : An official Publications of China, Germany and Portugal

Yellow Book : French official Book

White Paper : An official paper of the Government of Britain and India on a particular issue

Red Data Book: A book which contains lists of species whose continued existence is threatened

The New 7 Wonder of the World

Chichen Itza, Maxico	Petra, Jordan
Christ the Redeemer, Brazil	The Colosseum, Rome, Italy
Great Wall of China, China	The Taj Mahal, India
Machu Picchu, Peru	

World's Most Powerful Intelligence Agencies

Detective Agency	Country	Detective Agency	Country
Ministry of State Security	China	VAJA	Iran
Australian Secret Intelligence Service (ASIS)	Australia	MOSSAD	Israel
FSB	Russia	Egyption Homeland Security	Egypt
State Security Agency	South Africa	PSIA	Japan
Inter Service Intelligence (ISI)	Pakistan	Iraqi National Intelligence Service	Iraq
MI (Military Intelligence) 5 and 6, Special Branch, Joint Intelligence org.	UK	Central Intelligence Agency (CIA), Federal Bureau of investigation (FBI)	USA
Research and Analysis wing (RAW), Intelligence Bureau (IB)	India	DGSE (Direction General Dela Securite Exterieure.	France

Direction Generale De La Securite Exterieure (DGSE), France

The General Directorate for External Security (DGSE) is the intelligence agency of France. It was founded in 1982 to gather intelligence from foreign sources to assist in military and strategic decisions. It is not as famous as CIA or Mossad, but DGSE claims to have prevented more than 15 terrorist attacks in France since 9/11. The agency has a network of around 5000 agents spread across France and the world. Its head office is in the 20th arrondissement of Paris.

The Institute for Intelligence and Special Operations, MOSSAD, Israel

One of the most powerful secret service agencies in the world, the Mossad, meaning Institute for Intelligence and Special Operations, is the national intelligence agency of Israel. Mossad, like the CIA, has active agents spread across the world and are involved in intelligence gathering, covert operations and 'protecting Jews and Jewish interests'. Mossad was formed on December 13, 1949, as the Central Institute for Coordination at the recommendation of Prime Minister David Ben-Gurion to Reuven Shiloah.

Federal Security Services (FSB), Russia

Federal Security Services is the principal security agency of Russia and the foremost successor agency to the USSR's Committee of State Security(KGB). Its main responsibilities are within the country and include counter-intelligence, internal and border security, counter-terrorism, and surveillance as well as investigating some other types of grave crimes and federal law violations. It is headquartered in Lubyanka Square, Moscow's centre, in the main building of the former KGB. The Director of the FSB since 2008 is army general Aleksandr Bortnikov.

Ministry of State Security (MSS), China

The Ministry of State Security (MSS) is one of the most powerful and most active Chinese intelligence agencies. Its main objective is to keep track and neutralise "enemies" of the Communist Party of China. It is headquartered near the Ministry of Public Security of the People's Republic of China in Beijing. MSS holds the same authority to arrest or detain people as regular police for crimes involving state security with identical supervision by the procuratorates and the courts.

Military Intelligence Section 6 (MI6), United Kingdom

The Secret Intelligence Service (SIS), popularly referred to as the Directorate of Military Intelligence Section 6 (MI6), is known as the "the secret front line" of Britain`s national security. A century old organisation, the MI6's presence was not officially acknowledged till 1994. The agency is tasked with gathering foreign intelligence from across the globe that could impact political and economic interests in the UK. Since 1995, the SIS headquarters have been at Vauxhall Cross on the South Bank of the River Thames.

Inter Service Intelligence (ISI), Pakistan

Established in 1948, Pakistan's Directorate for Inter-Services Intelligence (ISI) is the premier military operated intelligence service of Pakistan. The ISI was established as an independent intelligence service in 1948 in order to strengthen the sharing of military intelligencebetween the three branches of Pakistan Armed Forces in the aftermath of the Indo-Pakistani War of 1947, which had exposed weaknesses in intelligence gathering, sharing and coordination between the Army, Air Force and Navy.The ISI has headquarters in Islamabad, Islamabad Capital Venue, and is currently headed by Lieutenant-General Rizwan Akhter, who succeeded Zaheerul Islam in October 2014.

Central Intelligence Agency, CIA, United States

The Central Intelligence Agency (CIA) of the United States of America is indeed the largest secret service with the maximum reach. The CIA is known to play a pivotal role in helping the US maintain its status as the world's sole super power. More importantly, CIA has been playing a central role in exchange of intelligence between countries to combat global terrorism.

Research and Analysis Wing (RAW, India)

Founded in 1968, the Research and Analysis Wing (RAW), initially, focused its activities in India's immediate neighbourhood but with the changing profile of New Delhi's geo-political interests, it has spread its wings to other regions across the world. The primary function of R&AW is gathering foreign intelligence and counter-terrorism. R&AW was formed in September 1968 under the guidance of its first Director, Rameshwar Nath Kao. Headquartered in New Delhi.

Canadian Security Intelligence Service (CSIS)

Canadian Security Intelligence Services is Canada's primary national intelligence service. It is responsible for collecting, analyzing, reporting and disseminating intelligence on threats to Canada's national security, and conducting operations, covert and overt, within Canada and abroad. It also reports to and advises the government of Canada on national security issues and situations that threaten the security of the nation. Its headquarters is located in Ottawa, Ontario, in a purpose-built facility completed in 1995.

Australian Secret Intelligence Service (ASIS)

The Australian Secret Intelligence Service (ASIS) is Australia's intelligence watchdog which keeps a close watch on developments across the world, especially in the Asia-Pacific region. Although Australia is relatively isolated from global terror, still ASIS works 24x7 to protect the country's political and economic interests. Interestingly, the existence of ASIS, founded in 1952, was a secret even from its own government for over twenty years. Its current Director-General is Nick Warner.

Inventors of Various fields

Field	Inventor	Field	Inventor
Atom Bomb	Dr. Robert Oppenheime	Computer	Charles Babbage
Aviation	Sir George Cayley	Biology	Aristotle
Chemistry	Robert Boyle	Microbiology	Louis Pasteur and Robert koch
Comedy	Aristophanes	Political Science	Aristotle
Economics	Adam Smith	Modern Philosphy	Rene Descartes
English Poetry	Geoffrey Chaucer	Psychology	Wilhelmam Wundt
Greek Tragedy	Aeschylus	Modern Observational Astronomy	Galileo Galilei
Immunology	Edward Jenner	Modern Physics Science	Galileo Galilei
Modern Chemistry	Antoini Lavoisier	Modern Science	Galileo Galilei
Nuclear Physics	Ernest Rutherford	Nano technology	Richard smalley
Sanskrit Grammar	Panini	Indian Nuclear Science	Homi Jehengir Bhabha
Geography	Eratosthenes	Anatomy	Andreas Vesalius
Sociology	Auguste Comte	Geometry	Euchid
Mathematics	Archimedes	Internet	Vinton Cerf

Some Important Symbols or Signs

Pen	Symbol of Cutural and Civilization
Lotus	Culture and Civilization
Red cross	Medical Aid and Hospital
Red flag	Revolution also sign of danger
Black flag	Symbol of Protest
Yellow flag	Floun on shops or vehicles carrying patients suffering
White flag	From infections diseases
Flag flower at half mast	Symbol of Truce
Pigeon or doke	Symbol of National Mourning
A blindfolded woman	Symbol of Peace
Holding a balanced scale one skull on two	Symbol of Justice
one skull on two bones crossing each other diagnally	Sign of Danger
Wheel (Chakru)	Symbol of Progress
Olive Branch	Symbol of Peace

List of Parliaments of Different Countries

Country	Name of Parliament
Afghanistan	Shora
Argentina	National Congress
Australia	Federal Parliament
Austria	National Assembly
Azerbaijan	Melli Majlis
Bahamas	General Assembly
Bahrain	Consultative Council
Bangladesh	Jatia Parliament
Bhutan	Tsogdu
Bolivia	National Congress
Botswana	National Assembly
Brazil	National Congress
Britain	Parliment (House Of Common's and House Of Lords)
Brunei	National Assembly
Bulgaria	Narodno Subranie
Cambodia	National Assembly
Canada	Parliament
China	National People's Assembly
Colombia	Congress
Congo	Democratic Rep. Of National Legislative Council
Crotia	Sabor
Cuba	National Assembly of People's Power
Denmark	Folketing
Ecuador	National Congress
Egypt	People's Assembly
Ethiopia	Federal Council and House of Representative
Fiji Islands	Senate & House of Representative
Finland	Eduskusta (Parliament)
France	National Assembly
Germany	Bundestag (Lower House) and Bundesrat (Upper House)
Great Britain	Parliament
Greece	Chamber of Deputies
Guyana	National Assembly
Hungary	National Assembly
Iceland	Althing
India	Sansad
Indonesia	People's Consultative Assembly
Iran	Majlis
Iraq	National Assembly
Ireland	Oireachtas
Israel	The Knesset
Italy	Chamber of Deputies and Senate
Japan	Diet
Jordan	National Assembly
Korea(North)	Supreme People's Assembly
Korea(South)	National Assembly
Kuwait	National Assembly
Luxembourg	Chamber of Deputies
Madagascar	National People's Assembly
Malaysia	Majilis
Maldives	Majilis
Myanmar	Pyithu Hluttaw
Nepal	Rashtriya Panchayat
Netherlands	States General (Staten-General)
New Zealand	Parliament (House of Representative)
Norway	Storting
Pakistan	National Assembly & Senate
Papua New Guinea	National Parliament
Philippines	The Congress
Russia	Duma & Federal Council
Saudi Arabia	Majlis Al Shura
South Africa	Parliament
Spain	Crotes
Taiwan	Yuan
Turkey	Grand National Assembly
USA	Congress
Vietnam	National Assembly

Sobriquets

A sobriquet is a nickname, Occasionally assumed and often given by another. The sobriquet can become more familiar than the original name.

Sobriquets Person	Primary Names
Angle of Death	Josef Mengele
Bard of Avon	William Shakespeare
Bard of Twickenham	Alexander Pope
Bloody mary	Mary I of England
Bonnie Prince Charlie	Charles Edward Stuart
Brangelina	Brad Pitt and Angelina Jolie
Caligula	Gaius Julius Caesar Augustus Germanicus
Canuck	Canadian, from Johnny Canuck
der Alte (the old man)	Konrad Adenauer
Desert Fox	Erwin Rommel
Diamond Dave	David Lee Roth, Singer
Digger	Australian soldier
Dr. Death	Jack Kevorkian, proponent of assisted suicide
Dubya	George W. Bush
EI Caudillo	Francisco Franco
Father of his country	George Washington
Fuhrer	Adolf Hitler
Genghis Khan	Temüjin
Grand Old Man of Britain	Willian Ewart Glandstone
Hanoi Jane	Jane Fonda
Honest Abe	Abraham Lincoln
Ike Dwight	David Eisenhower
Iron Duke	Duke of Wellington
Iron Lady	Margaret Thatcher
King James	LeBron James, American basketball player
Lady with the Lamp	Florence Nightingale
Little Richard	Rev. Richard Wayne Penniman, a prominent figure in rock n' roll.
Madge	Madonna
Madiba	Nelson Mandela
Maid of Orleans	Joan of Arc
Man of Blood and Iron	Otto Von Bismark
Man of Destiny	Napolean Bonaparte
Old Blood and Guts	George S. Patton
Old Blue Eyes	Frank Sinatra, entertainer
Old Hickory	Andrew Jackson, 7th President of the United States
Old Kinderhook (OK)	Martin Van Buren, 8th President of the United States
Old Nick	Santa
Old Rough and Ready	Zachary Taylor
Old St. Nick	Santa
Pelê	Edson Arantes do Nascimento
Prince of the Humanists	Desiderius Erasmus
Qaid-e-Azam	Mohammad Ali Jinnah
Saint Jimmy	Billie Joe Armstrong
Satchmo	Louis Armstrong
Slick Willy	U.S. President Bill Clinton
Slowhand	Eric Clapton
Sting	Gordon Summer, British rock musician
The Bard	William Shakespeare
The Bird	Mark Fidrych, Baseball pitcher
The Boss	Bruce Springsteen
The Cincinnatus of the Americans	George Washington
The Duke	John Wayne
The Fab Four	The Beatles
The Godfather of Soul	James Brown
The Golden Bear	Jack Nicklaus
The Great Commoner	William Pitt, 1st Earl of Chatham ("Pitt the elder") or William Jennings Bryan
The Greatest	Muhammad Ali, Boxer
The King (of golf)	Arnold Palmer
The King (of Rock and Roll)	Elvis Presley
The King of Pop	Michael Jackson
The Lion of the Round Top	Col. Joshua L. Chamberlain, commander of the 20th Maine Regiment, American Civil War
The Man from Tennessee	Andrew Jackson
The Material Girl	Madonna
The New Sinatra	Jay-Z
The Rat Pack	A group of American singers and entertainers from the late 1950s to the early 1970s
The Red Baron	Manfred von Richthofen, World War I, German flying ace
The Rock Chemeleon	David Bowie
The Tiger of France	Georges Clemenceau
Tricky Dick	Richard Nixon, 37th President of the United States
Uncle Sam	The U.S.A. or sometimes the government
Wizard of the North	Walter Scott
Yank (a short form of "Yankee")	Originally used derogatorily by Southerners but now only heard outside the USA

Places

Subsequent Place	Primary Names
Beantown	Boston, Massachusetts, USA
Blighty	Great Britain (used by British servicemen abroad and expatriates)
Brass Fountain	PPSh-41
Brew City	Milwaukee, Wisconsin
Brisvegas	Brisbane, Queensland, Australia
Britain of South	New Zealand
Chocolate City	Washington, D.C., so named because of its majority African-American population
City of Brotherly Love	Philadelphia
City of Dreaming Spires	Oxford, England
City of Golden Gate	San Francisco, USA
City of Magnificent Distances	Washington D.C., USA
City of Seven Hills	Rome, Italy
City of Skyscrapers	New York, USA
City of the Golder Gate	San Francisco
Cockpit of Europe	Belgium
Dark Continent	Africa
Empire City	New York, USA
Eternal City	Rome, Italy
Forbidden City	Lhasa, Tibet
Frisco	San Francisco, California
Garden of England	Kent, England
Garrincha	Manoel Francisco dos Santos
Gate of Tears	Bab-el-mandab, Jerusalem
Gift of Nile	Egypt
Gotham	New York
Granite City	Aberdeen, Scotland
Great White Way	Broadway, New York, USA
Hermit Kingdom	Korea
Herring Pond	Atlantic Ocean
Hogtown	Toronto, Ontario, Canada
Holy Land	Palestine
Humming Bird	Trinidad
Island of Cloves	Madagascar
Island of Pearls	Bahrain
Key of Mediterranean	Gibraltar
Land of Cakes	Scotland
Land of Canals	Netherlands
Land of Golden Pagoda	Myanmar (Burma)
Land of Lilies	Canada
Land of Maple	Canada
Land of Midnight Sun	Norway
Land of Morning Calm	Korea
Land of Rising Sun	Japan
Land of the Golden Fleece	Australia
Land of the Golden Pagoda	Myanmar
Land of Thousand Lakes	Finland
Land of Thunderbolt	Bhutan
Land of White Elephants	Thailand
Land of Windmills	Netherlands
Manchester of Japan	Osaka
Never Never Land	Prairies of N.Australia
Pearl of the Antilles	Cuba
Pearl of the Orient	Philippines
Perfidious Albion	Great Britain
Pillars of Hercules	Strait of Gibraltar
Playground of Europe	Switzerland
Port of Five Seas	Moscow
Powder Keg of Europe	Balkans
Quaker City	Philadelphia, USA
Queen of Adriatic	Venice, Italy
Roof of the World	Pamirs, Central Asia
Sick Man of Europe	Turkey
Sin City	Las Vegas, Nevada, USA
Sorrow of China	River Hwang Ho
Sugar Bowl of the World	Cuba
Taiwan	Republic of China
The Antipodes	Australia and New Zealand
The Battlefield of Europe	Belgium
The Bayou City	Houston, Texas, USA
The Big Apple	New York City
The Big D	Dallas, Texas, USA
The Big Easy	New Orleans, Louisiana
The Big Smoke	Toronto, Ontario, Canada
The City of Light	Paris
The City or The City by the Bay	San Francisco, California
The Dragon	China (as an economy)
The Emerald City	Seattle, Washington, USA
The Emerald Isle	Ireland and Puerto Rico
The Enchanted Isle	(from 'la isla del encanto') Puerto Rico
The Federal City	Washington D.C.
The Fourth Estate	The Press
The Mother-in-law of Europe	Denmark
The Old Bailey	The Central Criminal Court in England
The Old Lady of Threadneedle Street	The Bank of England

The Old Smoke	London
The Paris of the South	São Paulo and Buenos Aires
The Paris of the West	San Francisco, USA
Tie Rock (prison)	Alcatraz Prison
The Steel City	Pittsburgh, Pennsylvania.
The Windy City	Chicago, Illinois, USA
Tinseltown	Hollywood, California, USA
Venice of the North	Stockholm
Westminster	The British Parliament
White City	Belgrade, Yugoslavia
White House	The executive branch of the government of the United States
White Man's Grave	Guinea Coast
Whitehall	The British government including Parliament but excluding the monarchy
World's Breadbasket	Prairies of N. America
World's Loneliest Island	Tristan De Gunha (Mid-Atlantic)
Yellow River	Hang He (China)

Some Important Boundary Lines

Durand Line: between Pakistan and Afghanistan
Hindenberg Line: between Germany and Poland
49th Parallel: between USA and Canada
Mac Mahon Line: between India and Tibet/China
Maginot Line: between France and Germany
38th Parallel: between North and South Korea
Oder Neisse Line: between Germany and Poland
Radcliffe Line: between India and Pakistan
17th Parallel: between India and Pakistan (as claimed by Pakistan)

ADDITIONAL FACTS (WORLD)

- The largest Coffee growing Country in the world is - Brazil
- The Biggest Delta in the World is the - Sunderbans
- The Japanese call their country as - Nippon
- The Biggest Island of the World is - Greenland
- The river which carries maximum quantity of water into the sea is the - Amazon
- Mount Everest was named after Sir George - Everest
- The World's Largest Diamond producing Country is - Congo (Kinshara)
- The Eiffel tower was built by - Alexander Eiffel
- The Red Cross was founded by - Jean Henri Durant
- The permanent secretariat of the SAARC is located at - Kathmandu
- The earlier name of Sri Lanka was - Ceylon
- The founder of the Chinese Republic was - San Yat Sen

First in the World

The first person to reach Mount Everest	Sherpa Tenzing, Edmund Hillary
The first person to reach North Pole	Robert Peary
The first person to reach South Pole	Amundsen
The first religion of the world	Hinduism
The first country to print book	China
The first country to issue paper currency	China
The first country to commence competitive examination in civil services	China
The first President of the U.S.A	George Washington
The first Prime Minister of Britain	Robert Walpole
The first Governor General of the United Nations	Trigveli (Norway)
The first country to win football World cup	Uruguay
The first country to prepare a constitution	U.S.A
The first Governor General of Pakistan	Mohd. Ali Jinnah
The first country to host NAM summit	Belgrade (Yugoslavia)
The first European to attack India	Alexander, The Great
The first European to reach China	Marco Polo
The first person to fly aeroplane	Wright Brothers
The first person to sail round the world	Magellan
The first country to send man to the moon	U.S.A
The first country to launch Artificial satellite in the space	Russia
The first country to host the modern Olympics	Greece
The first city on which the atom bomb was dropped	Hiroshima (Japan)
The first person to land on the moon	Neil Armstrong followed by Edwin E. Aldrin
The first shuttle to go in space	Columbia
The first spacecraft to reach on Mars	Viking-I
The first woman Prime Minister of England	Margaret Thatcher

The first Muslim Prime Minister of a country	Benazir Bhutto (Pakistan)
The first woman Prime Minister of a country	Mrs. S. Bandamaike (Sri Lanka)
The first woman to climb Mount Everest	Mrs. Junko Tabei (Japan)
The first woman cosmonaut of the world	Velentina Tereshkova (Russia)
The first woman President of the U.N. General Assembly	Vijaya Lakshmi Pandit
The first man to fly into space	Yuri Gagarin (Russia)
The first batsman to score three test century in three successive tests on debut	Mohd. Azharuddin
The first man to have climbed Mount Everest twice	Nawang Gombu
The first U.S. President to resign Presidency	Richard Nixon

First in World-Male and Female

First men to climb Mt. Everest	Sherpa Tenzing Norgay & Sir Edmund Hillary (29th May, 1953)
First man to reach North Pole	Robert Peary
First man to reach South Pole	Ronald Amundsen
First religion of the world	Santosh Dharma
First country to print books	China
First country to issue paper currency	China
First country to start Civil Services Competition	China
First President of United States of America	George Washington
First prime Minister of great Britain	Robert Walpole
First secretary general of United Nations	Trigve Li
First country to make education compulsory	Prussia
First country to win the world cup Football	Uruguay (1930)
First country to make a constitution	United States of America
Pakistan's first Governor General	Mohammed Ali Jinnah
First Summit of NAM was organized in	Belgrade (former Yugoslavia)
First European to visit China	Marco Polo
First men to fly an aeroplane	Wright Brothers

First person to sail around the world	Ferdinand Magellan
First country to send human to Moon	United States of America
First country to launch satellite into space	Russia (former USSR)
First country to host the modern Olympic games	Greece
First President of the Republic of China	Dr. Sun Yat-sen
First city to be attacked with Atom bomb	Heroshima (Japan)
First Radio Telescope Satellite was launched into space by	Japan
First Russian (Soviet) Prime Minister to visit India	V.I. Bulganin
First University of the world	Taxila University
First man to set foot on the Moon	Neil Armstrong (U.S.A)
First man to go into space	Major Yuri Gagarin (USSR)
First Space Shuttle Launched	Columbia
First space ship landed on mars	Viking –I (July,1976)
First woman Prime Minister of England	Margaret Thacher
First woman Prime Minister of any Muslim country	Benazir Bhutto (Pakistan)
First woman Prime Minister of a country	S. Bhandarnayake (Sri Lanka)
First woman cosmonaut in space	Valentina Tereshkova (USSR)
First woman to climb Mt. Everest	Junko Tabei (Japan)
First deaf and dumb to cross the Srait of Gibraltar	Taranath Shenoy (India)
First woman president of UN General assembly	Smt. Vijayalakshmi Pandit (1953)
First European Invader of Indian soil	Alexander, The Great
First woman to reach the North pole	Ms. Fran
First woman to reach Antartica	Caroline Michaelson
First man to draw the map of earth	Anexemander
First man to compile Encyclopaedia	Aspheosis (Athens)
First eldest man to climb Mt. Everest	Richard Wass
First Asian to win Wimbledon Trophy	Arthur Ashe (U.S.A)

First man to win Nobel Prize for Literature	Rene F.A. & Suilt Pradhom (France)
First man to win Nobel Prize for Peace	Jin F. Dunant (Switzerland) & Frederic Peiry (France)
First man to win Nobel prize for Physics	W.K. Roentgen (Germany)
First man to win Nobel prize for Chemistry	J.H. Wenthoff (Holland)
First man to win Nobel Prize Medicine (Medical Science)	A.E. Wonn Behring (Germany)
First man to win Nobel Prize Economics	Ranger fish (Norway) & John Tinbergen (Holland)
First woman President of a country	Maria Estela Peron (Argentina)
First Space Tourist (Male)	Dennis Tito
First Space Tourist (Female)	Mrs. Anousheh Ansari

Superlatives

Tallest Animal on (land)	Giraffe
Biggest Bell	Great Bell at Moscow
Fastest Bird	Swift
Largest Bird	Ostrich
Smallest Bird	Humming Bird
Longest Bridge (Railway)	Lower Zambeji (Africa)
Tallest Building	Burj khalifa, Dubai (U.A.E)
Tallest office Building	Patronas Twin Towers Kuala Lampur (Malaysia)
Longest Big Ship Canal	Seuz Canal (Linkin red sea & Mediterranean)
Busiest Canal (Ship)	Baltic White Sea Canal (152 miles)
Biggest Cinema House	Roxy (New York)
Highest City	Wen Chuwan (Tibet, China) 16,732 ft.
Largest City (in population)	Tokyo [(3,42,00000), Est. population in 2006]
Biggest City in (area)	Mount Isa, Queensland, Australia (41225 sq. km.)
Largest Continent	Asia
Smallest Continent	Australia
Largest Country (in population)	China
Largest Country (in area)	Russia

Largest Coral Formation	The Great Barrier Reef (Australia)
Largest Dam	Grand Coulee- Concrete Dam (U.S.A)
Longest Day	June 21 (in Northern Hemisphere)
Shortest Day	Dec. 22(in Northern Hemisphere)
Largest Delta	Sundarbans, India (8000 sq. miles)
Longest Desert (World)	Sahara, Africa (84,00,000 sq. km.)
Largest Diamond	The Cullinan (over 1 ½ 1b.)
Biggest Dome	Gol Gumbaz (Bijapur), (Old archi) 144 ft. diameter.
Biggest Dome (New Archi)	Astrodome, Sports
Longest Epic	The Mahabharata
Largest Island	Greenland (renamed Kalaallit Nunaat)
Largest Lake (Artificial)	Lake Mead (Bouler)
Deepest Lake	Baikal (Siberia); average depth 2300 ft.
Highest Lake	Titicaca (Bolivia) 12645 ft. above sea level.
Largest Lake (Fresh Water)	Lake Superior, U.S.A
Largest Lake (Salt Water)	Caspian Sea 3,71,000 sq. km.)
Largest Mosque	Jama Masjid, Delhi, (area 10,000 sq.ft.)
Biggest Library	National Kiev Library, Moscow & Library of the Congress, Washington)
Highest Mountain peak (World)	Himalayas
Longest Mountain Range	Andes (S.America) 5,500 miles in length
Biggest Museum	British Museum (London)
Tallest Minaret (Free Standing)	Qutub Minar, Delhi 238 ft.
Tallest Minaret	Great Hassan Mosque, Casablanca, Morocco
Deepest & Biggest Ocean	The Pacific
Largest Palace	Imperial Palace (Gugong), Beijing (China)
Largest Park	National Park, Greenland
Largest Peninsula	Arabic (32,50,000 sq. km.)
Coldest Place or Region	Verkhoyansk (Syberia), Temperature – 85° C
Driest Place	Death Valley (California); rainfall 1.5 inch.

Hottest Place (World)	Al-Aziziyah (Libya, Africa) 136°F
Largest Planet	Jupiter
Brightest and Hottest Planet (also nearest to Earth)	Venus
Farthest planet (from the Sun)	Neptune
Nearest Planet (to the Sun)	Mercury
Smallest Planet	Mercury
Highest Plateau	Pamir (Tibet)
Longest Platform (Railway)	Kharagpur W.B, India (833m)
Largest Platform (Railway)	Grand Central terminal, New York (U.S.A)
Largest Port	Port of New York & New Jersey (U.S.A)
Busiest Port	Rotterdam (the Netherlands)
Longest Railway	Trans-Siberian Railway (6,000 miles Long)
Longest River	Nile (6690 km), Amazon (6570 km.)
Longest River Dam	Hirakund Dam (Orissa), India 15.8 miles.
Largest sea-bird	Albatross
Largest Sea (inland)	Mediterranean
Brightest Star	Sirius (also called Dog star)
Tallest statue	Statue of Liberty, New York (U.S.A), 150 ft. high.
Tallest Statue (Bronze)	Bronze Statue of Lord Buddha, Tokyo (Japan).
Longest Swimming Course	English Channel
Tallest Tower	C.N Tower Toronto (Canada)
Longest Train nonstop	Flying Scoutsman
Longest Tunnel (Railway)	Seikan Rail Tunnel (Japan), (53.85 km.)
Longest & Largest Canal Tunnel	Le Rove Tunnel (South of France)
Longest Tunnel (Road)	Laerdal, Norway
Highest Volcano	Ojos Del Salado, Andes Argentine-Chile (6,885 m.)
Largest Volcano	Mauna Lao (Hawaii)
Longest Wall	Great Wall of China (1500 miles)
Highest Waterfall	Salto Angel Falls (Venezuela)
Longest Strait	Tartar Strait (Sakhalin Island & the Russian mainland)
Broadest Strait	Davis Straits (Greenland & Baffin Island, (Canada)
Narrowest strait	Chaliks-45 yards (Between the Greek mainland the island of Euboea in the Aegean Sea)
Largest Bay	Hudson Bay, Canada (Shore line 7623 miles)
Largest Gulf	Gulf of Mexico, (shoreline 2100 miles)
Largest Archipelago	Indonesia (over 3,000 Islands)
Tallest Active Geyser	Giant (Geyser) yelowstone park U.S.A 200 ft. high
Largest River Basin	Amazon Basin- 27, 20,000 sq. mile.
World Rainiest Spot	Cherrapunji (Mawsynram), India
Largest Gorge	Grand Canyon, on the Colorado River, U.S.A
Lightest gas	Hydrogen
Lightest Metal	Lithium
Highest Melting Point	Tungsten, 3,410°C
Hardest Substance	Diamond
Longest Animal	Blue Whale, (recorded length 106 ft. weight-195 tons)
Longest Life Span of an Animal	190 to 200 years, (Giant tortoise)
Largest Land Animal	African Bush Elephant
Fastest Animal	Cheetah (Leopard) 70 m.p.h
Longest Jump Animal	Kangaroo
Longest wing Spread Bird	Albatross
Slowest Animal	Snail
Domestic Dog	Irish Wolf Hound
Fastest Dog	Persian Grey Hound (speed 43 m.p.h)
Longest poisonous snake	King cobra
Biggest Flower	Raffesia (Java)
Largest Stadium	Strahov stadium in prague, (the Czech Republic)
Largest Church	Basilica of st. peter, vetican city, Rome Italy
Largest Temple	Angkor Vat (Combodia)
Largest Diamond mine	Kimbarley (S.Africa)
Largest River in volume	Amazon, Brazil

Longest Corridor	Rameshwaram Temple's Corridor (5000 ft.)
Highest Straight Dam	Bhakhra Dam
Highest Capital City	La Paz (Bolivia)
Largest Asian Desert	Gobi, Mongolia
Largest Democracy	India
Longest Thoroughfare	Verazano-Narrows, New York City Harbour
Largest Neck Animal	Giraffe
Largest Animal of the Cat Family	Lion
Most Intelligent Animal	Chimpanzee
Bird, that never makes its nests	Cuckoo
Wingless Bird	Kiwi
Reptile which changes its colors	Chameleon
Largest Mammal	Whale

Famous Landmarks around the World

1. The Statue of Liberty in New Your: **USA**
2. The Eiffel tower in Paris: **France**
3. St. Basil's Cathedral in Moscow : **Russia**
4. The Great Sphinx at Giza, The Pyramids of Giza: **Egypt**
5. Neptune and the Place of Versailles: **France**
6. The Great wall of China : **China**
7. The Taj Mahal in Agra : **India**
8. Christ the Redeemer: **Rio de Janeiro**
9. Mecca: **Saudi Arabia**
10. Brandenburg Gate in Berlin: **Germany**
11. Acropolis of Athens: **Greece**
12. Niagara Falls : **Border of Ontario (Canada) and New York (USA)**
13. Angkor Wat : **Cambodia**
14. St. Peter's Cathedral : **Vatican City**
15. Mount Rushmore: **South Dakota**
16. The Grand Canyon : **Arizona**
17. Sydney Opera House : **Australia**
18. Forbidden City : **Beijing**
19. The Colosseum: **Rome, Italy**
20. The Empire State Building : **New York**
21. Abu Simbel : **Egypt**
22. Tower of Pisa : **Italy**
23. The Burj al Arab Hotel : **Dubai**
24. Stonehenge: **Wiltshire, United Kindom**
25. Big Ben : **London**

Continent's Highest and Lowest Points

Continent	Highest Point	Lowest Point
1. Asia	Everest (8848 m)	Dead Sea (−396.8m)
2. Africa	Kilimanjaro (5894 m)	Lake Assal (−156.1 m)
3. North America	Mckinley (6194 m)	Death Valley (−85.9 m)
4. South America	Aconcagua (6960 m)	Valdis Penin (−39.9 m)
5. Europe	Elbrus (5663 m)	Caspian Sea (−28.0 m)
6. Australia	Koscisko (2228 m)	Lake Eyre (−15.8 m)
7. Antarctica	Vinson Massif (5140 m)	(Unexplored)

Highest Mountain Peaks (World)

Name	Height (in metres)	Range
1. Mount Everest	8848	Himalayas
2. K2 (Godwin Austen)	8611	Karakoram
3. Kanchenjunga	8598	Himalayas
4. Lhotse	8511	Himalayas
5. Makalu	8481	Himalayas
6. Cho-Oyu	8201	Himalayas
7. Dhaulagiri	8167	Himalayas
8. Manaslu	8163	Himalayas
9. Nanga Parvat	8126	Himalayas
10. Annapurana	8091	Himalayas

Three Deepest Oceans

Name	Greatest depth (in metres)	Greatest depth location
1. Pacific Ocean	11,033	Mariana Trench
2. Atlantic Ocean	9,460	Puerto Pico Trench
3. Indian Ocean	7,542	Sunderdeep of Java Trench

Largest Deserts of the World

Subtropical

Sahara, North Africa	8,600,650 sq. km
Arabian, Middle East	2,300,000 sq. km
Great Victoria, Australia	418,750 sq. km
Kalahari	930,000 sq. km
Gibson	155,000 sq. km
Thar	200,000 sq. km

Cool Coastal

Atacama, Chile SA	105,000 sq. km
Namib, desert	80,900 sq. km

Cold Winter

Gobi, China	1,300,000 sq km
Patagonian, Argentina	673,374 sq km
Great Basin, USA	305,800 sq. km
Karakum, West Asia	350,000 sq. km
Taklamakan, China	320,000 sq. km

Deep-Sea Trenches

Name	Depth
Mariana Trench	10.91
Tonga Trench	10.88
Philipines Trench	10.54
Kuril-Kam Chatka Trench	10.5
Kermadec Trench	10.04
Izu-Ogasawara Trench	9.78
Japan Trench	9
Puerto Rico Trench	8.64
South Sandwich Trench	8.42
Peru-Chile Trench	8.06

Some Important Tribes and their Home

Aleuts : Alaska
Ainus : Japan
Aeta : Phillip Cines
Bushman : Kalahari
Buryak : Central Asia
Berbers : N. Africa
Bedouin : Sahara and Middle East
Koryaks : N. Siberia, Eurassian Tunda, N.E. Asia
Kalmuk : Central Asia
Kareus or Meos : Myanmar
Kirghiz : Asiatic steppes
Kazakhs : Kazakhistan
Lapps : N. Finland, Scandinavian, country
Bindibu or Aborigins : Australia
Chukchi : N.E. Asia, U.S.S.R., North Siberia
Eskimos : Greenland, North Canada, Alaska, N. Siberia
Fulani : Western Africa
Gobi Mongols : Gobi
Guicas : Amazon forest area
Hausa : North Nigeria
Hotten tots : Hot tropical Africa
Ibans : Equatorial rain forest region of South-East Asia
India Tribes : Amazon basin
Maoris : New Zealand
Masai : East and Central Africa
Orange Asli : Malaysia
Pygmies : Congo basin, Zaire
Red Indian : N. America
Somoyeds : Siberia
Semangs : East Sumatra
Turregs : Sahara
Tapiro : Papua New Guinea
Yoakuts : Siberia
Zulus : South Africa

Exercise -1

1. The first country to legalise medically assisted suicide is
   - (a) Switzerland
   - (b) New Zealand
   - (c) USA
   - (d) Netherlands
2. Which of the following places is called the 'Land of Golden Pagoda'?
   - (a) Japan
   - (b) Thailand
   - (c) Myanmar
   - (d) Java
3. With which one of the following countries, does India have the longest border?
   - (a) Bangladesh
   - (b) China
   - (c) Pakistan
   - (d) Myanmar
4. The main thrust of Panchsheel consists in
   - (a) Peaceful co-existence
   - (b) Non-alignment
   - (c) Disarmament agreements
   - (d) Trade agreements
5. Which one of the following pairs is not correctly matched?

City	River
(a) Berlin	Rhine
(b) London	Thames
(c) New York	Hudson
(d) Vienna	Danube

6. Which countries are separated by Mac Mohan Line?
   - (a) India and Pakistan
   - (b) China and Tibet
   - (c) India and China
   - (d) India and Bangladesh
7. The tallest minaret in the world (Sultan Hassan Mosque) is located in –
   - (a) Iran
   - (b) Iraq
   - (c) Turkey
   - (d) Morocco
8. In which country does Basque separatist group operate?
   - (a) Ireland
   - (b) Italy
   - (c) Spain
   - (d) Turkey
9. The currency of Sweden is ?
   - (a) Mark
   - (b) Franc
   - (c) Lira
   - (d) Krona
10. The currency used in Italy is ?
    - (a) Yen
    - (b) Euro
    - (c) Dinar
    - (d) Lira
11. Which one of the following was not part of the Panchsheel agreement between India and China?
    - (a) Adoption of socialistic pattern of society
    - (b) Mutual respect for each other's integrity and sovereignty.
    - (c) Non-interference with each other's internal affairs
    - (d) Peaceful co-existence
12. Cortes is the parliament of:
    - (a) Poland
    - (b) Sweden
    - (c) Iran
    - (d) Spain
13. The Radcliff Line demarcates the boundary between
    - (a) India & China
    - (b) India & Pakistan
    - (c) Pakistan & Afghanistan
    - (d) India & Afghanistan
14. Diet is the Parliament of:
    - (a) Israel
    - (b) Sweden
    - (c) Germany
    - (d) Japan
15. New York is located on the bank of river
    - (a) Potomac
    - (b) Fibe
    - (c) Hudson
    - (d) Spree
16. The European Union has adopted which of the following as a common currency?
    - (a) Dollar
    - (b) Dinar
    - (c) Yen
    - (d) Euro
17. Other than India and China, which of the following groups of countries border Myanmar?
    - (a) Bangladesh, Thailand and Vietnam
    - (b) Cambodia, Laos and Malaysia
    - (c) Thailand, Vietnam and Malaysia
    - (d) Thailand, Laos and Bangladesh
18. An individual going to Bangladesh will make payments in _____ .
    - (a) Rial
    - (b) Yuan
    - (c) Taka
    - (d) Rupee
19. East Timor was under whose colonial rule?
    - (a) Dutch
    - (b) Portugal
    - (c) The United Kingdom
    - (d) French
20. In which one of the following countries, is Tamil a major language?
    - (a) Myanmar
    - (b) Indonesia
    - (c) Mauritius
    - (d) Singapore
21. Which one of the following cities is not a former capital of the given country (Country given in the brackets)?
    - (a) Karachi (Pakistan)
    - (b) Auckland (New Zealand)
    - (c) Kyoto (Japan)
    - (d) Brisbane (Australia)
22. What is the new administrative capital proposed for Myanmar?
    - (a) Bassein
    - (b) Mandalay
    - (c) Myitkyina
    - (d) Pyinmana
23. The Basque separatist organization is active in:
    - (a) Russia
    - (b) Cyprus
    - (c) Portugal
    - (d) Spain
24. Which one of the following countries is the first country in the world to propose a carbon tax for its people to address global warming?
    - (a) Australia
    - (b) Germany
    - (c) Japan
    - (d) New Zealand
25. After the Soviet Union broke up, which one of the following states did not inherit part of the USSR's nuclear arsenal?
    - (a) Lithuania
    - (b) Belarus
    - (c) Ukraine
    - (d) Kazakhstan
26. Generally, which of the following is not an experience that Developing World states share?
    - (a) European colonialism
    - (b) sharply divided classes
    - (c) decent transportation and communication systems
    - (d) economic underdevelopment and poverty

27. What is a muted bipolar world?
    (a) a world system in which two super-powers tightly control their alliance systems.
    (b) world system in which two super-powers are joined by other power centers, each with its own sets of interests. However, the other power centers are not yet superpowers.
    (c) a world system in which two super-powers are having difficulty managing their alliance systems, but a fundamental bipolar structure still exists.
    (d) it is a term that has no meaning in the context of international affairs.
28. What is most favoured nation status?
    (a) Under international law, it is when one nation continually receives preferred rulings by the International Court of Justice.
    (b) An agreement by which any state party to the agreement receives the same terms of trade as the state that is most favoured by each.
    (c) It is term that refers to those states that have an excellent natural resource base. Because of that base, they are said to be "most favoured."
    (d) In international monetary theory, any country that has a "hard" currency that is convertible into gold is said to be "most favored."
29. Which among the following countries was the earliest to give women the right to vote?
    (a) Iceland   (b) India
    (c) New Zealand   (d) U.S.A.
30. "World Development Report" is an annual publication of
    (a) United Nations Development Programme
    (b) International Bank of Reconstruction and Development
    (c) World Trade Organisation
    (d) International Monetary Fund
31. Which one of the following statements is not correct? Dinar/New Dinar is the currency of :
    (a) Sudan   (b) Yugoslavia
    (c) U.A.E   (d) Tunisia

32. Which one of the following is known as the "Coffee port" of the world?
    (a) Sao Paulo   (b) Santos
    (c) Rio de Janeiro   (d) Buenos Aires
33. In which one of the following countries rupee is its currency?
    (a) Bhutan   (b) Malaysia
    (c) Maldives   (d) Seychelles
34. Which one of the following countries is land locked?
    (a) Bolivia   (b) Peru
    (c) Surinam   (d) Uruguay
35. Which one among the following languages has largest number of speakers in the world?
    (a) Bengali   (b) French
    (c) Japanese   (d) Portuguese
36. Which among the following countries has the largest population?
    (a) Indonesia   (b) Japan
    (c) Pakistan   (d) Sudan
37. Which one among the following was the first to legalize Euthanasia?
    (a) Austria   (b) Switzerland
    (c) Netherlands   (d) Canada
38. Which one of the following is the driest desert of the world?
    (a) Atacama   (b) Gobi
    (c) Sahara   (d) Kalahari
39. Mariana Trench is located in the ocean floor of
    (a) Southern Atlantic Ocean
    (b) Western Pacific Ocean
    (c) Eastern Pacific Ocean
    (d) Northern Atlantic Ocean
40. Taklamakan Desert is situated in
    (a) Western Asia
    (b) Southern fringe of Sahara in Africa
    (c) South America
    (d) Central Asia
41. Where is Mekong Delta located?
    (a) Thailand   (b) Cambodia
    (c) Myanmar   (d) Vietnam

Exercise -2

Statement Based MCQ

1. Consider the following statements:
   1. The Constitution of the United States of America came into force in year 1810.
   2. All revenue bills must originate in the House of Representative of the US Congress.
   3. George W. Bush is the only President in the history of the United States of America.
   Which of the statements given above is/are correct?
   (a) 1 only   (b) 2 only
   (c) 1 and 2   (d) 2 and 3

2. Consider the following statements:
   1. The Parliament of Russia is called Federal Assembly.
   2. The Council of the Federation in the Russian Parliament is the lower house.
   3. The name of the upper house in the Russian Parliament is state Duma.
   Which of the statements given above is/are correct?
   (a) 1, 2 and 3   (b) 1 and 2
   (c) 2 and 3   (d) 1 only
3. Australasia or Oceania comprises of
   1. Australia   2. New Zealand
   3. New Guinea   4. Pacific Islands
   5. Tasmania

(a) 1, 2 and 4   (b) 1, 2 and 5
(c) 1, 2, 3 and 4   (d) 1, 2, 3, 4 and 5

4. Consider the following statements:
   1. In Macedonia, ethnic Albanians are a minority.
   2. In Kosovo, Serbians are a majority.
   Which of these statements is/are correct?
   (a) 1 only   (b) 2 only
   (c) Both 1 and 2   (d) Neither 1 nor 2

5. Consider the following international language:
   1. Arabic   2. French
   3. Spanish
   The correct sequence of the language given above in the decreasing order of the number of their speakers is :
   (a) 3, 1, 2   (b) 1, 3, 2
   (c) 3, 2, 1   (d) 1, 2, 3

Matching Based MCQ

DIRECTIONS (Qs. 6 to 16) : Match **List-I** with **List-II** and select the correct answer using the codes given below the lists.

6.

List-I (Sobriquets)		List II (Names)	
(A)	Frontier Gandhi	(1)	Madan Mohan Malviya
(B)	Grand Old Man of India	(2)	Vallabhbhai Patel
(C)	Mahamana	(3)	Dadabhai Naoroji
(D)	Strong Man of India	(4)	Balgangadhar Tilak
		(5)	Abdul Gaffar Khan

(a) A – 4 ; B – 2 ; C – 3 ; D – 5
(b) A – 5 ; B – 3 ; C – 1 ; D – 2
(c) A – 4 ; B – 2 ; C – 5 ; D – 1
(d) A – 5 ; B – 3 ; C – 2 ; D – 4

7.

List-I (Countries)		List-II (Languages)	
(A)	Afghanistan	(1)	Khmer
(B)	Bhutan	(2)	Pushtu
(C)	Cambodia	(3)	Bahasa
(D)	Indonesia	(4)	Hebrew
		(5)	Dzongkha

(a) A – 3 ; B – 4 ; C – 5 ; D – 2
(b) A – 4 ; B – 2 ; C – 3 ; D – 1
(c) A – 2 ; B – 5 ; C – 1 ; D – 3
(d) A – 2 ; B – 5 ; C – 3 ; D – 4

8.

List-I (Countries)		List-II (Currencies)	
(A)	Israel	(1)	Euro
(B)	South Korea	(2)	Dollar
(C)	Maldives	(3)	Shekel
(D)	Italy	(4)	Rufiyaa
		(5)	Won

(a) A – 3 ; B – 2 ; C – 4 ; D – 1
(b) A – 4 ; B – 2 ; C – 3 ; D – 5
(c) A – 5 ; B – 1 ; C – 2 ; D – 3
(d) A – 3 ; B – 5 ; C – 4 ; D – 1

9.

List-I (Countries)		List-II (Currencies)	
(A)	Bangladesh	(1)	Cruzeiro Real
(B)	Bhutan	(2)	Riel
(C)	Brazil	(3)	Taka
(D)	Cambodia	(4)	Escudo
		(5)	Ngultrum

(a) A – 4 ; B – 3 ; C – 5 ; D – 1
(b) A – 3 ; B – 5 ; C – 1 ; D – 2
(c) A – 3 ; B – 4 ; C – 2 ; D – 5
(d) A – 4 ; B – 5 ; C – 1 ; D – 3

10.

List-I (Countries)		List-II (Currencies)	
(A)	China	(1)	Pound
(B)	Egypt	(2)	Yuan
(C)	Germany	(3)	Rial
(D)	Iran	(4)	Dinar
		(5)	Euro

(a) A – 2 ; B – 1 ; C – 5 ; D – 3
(b) A – 3 ; B – 4 ; C – 5 ; D – 2
(c) A – 3 ; B – 2 ; C – 4 ; D – 1
(d) A – 2 ; B – 5 ; C – 3 ; D – 4

11.

List-I (Countries)		List-II (Capitals)	
(A)	Austria	(1)	Brussels
(B)	Belgium	(2)	Nicosia
(C)	Cambodia	(3)	Vienna
(D)	Cyprus	(4)	Prague
		(5)	Phnom-Penh

(a) A – 3 ; B – 1 ; C – 5 ; D – 2
(b) A – 4 ; B – 2 ; C – 1 ; D – 3
(c) A – 4 ; B – 5 ; C – 2 ; D – 3
(d) A – 3 ; B – 4 ; C – 5 ; D – 2

12.

List-I (Service/Agency)		List-II (Country)	
(A)	Foreign Intelligence Service	(1)	Israel
(B)	Ministry of State Security	(2)	Britain
(C)	Secret Intelligence Service	(3)	China
(D)	The Mossad	(4)	Russia

(a) A – 4 ; B – 1 ; C – 2 ; D – 3
(b) A – 2 ; B – 3 ; C – 4 ; D – 1
(c) A – 4 ; B – 3 ; C – 2 ; D – 1
(d) A – 2 ; B – 1 ; C – 4 ; D – 3

13. Match List-I with List-II and select the correct answer using the codes given below the lists: [1998]

List-I		List-II	
A.	Ringgit	1.	Indonesia
B.	Baht	2.	South Korea
C.	Rupiah	3.	Thailand
D.	Won	4.	Malayasia

Codes :
(a) A-1; B-3; C-4; D-2   (b) A-4; B-3; C-1; D-2
(c) A-1; B-2; C-4; D-3   (d) A-4; B-2; C-1; D-3

14. Which of the following pairs are correctly matched?

  1. Dow Jones : New York
  2. Hang Seng : Seoul
  3. FTSE-100 : London

  Select the correct answer using the codes given below:

  Codes:
  (a) 1, 2 and 3   (b) 2 and 3
  (c) 1 and 2   (d) 1 and 3

15. Consider the following pairs:

Large Bank		Country of Origin
1. ABN Amro Bank	:	USA
2. Barclays Bank	:	UK
3. Kookmin Bank	:	Japan

Which of the above pairs is/are correctly matched?
(a) 1 only   (b) 2 only
(c) 1 and 2   (d) 2 and 3

16. Consider the following pairs:

Automobile Manufacturer		Headquarters
1. BMW AG	:	USA
2. Daimler AG	:	Sweden
3. Renault S.A.	:	France
4. Volkswagen AG	:	Germany

Which of the pairs given above is/are correctly matched?
(a) 1, 2 and 3   (b) 3 and 4
(c) 4 only   (d) 1, 2 and 4

Hints and Explanations

EXERCISE-1

1. (d) 2. (c) 3. (a) 4. (a) 5. (a) 6. (c)
7. (d) 8. (c) 9. (d) 10. (b) 11. (a) 12. (d)
13. (b) 14. (d) 15. (c) 16. (d) 17. (d)
18. (c) 19. (b)
20. (d) Tamil is the major language in Singapore.
21. (d) Karachi was the capital of Pakistan from 1947 – 1959. Kyoto was the capital of Japan before Tokyo.
22. (d)
23. (d) The Basque separatist movement is active in Spain.
24. (d) New Zealand is the first country in the world to propose a carbon tax for its people address global warming in the year 2005.
25. (a) 26. (c) 27. (c) 28. (b) 29. (c) 30. (b)
31. (a) Currency of U.A.E is Dinar; Sudan's currency is Sudanese Pound; Yugoslavia's currency is New Dinar Currency of Tunisia is Tunisian Dinar.
32. (b) Santos port Brazil is known as "coffee port" of world.
33. (d) The rupee is the currency of Seyhelles. It is locally called roupi, it is subdivided into 100 cents.
Currency of Bhutan is Ngultrum, Currency of Malaysia is Malaysian Ringget and Currency of Maldives is Maldives Rufiyaa.
34. (a) Bolivia is a land locked country, the surrounding countries are Peru, Chile, Argentina, Brazil and Paraguay. Other than Bolivia Peru, Uruguay, Surinam are the countries which one side any ocean or sea is present.
35. (a)
36. (a) Indonesia has the largest population in the given countries.
37. (c)
38. (a) 39. (b) 40. (d) 41. (d)

EXERCISE-2

1. (b) The Constitution of USA came in to force in 1787. George H. W. Bush (Father) was 41st President and George W. Bush (Son) was 43rd President of USA.
2. (d) Only statement (1) is correct as statements 2&3 are mismatched. Federation Council is Upper House of Russian Parliament and State Duma is the Lower House. Both are located in Moscow.
3. (d) 4. (c)
5. (a) Total speaker of Spanish in world is 420 million, Arabic speakers are 230 million and French speakers are 200 million. So, the correct sequence in decreasing order of the number of speakers are Spanish, Arabic and French.
6. (b) 7. (c) 8. (d) 9. (b)
10. (a) 11. (a) 12. (c)
13. (b) Ringgit is the currency of Malaysia. A baht is also a unit of weight for gold and is commonly used in jewellers and goldsmiths in Thailand. The currency was originally known as the tical and this name was used in the English language text on banknotes until 1925. The rupiah (Rp) is the official currency of Indonesia. The Won is the official currency of South Korea.
14. (d) Hang Seng is the stock market of Hong Kong not Seoul. Rest 1 and 3 are correctly matched.
15. (b) ABN AMRO Bank N.V. is a Dutch bank with headquarters in Amsterdam, the Netherlands. Barclays PLC is a global financial services company headquartered in London, United Kingdom. KB Kookmin Bank is the largest bank by both asset value and market capitalization in South Korea.
16. (b) BMW AG and Daimler AG are Head quartered in Germany.

INDIAN-PANORAMA

3

Chapter

INDIAN STATES AND UNION TERRITORIES

Andhra Pradesh

- **Also known as:** "Rice Bowl of India", "Egg Bowl of Asia"
- **Capital:** Hyderabad
- **Largest City:** Visakhapatnam
- **No. Of Districts:** 13

Chief Minister: Nara Chandrababu Naidu
Governor: E. S. L. Narasimhan
Area: 160,205sq. km(61,855 sq mi)
Language: Telugu and Urdu
Date of Establishment:1st October 1953
Population: 49,386,799
Sex ratio: 992 females per 1000 males
Literacy Rate: 67.7%
Population Density(per sq km): 308
Total Forest Cover Area: 28,147 sq. km.

Agriculture: An exporter of many agricultural products and about 60 percent of population is engaged in agriculture and related activities. Rice is the major food crop and staple food of the state. Also grow wheat, jowar, bajra, maize, minor millet, coarse grain, many varieties of pulses, oil seeds, sugarcane, cotton, chilli-pepper and tobacco.

Industry: Home to firms like PepsiCo, Isuzu Motors, Cadbury India, Kellogg's, Colgate-Palmolive, Kobelco etc. Along with the largest PepsiCo plant in India.

Neighbouring states: Telangana in the North-West, Chhattisgarh in the north, Odisha in the North-East, Karnataka in the West, Tamil Nadu in the South and the water body of Bay of Bengal in the East.

Art & Culture:

(a) Classical dance forms (Sastriya Nrutyam) such as Kuchipudi, Bhamakalapam, Veeranatyam; and folk dances such as Butta bommalu, Tappeta Gullu, Lambadi, Dhimsa, and Chindu exists in Andhra Pradesh.

(b) Festivals : Sankranti,Maha Shivaratri,Ugadi or the Telugu NewYear,SriRamaNavami,Varalakshmi Vratam, Vinayaka Chaviti, Dasara, Atla Tadde, Deepavali, Deepothsavam during the Deepavali season.

Religious places: Tirupati or Tirumala is the richest pilgrimage centre in the world, dedicated to the god Venkateswara; Simhachalam is believed to be abode of the saviour-god Narasimha, who rescued Prahlada from abusive father Hiranyakasipu; Srisailam is dedicated mainly to Lord Shiva and is famous as one of the locations of the various Jyotirlingams.

Tribes: Andh, Bagata, Bhil, Chenchu, Gadabas, Bodo, Nakkala, Dhulia, Koya, Kotia, Jatapus, Kulia, Malis, Valmiki, Manna, Mukha, Pardhan, Porja.
Cuisines: Mutton Biryani, Mirchi Salan, Ghongpura Pickle, Korikoora
Animal: Blackback (Antilope *cervicapra*)
Bird: Indian Roller (Coracias *benghalensis*)

Arunachal Pradesh

Also known as: "The Orchid State of India" or "the Paradise of the Botanists"
Capital: Itanagar
Largest City: Itanagar
No. Of Districts: 23
Chief Minister: Pema Khandu
Governor: Brig. (Dr.) B.D. Mishra (Rtd)
Area: 83,743 sq. km
Language: English
Date of Establishment: 20 February 1987
Population: 1,383,727
Sex Ratio: 938 females per 1000 males
Literacy Rate: 65.38%
Population density:17 per sq. km
Total Forest Area: 66.964 sq. km.

Agriculture: Main crops:rice, maize, millet, wheat, pulses, sugarcane, ginger, and oilseeds. Also ideal for horticulture and fruit orchards.

Industry: Arts and Crafts, weaving, cane and bamboo, carpet weaving, wood carving, ornaments, tourism and horticulture.

Neighbouring States: Borders with the states of Assam and Nagaland to the south, and international borders with Bhutan in the west, Burma in the east and China in the north.

Art & Culture:

(a) **Dance:** Bardo Chham is a folk dance which depicts the victory of good over evil.

(b) **Festivals:** Losar or The New Year festival, is the most important festival of Tawang District in Arunachal Pradesh.

Religious places: Parasuram Kunda attracts lots of devotees in January during the Parasuram mela Akashganga Temple is also called Malinithan temple and associated with the legend of Daksha Yagya and Sati's self-immolation.

Tribes: Abor, Aka, Apatani, Momba, Naga, Sherdukp, Nyishi, Galo, Khampti, Khowa, Mishmi, Idu, Hrusso, Tagin, Khamba, Adi
Cuisines: Chinese Cuisine & Apong (Local Beer)
Animal- Gayal (Bos *frontalis*)
Bird- Great Hornbill (Buceros *bicornis*)

Asom

Capital: Dispur
Largest City: Guwahati
No. Of Districts: 33
Chief Minister: Sarbananda Sonowal
Governor: Jagdish Mukhi
Area: 78,438 sq. km
Language: Assamese, Bengali, Bodo
Date of Establishment: 1st April 1912
Population: 31,205,576
Population density: 398 per sq km.
Sex Ratio: 958 females per 1000 males
Literacy Rate: 72.19%
Total Forest Cover Area: 28,105 sq. km

Agriculture: Asom's biggest contribution to the world is Asom tea and has its own variety of Camellia assamica. The state produces rice, rapeseed, mustard seed, jute, potato, sweet potato, banana, papaya, areca nut, sugarcane and turmeric.
Industry: The industries housed by the state include a chemical fertiliser plant at Namrup, petrochemical industries at Namrup and Bongaigaon, Paper mills at Jagiroad, Hindustan Paper Corporatio Ltd. Township Area Panchgram and Jogighopa, sugar mills at Barua Bamun Gaon, Chargola, Kampur, Cement plant at Bokajan and Badarpur, cosmetics plant of Hindustan Unilever (HUL) at Doom Dooma, etc.
Neighbouring States: Asom is surrounded by six of the other Seven Sister States: Arunachal Pradesh, Nagaland, Manipur, Mizoram, Tripura, and Meghalaya.
Art & Culture:
(a) Ankia Naat (Onkeeya Naat), a traditional Vaishnav dance-drama (Bhaona) popular since the 15th century AD. Folk dances like Bihu and the Bagurumba (both danced during festivals held in the spring), the Bhortal dance, the Ojapali dance etc.
(b) Festivals: Bihu is the most important and common and celebrated all over Asom. Durga Puja is another festival celebrated with great enthusiasm. Muslims celebrate two Eids (Eid ul-Fitr and Eid al-Adha) with great zeal.
Religious places: Kamakhya Temple is one of the most famous temples.
Tribes: Mikirs, Khasis, Nagas, Barmans, Boro, Borokachari, Deori, Hojai, . Kachari, Sonwal, Lalung, Mech, Miri, Rabha, Dimasa, Hajong, Singhpho, Khampti, Garo.
Cuisines: Masor Tenga, Pitha
Animal: One-horned rhino (Rhinoceros *unicornis*)
Bird: White-winged wood duck (Cairina *scutulata*)

Bihar

Capital: Patna
Largest City: Patna
No. Of districts: 38
Chief Minister: Nitish Kumar
Governor: Satya Pal Malik
Area: 94,163 sq. km
Language: Hindi, Bhojpuri, Magadhi, Maithili, Urdu
Date of Establishment: 1st April 1936
Population: 104,099,452
Sex Ratio: 918 females per 1000 males
Literacy Rate: 61.8%
Population density: 1,106 per sq km.
Total Forest Cover Area: 7299 sq km.

Agriculture: Largest producer of vegetables, especially potatoes, onions, brinjal/egg-plant, and cauliflower. Largest producer of litchi, the third largest producer of pineapples and a major producer of mangoes, bananas, and guava. Sugarcane,jute cash crops

Industry: Three major firms — United Breweries Group, Danish Brewery Company Carlsberg Group and Cobra Beer — are to set up new units in Patna and Muzaffarpur in 2012.
Neighbouring States: It is contiguous with Uttar Pradesh to its west, Nepal to the north, the northern part of West Bengal to the east, and with Jharkhand to the south.
Art & Culture:
(a) Mithila painting is a style of Indian painting practised in the Mithila region of Bihar
(b) Festivals: Chhath, also called Dala Chhath, is an ancient and major festival in Bihar.Shravani mela,Teej and Chitragupta Puja along with all the major festivals of India are celebrated in Bihar.
Religious Places: Mahabodhi Temple is a Buddhist shrine and UNESCO World Heritage Site;
Mahavir Mandir in Patna; Takht Shri Harmandir Saheb in Patna and many more.
Tribes: Gonda, Mundas, Oraon, Gorait, Ho, Karmali, Kharia , Kha, Omitted, Binjhia, Birhor, Birjia, Chero.
Cuisines: Litti-Chokha, Sattu Paratha, Khaja, Khubi Ka Lai, Anarasa, Tilkut
Animal: Gaur (Bos *gaurue*)
Bird: House Sparrow (Passer *domesticus*)

Chhattisgarh

Also Known as: "Rice bowl of central India"
Capital: Raipur
Largest City: Raipur
No. Of Districts: 27
Chief Minister: Raman Singh
Governor: Anandiben Patel
Area: 135,192 sq. km.
Language: Chattisgarhi, Hindi
Date of Establishment: 1st November 2000
Population: 25,545,198
Sex Ratio: 991 females per 1000 males
Literacy Rate: 70.28%
Population density: 189 per sq km.
Total Forest Cover Area: 55547 sq km.

Agriculture: The main crops are rice, maize, kodo-kutki and other small millets and pulses oilseeds, such as groundnuts (peanuts), soybeans and sunflowers, are also grown. Horticulture and animal husbandry also engage a major share of the total population of the state.
Industry: Industries: Bhilai Steel Plant, Jindal Steel and Power, Bharat Aluminium Company, Baldev Alloys Pvt Ltd,Indian Oil Corporation
Engineering: Simplex Casting Ltd, CHPL-Dream-Homes (Chouhan Housing Pvt Ltd.), NMDC, South Eastern Coalfields, NTPC, Lanco Infratech, KSK Energy Ventures, Vandana Vidyut, Chhattisgarh State Power Generation Company and Jindal Power Limited.
Neighbouring States: Borders the states of Madhya Pradesh in the northwest, Maharashtra in the southwest Telangana and Andhra Pradesh in the south, Odisha in the east, Jharkhand in the northeast and Uttar Pradesh in the north.
Art & Culture: (a) **Dances:** Panthi, Rawat Nacha Pandwani, Chaitra, Kaksar, Saila and Soowa are the several indigenous dance styles of Chhattisgarh.
Festival– Bastar Dussere, Bhoramdeo Festival, Madai Festival. Hariyali, Kora, Navakhani are the major festival Religious
Places: Bhoramdeo temple, Rajivlochan temple, Chandrahasini Devi temple, Vishnu temple, Damudhara (Rishab Tirth) and

Sivarinarayana Laxminarayana temple, Bambleshwari Temple, Danteshwari Temple and many more other ancient temples.
Tribes: Agariya, Andh, Baiga, Bhaina, Bharia, Halba, Kamar, Karku, Saur, Sawar, Sawara, Sonr , Majhi, Majhwar, Mawasi, Munda, Kharia, Kondh, Kol, Kolam, Pao.
Cuisines: Bafauri, Kusli, Red Ant Chutney
Animal: Wild buffalo (Bubalis *arnee*)
Bird: Bastar Hill myna (Gracula *religiosa*)

Goa

Capital: Panaji
Largest City: Vasco da Gama
No. Of districts: 2
Chief Minister: Manohar Parrikar
Governor: Mridula Sinha
Area: 3,702 sq km
Language: Konkani
Date of Establishment: 30th May, 1987
Population: 14,58,545
Sex ratio: 973 females per 1000 males
Literacy Rate: 88.70%
Population density: 394 per sq km.
Total Forest Cover Area: 2229 sq km.

Agriculture: Rice the main agricultural crop, followed by areca, cashew and coconut.
Industry: Tourism is Goa's primary industry as it handles 12% of all foreign tourist arrival in India.
Neighbouring States:It is bounded by the state of Maharashtra to the north and by Karnataka to the east and south, while the Arabian Sea forms its western coast.
Art & Culture:
(a) **Dance:** Some of the traditional Goan dance art forms are Dekhnni, Fugdi, Corridinho, Mando, Dulpod and Fado.
(b) **Festivals:** The most popular celebrations in the Indian state of Goa are Ganesh Chaturthi, Diwali, Christmas, Easter, Samvatsar Padvo or Sanvsar Padvo, Shigmo, Goa Carnival. Goa known for its New Year's celebrations along with the Goan Carnival is known to attract a large number of tourists.

Religious places: Goa has two holy World Heritage Sites: the Bom Jesus Basilica and churches and convents of Old Goa. The Basilica holds the mortal remains of St. Francis Xavier, who is the patron saint of Goa.
Tribes: Dhodia, Dubla (Halpati), Naikda, Siddi, Varli, Kunbi, Gawda, Velip.
Cuisines: Vindaloo, Xacuti, Bibinca, Prawn Balchao
Animal: Gaur (Bos *gaurus*)
Bird: Black-crested bulbul (Pycnonotus *gularis*)

Gujarat

Also known as: Jewel of the Western part of India
Capital: Gandhinagar
Largest City: Ahmedabad
Ahmedabad has been declared India's first world Heritage city by UNESCO
No. Of districts: 33
Chief Minister: Vijay Rupani
Governor: Om Prakash Kohli
Area: 196,024 sq km
Language: Gujarati
Date of Establishment: 1 May 1960
Population: 60,439,692
Sex Ratio: 919 females per 1000 males
Literacy Rate: 78.03%
Population Density: 308 sq km.
Total Forest Cover Area: 14,757 sq km

Agriculture: Gujarat's agriculture is majorly focussed on cotton production, livestock, fruits and vegetables, and wheat production.
Industry: Large scale industries such as Agro Marine Exports, Creative Castings Ltd., Gujarat Dairy Development Corporation, Austin Engineering and JSW Power Co. The Alang Ship Recycling Yard (the world's largest), General Motors manufactures, Tata Motors manufactures the Tata Nano and AMW trucks are made near Bhuj. Surat is the hub of the global diamond trade. According to Forbes list Ahmedabad ranks 3rd in the world's fastest growing cities in the world.
Neighbouring states: The state is bordered by Rajasthan to the north, Maharashtra to the south, Madhya Pradesh to the east, and the Arabian Sea as well as the Pakistani province of Sindh to the west.
Art & Culture:
(a) Rass-garba is a folk dance which is done as celebration of Navratri.
(b) Festivals: Makar Sankranti, Navratri, Uttarayana, Diwali, Holi, Tazia and others are celebrated with great enthusiasm.
Religious places: Somnath temple and the Sun Temple are some of the renowned Hindu temples. Palitana templesfor the Jain community; Sidi Saiyyed Mosque and Jama Masjid are holymosques for Muslims.
Tribes: Bhils, Barda, Bavacha, Charan, Gond, Dubla, Dhanka, Chodhara, Chaudhr, Charan, Gamit, Kunbi, Patelia, Pomla, Rabar, Rathawa, Siddi.
Cuisines: Thepla, Dhokla, Khandvi, Handvo, Panki
Animal: Asiatic lison (Panthera leo *persica*)
Bird: Greater Flamingo (Phoenicopterus *roseus*)

Haryana

Capital: Chandigarh
Largest City: Faridabad
No. Of Districts: 22
Chief Minister: Manohar Lal Khattar
Governor: Satyadev Narayan Arya
Area: 44,212 sq. km
Language: Hindi, Punjabi, Haryanvi
Date of Establishment: 1 November 1966
Population: 25,351,462
Sex Ratio: 879 females per 1000 males
Literacy Rate: 75.55%
Population Density: 573 per sq km
Total Forest Cover Area: 1588 sq km.

Agriculture: Wheat and rice are the major crops making Haryana, the second largest contributor to India's central pool of food grains. The main crops are wheat, rice, sugarcane, cotton,oilseeds, gram, barley, corn, millet and many more.
Industry: National and international companies like Samsung, DB Schenker, Damco Solutions, Abacus Softech, Nokia Networks, Mitsubishi Electric, IBM, Huawei, General Electric, Tata Consultancy Services and Amdocs have their branch offices and contact centres in Faridabad and Gurgaon(also known as City of millennium). Large-scale companies like Orient Paper & Industries, JCB India Limited, Nirigemes, Agri Machinery Group (Escorts Limited), India Yamaha Motor Pvt. Ltd., Whirlpool, ABB Group, Goodyear Tyres and Knorr Bremse India Pvt. Ltd.
Neighbouring States: It is bordered by Punjab and Himachal Pradesh to the north, by Rajasthan to the west and south. The river Yamuna defines its eastern border with Uttar Pradesh.

Art & Culture: Festivals: Haryali Teej, Lohri, Gangore, Makar Sankranti, Gugga Naumi, Baisaki are some of the famous festivals of Haryana
Tourism: Surajkund International Crafts Mela, Sultanpur National Park, Kalesar National Park, Pinjore Gardens Resort, and Nahar Singh Mahal are some of the major tourist attraction.
Cuisine: Rabadi, Bajre ki Khichdi, Cholia, Chaach-Lassi, Kachri ki Sabzi
Animal: Blackbuck (Antilope *cervicapra*)
Bird: Black Francolin (Francolinus *francolinus*)

Himachal Pradesh

Name: Himachal Pradesh
Also known as: State of Apples, Dev Bhoomi(Abode of Gods)
Capital: Shimla
Largest City: Shimla
No. Of Districts: 12
Chief Minister: Jai Ram Thakur
Governor: Acharya Dev Vrat
Area: 55,673 sq. km
Language: Hindi, English
Date of Establishment: 25th January 1971
Population: 6,864,602
Sex Ratio: 972 females per 1000 males
Literacy Rate: 82.8%
Population Density: 123 per sq km
Total Forest Cover Area: 15,100 sq km.

Agriculture: Agriculture contributes nearly 45% to the net state domestic product and 93% of the state population depends directly upon agriculture. The main cereals grown in the state are wheat, maize, rice and barley. Fruit cultivation has also proved to be an economic boon,with Apple farming producing the maximum income.
Industry: Textiles, pharmaceuticals, food procurement and processing, light engineering, IT and electronics, cement, tourism and hydropower are the key industries resident in the state with Himachal accounting for about 25 per cent of the country's total hydro power potential.
Neighbouring States: It is bordered by Jammu and Kashmir on the north, Punjab on the west, Haryana on the south-west, Uttarakhand on the south-east and by the Tibet Autonomous Region on the east.
Art & Culture:
(a) **Dances:** Losar Shona Chuksam, Dangi, Gee Dance and Burah dance, Naati, Kharait, Ujagjama and Chadhgebrikar and Shunto are some of the known dance forms.
(b) **Festivals:** Kullu Dussehra, Shivratri Fair, Shoolini Mela (Solan), Minjar Fair, Mani Mahesh Chhari Yatra, Renuka fair, Lavi Trade Fair, Vrajeshwari fair, Jwalamukhi Fair, Holi Fair, and Naina Devi Fair, and Fulaich are some of the most celebrated festivals.
Tourism: The state is home to many famous hill stations such as Dalhousie, Kullu, Manali, Shimla, Nainital, Dharamsala, Mcleodganj and many more.
Tribes: Bhot, Bodh, Gaddi, Gujjar, Jad, Lamba, Khampa, Kanaura, Kinnara, Lahaula, Pangwala, Swangla, Beta, Beda, Domba.
Cuisines: Sidu, Aktori, Dham, Seppu Vadi, Badana, Babru
Animal: Snow Leopard (Uncia uncia or *Panthna uncia*)
Bird: Jujurana Western Irogapa (Trogopan *melanocephalus*)

Jammu and Kashmir

Also known as: Heaven on Earth
Capital: Srinagar
Largest City: Srinagar
No. Of Districts: 22
Chief Minister:
Governor: Narinder Nath Vohra
Area: 222,236 sq. km
Language: English, Urdu, Dogari, Ladakhi
Date of Establishment: 26th October 1947
Population: 12,541,302
Sex Ratio: 889 females per 1000 males
Literacy Rate: 67.16%
Population Density: 124 per sq. km (150/sq mi)
Total Forest Cover Area: 23241 sq km.

Agriculture: Known for its sericulture and cold-water fisheries. Wood to make high-quality cricket bats known as Kashmir Willow. Kashmiri saffron. Horticultural includes apples, apricots, cherries, pears, plums, almonds and walnuts.
Industry: Horticulture plays a pivotal role in the economy of the country.
Neighbouring States: It shares border with the states of Himachal Pradesh and Punjab to the south, an international border with China in the north and east, and the Line of Control separates it from the Pakistani-controlled territories of Azad Kashmir and Gilgit–Baltistan in the west and northwest respectively.
Art & Culture: Dances: The Dumhal is a famous dance in the Kashmir Valley, performed by men of the Wattal region whereas women perform the Rouff, another traditional folk dance of the region.
Religious places: Vaishno Devi temple, Amarnath, and Raghunath temple.
Nature Tourism: Gulmarg, Sonamarg, Leh, Pahalgam and many more are some of the most frequented hill stations.
Tribes: Balti, Beda, Bot, Boto, Brokpa, Drokpa, Dard, Shin, Changpa, Garra, Mon, Purigpa, Gujjar, Bakarwal, Gaddi, Sippi.
Cuisines: Gustaba, Tbak Maz, Dum Aloo, Haak or Karam ka Saag
Animal: Kashmir Stag (Cervus elaphus *hanglin*)
Bird: Black-necked crane (Grus *nigricollis*)

Jharkhand

Also known as: "the Land of jungles" and "jharis"(bushes)
Capital: Ranchi
Largest City: Jamshedpur
No. Of Districts: 24
Chief Minister: Raghubar Das
Governor: Draupadi Murmu
Area: 79,716 sq. km
Language: Hindi, Santhali, Mundari, Ho
Date of Establishment: 15th November 2000
Population: 32,988,134
Sex Ratio: 948 females per 1000 males
Literacy Rate: 66.41%
Population Density: 414 per sq km
Total Forest Cover Area: 23,553 sq km.

Agriculture: Rice, Pulses, Jackfruit, Blackberry, Mango and Litchi
Industry: Mining is the primary and most important source of economy for the state as it accounts to 40% of mineral resources of the state.

Neighbouring States: The state shares its border with the states of Bihar to the north, Uttar Pradesh and Chhattisgarh to the west, Odisha to the south, and West Bengal to the east.

Art & Culture: Dance: The most popular foll dances of Jharkhand are Jhumar, Paika, Chau, Agni, Santhal, Nanhai, Jamda, Ghatwari, Natwa, Chaukare, Sohrai, Lurisayro, Uatha Festivals: Karam festival, Vat savitri puja, Teej, Sohrai, Jitia Puja, Sarhul, Makar Sankranti, Deepavali, Durga Puja and many more are some of the most celebrated festivals.

Tourism: Sanctuaries: Palamau Tiger Reserves, Hazaribag Wildlife Sanctuary, Jawaharlal Nehru Biological Park, and Betla National Park

Tribes: Asur, Agaria, Baiga, Banjara, Bathudi, Bedia, Binjhia, Chero, Chik Baraik, Gond, Gorait, Ho, Karmali, Kharia, Kora, Kharwar, Khond, Kisan, Mudi-Kora, Korwa, Munda, Oraon, Lohra Santal, Sauria Paharia, Savar, Bhumij, Kawar, Kol

Cuisines: Thekua, Pua, Pittha, Marua-ka-Roti

Animal: Indian Elephant (Elephas maximus *indicus*)

Bird: Asian koel (Eudynamys *scolopacea*)

Karnataka

Capital: Bengaluru
Largest City: Bengaluru
No. Of Districts: 30
Chief Minister: H.D. Kumaraswamy
Governor: Vajubhai Vala
Area: 191,791 sq. km
Language: Kannada
Date of Establishment: 1st November 1956
Population: 61,095,297
Sex Ratio: 948 females per 1000 males
Literacy Rate: 75.36%
Population Density: 319/ sq. km
Total Forest Cover Area: 37550 sq km

Agriculture: The main crops: rice, ragi, jowar, maize, and pulses (Tur and gram) besides oilseeds and number of cash crops. Cashews, coconut, arecanut, cardamom, chillies, cotton, sugarcane and tobacco are among the other crops produced in the state. Karnataka is the largest producer of coarse cereals, coffee, raw silk and tomatoes among the states in India. Karnataka occupies the second position in India in terms of production and 700 tons of flowers (worth Rs.500 million) were produced in 2004–05.

Industry: National Aerospace Laboratories, Bharat Heavy Electricals Limited, Indian Telephone Industries, Bharat Earth Movers Limited (BEML), Bharat Electronics Limited, Hindustan Machine Tools and Indian subsidiaries of Volvo and Toyota are headquartered in Bangalore.

Neighbouring States: Karnataka is bordered by the Arabian Sea and the Laccadive Sea to the west, Goa to the north west, Maharashtra to the north, Telangana to the North east, Andhra Pradesh to the east, Tamil Nadu to the south east, and Kerala to the south west.

Art & Culture: (a) Dance: Mysore style of Bharatanatyam is the oldest and most popular dance form and is widely performed in Karnataka. Bolak-aat, Ummatt-aat and Komb-aat are some of the other forms of folk dances in the state.

(b) Festivals: Mysore Dasara is celebrated as the state festival of Mysore. Ugadi (Kannada New Year), Makar Sankranti (the harvest festival), Ganesh Chaturthi, Nagapanchami, Basava Jayanthi, Deepavali, and Ramzan are the other major festivals of Karnataka.

Tourism:

National Parks: Bandipur National Park, Bannerghatta National Park and Nagarhole National Park.Waterfalls: Gokak Falls, Unchalli Falls, Magod Falls, Abbey Falls, Jog falls and Shivanasamudra Falls

Tribes: Adiyan, Barda, Bavacha, Bhil, Chenchu, Chodhara, Dubla, Konda, Koraga, Kurumans, Maha Malasar, Malaikudi, Malasar, Malayekandi, Maleru, Maratha Patelia, Rathawa, Siddi, Sholaga, Soligaru , Toda, Varli, Vitolia

Cuisines: Bisi Bele Bhaat, Kesari Bath, Mysore Pak, Dharwad Pedha, Chiroti

Animal: Indian Elephant (Elephas maximus *indicus*)

Bird: Indian Roller (Coracias *benghalensis*)

Kerala

Also known as: God's own country
Capital: Thiruvananthapuram
Largest City: Kochi
No. Of Districts: 14
Chief Minister: Pinarayi Vijayan
Governor: P. Sathasivam
Area: 38,852 sq.km
Language: Malayalam, English
Date of Establishment: 1st November 1956
Population: 33,406,061
Sex Ratio: 1,084 females per 1000 males
Literacy Rate: 94%
Population Density: 860/sq. km
Total Forest Cover Area: 20321 sq km

Agriculture: Kerala produces 97% of the national output of black pepper and accounts for 85% of the area under natural rubber in the country. Coconut, tea, coffee, cashew, and spices—including cardamom, vanilla, cinnamon, and nutmeg comprise a critical agricultural sector. The key agricultural staple is rice, with varieties grown in extensive paddy fields.

Industry: Software giants like Infosys, Oracle, Tata Consultancy Services, Capgemini, HCL, UST Global, Nest, Suntec and IBS have offices in the state. Thiruvananthapuram is also the "IT Hub of Kerala" and accounts for around 80% of the software exports. The Grand Kerala Shopping Festival (GKSF) claimed to be "Asia's largest shopping festival" was started in the year 2007.

Neighbouring States: It is bordered by Karnataka to the north and north east, Tamil Nadu to the east and south, and the Lakshadweep Sea to the west.

Art & Culture:

(a) **Dance:** The classical dance forms of Kerala are Kathakali, Mohiniyattam, Koodiyattom, Thullal and Krishnanattam.

(b) **Festivals:** Onam is a harvest festival celebrated by the people of Kerala.

Tourism:

Beaches: Kovalam, Varkala, Fort Kochi, Cherai, Payyambalam, Kappad, Muzhappilangad.

Hill stations: Munnar, Wayanad, Wagamon, Peermade, Paithalmala, Nelliampathi and Ponmudi.

National parks and sanctuaries: Periyar Tiger Reserve, Parambikulam Wildlife Sanctuary, Chinnar Wildlife Sanctuary, Thattekad Bird Sanctuary, Wayanad Wildlife Sanctuary, Muthanga Wildlife Sanctuary, Aralam Wildlife Sanctuary, Eravikulam National Park, and Silent Valley National Park.

Tribes: Adiyan, Arandan, Irular, Kadar, Cholanaickan, Paniyan, Ulladan , Ullatan, Uraly Mavilan, Karimpalan, Vetta Kuruman, Mala Panickar

Cuisines: Puttu-Kadala, Kappa-Meen Kari, Sadya Meal, Avial, Malabar Parotha, Payasam, Irachi Stew, Karimean Kari

Animal: Indian Elephant (Elephas maximus *indicus*)

Bird: Great Hornbill (Buceros *bicornis*)

Madhya Pradesh

Also known as: "Heart of India"
Capital: Bhopal
Largest City: Indore
No. Of Districts: 51
Chief Minister: Shivraj Singh Chauhan
Governor: Smt. Anandiben Patel
Area: 308,2252 sq.km
Language: Hindi
Date of Establishment: 1st November 1956
Population: 72,626,809
Sex Ratio: 931 females per 1000 males
Literacy Rate: 69.32%
Population Density: 236/sq.km
Total Forest Cover Area: 77414 sq km.

Agriculture: The state has an agrarian economy. The major crops of Madhya Pradesh are wheat, soybean, gram, sugarcane, rice, maize, cotton, rapeseed, mustard and arhar

Industry: Mining and Ordinance factories comprise the major industries.

Neighbouring States: It borders the states of Uttar Pradesh to the north-east, Chhattisgarh to the south-east, Maharashtra to the south, Gujarat to the west, and Rajasthan to the northwest.

Art & Culture:

(a) **Dances:** Badhai, Rai, Saira, Jawara, Sher, Akhara, Shaitan, Tertali, Charkula, Jawara, and Maanch are some of the majore dance forms.

(b) **Festivals:** Shivratri, Navratri, Dussehra, Diwali, Bahgoriya, Shab-I-Barat, Krishna Janamashtmi and many more.

Tourism:

National parks and sanctuaries: Kanha, Bandhavgarh, Pench, Panna, and Satpura National Park.

Hill Station: Pachmarhi and Amarkantak

Tribes: Bhil, Bhunjia, Biar, Binjhwar, Birhul, Damor, Dhanwar, Gadaba, Gond, Halba, Kamar, Karku, Kawar, Kondar, Kharia, Kondh, Kol, Kolam, Korku, Munda, Oraon, Panika, Pao, Pardhan, Saonta, Saur, Sawar, Sonr.

Cuisines: Lapsi, Bafla, Bhutte ki Khees, Bhopali Kabab

Animal: Barasingha (Rucervus *duvaucelii*)

Bird: Asian Paradise Flycatcher (Trepsiphone *paradisi*)

Maharashtra

Capital: Mumbai
Largest city: Mumbai
No. Of districts: 36
Chief Minister: Devendra Fadnavis
Governor: C. Vidyasagar Rao
Area: 307,713 sq. km
Language: Marathi
Date of establishment: 1st May 1960
Population: 112,374,333
Sex Ratio: 929 females per 1000 males
Literacy Rate: 82.34%
Population Density: 365/sq.km
Total Forest Cover Area: 50682 sq km

Agriculture: Agriculture and allied activities contributes 12.9% to the state's income. Staples such as rice and millet are the main monsoon crops. Cash crops include sugarcane, cotton, oilseeds, tobacco, fruit, vegetables and spices such as turmeric.

Industry: Mumbai is also known as the financial capital of India and houses major corporate and financial institutions. Maharashtra contributes about 25% of the country's industrial output and is manufacturing hub for some of the largest public sector industries in India, including Hindustan Petroleum Corporation, Tata Petrodyne and Oil India Ltd.

Neighbouring States: It shares its border with Arabian Sea to the west and states of Karnataka, Telangana, Goa, Gujarat, Chhattisgarh, Madhya Pradesh and the Union territory of Dadra and Nagar Haveli.

Art & Culture:

(a) **Dances:** Lavani is the most popular form of dance in the state. Koli dance is yet another form of folk dance.

(b) **Festivals:** Vijayadashami or Dasara, Navaratri, Holi, Diwali, Eid, Simollanghan is a ritual performed on Dasara or Viajaya Dashami day in Maharashtra.

Religious Tourism: Shirdi, Haji Ali Dargah, Tuljabhavani temple, Parvati temples, Chaturshringi Temple, Pataleshwar.

Nature Tourism: Amboli, Chikhaldara, Igatpuri, Jawhar, Karjat, Khandala, Lavasa, Lonavala, Mahabaleshwar, Matheran, Panchgani, Panhala, Toranmal

Tribes: Andh, Baiga, Barda, Bavacha, Bhaina, Bhunjia, Birhul, Kol, Halba, Kamar, Kathodi, Kolam, Khairwar, Kharia, Kokna, Parja, Patelia, Pomla, Rathawa, Sawar, Thakur, Varli, Vitolia

Cuisines: Shrikhand, Thalipeeth, Vada Pao, Modak

Animal: Indian Giant Squirrel (Ratufa *indica*)

Bird: Yellow footed green pigeon (Treron *phoenicoptera*)

Manipur

Also known as: "Gateway to the East"
Capital: Imphal
Largest city: Imphal
No. Of districts: 16
Chief Minister: N. Biren Singh
Governor: Najma Heptulla
Area: 22,327 sq.km
Language: Meeteilon (Manipuri)
Date of establishment: 21st Jan. 1972
Population: 2,570,390
Sex Ratio: 992 females per 1000 males
Literacy Rate: 79.21%
Population Density: 115/sq.km
Total Forest Cover Area: 17346 sq km

Agriculture: Manipur's climate and soil conditions are ideally suited for horticultural crops. It is home for variety of rare and exotic medicinal and aromatic plants. Some cash crops suited for Manipur include litchi, cashew nuts, walnuts, orange, lemon, pineapple, papaya, passion fruit, peach, pear and plum.

Industry: Its economy is primarily agriculture, forestry, cottage and trade driven. Manipur has the highest number of handicrafts units and number of craftspersons, in the entire northeastern region of India. The state is covered with over 3,000 square km of bamboo forests, making it one of India's largest contributors to its bamboo industry.

Neighbouring States: It is bounded by Nagaland to the north, Mizoram to the south, and Assam to the west; Burma lies to its east.

Art & Culture:
(a) **Dances:** Manipuri dance (Ras Lila)
(b) **Festivals:** The various festivals of Manipur are Lui-ngai-ni Ningol Chakouba, Yaoshang, Ganngai, Chumpha, Christmas, Cheiraoba, Kang and Heikru Hidongba.

Nature Tourism: Loktak Lake, Kaina, Keibul Lamjao National Park, Sadu Chiru waterfall and Thalon Cave.

Tribes: Aimol, Anal, Angami, Chiru, Chothe, Gangte, Hmar, Kabui, Koireng, Kom, Lamgang, Mao, Maram, Maring, Mizo, , Suhte, Tangkh, Thadou, Vaiphui, Zou, Kuki.

Cuisines: Iromba, Kabok, Chakkounba

Animal: Sangai (Cervus *eldi*)

Bird: Mrs. Humes Pheasant (Syrmaticus *humiae*)

Meghalaya

Also known as: "the abode of the clouds"
Capital: Shillong
Largest city: Shillong
No. Of districts: 11
Chief Minister: C.K. Sangma
Governor: Ganga Prasad
Area: 22,429 sq.km
Language: English, Khasi and Garo
Date of establishment: 21 January 1972
Population: 2,966,889
Sex Ratio: 989 females per 1000 males
Literacy Rate: 74.43%
Population Density: 132/sq.km (340/sq mi)
Total Forest Cover Area: 17146 sq km

Agriculture: Basically an agricultural state with about 80% of population depending entirely on agriculture for their livelihood. Rice, maize, wheat and a few other cereals and pulses. The important cash crops potato, ginger, turmeric, black pepper, areca nut, tezpatta, betelvine, short-staple cotton, jute, mesta, mustard and rapeseed etc. Horticultural crops like orange, lemon, pineapple, guava, litchi, banana, jack fruits and fruits such as plum, pear and peach.

Industry: Meghalaya has a rich base of natural resources which include minerals such as coal, limestone, sillimanite, Kaolin and granite among others.

Neighbouring States: This state is bounded to the south by the districts of greater Mymensingh and the Division of Sylhet and the west by the Division of Rangpur of Bangladesh and the north and the east by Assam.

Art & Culture:
(a) **Dances:** Nongkrem` is an important folkdance from the Meghalaya.
(b) **Festivals:** Shivratri, Nongkrem Dance Festival, and Wangala or the harvest Festival.

Tourism: Mawphlang sacred forest, limestone and sandstone caves, and some of the popular waterfalls like the Elephant Falls, Shadthum Falls, Weinia falls, Bishop Falls, Nohkalikai Falls, Langshiang Falls and Sweet Falls.

Tribes: Chakma, Dimasa, Garo, Hajong, Hmar, Khasi, Jaintia, Kuki, Pawi, Synteng, Boro, Koch, Raba, Lakher, Man, Naga, Mikir, Mizo.

Cuisines: Jadoh, Kyat (local beer). Bitchi

Animal: Clouded Leopard (Neofelis *nebulosa*)

Bird: Hill Myna (Gracula *religiosa*)

Mizoram

Also known as: "land of the hill people"
Capital: Aizawl
Largest city: Aizawl
No. Of districts: 8
Chief Minister: Pu Lal Thanhawla
Governor: K. Rajesh Kharan
Area: 21,081 sq.km
Language: Mizo
Date of establishment: 20th February 1987
Population: 1,097,206
Sex Ratio: 976 females per 1000 males
Literacy Rate: 91.33%
Population Density: 52/sq.km
Total Forest Cover Area: 18,186 sq km

Agriculture: 55% to 60% of the working population of the state is annually deployed on agriculture. Rice remains the largest crop grown in the state; fruits are the second largest category, followed by condiments and spices.

Industry: Handloom, horticulture industries, forestry, fisheries and sericulture

Neighbouring States: The state shares borders with three of the seven sister states, namely Tripura, Assam, Manipur and a 722 km border with the neighbouring countries of Bangladesh and Myanmar.

Art & Culture:
(a) **Dances:** Cheraw, Khuallam, Chheihla, Chai
(b) **Festivals:** Chapchar Kut, Thalfavang Kut, Mim Kut, Pawl Kut, Christmas and Easter.

Tourism:
National parks and sanctuaries: Murlen National Park, Dampa Tiger Reserve, Khawnglung Wildlife Sanctuary.
Hill stations: Hmuifang Tlang, Reiek Tlang
Tribes: Chakma, Dimasa, Garo, Hajong, Hmar, Khasi, Jaintia, Kuki, Mikir, Naga, Pawi, Synteng, Paite, Lakher, Man.

Cuisines: Zu (a special tea)

Animal: Hoolock gibbon (Hoolock *hoolock*)

Bird: Mrs. Humes pheasant (Syrmaticus *humaie*)

Nagaland

Also known as: "falcon capital of the world"
Capital: Kohima
Largest city: Dimapur
No. Of districts: 11
Chief Minister: T. R. Zeliang
Governor: Padmanabha Acharya
Area: 16,579 sq.km
Language: English
Date of establishment: 1st December 1963
Population: 1,978,502
Sex Ratio: 931
Literacy Rate: 79.55%
Population Density: 119/sq.km
Total Forest Cover Area: 12489

Agriculture: The main crops of the state are rice, millet, maize, and pulses. Cash crops, like sugarcane and potato, are also grown in some parts. Plantation crops such as premium coffee, cardamom, and tea are grown in hilly areas in small quantities.

Industry: Forestry is also an important source of income. Cottage industries such as weaving, woodwork, and pottery are also an important source of revenue.

Neighbouring States: It borders the state of Assamto the west, Arunachal Pradesh and part of Assam to the north, Burma to the east and Manipur to the south.

Art & Culture:

(a) **Dances:** Zeliang is the one of the most artistic dance forms.

(b) **Festivals:** Nagaland is known as the land of festivals. The Hornbill Festival in December, Sekrenyi, Tsukhenyie, Mimkut, Bishu, Aoling, Moatsu, Tuluni, Nyaknylum, Mongmong, Tokhu Emong and Yemshe are some of the important festivals celebrated by the various Naga tribes.

Tribes: Naga, Kuki, Kachari, Mikir, Garo
Cuisines: Momos, Rice Beer, and Cherry Wine
Animal: Gaur (Bos *gaurus*)
Bird: Blyth's Tragopan (Tragopan *blythii*)

Odisha

Capital: Bhubaneshwar
Largest city: Bhubaneshwar
No. Of districts: 30
Chief Minister: Naveen Patnaik
Governor: Ganeshi Lal
Area: 155,707 sq.km
Language: Odia, English
Date of establishment: 1st April 1936
Population: 41,974,218
Sex Ratio: 979 females per 1000 males
Literacy Rate: 72.87%
Population Density: 270/sq.km
Total Forest Cover Area: 51,345 sq. km

Agriculture: Rice is the dominant crop in Odisha and is grown on 77% of the area under cultivation. The state is the fourth largest shrimp producing state in India.

Industry: Industries like manufacturing; mining and quarrying; electricity, gas and water supply; and construction are dominant in the state. NALCO and Vedanta, two of the biggest aluminium plants are in Odisha which makes the state leading producer of aluminium in the state.

Neighbouring States: It shares its borders with states of West Bengal to the north-east, Jharkhand to the north, Chhattisgarh to the west and north-west, Telangana to the south-west and Andhra Pradesh to the south.

Art & Culture:

(a) **Dances:** Odissi is one of the oldest and most important classical dance forms in the state. Other dance forms include: Ghumura Dance, Chhau dance, Mahari dance, and Gotipua.

(b) **Festivals:** Durga Puja, Kumar Purnima, Deepabali, Prathamastami, Vasant Panchami, Maha Shivaratri, Ratha Yatra, Ganesh Chaturthi, Raja Parba are some of the major festivals celebrated across Odisha.

Religious Places: Lingaraja Temple at Bhubaneswar, Jagannath Temple, Puri and the Konark Sun Temple and Maa Sarala Temple at Tirtol town.

Nature Tourism: Udayagiri and Khandagiri Caves, Dhauli, Chilika Lake, Bhitarkanika National Park, Simlipal National Park.

Tribes: Bagata, Bathudi, , Birhor, Didayi, Didayi, Chenchu, Dal, Desua, Gandia, Ghara, Gond, Ho, Holva, Kandha, Munda, Kol, Kolah Laharas, Kol Loharas, Kolha, Koli, Mahali, Mankidi, Mankirdia, Pentia, Rajuar, Santal, Saora,

Cuisines: Fish Orly, Khirmohan, Rsabali, Chhenapodapitha
Animal: Sambar (Rusa *unicolor*)
Bird: Indian Roller (Coracias *benghalensis*)

Punjab

Also known as: "Granary of India", "India's bread-basket"
Capital: Chandigarh
Largest city: Ludhiana
No. Of districts: 22
Chief Minister: Capt. Amarinder Singh
Governor: V.P. Singh Badnore
Area: 50,362 sq.km
Language: Punjabi
Date of establishment: 1st November 1966
Population: 27,743,338
Sex Ratio: 895 females per 1000 males
Literacy Rate: 75.84%
Population Density: 551/sq. km
Total Forest Cover Area: 1837 sq. km

Agriculture: Wheat is the most important crop of the state. Rice, sugarcane, fruits and vegetables are also grown. The state produces 10.26% of India's cotton, 19.5% of India's wheat, and 11% of India's rice.

Industry: Industries include the manufacturing of scientific instruments, agricultural goods, electrical goods, financial services, machine tools, textiles, sewing machines, sports goods, starch, tourism, fertilisers, bicycles, garments, and the processing of pine oil and sugar. Punjab also has the largest number of steel rolling mill plants in India, which are located in "Steel Town"—Mandi Gobindgarh in the Fatehgarh Sahib district.

Neighbouring States: The state is bordered by the Indian states of Himachal Pradesh to the east, Haryana to the south and southeast, Rajasthan to the southwest, and the Pakistani province of Punjab to the west. To the north it is bounded by the Indian state of Jammu and Kashmir.

Art & Culture:

(a) **Dances:** Bhangra and Giddha are the major dance forms of the state.

(b) **Festivals:** Bandi Chhor Divas (Diwali), Mela Maghi, Hola Mohalla, Rakhri, Vaisakhi, Lohri, Teeyan and Basant.

Religious Places: The Golden Temple in Amritsar and Sri Anandpur Sahib are the major religious attraction of the state.

Cuisines: Dal Makhni, Makke di Roti-Sarson da Saag, Chana Bhature
Animal: Blackbuck (Antilope *cervicapra*)
Bird: Northern Goshawk (Accipiter *gentilis*)

Rajasthan

Name: Rajasthan
Capital: Jaipur
Largest city: Jaipur
No. Of districts: 33
Chief Minister: Smt. Vasundhara Raje
Governor: Kalyan Singh
Area: 342,239 sq.km
Language: Hindi, Rajasthani
Date of establishment: 1st November 1956

Population: 68,548,437
Sex Ratio: 928 females per 1000 males
Literacy Rate: 66.11%
Population Density: 200/sq.km
Total Forest Cover Area: 16572 sq km

Agriculture: Wheat, barley, pulses, sugarcane and oilseeds are cultivated over large areas. Cotton and tobacco are the main cash crops. The largest producers of edible oils in India and the second largest producer of oilseeds. The biggest wool-producing state in India and the main opium producer and consumer.

Industry: Main industries are mineral, agriculture, and textile based. The second largest producer of polyester fibre in India.

Neighbouring States: It shares a border with the Pakistani provinces of Punjab to the northwest and Sindh to the west, along the Sutlej-Indus river valley. Elsewhere it is bordered by the other Indian states: Punjab to the north; Haryana and Uttar Pradesh to the northeast; Madhya Pradesh to the southeast; and Gujarat to the southwest.

Art & Culture:

(a) **Dances:** Ghoomar dance from Udaipur and Kalbeliya dance of Jaisalmer

(b) **Festivals:** Deepawali, Holi, Gangaur, Teej, Gogaji, Shri Devnarayan Jayanti, Makar Sankranti and Janmashtami

Religious Places: The Brahma temple at Pushkar, Dilwara Temples of Mount Abu, Ranakpur Temple in Pali District, Mehandipur Balaji Temple, Karni Mata Temple of Bikaner, Ajmer Sharif Dargah are some of the important religious places in the state.

Cuisines: Dal-Bati-Churma, Ker Sangari, Lal Maas, Gatte
Animal: Chinkara (Gazella *bennettii*)
Bird: Great Indian Bustard (Ardeotis *nigriceps*)

Sikkim

Capital: Gangtok
Largest city: Gangtok
No. Of districts: 4
Chief Minister: Pawan Chamling
Governor: Ganga Prasad
Area: 7,096 sq.km
Language: Nepali, Bhutia, Gurung, Lepcha, Limbu, Manggar, Newari, Sherpa, Sunwar, Tamang
Date of establishment: 16th May 1975
Population: 610,577
Sex Ratio: 890 females per 1000 males
Literacy Rate: 81.42%
Population Density: 86/sq.km
Total Forest Cover Area: 3344 sq km

Agriculture: Crops such as Rice, maize, millet, wheat, barley, oranges, tea and cardamom are grown here. Sikkim is the leading producer of cardamom in India

Industry: Brewing, distilling, tanning and watches are the main industries. The state has also invested in a fledgling gambling industry, promoting both casinos and online gambling. The Playwin lottery has been a notable success in the state.

Neighbouring States: The state is bordered by Nepal to the west, China's Tibet Autonomous Region to the north and east, and Bhutan to the east. The Indian state of West Bengal lies to the south.

Art & Culture:
(a) **Dances:** Singhi Chham is a masked dance of Sikkim.
(b) **Festivals:** Diwali, Dussera, Maghe Sankranti, Bhimsen Puja, Losar, Loosong, Saga Dawa, Lhabab Duechen, Drupka Teshi, Bhumchu, Eid ul-Fitr, Muharram and Christmas are the major festivals celebrated in the state.

Religious Places: Rumtek Monastery, Tsongmo Lake, Nathu la pass, Gurudongmar Lake
Tribes: Bhutia, Lepcha, Limboo, Tamang
Cuisines: Momos, Thukpa, Gundruk, Phagshapa and Seal Roti
Animal: Red panda (Ailurus *fulgens*)
Bird: Blood pheasant (Ithaginis *cruentus*)

Tamil Nadu

Capital: Chennai
Largest city: Chennai
No. Of districts: 32
Chief Minister: E.K. Palaniswami
Governor: Banwarilal Purohit
Area: 1,30,060 sq.km
Language: Tamil
Date of establishment: 26th January 1950
Population: 72,147,030
Sex Ratio: 996 females per 1000 males
Literacy Rate: 80.09 %
Population Density: 555/sq.km
Total Forest Cover Area: 26,281

Agriculture: Rice is the leading crop and the Cauvery delta region is known as the Rice Bowl of Tamil Nadu. Mango and banana are the leading fruit crops. The main vegetables grown are tapioca, tomato, onion, brinjal(eggplant), and drumstick.

Industry: Textiles, leather, electronics, heavy industries, engineering, software, and automobiles are the leading industries of the state. Integral Coach Factory which is located in Perambur is the largest producer of railway coaches in Asia.

Neighbouring States: The state is bordered by the union territory of Puducherry and the south Indian states of Kerala, Karnataka, and Andhra Pradesh. It also shares a maritime border with the nation of Sri Lanka.

Art & Culture:
(a) **Dances:** Bharatanatyam is the famous dance forms of Tamail Nadu. Other forms of folk dances are Karakattam,Mayilam.
(b) **Festivals:** Pongal is the most celebrated festival of the state. Other major festivals are Deepavali, Ayudha Poojai, Saraswathi Poojai (Dasara), Krishna Jayanthi and Vinayaka Chathurthi, Eid ul-Fitr, Bakrid, Milad un Nabi, Muharram, Good Friday, Easter are celebrated in the state.

Religious Places: Chidambaram, Thiruvannaamalai, Brihadishwara Temple, Gangaikonda Cholapuram, Madurai Meenakshi Amman Temple, Sri Ranganathaswamy Temple, Srirangam, Tiruchirappalli, and Rameshwaram are the famous religious places of the state.

Tribes: Adiyan, Aranadan, Eravallan, Irular, Kadar, Kammara, Kaniyan, Kanyan, Kattunayakan, Kochu, Konda, Kondareddis, Koraga, Kota Muthuvan, Malai, Malakkuravan, Malasar, Malayali , Palliyar, Paniyan, Sholaga, Toda.

Cuisines: Appam, Dosai, Idli, Sambhar, Rasam, Chettinad Chicken, Pongal
Animal: Nilgiri Tahr (Nilgiritragus *hylocrius*)
Bird: Emerald Dove (Chalcophaps *indica*)

Telangana

Capital: Hyderabad
Largest city: Hyderabad
No. Of districts: 31
Chief Minister: Kalvakuntla Chandrashekar Rao
Governor: E. S. L. Narasimhan
Area: 114,840 sq.km
Language: Telugu, Urdu
Date of establishment: 2nd June 2014
Population: 35,193,978
Sex Ratio: 988 females per 1000 males
Literacy Rate: 66.50%
Population Density: 307/sq.km
Total Forest Cover Area: 20,419 sq km

Agriculture: Rice is the major food crop and staple food of the state. Other important crops are Maize, Tobacco, Mango, Cotton and Sugar cane

Industry: Automobiles and auto components industry, spices, mines and minerals, textiles and apparels, pharmaceutical, horticulture, poultry farming

Neighbouring States: The state shares its borders with Maharashtra, Chhattisgarh to the north, and Karnataka to the west, and Andhra Pradesh to the south, east and north east.

Art & Culture:

(a) Classical dance forms (Sastriya Nrutyam) such as Kuchipudi, AndhraNatyam, Bhamakalapam, Veeranatyam; and folk dances such as Butta bommalu, Tappeta Gullu, Lambadi, Dhimsa, and Chindu.

(b) **Festivals:** Sankranti, Maha Shivaratri, Ugadi or the Telugu New Year, Sri Rama Navami, Varalakshmi Vratam, Vinayaka Chaviti, Dasara, Atla Tadde, Deepavali, Deepothsavam during the Deepavali season.

Religious Places: Alampur Jogulamba temple, Gnana Saraswati Temple, Bhadrachalam Temple, Sri Raja Rajeswara Swami temple and the Thousand Pillar Temple are some of the famous temples of the state.

Cuisines: Gongura Ghosht, Pappuchura, Gongura Pappu, Hyderabadi Biryani
Animal: Chital (Zinka)
Bird: Pala Pitta (Coracias *benghalensis*)

Tripura

Capital: Agartala
Largest city: Agartala
No. Of districts: 8
Chief Minister: Biplab Kumar Deb
Governor: Tathagata Roy
Area: 10,486 sq.km
Language: Bengali and Kokborok
Date of establishment: 21st Jan. 1972
Population: 3,673,917
Sex Ratio: 960 females per 1000 males
Literacy Rate: 87.22%
Population Density: 350/sq.km
Total Forest Cover Area: 7726 sq km

Agriculture: Rice, potato, sugarcane, mesta, pulses, and jute are some of the crops grown in the state. Jackfruit and pineapple are among the horticultural products.

Industry: Brickfields and tea industry
Neighbouring States: The state is bordered by Bangladesh to the north, south, and west, and Assam and Mizoram to the east.
Art & Culture: Goria dance, Jhum dance, lebang dance, mamita dance, and mosak sulmani dance are some of the dance forms of the state.
Tourism: Ujjayanta Palace, Kunjaban Palace, Neermahal – Lake Palace, Laxminarayan Temple, Uma Maheswar Temple, Jagannath Temple, Benuban Bihar, Gedu Mian Mosque, Malancha Niwas, Rabindra Kanan, Purbasha, Handicrafts Designing Centre, Fourteen Goddess Temple, and Portuguese Church are some of major tourist attractions.
Tribes: Bhil, Bhutia, Chaimal, Chakma, Garoo, Halam, Khasia, Kuki, Mag , Munda, Noatia, Orang, Riang, Santal, Tripura
Cuisines: Chakhwi, Mwkhwi, Muitru
Animal: Phayre's Langur (Trachypithecus *phayrel*)
Bird: Green Imperial Pigeon (Dacula *genea*)

Uttarakhand

Also known as: "Land of the Gods"
Capital: Dehradun
Largest city: Dehradun
No. Of districts: 13
Chief Minister: Trivendra Singh Rawat
Governor: Krishan Kant Paul
Area: 53,483 sq.km
Language: Hindi, Sanskrit, Garhwali, Kumaoni
Date of establishment: 9th November 2000
Population: 10,086,292
Sex Ratio: 963 females per 1000 males
Literacy Rate: 78.82%
Population Density: 189/sq.km
Total Forest Cover Area: 24295 sq km

Agriculture: Basmati rice, wheat, soybeans, groundnuts, coarse cereals, pulses, and oil seeds are the major crops grown in the state.

Industry: Tourism and hydropower are the major industries of the state.

Neighbouring States: It borders Tibet on the north; the Mahakali Zone of the Far-Western Region, Nepal on the east; and the Indian states of Uttar Pradesh to the south and Himachal Pradesh to the northwest.

Art & Culture:

(a) **Dances:** Langvir Nritya, Barada Nati, Hurka Baul, Jhora-Chanchri, Jhumaila, Chauphula, and Chholiya.

(b) **Festivals:** Kumbh Mela, Kanwar Yatra, Kandali Festival, Ramman, Harela mela, Nauchandi mela, Uttarayani mela and Nanda Devi Mela take place.

Tourism: It is home to some most frequented hill stations like Mussoorie, Nainital, Dhanaulti, Lansdowne, Pauri, Sattal, Almora, Kausani, Bhimtal, and Ranikhet. National parks in the state include Jim Corbett National Park, Rajaji National Park, Nanda Devi National Park, and Valley of Flowers National Park. Badrinath and Kedarnath are one of the most auspicious and holy pilgrimages housed by the state.
Tribes: Bhotia, Buksa, Jaunsari, Raji, Tharu
Cuisines: Aloo ke Gutke, Kaapa, Jhangora (millets) ki Kheer, Chainsoo
Animal: Musk deer (Moschus *cupreus*)
Bird: Himalayan Monal (Lophophorus *impejanus*)

Uttar Pradesh

Also known as: 'Hindi heartland of India'
Capital & Largest city: Lucknow
No. Of districts: 75
Chief Minister: Yogi Adityanath
Governor: Ram Naik
Area: 240,928 sq.km
Language: Hindi, Urdu
Date of establishment: 1st April 1935 as the United Provinces
Population: 19,98,12,341
Sex Ratio: 912 females per 1000 males
Literacy Rate: 67.68%
Population Density: 829/sq.km
Total Forest Cover Area: 14679 sq km

Agriculture: Wheat is the major food crop; and sugarcane is the main commercial crop with 70% of sugar produce from the state.

Industry: Major industries include electronics, electrical equipment, cables, steel, leather, textiles, jewellery, frigates, automobiles, railway coaches, etc

Neighbouring States: The state shares its border with Rajasthan to the west, Haryana and Delhi to the northwest, Uttarakhand and the country of Nepal to the north, Bihar to the east, Jharkhand to the southeast, Chhattisgarh to the south and Madhya Pradesh to the southwest.

Art & Culture:

(a) **Dances:** Kathak is most popular dance form.

(b) **Festivals:** Diwali, Buddha Purnima, Christmas, Rama Navami, Vijayadashami, Makar Sankranti, Vasant Panchami, Ayudha Puja, Ganga Mahotsava, Janmashtami, Sardhana Christian Fair, Maha Shivaratri, Mahavir Jayanti, Moharram, Barah Wafat, Eid, Bakreed, Chhath puja, Lucknow Mahotsav, Kabob and Hanuman Jayanti.

Tourism: Taj Mahal, Agra Fort, Bara Imambara, Fatehpur Sikri, Sarnath, Kushinagar, Patna Bird Sanctuary and many more are the major tourist attractions of the state.

Tribes: Bhotia, Buksa, Jaunsari, Raji, Tharu, Gonda, Baiga, Parahiya, Saharya, Chero, Kharwar, Bhuiya, Pankha, Baiga.

Cuisines: Kabab, Biryanis, Bedmi Aloo, Kachori, Banarasi Chaat

Animal: Swamp Deer (Rucervus *duvaucelii*)
Bird: Sarus Crane (Grus *antigone*)

West Bengal

Capital & Largest city: Kolkata
No. Of districts: 23
Chief Minister: Mamata Banerjee
Governor: Keshari Nath Tripathi
Area: 88,752 sq.km
Language: Bengali and English
Date of establishment: 1st Nov. 1956
Population: 91,276,115
Sex Ratio: 950 females per 1000 males
Literacy Rate: 76.26%
Population Density: 1028/sq.km
Total Forest Cover Area: 16847 sq km

Agriculture: Rice, potato, jute, sugarcane and wheat

Industry: steel, leather, textiles, jewellery, frigates, automobiles, electronics, electrical equipment etc are the major manufacturing industries of West Bengal.

Neighbouring States: The state is surrounded by the countries of Bangladesh, Nepal and Bhutan, and the states of Odisha, Jharkhand, Bihar, Sikkim, and Assam

Art & Culture:

(a) **Dances:** Chau dance and many other folk dances.

(b) **Festivals:** Durga Puja, Poila Baishakh (the Bengali New Year), Rathayatra, Dolyatra or Basanta-Utsab, Nobanno, Poush Parbon, Kali Puja, Saraswati Puja, Laxmi Puja, Christmas, Eid ul-Fitr, Eid ul-Adha, Buddha Purnima, Muharram, Christmas

Tourism: Dakshineswar Kali Temple, Tipu Sultan Mosque, St Paul's Cathedral, Victoria Memorial, Howrah Bridge, Vidyasagar Setu are some of the major tourist attractions. Popular national parks include Sundarbans National Park, Buxa Tiger Reserve, Gorumara National Park, Neora Valley National Park, Singalila National Park, and Jaldapara National Park.

Tribes: Asur, Baiga, Bedia, Chero, Chik Baraik, Garo, Gond, Gorait, Haja Mru, Munda, Nagesia, Oraon, Parhaiya, Rabha, Santal, Sauria Paharia, Savar, Limbu

Cuisines: Rosogulla, Mishti Doi, Bhapa Illish

Animal: Fishing cat (Prionailurus *viverrinus*)
Bird: White-breasted Kingfisher (Halcyon *smyrnensis*)

Andaman and Nicobar Islands

Capital & Largest city: Port Blair
No. Of districts: 3
Area: 8249 sq.km
Language: English, Hindi, Nicobarese
Date of establishment: 1st November 1956
Lieutenant Governor: Jagdish Mukhi
Population: 380,581
Sex Ratio: 876 females per 1,000 males
Literacy Rate: 86.63%
Population Density: 46 per sq.km
Total Forest Cover Area: 6742 sq km

Agriculture: Paddy, oilseeds and vegetables

Industry: Small scale industries and handicraft units; Tourism plays an important role in the economy of the union territory.

Tourism: The island serves as an excellent tourist destination with major attractions like Havelock island, Cellular Jail, Mahatma Gandhi Marine National Park, Andaman Water sports complex, Chatham Saw Mill, Mini Zoo, Corbyn's cove, Chidiya Tapu, Wandoor Beach, Forest Museum, Cinque island, Mt Harriet and Mud Volcano, Neil Island and many more.

Tribes: Andamanese, Chariar, Chari, Kora, Tabo, Bo, Yere, Kede, Bea, Balawa, Bojigiyab, Juwai, Kol, Jarawas, Nicobarese, Onges, Sentinelese, Shom.

Chandigarh

Also known as: "Wealthiest Town of India"
Administrator: V.P. Singh Badnore
Area: 114 sq.km
Language: English, Hindi, Punjabi

Date of establishment: 1st Nov, 1966
Population: 1,055,450
Total Forest Cover Area: 114 sq km
Sex Ratio: 818 females per 1000 males
Literacy Rate: 86.05%
Population Density: 9,258/sq.km
Industry: Pharmaceuticals, machinery, food products, and electrical appliances are some of the major industries.
Neighbouring states: The union territory shares its border with Haryana and Punjab.
Tourism: Kasauli, Sukhna Lake, Leisure Valley, Rock Garden and many more are the major tourist attraction.
Cuisines: Butter Chicken, Tandoori Chicken, Mutton Pulao

Dadra and Nagar Haveli

Capital: Silvassa
Administrator: Praful Patel
Area: 491 sq.km
Language: English, Gujarati, Hindi, Marathi
Date of establishment: 11th August 1961
Population: 343,709
Sex Ratio: 774 females per 1000 males
Literacy Rate: 76.24%
Population Density: 700 per sq.km
Total Forest Cover Area: 207 sq km

Agriculture: paddy, ragi, small millets, jowar, sugarcanes
Industry: Agriculture, Industries, Forestry, Animal Husbandry and Tourism
Neighbouring states: It is surrounded by Valsad District of Gujarat on the West, North and East and by Thane District of Maharashtra on the South and South-East.
Tourism: Vanganga Lake Garden, Hirwavan garden, Piparia, Tribal Museum, Vandhara Udyan, Mini Zoo and Bal Udyan, Ayyappa Temple ,Silvassa, Tapovan Tourist Complex, Bindrabin are the major tourist attractions.

Daman and Diu

Capital: Daman
Administrator: Praful Patel
Area: 111 sq.km
Language: English, Gujarati, Hindi, Marathi
Date of establishment: 30 May 1987
Population: 243,247
Sex Ratio: 618 females per 1000 males
Literacy Rate: 87.07%
Population Density: 2172 per sq.km
Total Forest Cover Area: 20.49 sq km

Industry: Major industries include distillery, fishing andtourism
Neighbouring states: Gujarat
Tribes: Dhodia, Dubla (Halpati), Naikda (Talavia), Siddi, Varli.

Lakshadweep

Capital: Kavaratti
Largest city: Andrott
No. Of districts: 1
Administrator: Farooq khan
Area: 30 sq.km

Language: English, Malayalam
Date of establishment: 1st November 1956
Population: 64,473
Total Forest Cover Area: 27.10 sq km
Sex Ratio: 946 females per 1000 males
Literacy Rate: 91.85%
Population Density: 2015 per sq.km
Total Forest Cover Area: 27.10 per sq km

Agriculture: fishing and coconut cultivation
Industry: Fisheries, production of fibre products, tourism and desalination are major industries
Neighbouring states: Kerala and Karnataka
Art & Culture: Festivals: Eid-Ul-Fitr, Muharram, Bakra Eid and Milad-Un-Nabi are the most celebrated festivals.
Tourism: Bangaram and Kadmat islands are the most frequented tourist destinations.
Animal: Butterfly fish (Chaetodon *decussatus*)
Bird: House Sparrow (Passer domesticus)
Bird: Soofy Tern (onychoprion *fuscata*)

National Capital Territory of Delhi

Capital: New Delhi
No. Of districts: 11
Chief Minister: Arvind Kejriwal
Lieutenant Governor: Anil Baijal
Area: 1,483 sq.km
Language: Hindi, Punjabi, Urdu, English
Date of establishment: 1st Feb 1956
Population: 16,787,941
Sex Ratio: 868 females per 1000 males
Literacy Rate: 86.21%
Population Density: 11,320 per sq. km
Total Forest Cover Area: 192 sq km

Industry: Information technology, sports goods, medicines, leather goods, telecommunications, hotels, banking, media and tourism
Neighbouring states: Haryana and Uttar Pradesh
Art & Culture: Festivals: Diwali (the festival of lights), Mahavir Jayanti, Guru Nanak's Birthday, Raksha Bandhan, Durga Puja, Holi, Lohri, Krishna Janmastami, Maha Shivratri, Eid ul-Fitr, Moharram and Buddha Jayanti.
Tourism: Red Fort, Qutab Minar, Humayun's Tomb, India Gate, Jantar Mantar, Laxminarayan temple, Akshardham temple, Lotus temple, Iskcon temple, Safdarjung's Tomb, and Jama Masjid are the prominent tourist attractions.
Cuisines: Chaat, Tandoori Chicken, Paranthe, Chole Bhature
Bird: House Sparrow (Passer domesticus)

Puducherry

Capital & Largest city: Pondicherry
No. Of districts: 4
Chief Minister: V. Narayanasamy
Area: 490 sq.km
Language: French, Malayalam, Tamil, Telugu
Date of establishment: 7 Jan 1963
Population: 1,247,953
Sex Ratio: 1,037 females per 1000 males
Literacy Rate: 85.85%
Population Density: 2,605/sq.km
Total Forest Cover Area: 53.67 sq km

Agriculture: Rice, pulses, sugarcane, coconuts, and cotton

Industry: Fisheries, textile, automobile parts, computer hardware, cotton yarn and tourism are the major industries.

Tourism: Promenade Beach, Sri Aurobindo Ashram, Auroville Beach, Serenity Beach, French War Memorial, 19th Century Light House, Bharathi Park, Governors Palace, Romain Rolland Library, Legislative Assembly, Pondicherry Museum, Thirukaameeswarar Temple and many more are the famous tourist spots in Puducherry.

Cuisines: Kadugu yerra, Vendakkai, Patchaddy

Animal: Squirrel Sciuridae *ratufinae*

Bird: Asian Koel (Eudynamys *scolopaceus*)

Four Ends of India

Easternmost point of India is known as Kibithu; situated on right bank of river Lohit separating India from China-Tibet region. It is a small village with the population at the altitude of 3,350 metre in Arunachal Pradesh. **Westernmost point** is situated in Kuch area of Gujarat called as Ghuar Mota. The region is famous for its harsh climate with 45°C in summer and 20°C in winter. During monsoon season this region looks like tortoise surrounded by seawater. **Northernmost** point of India has been in controversies ever since India's independence. The Siachen Glacier in the state of J&K is the northern boundary of India according to the official division of India during the time of Independences. The **Southernmost** point of the mainland of India is Kanyakunar District in the state of Tamil Nadu. Kanniyakumari, formerly was known as Cape Comorin. It is the second largest and urbanized of Tamil Nadu. Indira Point is a village in the Nicobar district of Andaman and Nicobar Islands, India. It is located in the Great Nicobar tehsil. It is the location of the southernmost point of India's territory.

National Symbols of India

National Flag

The national flag consists of a horizontal rectangular tricolour with saffron at the top, white in the middle and India green at the bottom. The centre has a navy blue wheel with twenty-four spokes, known as the Ashoka Chakra. The flag is designed by Pingali Venkayya.

It was adopted in its present form during a meeting of the Constituent Assembly held on **22 July 1947**, when it became the official flag of the Dominion of India.

- The tricolour was hoisted for the first times on the ramparts of the Red fort on August 16th 1947.
- The design and manufacturing process for the national flag is regulated by three documents issued by the Bureau of Indian Standards.
- All of the flags are made out of khadi cloth of silk or cotton. There are two kinds of khadi used: The first is the khadi-bunting which makes up the body of the flag, and the second is the khadi duck, which is a beige coloured cloth that holds the flag of the pole.

History

- Various proto-types of the National flag was presented by different individuals before the design was finalised. Margaret Noble or 'Sister Nivedita' designed one of the earliest proto-types of the national flag in 1905. It was displayed by the Indian National Congress in its annual session at Calcutta in December 1906.

- Another flag named as the **"Calcutta Flag"** was designed by Sachindra Prasad Bose and Sukumar Mitra and unfurled on 7th August 1906 at the Parsee Began Square (green park) in calcutta.
- **Pengali Venkayya**, who started the Indian National Flag mission in 1916, presented thirty different designs for the national flag, of which one presented in 1921 contained a spinning wheel on a red and green background.
- In 1921 Gandhi ji first proposed a flag to the Indian National Congress.
- Former, there was a traditional spinning wheel in the centre of flag. The design was then modified to include a white strip in the centre for other religious communities, and provide a background for the spinning wheel.
- A few days before India became independent a modified version of the *swaraj flag* was chosen, the tricolour remained the same saffron, white and green. However, the charkha was replaced by the Ashoka chakra representing the eternal wheel of law.
- The philosopher and second president of India Sarvepalli Radhakrishnan clarified the adopted flag and described its signficance as follows.
- "Bhagwa or saffron (Kesari) colour denotes renunciation.
- The white in the centre is light, the path of truth guide our conduct.
- The green shows our relation to soil and plant life.
- The "Ashoka Chakra" in the centre of the white is the wheel of law of dharma".

National Emblem

- The National Emblem depicts four lions, standing back to back. It is an adaptation from the Sarnath Lion Capital of Ashoka, near Varanasi in Uttar Pradesh.
- It was adopted on **26 January 1950**, the day that India became a republic.
- The four lions symbolizing power, courage, pride and confidence, rest on a circular abacus.
- The abacus is girdled by four smaller animals, guardians of the four directions : the lion of the north, the elephant of the east, the horse of the south and the bull of the west.
- The abacus rests on a lotus in full bloom, examplifying the fountainhead of life and creative inspiration.

The words **Satyameva Jayate** (meaning truth alone triumphs') from Mundaka Upanishad are inscribed below the abacus in Devanagari script.

- The usage of the emblem is regulated and restricted under state Emblem of India Act, 2005.

National Anthem

- The song **Jana-gana-mana**, composed originally in highly Sanskritised (Tatsama) Bengali by Rabindranath Tagore, was adopted in its Hindi version by the Constituent Assembly as the National Anthem of India on 24 January 1950.
- The complete song (Jana-gana-mana) consists, of five stanzas. The first stanza contains the full version of the national Anthem.

- Playing time of the full version of it is 52 seconds.
- A short version which consists of the first and the last lines of the stanza takes 20 seconds, is also played on certain occasions.
- Jana Gana Mana was written on 11 December 1911. Rabindernath Tagore translated the song from Bengali to English and also set it to music in *Madanapalle*, a town located in the chittoor district of Andhra Pradesh State India.
- It was first sung on 27th December 1911 at Calcutta session of the Indian National Congress.
- Jana Gana Mana was first published under the title "Bharat Vidhata" in the Tatva bodhini Patrika, the offical organ of Maharishi Debenranath Tagore's *Brahmo Samaj* in January 1912. The song was sub titled *Brahmo-Sangeet*.
- The National Anthem was first played as an orchestral arrangement in the united nations at New York in 1947.

National Song of India

- The song Vande Mataram composed in Sanskrit by Bankimchandra Chatterji on November 7th, 1875, was incorporated in his famous novel Ananda math (1882).
- It was first song in a political context by Rabindranath Tagore at the 1896 session of the Indian National Congress.
- It was declared as the National song in 1937 through a resolution.
- The original Vande Mataram consists of six stanzas and the translation in prose for the complete poem by Shri Aurobindo appeared in *Karmayogin*, 20 November 1909.
- Bhikaji Cama created the first version of India's National flag in *stuttgart*, *Germany* in 1907. It had Vande Mataram written on it in the middle band.

Indian National Calendar

- The National Calendar is based on the *Saka Era* with Chaitra being its first month.
- It consists of 365 days in a normal year. It was adopted from 22nd march 1957 it alongside the Gregorian calendar, by *The Gazette of India*, in news broadcasts by All India Radio and in calendars and communications issued by the Government of India.

National Pledge

- The National Pledge, an oath of allegiance to the Republic of India. was originally composed in Telugu language by writer *Pydimarri Venkata Subba Rao* in 1962.
- It was first read out in a school in Visakhapatnam in 1963.
- The Indian National Pledge is commonly recited by Indians at public events, during daily assemblies in many Indian schools and during the Independence Day and Republic Day Commemoration ceremonies.

National Bird of India

- The colourful, swan sized Indian peacock (Pavocristatus) having a fan-shaped crest of feathers, a white patch under the eye and a long, slender neck was named as the National Bird of India in 1963.

- *Carl Linnaeus* in his work systema Naturae in 1758 assigned to the Indian peacock the technical name of *Pavo Cristatus*.
- The peacock, known as *mayura* in Sanskrit, is frequently depicted in temple art, mythology, poetry, folk music and traditions.

National Flower of India

- Lotus (Nelumbo nucifera) is the National flower of India.
- The lotus plant is cited extensively within puranic and vedic literature. Most deities of Asian religions are depicted as seated on a lotus flower. Vishnu and lakshmi often portrayed on a pink lotus in iconography.

National Tree of India

- Ficus benghalensis with the common name Indian banyan in Bengali, is a tree which is native to the Indian subcontinent.
- The banyan tree is also considered sacred and is called "Vat Vriksha" in Sanskrit, in Telugu known as *Marri Vrikshamu* and in Tamil known as, Ala Maram.
- It is described as 'Kalpavirksha' in ancient texts, which means a tree that fulfils wishes.

National Fruit of India

- Mango (Mangifera Indica) which is known as the 'king of fruits', is considered as the National fruit of India. It is National fruit of Pakistan and the Phillippines also, and the national tree of Bangladesh.

National River

- The Ganga is a trans-boundary river of Asia which flows through the nations of India and Bangladesh.
- The Ganga begins at the confluence of the Bhagirathi and Alaknanda rivers at Devprayag.
- The 2,525 km river rises in the western Himalayas in the Indian state of Uttarakhand and flows south and east through the Gangetic plain of North India into Bangladesh, where it empties into the Bay of Bengal.
- The six headstreams of Ganga are the Alaknanda, Dhauliganga, Nandakini, pindar Mandakini, and Bhagirathi rivers.
- The five confluences, known as the *Panch Prayag*, are all along the Alaknanda. They are in down stream order :

(1) *Vishnu prayag*, where the Dhauliganga joins the Alaknanda;
(2) *Nandprayag*, where the Nandakini joins;
(3) *Karnaprayag*, where the Pindar joins;
(4) *rudraprayag*, where the Mandakini joins;
(5) *Deva prayag*, where the Bhagirathi joins the Alaknanda.

The *Ganger river dolphin* has been recognised by the government of India as its National Aquatic Animal.

National Animal of India

- The Bengal tiger, also called the royal Bengal tiger, is the national animal of both India and Bangladesh.

- Since 2010, it has been classified as endangered by IUCN. In 1973, Project Tiger was launched aiming at ensuring a viable population of tigers in the country.

National Game of India

- Despite the ever-growing popularity of cricket and Hockey, there is no official national game of India.

- Although some experts believe that Hockey is our national game but the fact is none of the games or sports played in the country has the status of "national game."
- The peak time of Indian hockey team was from 1928 to 1956, when it brought all the six consecutive Olympic gold medals.

First in India

Air Mail	Allahabad to Naini (1911)
Telegraph Line	Diamond Harbour to Kolkata
Telephone line introduced in india	1851
International Telephone Service	Mumbai to London (1851)
Newspaper	Bengal Gazette (James Hickey)
Vernacular Daily	Samachar Darpan
Hindi Newspaper	Udant Martand
Passenger Train	Bombay to Thane (1853)
Train with Wi-Fi Facility	Delhi Howrah Rajdhani Express
Metro Train	Kolkata Metro (1984)
Expressway	Mumbai-Pune (2000)
Silent Movie	Raja Harish Chandra (Dadasaheb Phalke (1913)
Talkie Movie	Alam Ara (Ardeshir Irani-1931)
3-D Movie	My Dear Kuttichathan (1984)
Coloured Movie	Kisan Kanya (1937)
Indian English Film	Nur Jahan
Technicolour Film	Jhansi ki Rani
Census	1872
Regular Decadal Census	1881 Onwards
Satellite	Aryabhatta (19th April, 1975)
Aircraft Carriage Warship	INS Vikrant
Indigenously made Satellite	INSAT 2-A (1992)
Battle Tank	Arjun
Fighter Jet	Tejas
Satellite dedicated exclusively for Education Purposes	EDUSAT
Successful Indigenous Launch Vehicle	SLV-3
Military Satellite	G-SAT- 7 or Rukmini
Indigenous Missile	Prithvi (1988)
Antarctica Mission	In 1982, under the leadership of Dr SZ Qasim
Nuclear Reactor	Apsara (1956) Trombay
Atomic Research Centre	Tarapur
Lunar Mission	Chandrayaan-I (October, 2008)

Mars Orbitar Mission	5th November, 2013
Hydroelectric Project	Sidrapong (1898)
Marine National Park	Kutch (Gujarat)
National Park	Hailey National Park (Jim Corbett), 1936
Biosphere Reserve	Nilgiri
Open University	Dr Bhim Rao Ambedkar Open University (formerly known as Andhra Pradesh Open University)
State to Establish Central Agricultural University	Manipur
Sports University	Pune (1996)
Defence University	Binola, Gurgaon (Haryana)
Football Club	Mohun Bagan, Kolkata (1889)
Cricket Tournament	The Bombay Triangular
Formula One Team	Force India F1
General Post-Office of India	Madras GPO (1786)
State to appoint Lokayukta	Maharashtra (1971)
State to Implement the Panchayati Raj Institution	Rajasthan
First E-court	Ahmedabad
Court exclusively dedicated to women	Malda (WB)
Bank	Bank of Hindustan (1770)
Wax Statue at Madame Tussauds Museum	Mahatma Gandhi
Hospital on wheels	Jeevan Rekha
Chairman of UPSC	Ross Barker
The Prime Minister of India, who did not face the Parliament	Chaudhary Charan Singh
The Indian Member of the Viceroy's Executive Council	SP Sinha
Army General of India	MM lockhart
Ultra Mega Power Project (UMPP)	Mundra (Gujarat)
To implement Right to Recall	Mangrol Nagar (Rajasthan)
To implement Aadhar Project (UID)	Tembhali (2010), Maharashtra
To implement MGNREGA	Anantpur (Andhra Pradesh) (2006)
Language to get classical language status	Tamil (2004)

First in Male

First governor of Bengal	Lord Clive(1757-60)
Last governor of Bengal	Warren Hastings(1772-74)
The first British Governor General of Bengal	Lord Warren Hasting(1774-1885)
The first British Governor General of India	Lord William Bentinck(1833-1835)
The first British Viceroy of India	Lord Canning(1856-62)
The first Governor General of free India	Lord Mountbatten(1947-1948)
The first and the last Indian to be Governor General of free India	C. Rajgopalachari (1948-1950)
The first President of Indian Republic	Dr. Rajendra Prasad
The first Prime Minister of free India	Pt. Jawahar Lal Nehru
The first Indian to win Nobel Prize	Rabindranath Tagore
The first President of Indian National Congress	W.C. Banerjee
The first Muslim President of Indian National Congress	Badruddin Tayyabji
The first Muslim President of India	Dr. Zakir Hussain
The first man who introduced printing press in India	James Hicky
The first Indian to join the I.C.S	Satyendra Nath Tagore
India's first man in Space	Rakesh Sharma
The first Prime Minister of India who resigned without completing the full term	Morarji Desai
The first Indian Commander-in-Chief of India	General Cariappa
The first Chief of Army Staff	Gen. Maharaj Rajendra Singhji
The first Indian Member of the Viceroy's executive council	S.P.Sinha
The first President of India who died while in office	Dr. Zakhir Hussain
The first Muslim President of Indian Republic	Dr. Zakhir Hussain
The first Prime Minister of India who did not face the Parliament	Charan Singh
The first Field Marshal of India	S.H.F. Manekshaw
The first Indian to get Nobel Prize in Physics	C.V.Raman
The first Indian to receive Bharat Ratna award	Dr. Radhakrishnan
The first Indian to cross English Channel	Mihir Sen
The first Person to receive Jnanpith award	Sri Shankar Kurup
The first Speaker of the Lok Sabha	Ganesh Vasudeva Mavalankar
The first Vice-President of India	Dr. Radhakrishnan
The first Education Minister	Abdul Kalam Azad
The first Home minister of India	Sardar Vallabh Bhai Patel
The first Indian Air Chief Marshal	S. Mukherjee
The first Indian Naval Chief	Vice Admiral R.D. Katari
The first Judge of International Court of Justice	Dr. Nagendra Singh
The first person to reach Mt. Everest without oxygen	Sherpa Anga Dorjee
The first person to get Param Vir Chakra	Major Somnath Sharma
The first Chief Election Commissioner	Sukumar Sen
The first person to receive Magsaysay Award	Acharya Vinoba Bhave
The first person of Indian origin to receive Nobel Prize in Medicine	Hargovind Khurana
The first Chinese traveller to visit India	Fa-hein
The first person to receive Stalin Prize	Saifuddin Kitchlu
The first person to resign from the Central Cabinet	Shyama Prasad Mukherjee
The first person to receive Nobel Prize in Economics	Amartya Sen
The first Chief Justice of Supreme Court	Justice Hirala J. Kania
The first Indian Pilot	J.R.D. Tata (1929)

First in Female

The first lady to become Miss World	Rita Faria
The first woman judge in Supreme Court	Mrs. Meera Sahib Fatima Bibi
The first woman Ambassador	Miss C.B. Muthamma
The first woman Governor of a state in free India	Mrs Sarojini Naidu
The first woman Speaker of a State Assembly	Shanno Devi
The first woman Prime Minister	Mrs Indira Gandhi
The first woman Minister in a Government	Rajkumari Amrit Kaur
The first woman to climb Mount Everest	Bachhendri Pal
The first woman to climb Mount Everest twice	Santosh Yadav

The first woman President of Indian National Congress	Mrs Annie Besant
The first woman pilot in Indian Air Force	Harita Kaur Dayal
The first woman Graduates	Kadambini Ganguly and Chandramukhi Basu, 1883
The first woman Airline Pilot	Durga Banerjee
The first woman Honours Graduate	Kamini Roy, 1886
The first woman Olympic medal Winner	Karnam Malleswari, 2000
The first woman Asian Games Gold Medal Winner	Kamlijit Sandhu
The first woman Lawyer	Cornelia Sorabjee
The first woman President of United Nations General Assembly	Mrs Vijaya Laxmi Pandit
The first woman Chief Minister of an Indian State	Mrs Sucheta Kripalani
The first woman Chairman of Union Public Service Commission	Roze Millian Bethew
The first woman Director General of Police	Kanchan Chaudhary Bhattacharya
The first woman Judge	Anna Chandy (She became judge in a district court in 1937)
The first woman Cheif Justice of High Court	Mrs Leela Seth (Himachal Pradesh High Court)
The first woman Judge in Supreme Court of India	Kumari Justice M. Fathima Beevi
The first woman Lieutenant General	Puneeta Arora
The first woman Air Vice Marshal	P. Bandopadhyaya
The first woman chairperson of Indian Airlines	Sushma Chawla
The first woman IPS officer	Mrs. Kiran Bedi
The first and last Muslim woman ruler of India	Razia Sultan
The first woman to receive Ashoka Chakra	Nirja Bhanot
The first woman to receive Gyanpith Award	Ashapurna Devi
The first woman to cross English Channel	Aarti Saha
The first woman to receive Nobel Prize	Mother Teresa
The first woman to receive Bharat Ratna	Mrs Indira Gandhi
The first fighters pilots	Avani Chaturvedi

First in Others

First Wax statue of a Living Indian	Mahatma Gandhi at Madame Tussaud's in 1939
First Exclusive internet magazine	Bharat Samachar
First Miss India to participate in Miss Universe	Indrani Rehman
First Judge in International Court of Justice	Dr. Nagender Singh
First Graduate in Medicine	Soorjo Coomar Goodeve Chukerbutty
India's First University	Nalanda University
India's First Open University	Andhra Pradesh Open University
India's First Lok Sabha Member to be elected with a record maximum number of votes	P.V.Narasimha Rao
First Indian to reach Antarctica	Lt. Ram Charan
First British to Visit India	Hawkins
First Test tube baby of India	Indira (Baby Harsha)
First Post Office Opened in India	Kolkata(1727)

Superlatives
Structures

Highest Tower (Minaret) – Qutub Minar

Higher Gateway – Buland Darwaza at Fatehpur Sikri near Agra. Built by Akbar (53.5 m /175 ft High)

Highest Dam – Bhakra Dam

Highest Bridge – Chenab Bridge

Highest Airport- Leh Air Port in Ladakh (3256m/ 16080 ft high)

Highest Hydel Power Station- Rongtong Hydel Project in Kinnaur district of Himachal Pradesh.

Highest Mountain Peak- Kanchenjunga

Highest Road- Road at Khardungla in the Leh-Manali Sector

Highest Waterfall- Jog Waterfall, Karnataka

Largest Residence – Antilia Bhawan built by Mukesh Ambani

Largest Cinema Hall – Prasad Max, Hyderabad

Largest Museum – National Museum Delhi

Largest River Barrage – Farakka Barrage

Biggest Auditorium (Mumbai) – Sri Shanmukhanand Hall

Largest zoo – Arignar Anna Zoological Park

Largest Cave Temple – Ellora

Largest Gurudwara – Golden Temple, Amritsar

Largest Mosque – Jama Masjid, Delhi (built by Shah Jahan in 1644-58)

Largest Man-made Lake – Govind Sagar (Bhakra)

Largest Dome – Gol Gumbaz   (Karnataka)

Largest Cantilever Bridge – Howrah Bridge

Longest Railway Tunnel- Pir Panjal Railway Tunnel (11 km)

Longest Road Tunnel - 9.2 km long tunnel on Jammu-Srinagar National Highway

Largest Public Sector Bank- State Bank of India

Largest Botanical Garden - National Botanical Garden in Kolkata

Largest Church- Se Cathedral at Old Goa, 10 km from Panaji.

Largest Delta- Sunderbans (75,000 sq km) formed by the Ganga and Brahmaputra in West Bengal and Bangladesh

Largest Stupa- Kesariya Stupa in Bihar

Largest Library- National Library, Kolkata

Largest Planetarium- Birla Planetarium, Kolkata.

Largest Prison- Tihar Jail, Delhi

Largest Concentration of Scheduled Tribes- Madhya Pradesh

Largest Scheduled Caste- Community Santhal

Longest River Bridge – Bandra-Worli sea link which is 5.6 km.

Largest Corridor – Rameshwaram Temple Corridor

Largest irrigation Canal-Indira Gandhi Canal or Rajasthan Canal (959 km long)

Longest Dam-Hirakund Dam on Mahanadi river in Orissa (24.4 km long)

Longest Glacier-Siachen Glacier on the Indo-pakistan border (75.6 km long and 2.8 km wide)

Longest Railway Bridge Nehru Setu Bridge (4.62 km) long

Fastest Train-Shatabdi Express between New Delhi and Bhopal at a speed of 140 kmph

Tallest Light House – Jakhau, light hour, Gujarat

Tallest Statues – Statue of Jain Saint Gomateswara at Sravanabelagola in Karnataka

Tallest Chimber – Hanuman Swami statue with 135ft. tall.

Oldest Church- St. Thomas Church at Palayar in Trichur district in Kerala built in 52 AD.

Oldest Monastery- Buddhist Monastery, (situated at an altitude of 3,048 m /10,000 ft) at Tawang in Arunachal Pradesh.

Largest mall- Lulu Mall Kochi

Most Populous City- Mumbai

Natural

Longest River – Ganges

Largest Desert – Thar (Rajasthan)

Largest Lake – Wular Jammu and Kashmir

Largest Fresh Water Lake-Kolleru in Andhra Pradesh

Largest Cave- Amarnath (about 44 km from Pahalgam in Jammu and Kashmir)

Founders of Indian Institutions

Arya Samaj-Swami Dayanand Saraswathi

Athmiya Sabha-Raja Ram Mohan Roy

Brahma Samaj-Raja Ram Mohan Roy

Deccan Education Society-G.G.Agarkar, M.G.Ranade, V.G.Gibhongar

Dharma Sabha-Radhakanthadev

Indian Brahma Samaj-Keshav Chandra Sen

Manavadharma Sabha-Durgaram Manjaram

Prarthana Samaj-Athmaram Pandurang

Pune Sewa Sadan-Smt.Remabhai Ranade, G.K.Devdhar

Ramakrishna Mission-Swami Vivekananda

Sadharan Brahma Samaj-Shivananda Sashtri, Anand Mohan Bose

Servants of India Society-Gopalakrishna Gokhale

Sewa Sadan-Bahuramji M.Malabari

Sewa Samithi-H.N.Kunsru

Social Service League-N.M.Joshi

Thathwabodhini Sabha-Debendranatha Tagore

Theosophical Society-Madam H.P.Blavadski, Col.H.L.Olkott

Leader of Nations-Famous Father

America—George Washington

Bangladesh—Mujibur Rehuman

China—Sunyatsen

India—Gandhiji

Indonesia—Sukarno

Mouritius—Ramgoolam

Namibia—Sam Nujoma

Pakistan—Muhammad Ali Jinna

SriLanka—D.S.Senanayeke

Tanzania—Julius Nerera

Turkey—Musthafa Kamal

Founders of Towns in India

Agra- Sikkandar Lodhi

Ahmedabad - Ahmed Shah

Ajmer- Ajayaraja

Allahabad- Akbar

Culcutta- Job Charnok

Delhi- Anangpal

Fathepur Sikri - Akbar

Hisar- Ferozshah Tuglaq

Hyderabad - Quli Qutabshah

Jodhpur- Rao Jodha

Mahabalipuram - Narasimhawarman

Siri- Alaudden Khilji

Vijayanagaram - Hariharan 1

List of Revolutions Relating to Products

Blue Revolution - Fisheries Development

Brown Revolution - Leather Production

Grey Revolution - Housing Development

Green Revolution - Agriculture Production

Pink Revolution - Meat and Poultry Processing sector

Silver Revolution - Egg Production

White Revolution - Dairy Development

Yellow Revolution - Oil Seed Production

Properties Inscribed on the World Heritage List (37)

Culture (29)

Agra Fort (1983)

Ajanta Caves (1983)

Archaeological Site of Nalanda *Mahavihara* at Nalanda, Bihar (2016)

Buddhist Monuments at Sanchi (1989)

Champaner-Pavagadh Archaeological Park (2004)

Chhatrapati Shivaji Terminus (formerly Victoria Terminus) (2004)

Churches and Convents of Goa (1986)

Elephanta Caves (1987)

Ellora Caves (1983)

Fatehpur Sikri (1986)

Great Living Chola Temples (1987, 2004)

Group of Monuments at Hampi (1986)

Group of Monuments at Mahabalipuram (1984)

Group of Monuments at Pattadakal (1987)

Hill Forts of Rajasthan (2013)

Historic City of Ahmadabad (2017)

Humayun's Tomb, Delhi (1993)

Khajuraho Group of Monuments (1986)

Mahabodhi Temple Complex at Bodh Gaya (2002)

Mountain Railways of India (1999, 2005, 2008)

Qutb Minar and its Monuments, Delhi (1993)

Rani-ki-Vav (the Queen's Stepwell) at Patan, Gujarat (2014)

Red Fort Complex (2007)

Rock Shelters of Bhimbetka (2003)

Sun Temple, Konârak (1984)

Taj Mahal (1983)

The Architectural Work of Le Corbusier, an Outstanding Contribution to the Modern Movement (2016)

The Jantar Mantar, Jaipur (2010)

Victorian Gothic and Art Deco Ensembles of Mumbai (2018)

Natural (7)

Great Himalayan National Park Conservation Area (2014)

Kaziranga National Park (1985)

Keoladeo National Park (1985)

Manas Wildlife Sanctuary (1985)

Nanda Devi and Valley of Flowers National Parks (1988, 2005)

Sundarbans National Park (1987)

Western Ghats (2012)

Mixed (1)

Khangchendzonga National Park (2016)

Sites on the Tentative List (41)

A Tentative List is an inventory of those properties which each State Party intends to consider for nomination.

Temple at Bishnupur, West Bengal (1998)

Mattanchery Palace, Ernakulam, Kerala (1998)

Group of Monuments at Mandu, Madhya Pradesh (1998)

Ancient Buddhist Site, Sarnath, Varanasi, Uttar Pradesh (1998)

Sri Harimandir Sahib, Amristar, Punjab (2004)

River Island of Majuli in midstream of Brahmaputra River in Assam (2004)

Namdapha National Park (2006)

Wild Ass Sanctuary, Little Rann of Kutch (2006)

Neora Valley National Park (2009)

Desert National Park (2009)

Silk Road Sites in India (2010)

Santiniketan (2010)

The Qutb Shahi Monuments of Hyderabad Golconda Forst, Qutb Shahi Tombs, Charminar (2010)

Mughal Gardens in Kashmir (2010)

Delhi - A Heritage City (2010)

Monuments and Forts of the Deccan Sutanate (2014)

Cellular Jail, Andaman Islands (2014)

The Glorious Kakatiya Temples and Gateways (2014)

Iconic Saree Weaving Clusters of India (2014)

Dholavira: A Harappan City (2014)

Apatani Culture Landscape (2014)

Sri Ranganathaswamy Temple, Srirangam (2014)

Monuments of Srirangapatna Island Town (2014)

Chilika Lake (2014)

Padmanabhapuram Palace (2014)

Sacred Ensembles of the Hoysala (2014)

Sites of Saytagrah, India's non-violent freedom movement (2014)

Thembang Fortified Village (2014)

Narcondam Island (2014)

Moidams – the Mound-Burial system of the Ahom Dynasty (2014)

Ekamra Kshetra – The Temple City, Bhubaneswar (2014)

The Neolithic Settlement of Burzahom (2014)

Archaeological remains of a Harappa Port-Town, Lothal (2014)

Mountain Railways of India (Extension) (2014)

Chettinad, Village Clusters of the Tamil Merchants (2014)

Bahá'í House of Worship at New Delhi (2014)

Evolution of Temple Architecture – Aihole-Badami-Pattadakal (2015)

Jaipur city, Rajasthan India (2015)

Cold Desert Cultural Landscape of India (2015)

Sites along the Uttarapath, Badshahi Sadak, Sadak-e-Azam, Grand Trunk Road (2015)

Keibul Lamjao conservation Area (2016)

Sobriquets

A sobriquet is a nickname, Occasionally assumed and often given by anther. It is usually a familiar name. This significant distinctive is a ample familiarity that the sobriquet can become more familiar than the original name.

Person	Primary Names
Anna	C N Annadurai
Badshah Khan/ Frontier Gandhi	Abdul Ghaffar Khan
Buddha	Siddhartha Gautama
Chacha	Jawaharlal Nehru
Deenabandhu	C F Andrews
Deshbandhu	C. R. Das
Father of the Nation	Mohandas Karamchand Gandhi
Frontier Gandhi	Abdul Gaffar Khan
Grand Old Man of India	Dadabhai Naoroji
Gurudev	Rabindranath Tagore
Guruji	M S Gohlwalkar
Kaviguru	Rabindranath Tagore
Lokmanya	Bal Gangadhar Tilak
Loknayak	Jayaprakash Narayan
Mahatma Gandhi	Mohandas K. Gandhi
Man of Peace	Lal Bahadur Shastri
Manitas de Plate	Flamenco guitarist Ricardo Baliardo
Netaji	Subhash Chandra Bose
Nightingale of India	Sarojini Naidu
Panditji	Jawaharlal Nehru

Punjab kesari	Lala Lajpat Rai
Rajaji	C Rajagopalachari
Saint of the Gutters	Mother Teresa
Father of the Nation	Mohandas Karamchand Gandhi
Haryana Hurricane	Kapil Dev
Prince of Kolkata	Saurav Ganguly

Places	Primary Names
Bengal's Sorrow	Damodar Rever, India
Blue Mountain	Niligiri Hills, India
City of Golden Temple	Amritsar, India
City of Palaces	Kolkata, India
Diamond City in India	Surat, Gujarat
Garden City of India	Bengaluru
Garden of India	Kashmir
Gateway of India	Mumbai
God's Own Country	Kerala
Land of Five Rivers	Punjab, India
Pink City	Jaipur, India
Queen of Arabian Sea	Kochi, India
Spice Garden of India	Kerala
The City of Joy	Kolkata, India
The City of Palaces	Kolkata, India
Venice of East	Alleppey, India
Queen of Arabian Sea	Kochi, India
Garden City of India	Bangalore
Blue Mountains	Niligiri Hills, India

River Side Cities of India	
City	River
Hyderabad	Musi
Ahmedabad	Sabarmati
Badrinath	Alaknanda
Cuttack	Mahanadi
Kurnool	Tungabhadra
Ujjain	Shipra
Panchmarhi	Denwa
Leh	Indus
Dibrugarh	Brahmaputra
Ferozpur	Sutlej
Srinagar	Jhelum
Mandi	Beas
Hamirpur	Yamuna
Mysore	Cauvery

Ratlam	Chambal
Jabalpur	Narmada
Jamshedpur	Subarnarekha
Kota	Chambal
Ludhiana	Sutlej
Pandharpur	Bhima
Khandwa	Narmada
Nasik	Godavari
Surat	Tapi
VijayawadA	Krishna
Moradabad	Ramganga
Jaunpur	Gomti
Tiruchirapalli	Cauvery
Madurai	Vaigai
Gorakhpur	Rapti
Koshambi	Yamuna
Ayodhya	Saryu
Vrindavan	Yamuna
Kolhapur	Panchganga
Rajkot	Aji
Vadodara	Vishwamitra
Bengaluru	Vrishabhavathi
Mangalore	Netravati
Shimoga	Tunga
Gwalior	Chambal
Malegaon	Girna
Rourkela	Brahmani
Pune	Mula-Mutha
Chennai	Adyar
Patna	Ganges

Famous Establishments and their Founders

Established	Founder
Kashi Hindu University	Pandit Madan Mohan Malviya
Shanti Niketan	Rabindranath Tagore
Swaraj Party	CR Das and Motilal Nehru
Auroville Ashram	Aurobindo Ghosh
Indian Association	Surendranath Banerjee
Theosophical Society	Madem Blavethshki
Asiatic Society	William Jones
Indian National Congress	AO Hume
Ramakrishna Mission	Swami Vivekananda
Sikh Dharam	Guru Nanak
Prarthana Samaj	Keshav Chandra Sen
Nyay Darshan	Gautam
Samkhya Darshan	Kapil
Yog Darshan	Patanjali
Khalsha Panth	Guru Gobind Singh
Anand Van	Baba Amte
Chipko Movement	Sunder Lal Bahuguna
Widow Remarriage	Ishwar Chandra Vidhyasagar
Arya Samaj	Swami Dayanand
Paunar Ashram Bhoodan Movement	Aacharya Vinoba Bhave
Sadakat Ashram	Dr Rajendra Prasad
Sabarmati Ashram	Mahatma Gandhi
Nirmal Hriday	Mother Teresa
Forward Bloc	Subhash Chandra Bose
Anand Milk Cooperative	VJ Kurien
Vikram Samvat	Chandra Gupta Vikramaditya
Servants of Indian Society	Gopal Krishna Gokhale
Khudali khidmatgar	Khan Abdul Gaffar Khan
Home Rule League	Annie Besant/Bal Gangadhar Tilak
Brahmo Samaj	Raja Ram Mohan Roy
Gadar Party	Lala Hardayal

India's International Airports

Airport	City/State
Indira Gandhi International Airport	New Delhi
Jaipur International Airport	Jaipur, Rajasthan
Srinagar Airport (Gugu Ramdas)	Srinagar
Amritsar International Airport (Guru Ramdas)	Amritsar, Punjab
Netaji Subhash Chandra Bose International Airport	Kolkata, Paschim Banga
Dr Bhimrao Ambedkar International Airport	Nagpur, Maharashtra
Rajiv Gandhi International Airport	Hyderabad, Andhra Pradesh
Goa International Airport (Vasco-de-Gama)	Dabolim, Goa

Kempegowda International Airport	Bengaluru, Karnataka
Veer Savarkar International Airport	Port Blair, Andaman and Nicobar Island
Sardar Vallabhbhai Patel International Airport	Ahmedabad, Gujarat
Lokpriya Gopinath Bordoloi International Airport	Guwahati, Asom
Meenambakkam International Airport (Kamraj)	Mumbai, Maharashtra
Chhatrapati Shivaji International Airport (Santacruz)	Chennai, Tamil Nadu
Calicut International Airport	Calicut, Kerala
Cochin International Airport (Nedumbassery)	Cochin, Kerala
Thiruvananthapuram International Airport	Thiruvananthapuram, Kerala
Chaudhary Charan Singh International Airport (Amausi)	Lucknow, Uttar Pradesh
Lal Bahadur Shastri Airport	Varanasi, Uttar Pradesh
Mangalore Airport (Bajpe)	Mangalore, Karnataka
Tiruchirapalli International Airport	Tiruchirapalli
Coimbatore International Airport	Coimbatore, Tamil Nadu

Exercise -1

1. National Institute of Oceanography is located in :
   - (a) Calcutta
   - (b) Chennai
   - (c) Mangalore
   - (d) Panaji

2. At Which one of the following places , East-West Corridor Connecting Silchar and Porbandar and North -south Corridor Connecting Srinagar and Kanyakumari Intersect Each other?
   - (a) Jhansi
   - (b) Agra
   - (c) Jabalpur
   - (d) Nagpur

3. In which State is the Buddhist site Tabo Monastery located?
   - (a) Arunachal Pradesh
   - (b) Himachal Pradesh
   - (c) Sikkim
   - (d) Uttarakhand

4. Where is the headquarters of the Reserve Bank of India?
   - (a) Mumbai
   - (b) Delhi
   - (c) Chennai
   - (d) Kolkatta

5. Which one of the following pairs is not correctly matched?
   - (a) Indira Gandhi Rashtriya Manav Sangrahalaya : Bhopal
   - (b) Ramakrishna Mission Institute of Culture : Kolkata
   - (c) Khuda Bakhsh Oriental Public Library : Lucknow
   - (d) Anthropological Survey of India (Headquarters) : Kolkata

6. Jharkhand does not share boundary with –
   - (a) West Bengal
   - (b) Odisha
   - (c) Chhattisgarh
   - (d) Madhya Pradesh

7. Bhimbetka which was been conferred the status of World Heritage Site is situated in:
   - (a) Odisha
   - (b) Rajasthan
   - (c) Madhya Pradesh
   - (d) Bihar

8. The Radcliffe line is a boundary between
   - (a) India and Pakistan
   - (b) India and China
   - (c) India and Myanmar
   - (d) India and Afghanistan

9. Who was the first Indian woman to swim across the English Channel?
   - (a) Shanta Rangaswami
   - (b) Arati Saha
   - (c) Santosh Yadav
   - (d) Kamaljit Sandhu

10. Gol Gumbaz, the largest dome in India is located in the state of –
    - (a) Karnataka
    - (b) Maharashtra
    - (c) Madhya Pradesh
    - (d) Bihar

11. Which of the following is not correctly matched with regard to the Indians who have won the Nobel Prize (in the mentioned years)?
    - (a) Rabindranath Tagore - 1913
    - (b) C V Raman - 1930
    - (c) Hargobind Khorana - 1968
    - (d) Mother Teresa - 1978

12. The oldest church (St. Thomas Church) in India is located in the state of
    - (a) Goa
    - (b) Kerala
    - (c) West Bengal
    - (d) Assam

13. Compulsory Education Act will ensure education to children upto the age of:
    - (a) 10 yr
    - (b) 14 yr
    - (c) 8 yr
    - (d) 17 yr

14. Which one of the following is not correctly matched?
    - (a) White Revolution – Dairy
    - (b) Green Revolution – Agriculture
    - (c) Blue Revolution – Fishery
    - (d) Red Revolution – Wool

15. India is **not** a member of which one of the following?
    - (a) Commonwealth of Independent States
    - (b) South Asian Association for Regional Cooperation
    - (c) South Asian Free Trade Agreement
    - (d) World Trade Organization

16. The National Commission for Protection of Child Rights (NCPCR) is going to start a program to mobilise community youth to protect child rights in the Naxal-affected areas. The program has been named as
    - (a) Sakha-Bandhu scheme
    - (b) Bal Bandhu scheme
    - (c) Bal Uttaradhikari scheme
    - (d) Bhavishya Ujjwal scheme

17. 'Eco mark' is given to the Indian products that are:
    - (a) pure and unadulterated
    - (b) rich in proteins
    - (c) environment friendly
    - (d) economically viable

18. Which one of the following is not a Central University?
    - (a) Pondicherry
    - (b) Maulana Azad National Urdu University, Hyderabad
    - (c) Vishva Bharti, Shanti Niketan
    - (d) University of Madras, (Chennai)

19. National Institute of Nutrition is located at
    - (a) Chennai
    - (b) Bangalore
    - (c) New Delhi
    - (d) Hyderabad

20. National Library, the largest in India is located at
    - (a) Chennai
    - (b) Mumbai
    - (c) Delhi
    - (d) Kolkata

21. Which among the following cities of India will have mid-day Sun exactly overhead only once a year?
    (a) Delhi and Chennai
    (b) Srinagar and Darjeeling
    (c) Hyderabad and Kohima
    (d) Nagpur and Kolkata

22. Which one among the following cities is called the 'zero-mile centre' of India?
    (a) Kanpur
    (b) Allahabad
    (c) Nagpur
    (d) New Delhi

23. Which one of the following statements is NOT correct?
    (a) The Press Council of India is an autonomous quasi-judicial body established under an Act of Parliament
    (b) The Press Information Bureau provides accreditation to media person so as to have easy access to information from government sources
    (c) Among all the states of India, Maharashtra publishes the largest number of newspapers
    (d) Press Trust of India is the largest news agency in the country

24. Survey of India is under the Ministry of
    (a) Defence
    (b) Environmental & Forests
    (c) Home Affairs
    (d) Science & Technology

25. Norman Ernest Borlaug who is regarded as the father of the Green Revolution in India is from which country?
    (a) United States of America
    (b) Mexico
    (c) Australia
    (d) New Zealand

Exercise -2

Statement Based MCQ

1. As a policy to boost the agricultural sector, the GOI has taken special measures over time. Which of the following are **not** a measure with a direct impact on the agricultural sector?
    1. Setting up of a National Food Processing Bank
    2. Opening irrigation, sanitation and water projects for Private Participation.
    3. Efforts to reduce fiscal deficit to 5.5 per cent level of GDP
    (a) 1 only
    (b) 2 only
    (c) 3 only
    (d) 1 and 2

2. Workers from poor states migrate to high wage states as agricultural labour. What are reason behind their migration?
    1. Lack of irrigation facilities, low productivity of land and uncertain monsoon.
    2. Non-availability of fertilizers and other inputs at subsidized rates.
    3. Single crop cultivation.
    (a) 1 and 2
    (b) 2 only
    (c) 3 only
    (d) All the three

3. Consider the following statements?
    1. Hariyali is a watershed development project sponsored by the Central Government.
    2. Hariyali also aims at enabling the urban population to conserve rain water.
    Which of the statements gtiven above is/are correct ?
    (a) 1 only
    (b) 2 only
    (c) Both 1 and 2
    (d) Neither 1 nor 2

4. At which of the following places, Kumbh Mela is held?
    1. Nasik
    2. Hardwar
    3. Prayag
    4. Ujjain
    (a) 1 and 2
    (b) 2, 3 and 4
    (c) 2 and 4
    (d) 1, 2, 3 and 4

5. Consider the following sites/monuments:
    1. Champaner-Pavagadh Archaeological Park
    2. Chhatrapati Shivaji Railway Station, Mumbai
    3. Mamallapuram
    4. Sun Temple (Konark Temple)
    Which of the above are included in the World Heritage List of UNESCO?
    (a) 1, 2 and 3
    (b) 1, 3 and 4
    (c) 2 and 4
    (d) 1, 2, 3 and 4

6. In which of the following International Organisations is India a member?
    1. Indian Ocean Rim Association for Regional Cooperation.
    2. Organisation for Economic Cooperation and Development.
    Select the correct answer using the codes given below
    (a) 1 only
    (b) 2 only
    (c) Both 1 and 2
    (d) Neither 1 nor 2

7. Which among the following is/are example/examples of youth unrest in India?
    1. Naxalite movement
    2. Anti-foreigners movement in Asom
    3. Anti-Mandal Commission agitation

Select the correct answer using the code given below
(a) 1, 2 and 3   (b) 2 and 3
(c) 2 only   (d) 3 only

8. Consider the following statements UNESCO's World Heritage mission is to
   1. take over the management, maintenance and preservation of World Heritage sites.
   2. encourage state parties to the Convention concerning the Protection of the World Cultural and Natural Heritage to nominate sites within their national territory for inclusion on the World Heritage List.
   3. provide emergency assistance for World Heritage sites in immediate danger.
   Which of the statements given above are correct?
   (a) 1, 2 and 3   (b) 1 and 3
   (c) 1 and 2   (d) 2 and 3

9. Who among the following recently became the first woman pilot in Indian Navy?
   (a) Astha Segal   (b) Roopa A
   (c) Sakthi Maya S   (d) Shubhangi Swaroop

Matching Based MCQ

DIRECTIONS (Qs. 10 to 15) : Match List-I with List-II and select the correct answer using the codes given below the lists.

10.
List-I (Centre of Handicrafts)	List-II (State)
(A) Mon	(1) Arunachal Pradesh
(B) Nalbari	(2) Assam
(C) Pasighat	(3) Meghalaya
(D) Tura	(4) Nagaland

(a) A – 4; B – 2; C – 1; D – 3
(b) A – 1; B – 3; C – 4; D – 2
(c) A – 4; B – 3; C – 1; D – 2
(d) A – 1; B – 2; C – 4; D – 3

11.
List-I	List-II
(A) Rashtriya Mahila Kosh	(1) Empowerment of women
(B) Mahila Samridhi Yojana	(2) Education for women's equality
(C) Indira Mahila Yojana	(3) Promotion of savings among rural women
(D) Mahila Samakhya Programme	(4) Meeting credit needs of the poor women

(a) A – 3; B – 2; C – 1; D – 4
(b) A – 1; B – 3; C – 4; D – 2
(c) A – 4; B – 3; C – 2; D – 1
(d) A – 4; B – 1; C – 2; D – 3

12.
List-I (Institute)	List-II (Location)
(A) Central Institute of Higher Tibetan Studies	(1) Hyderabad
(B) Indira Gandhi Institute of Development Research	(2) Mumbai
(C) National Institute of Mental Health and Neuro-sciences	(3) Bangalore
(D) Central Institute of English and Foreign Languages	(4) Dharamshala
	(5) Varanasi

(a) A – 5; B – 3; C – 4; D – 1
(b) A – 5; B – 2; C – 3; D – 1
(c) A – 3; B – 2; C – 4; D – 5
(d) A – 4; B – 5; C – 1; D – 2

13.
List-I (Hill Station)	List-II (Location in Map)
(A) Dharamsala	
(B) Almora	
(C) Naintal	
(D) Darjeeling	

(a) A – 1; B – 2; C – 3; D – 4
(b) A – 1; B – 3; C – 2; D – 4
(c) A – 2; B – 1; C – 4; D – 3
(d) A – 2; B – 4; C – 1; D – 3

14. Match the following

List I (City)	List II (Stadium)
A. Bengaluruw	1. Sawai Mansingh
B. Chennai	2. Sardar Patel
c. Motera	3. Chinnaswami
D. Jaipur	4. Chidambaram

Codes
	A	B	C	D
(a)	1	2	3	4
(b)	3	4	2	1
(c)	1	3	2	4
(d)	3	2	4	1

15. Match List I with List II and select the correct answer using the code given below the Lists :

List-I (World Heritage Site)	List-II (State)
A. Brihadisvara Temple	1. Maharashtra
B. Ellora Caves	2. Karnataka
C. Hampi	3. Tamil Nadu
D. Mahabodhi Temple	4. Bihar

Code :
	A	B	C	D
(a)	4	1	2	3
(b)	4	2	1	3
(c)	3	2	1	4
(d)	3	1	2	4

Hints and Explanations

1. (d)   2. (d)   3. (b)   4. (a)   5. (c)   6. (d)

7. (c)   8. (a)   9. (b)   10. (a)   11. (d)   12. (b)

13. (b)   14. (d)

15. (a) The Commonwealth of Independent States is the Internatinoal Organization, or alliance.

16. (b)   17. (c)   18. (d)   19. (d)   20. (d)   21. (d)

22. (c)   23. (c)   24. (d)   25. (a)

1. (c)   2. (d)   3. (a)   4. (d)   5. (d)

6. (a) Indian Ocean Rim Association for Regional Co-operation is an international organization with 18 member states. It organization for Economic co-operation and Development (OECD) is an international economic organization of 34 Countries foundes in 1961. India is one of the Candidate of OECD, not a member.

7. (d) Mandal Commission protests of 1990 were against giving government jobs to certain casters are basis of birth rather than merits of candidate. It led to interspersed youth unrest in India.

8. (d) UNESCO's World Heritage mission is to-

·Encourage countries to sign the World Heritage Convention; nominate sites within their national territory; establish management plans and set up reporting systems on the state of conservation of their World Heritage Sites;

Help national governments to safeguard World Heritage properties by providing technical assistance and professional training;

Provide emergency assistance for the World Heritage sites in immediate danger;

Carry out public awareness activities for World Heritage conversation;

Support participation of the local population in the preservation of their cultural and natural heritage;

Encourage international cooperation in the conservation of world's cultural and natural heritage.

9. (d)   10. (a)   11. (c)

12. (b)
- Central institute of Higher Tibetan studies is present at Varanasi of Uttarpradesh in the year 1967.
- Indira Gandhi Institute of Development Research is located in Mumbai of Maharastra.
- National Institute of Mental Health and Neurosciences is located in Banglore and
- Central institute of English and foreign languages is located in Hyderabad of Andhra Pradesh.

13. (a)

14. (b)

Bengluru	-	Chinnaswami
Chennai	-	Chidambaran
Motera	-	Sardar Patel
Jaipur	-	Sawai Mansingh

15. (d) Brihadiswara temple is located at Tanjore in Tamil Nadu. Ellora Caves are situated in the district of Aurangabad in Maharashtra. Hampi is a historical city in Karnataka. Mahabodhi Temple is located at Gaya district of Bihar.

ART AND CULTURE

4
Chapter

Culture plays an important role in the development of any nation. It represents a set of shared attitudes, values, goals and practices. Culture and creativity manifest themselves in almost all economic, social and other activities. A country as diverse as India is symbolized by the plurality of its culture.

India has one of the world's largest collections of songs, music, dance, theatre, folk traditions, performing arts, rites and rituals, paintings and writings that are known, as the 'Intangible Cultural Heritage' (ICH) of humanity.

Indian Painting

Painting as an art form has flourished in India from very early periods as is evident from literary sources and from the remnants that have been discovered. Numerous paintings or *Patas* are mentioned in the *Mudrakshaka*. There are isolated paintings like the Yama–pata; isolated framed drawings like *Cauka–patas* and the *Dighala–patas* or long scroll of paintings, representing a complete legend. In another book *Vishnudharmottara*, the section *Chitrasutra* describes the basic tenets of painting. The six limbs of painting are: variety of form, proportion, infusion of emotions, creation of luster and iridescence, portrayal of likeness and colour mixing to produce the effect of modelling.

Ancient Indian Paintings

- Ancient Indian art has seen the rise of the Bengal School of art in 1930s pursued by a lot of forms of experimentations in European and Indian styles. With the development of the economy the forms and styles of art also undergo many changes.
- Monuments of the exceptional value are Bhimbetka Rock Shelters, here, more than 500smaller rocks and caves contains thousands of paintings. Some of the oldest paintings here are more than 15000 years old, and in some cases it is 30,000 years old.
- The prehistoric art from is spread all over India from snow covered Himalayas to south of Tamil Nadu.

- Indian Cave Paintings are regarded as the earliest evidences of Indian paintings which are made on cave walls and palaces while miniature paintings are small-sized colourful, intricate handmade illumination.
- This starts from prehistoric cave painting of Bhimbetka and flourishes through cave paintings of Ajanta caves, Ellora caves and Bagh.

Medieval Indian Paintings

- During the Medieval period, India observed important development in the field of art of painting. The Medieval India is the part of Indian history between the 8th century and the 18th century A.D.
- The Persian tradition of miniature painting was also first introduced by the local rulers. It was during Akbar's supremacy that the painting was organized by a grand concern which brought jointly Hindu and Muslim painters and artisans from diverse parts of India, particularly, from regions like Gujarat and Malwa where manuscripts and miniature paintings had developed.

Mughal Paintings mainly describes Indo-Islamic design of painting and flourished in the ateliers of Mughal emperors including Akbar, Jahangir and Shah Jahan. Tanjore Paintingsare classical South Indian form of painting which evolved in the village of Thanjavur.

Rajasthani paintings are miniature paintings of the finest quality, which are made both on paper and on large pieces of cloth. A number of famous schools of painting are Mewar, Hadoti, Marwar, Kishangarh, Alwar and Dhundhar. It is also known as Rajput Paintings and has clear influence of Mughal paintings though it quite unique in its own way. Pahari Painting is the miniature painting evolved in the hilly states of Himachal Pradesh, Punjab, Jammu and Kashmir during the period of Rajputs. These paintings have beautiful scenes of Himalaya as the backdrop.

Modern Indian Paintings

Glass Painting in India is a new concept and is extremely wonderful for its clarity and richness of colours. Patachitra flourished in the state of Odisha and is made on cloth with extremely vivid colours and mythology-based subject. Kalighat pots are another form, which are made on earthen pot or cloth. These are mainly used as wall hangings. Marble Painting is also a type of modern Indian painting which is made on exquisite marble stones. Marble paintings are mainly used for decorative purpose, especially on tabletop, furniture and flower vases. The Indian artists adopted Indian Oil painting as a unique technique of art and Raja Ravi Verma was considered to be the pioneer who made this new medium popular in India.

The tradition of painting has been carried on in the Indian subcontinent since the ancient times. Standing as a testimony to this fact are the exquisite murals of Ajanta and Ellora, Buddhist palm leaf manuscripts, Mughal and Kangra schools of miniature Indian paintings, etc. In fact records have been found that indicate the usage of paintings for decorating the doorways, guest rooms, etc. Some traditional Indian paintings, like those of Ajanta, Bagh and Sittanvasal, depict a love for nature and its forces.

With time, Indian classical paintings evolved to become a sort of blend of the various traditions influencing them. Even the folk painting of India has become quite popular amongst art lovers, both at the national as well as the international level. Most of the folk paintings reflect a heavy influence of the local customs and traditions. In the following lines, we have provided information on the famous paintings of India.

Famous Indian Paintings

Patachitra

- The patachitra of Orissa depicts stories from the famous poem, the Geet Govind, and devotional stanzas by ancient poets, singers and writers.
- Stories are drawn in sections on palm leaf as etchings or as paintings on paper and silk.
- Modern developments have encouraged them to paint on wooden boxes, picture frames etc. for contemporary use.
- Paintings are based on Hindu Mythology and specially inspired by Jagannath and Vaishnava cult.
- Paintings are done on small strips of cotton cloth. The canvas is prepared by coating the cloth with a mixture of chalk and gum made from tamarind seeds. Women traditionally make this gum and application.
- The master hand, mostly the male member, draws the initial line and gives the final finishing.
- The painting is held over a fire-place so that the back of the painting is exposed to heat. On the surface of the painting fine lacquer is applied.
- Natural colours are used.
- Tala Pattachitra is one variant of this form, drawn on palm leaf.

Bengal Painting

- The Bengal School of Art was an influential style of art that flourished in India during the British Raj in the early 20th Century.
- It was associated with Indian nationalism, but was also supported and promoted by many British art administrators.
- The Bengal School's influence in India declined with the spread of modernist ideas in the 1920s.
- The indigenous art from belongs to Bengal and very interestingly it depicts spoof on retrograde social practices, thus attempting to highlight them for change.
- Artists use dye that are made of spices, earth, soot etc. and particularly red, indigo, green , black and ochre colours are seen widely in such painting.

Madhubani Painting

- Madhubani painting originated in a small village known as Maithili of Bihar. Initially, the women folk of the village drew the paintings on the walls of their home, as an illustration of their thoughts, hopes and dreams.
- The brush used for Madhubani paintings of Bihar was made of cotton, wrapped around a bamboo stick.
- The artists prepare the colours that are used for the paintings. Black color is made by adding soot to cow dung; yellow from combining turmeric (or pollen or lime) with the milk of banyan leaves; blue from indigo; red from the kusam flower juice or red sandalwood; green from the leaves of the wood apple tree; white from rice powder and orange from palasha flower.
- No space is left empty: gaps are filled in with paintings of flowers, animals, birds and geometric designs.
- Artists use natural dyes and pigment extracted from leaves, herbs and flowers.

Miniature Painting

- Miniature paintings are handmade paintings, which are quite colourful, but small in size.
- The peculiarity of these paintings is the intricate and delicate brush work, which lends them a unique identity.
- The Palas of Bengal were the pioneers of miniature painting in India.
- The highlight of these paintings is the intricate and delicate brushwork, which lends them a unique identity.
- The colours are handmade, from minerals, vegetables, precious stones, indigo, conch shells, pure gold and silver.
- The most common theme of the Miniature painting of India comprises of the Ragas i.e., the musical codes of Indian classical music. There were a number of miniature schools in the country, including those of Mughals, Rajputs and the Deccan.
- The Ragamala paintings also belong to this school, as does the Company painting produced for British clients under the British Raj.

Tanjore Painting

- Tanjore Painting is one of the most popular forms of classical South Indian painting.
- It is the native art form of Thanjavur (also known as Tanjore) city of Tamil Nadu. The dense composition, surface richness and vibrant colors of Thanjavur Paintings distinguish them from the other types of paintings. Then, there are embellishments of semi-precious stones, pearls and glass pieces that further add to their appeal.
- The relief work gives them a three dimensional effect. Tanjore Painting of India originated during the 16th century, under the reign of the Cholas.
- Vishnu, Shiva & Krishna favorite of artist
- Made for ritual & worship and not for display
- Paintings were made on Jack wood posted with unbleached cloth brilliant colour schemes, jewellery with stones and copper glasses & remarkable gold leaf work to which a mixture of list, chalk, gum honey are applied in layers on a sketch of the icon.
- Background always painted Red/Green.
- Baby Krishna is white but as an adult blue.
- Outlines of figures are in a dark reddish brown.
- Belong to Maratha Period them mythological.

Kalamkari Painting

- Kalamkari or "pen craft" of Srikalahasti, is executed with a kalam or pen, used for free hand drawing of the subject and filling in the colours, entirely by hand. Paintings are usually hand-painted or block-printed on cotton textile.
- This style grew around temples and had a distinctly religious identity - scrolls, temple hangings, deities and scenes from the great Hindu epics.
- The Machilipatnam style tends to have more block printing. However, both use only vegetable colours.
- These paintings are made in Andhra Pradesh.
- It is hand painted as well as block printing with vegetable dyes applied on cloth.
- Vegetable dyes are used for colour in the Kalam Kari work.
- A small place Sri-Kalahasti is the best known centre of Kalamkari art.
- This art is mainly related to decorating temple interiors with painted cloth panels, which was developed in the fifteenth century under the patronage of Vijaynagar rulers.
- Every scene is surrounded by floral decorative patterns.
- These paintings are made on cloth. They are very durable and flexible in size and made according to theme.
- The artists use a bamboo or date palm stick pointed at one end with a bundle of fine hair attached to the other end to serve as brush or pen.
- The kalamkari dyes are obtained by extracting colours from plant roots, leaves, along with salts of iron, tin, copper, alum etc.

Warli Paintings

- Warli folk art has its origins in Maharashtra.
- It is widely practised in the Northern Sahyadri region by the Adivasis (tribes).
- Elements of nature are the focal points of Warli folk paintings. A mixture of rice paste, gum and water is used as paint by the warlis. A bamboo stick is used as the brush.
- It is vivid expression of daily & social events of Warli tribe, used by then to embellish the walls of village houses. Women are mainly engaged don't depict mythological character/images of deities but depict social life.
- It uses very shapes: a circle, a triangle and a square. The circle represents the sun and the moon, the triangle derived from mountains and pointed trees, the square indicates a sacred enclosure or a piece of land.
- Painted on austre mud base using one color. In this sax to see straight line.
- Human and animal bodies are represented by two triangles joined at the tip; the upper triangle depicts the trunk and the lower triangle the pelvis. Their precarious equilibrium symbolizes the balance of the universe.

Gond Art

- Gond art encompasses life as the central theme of art. It is practised by "Gondi" tribe of Central India.
- The art form celebrates life i.e., hills, streams, animals, birds etc. The tribes traditionally painted on the mud walls of their house.
- Produced by the Santhals in India.
- Mainly found in Gond tribe of the Godavari belt.
- Highly sophisticated and abstract form of Art works.

Basholi Paintings

- Basholi is a small town in Kathua district of Jammu and Kashmir. It was founded by Raja Bhupat Pal in circa 1635 and is renowned for a special and vibrant style of Pahari miniature paintings.
- Basholi Paintings are considered the first school of Pahari paintings. This style evolved into the much prolific Kangra paintings school by mid-eighteenth century. It is marked by bold stokes of primary colours and deep set facial patterns.
- Basholi Paintings Geometrical patterns, bright colors and glossy enamel characterize Basohli paintings.
- The style developed under the patronage of Raja Kripal Pal and was truly unconventional, rich and highly vigorous.
- It is endowed with intricate geometrical designs, monochrome background, gloss finishes and dramatic compositions with imposing figures with decorative attire, a special focus on eyes, use of beetles wings for showing diamonds in ornaments, narrow sky and red border.
- The wondrous paintings have also given shape to many illustrations of Hindu Gods viz. Radha-Krishna; Madhava-Malti and even themes from Bhagvata Purana.

Bundi Paintings

- The Bundi style of painting is very close to the Mewar style, but the former excels the latter in quality.
- Bundi School Concentrated on court scheme, many scenes of nobles, lovers & ladies in palaces were produced.
- The peculiar characteristics of the Bundi painting are the rich and glowing colors, the rising sun in golden colour, crimson-red horizon, overlapping and semi-naturalistic trees.
- The Mughal influence is visible in the refined drawing of the faces and an element of naturalism in the treatment of the trees. The text is written in black against yellow background on the top.
- Prominent features → Rich and glowing colours, the rising sun in golden colour, crimson-red horizon, border in brilliant red colour (in Rasikpriya series)
- Notable examples → Bhairavi Ragini (Allahabad Museum), illustrated manuscript of the Bhagawata Purana (Kota Museum) & a series of the Rasikapriya (National Museum, Delhi)

Kalighat Painting

- Patua painters from rural Bengal came and settled in Kalighat to make images of gods and goddesses in the early 19th century
- They evolved a quick method of painting on mill-made paper
- Used brush and ink from the lampblack
- Has five distinctive styles – Bharni, Katchni, Tantrik, Godna and Gobar
- Bharni, Kachni and Tantrik style were mainly done Brahman & Kayashth women, who are upper caste women in India and Nepal
- Godna & Gobar style is done by the Dalit & Dushadh communities
- These paintings on paper made with water colours comprise clear sweeping line drawings using bright colours and a clear background. Subjects are images of Kali, Lakshmi, Krishna, Ganesha, Shiva, and other gods and goddesses.
- This painting form has its roots in the culture upheavds of 19th century colonial Bengal.
- Kalighat paintings became the best mirror of this cultural and aesthetic shift.

Kangra Painting

- The Kangra style is developed out of the Guler style & possesses its main characteristics, like the delicacy of drawing & naturalism
- The Kangra style continued to flourish at various places namely Kangra, Guler, Basohli, Chamba, Jammu, Nurpur and Garhwal etc.
- However, Named as Kangra style as they are identical in style to the portraits of Raja Sansar Chand of Kangra
- In these paintings, the faces of women in profile have the nose almost in line with the forehead, the eyes are long & narrow, & chin is sharp.
- There is, however, no modelling of figures and hair is treated as a flat mass.
- Paintings of the Kangra style are attributed mainly to the Nainsukh family

Kishangarh (Banithani) Painting

- Offshoot of Jodhpur school, rose around the personality of Raja Samant Singh (1748-64)
- Popular subject loves of 'Radha & Krishna'
- Nihalchand developed 'Mannerist' style which exaggerated the slender curves and almond eyes of his figures the facial type, though idealized, is extremely lyrical in the beauty contest.
- The painting is marked by delicate drawing, fine modelling of the human figures and cows and the broad vista of landscape showing a stream, rows of overlapping trees, and architecture.
- The artist has displayed a masterly skill in the grouping of many figures in the miniature. The painting has a golden inner border.
- Distinguished by its individualistic facial type and its religious intensity
- Men and women are drawn with pointed noses and chins, deeply curved eyes, and serpentine locks of hair
- Their action is frequently shown to occur in large panoramic landscapes

Rajput Painting

- The art of the independent Hindu feudal states in India
- Unlike Mughal paintings which were contemporary in style, Rajput paintings were traditional & romantic
- Rajput painting is further divided into Rajasthani painting and Pahari painting (art of the Himalayan kingdoms)

Mysore Painting

- Mysore Painting is a form of classical South Indian painting, which evolved in the Mysore city of Karnataka.
- During that time, Mysore was under the reign of the Wodeyars and it was under their patronage that this school of painting reached its zenith.
- Quite similar to the Tanjore Paintings, Mysore Paintings of India make use of thinner gold leaves and require much more hard work. The most popular themes of these paintings include Hindu Gods and Goddesses and scenes from Hindu mythology.
- The grace, beauty and intricacy of Indian Mysore Paintings leave the onlookers mesmerized.
- Indian Mysore School of paintings exists in Mysore, Bangalore, Narasipura, Tumkur, Sravanabelagola and Nanjangud.

Mughal Painting

- Mainly confined to miniature illustrations on the books or as single works to be kept in an album
- Mughal paintings were a unique blend of Indian, Persian (Safavi) and Islamic styles
- Marked by supple naturalism → Primarily aristocratic and secular

- Tried to paint the classical ragas and Seasons or baramasa
- Tuti-nama - first art work of the Mughal School.
- Akbar's reign (1556–1605) ushered a new era in Indian miniature painting.
- At Zenith under Jahangir who himself was a famous painter
- Jahangir encouraged artists to paint portraits and durbar scenes.
- Shah Jahan (1627–1658) continued the patronage of painting.
- Aurangzeb had no taste for fine arts.
- Most significant are Hamza Nama, Razm-Nama or "The Book of War", Akbar Nama
- Finest example of this school includes Hamzanama series, started in 1567 & completed in 1582
- Hamzanama → Stories of Amir Hamza, illustrated by Mir Sayyid Ali
- 1200 paintings on themes of Changeznama, Zafarnama & Ramayana
- The paintings of the Hamzanama are of large size, 20" × 27" and were painted on cloth.
- They are in the Persian safavi style with dominating colours being red, blue and green
- Indian tones appear in later work, when Indian artists were employed.
- Akbar and Jehangir encouraged the illustration of epics and histories, Ramayana, Mahabharata, Akbarnama and Hamzanama.
- Experiments on rich colour schemes and varied expressions happened during this period.

- Hamza-nama (illustrations on cloth)- more developed and refined than Tuti-nama.
- Akbar was the first monarch to establish an atelier in India under the supervision of two Persian master artists, Mir Sayyed Ali & Abdus Samad. More than a hundred painters were employed, most of whom were Hindus from Gujarat, Gwalior and Kashmir, who gave a birth to a new school of painting, popularly known as the Mughal School of miniature Paintings.

Mural Painting

- Mural is inherently different from all other forms of pictorial art & is organically connected with architecture.
- Mural is the only form of painting that is truly three-dimensional, since it modifies and partakes of a given space.
- Mural paintings are applied on dry wall with the major use of egg, yolk, oil, etc.
- A mural artist must conceive pictorially a theme on the appropriate scale with reference to the structural exigencies of the wall & to the idea expressed.
- The history of Indian murals starts in ancient & early medieval times, from 2nd century BC to 8th – 10th century AD.
- Notable examples → Ajanta Caves, Bagh Caves, Sittanavasal Caves, Armamalai Cave (Tamil Nadu), Kailasa temple (Ellora Caves)
- Murals from this period depict mainly religious themes of Buddhist, Jain and Hindu.

Paintings	Themes
Ajanta Paintings	The themes of most of these paintings revolve around the life and teachings of Lord Buddha. This includes the Jataka stories related to the various lives and incarnations of Buddha.
Ellora Paintings	The rock paintings of Ellora were painted in two different series. The first series, which were done when the caves were carved, revolve around Lord Vishnu and Goddess Lakshmi. The second series, painted centuries later, illustrate procession of Shaiva holy men, Apsaras, etc. It also included Jataka tales and Jain text
Bagh Paintings	Paintings are both secular and religious (Buddhism is main inspiration). Painting style is influenced by Ajanta.
Sittanavasal Paintings	The themes of these paintings include animals, fish, ducks, people collecting lotuses from a pond, two dancing figures, etc. Apart from that, one can also find inscriptions dating back to the 9th and 10th century. Jainism is main inspiration.
Badami Paintings	Petronised by Chalukyas. It was inspired by Vaishaivism. Paintings in this cave depict palace scenes.
Pandyas paintings	Jains texts, female figures, etc.
Pallavas paintings	Beautiful lotus pond and flowers, dancing figures, lilies, fish, geese, buffaloes and elephants.
Chola paintings	The paintings celebrate Lord Shiva.
Vijayanagara Paintings	The paintings about the life and times of the Vijayanagara court.
Nayaka Paintings	Depicting the story of Mucukunda, a legendary Chola king

Kolam Painting

- Kolam is a ritualistic design drawn at the threshold of households and temples.
- It is drawn everyday at dawn and dusk by women in South India.
- Kolam marks festivals, seasons and important events in a woman's life such as birth, first menstruation and marriage.
- Kolam is a free-hand drawing with symmetrical and neat geometrical patterns.

Phad Painting

- Phad is a type of scroll painting.
- This type of painting is a most famous painting of Rajasthan, mainly found in the Bhilwara district.
- The main themes of the phad paintings depict the deities and their legends and the stories of erstwhile Maharajas.
- The unique features of phad paintings are the bold lines and a two dimensional treatment of figures with the entire composition arranged in sections.

Personalities of Indian Painting

Rabindranath Tagore	1861 -1941	He started painting from 1893 onwards and emerged as a creative exponent of graphic art in 1928. Tagore's best known painting, Bharat Mata, depicted a young woman, portrayed with four arms in the manner of Hindu, deities, holding objects symbolic of India's national aspirations
Abanindranath Tagore	1871 -1951	His first expression of paintings was Radhakrishna series. His set of paintings called Krishnalila (1896) is a synthesis of the Indian and European styles. His Arabian Nights series (1930) is among his most renowned works. He established the Indian Society of Oriental Art in 1907.
Nandlal Bose	1882 -1966	He was the student of Abanindranath Tagore. He was influenced by the Upanishads, Ajantha Paintings, Mughal Miniatures. He focused on the different levels of individual creativity and created a new conceptual base for Indian Art. His work Suttee won him a prize in the exhibition of Indian Society of Oriental Arts.
Jamini Roy	1887 -1972	He was greatly impressed by the kalighat paintings. His pictures are bold and statre. He used mineral and vegetable dyes popularly used in the villages to identify with the village ethos. He used cloth, wood and other materials in place of the canvas. He is the recipient of the Padma Bhushan Award (1955).
Amrita Shergil	1913 -1941	She was one of India's first modernist painters. Her work showed the fusion of the Eastern and Western style. Her painting shows her concern for poverty. She used real models and monochromatic colour at times for her paintings. Some of her famous paintings are Bride's Toilet, Hill women, Siesta, Nudes, Brahmacharis etc. She died at the age of 28.
S.H. Raza	1922-2016	Syed Haider Raza is an eminent Indian Artist who has lived and worked in France since 1950. His works are mainly abstracts in oil or acrylic, with a very rich use of colour. He was awarded the Padmashree and Fellowship of the Lalit Kala Academy in 1981 and Padma Bhushan in 2007.
M.F. Hussain	1915-2011	He is considered as India's leading artist. He paints in black social environment, often using distorted human figures, horses and objects. A times he uses highly violent distortions in form and colour to display emotions
Tyeb Mehta	1925 -2009	He was a famous Indian painter. His noted works were the 'Diagonal Series' Santiniketan, Kali, Mahishasura etc. He was part of the noted Bombay progressive Artists Group
Satish Gujral	1925	He is a painter, sculptor, muralist and architect in one. He works with several mediums like paint, clay, ceramic, wood, glass and metal. His dynamic social - realistic paints can be seen in the paintings of partition (revolution) which shows influence of Mexican grotesque distortion. He was awarded Padma Vibhushan in 1999.
Raja Ravi Varma	1848 - 1906	He introduced oil painting in India. Ravi Varma is particularly noted for his paintings depicting episodes from the story of Dushyanta and Shakuntala, and Nala and Damayanti, from the Mahabharata. His paintings are considered to be among the best examples of the fusion of Indian traditions with the techniques of European academic art.

Indian Music

Origin And History of Indian Music

Indian music has a very long, unbroken tradition and is an accumulated heritage of centuries. It is believed that sage Narada introduced the art of music to the earth and the sound that pervades the whole universe, The '*Samaveda*' is believed to contain all the seven notes of the raga '*karaharapriya*'. The earliest reference to musical theory is found in '*Rikpratisakhya*' (400 B.C,). Bharata's '*Natya Shastra*' (4th century A. D.) contains several chapters on music and it is probably the first work that clearly elaborated the octava and divided it into twenty two keys. Saranga Deva in his work '*Sangeeta Ratnakara*' defined almost 264 ragas and described the various 'microtones'. The other significant works on Indian music include Matanga's '*Brihaddesi*' (9th century A.D.), Narada's '*Sangeeta Makaranda*' (11th century A.D.), Ramamatya's '*Swaramela Kalanidhi*' (16th century A.D.) and Venkatamakhi's '*Chaturdandi-prakssika*' (17th century A.D.).

Raga & Tala Concept in Indian Music

In the Indian *Classical Music*, Raga is the basis of melody and Tala is the basis of rhythm. *Ragas* involve several important elements. The first element is sound – metaphysical and physical, which is referred to as *nada*. There are two types of nada, *anahata nada* or un-struck sound and *ahata nada* or struck sound. The next element of raga is *pitch*, relegated into *swara* (whole and half tones), and *sruti* (microtones). Raga also involves the production of emotional effects in the performer and listener, which are known as *rasa*. The aim of raga is to elicit emotional and psychological responses from the listener. There are nine *rasas*. Love (Shringar), Humour (Hasya), Pathos (Karuna), Anger (Rudra), Heroism (Vir), Terror (Bhayanaka), Disgust (Veebhatsa) and Wonder (Abdhuta).

Raga is the basis of classical music. It is based on the principle of a combination of notes selected out the 22 note intervals of the octave. There are 72 '*melas*',or parent scales, on which Ragas are based. Every Raga is derived from some *Thaat* or Scale.

Ragas are placed in three categories: (a) *Odava* or pentatonic, a composition of five notes, (b) *Shadava* or hexatonic, a composition of six notes and (c) *Sampoorna* or heptatonic, a composition of seven notes.

Every Raga must have at least five notes, starting at *Sa*, The speed of a raga is divided into three parts: *Vilambit* (slow), *Madhya* (Medium) and *Drut* (fast).

Another aspect of the ragas is the appropriate distribution in time during the 24 hours of the day for its performance, *i.e.* the time of the day denotes the type of the raga to be sung. Based on this, the ragas are divided into four types: *Sandi–prakash* ragas or twilight ragas, Midday and Midnight ragas, Ragas for the first quarter of the morning and night and Ragas for the last quarter of the day and night. All the ragas are divided into the broad groups -- Poor Ragas and Uttar Ragas.

Another division of ragas is the classification of ragas under six principal ragas -- *Hindol, Deepal, Megh, Shree* and *Maulkauns*.

Tala: Tala is the rhythmical groupings of beats. These rhythmic cycles range from 3 to 108 beats. It is the theory of time measure and has the same principle in Hindustani and Carnatic music, though the names and styles differ. There are over a 100 Talas, but only 30 Talas are known and only about 10–12 talas are actually used. The most commonly encountered one is the one with sixteen beats called the teentaal. The Laya is the tempo, which keeps the uniformity of time span. The Matra is the tempo, which keeps the uniformity of time span. The Matra is the smallest unit of the tala.

Hindustani Music

- The Hindustani music originated in North India in the 13th and 14th century. The Hindustani music has elements of ancient Hindu tradition, Vedic philosophy and Persian tradition as well.
- It is based on Raga system. The Raga is a melodic scale comprising of basic seven notes. Hindustani Music is vocal-centric.
- The major vocal forms associated with Hindustani classical music are the Khayal, Ghazal, Dhrupad, Dhammar, Hori, Tarana, Tappa, Chaturang, Ragasagar and Thumri.
- Medieval period: Hindustani music prevalent in North India & Carnatic music in South India
- Traced back to Delhi Sultanate → Amir Khusrau (AD 1253-1325) invented Sitar and Tabla, invented new Ragas like Ghora & Sanam evolved Qawwali mixing Indian & Iranian music
- New music instruments such as Sarangi & Rabab were introduced in this period
- Most of the Hindustani musicians trace their descent to Tansen
- Prominent Styles → Dhrupad, Dhamar-Hori, Khayal, Tarana, Sargam, Thumri & Ghazal

(A) Dhrupad

- Dhrupad is the oldest and perhaps the grandest form of Hindustani vocal music. Dhrupad is essentially a poetic form incorporated into an extended presentation style marked by precise and orderly elaboration of a raga.
- The exposition preceding the composed verses is called alap, and is usually the longest portion of the performance. Dhrupad is in decline since the 18th century.

(B) Khayal

- Khayal literally means 'a stray thought', 'a lyric' and 'an imagination'.
- This is the most prominent genre of Hindustani vocal music depicting a romantic style of singing.
- Khayal is dependent to a large extent on the imagination of the performer and the improvisations he is able to incorporate.
- Khayal is also composed in a particular raga and tala and has a brief text. The Khayal texts range from praise of kings or seasons, description of seasons to the pranks of Lord Krishna, divine love and sorrow of separation.

- There are six main gharanas in khayal: Delhi, Patiala, Agra, Gwalior, Kirana and Atrauli-Jaipur. Gwalior Gharana is the oldest and is also considered the mother of all other gharanas.

(C) Thumri

- Thumri originated in the Eastern part of Uttar Pradesh, mainly in Lucknow and Benares, around the 18th century AD.
- It is believed to have been influenced by hori, kajri and dadra.Thumri is supposed to be a romantic and erotic style of singing and is also called "the lyric of Indian classical music". The song compositions are mostly of love, separation and devotion.
- Its most distinct feature is the erotic subject matter picturesquely portraying the various episodes from the lives of Lord Krishna and Radha.
- A Thumri is usually performed as the last item of a Khayal concert. There are three main gharanas of thumri -- Benaras, Lucknow and Patiala.

(D) Dadra

- Dadra bears a close resemblance to the Thumri. The texts are as amorous as those of Thumris.
- The major difference is that dadras have more than one antara and are in dadra tala. Singers usually sing a dadra after a thumri.

(E) Dhamar-Hori

- These compositions are similar to Dhrupad but are chiefly associated with the festival of Holi. Here the compositions are specifically in praise of Lord Krishna.
- This music, sung in the dhamar tala, is chiefly used in festivals like Janmashthami, Ramnavami and Holi.
- The compositions here describe the spring season. These compositions are mainly based on the love pranks of Radha-Krishna.

(F) Tappa

- The tappa is said to have developed in the late 18th Century AD from the folk songs of camel drivers. Tappa literally means 'jump' in Persian.
- They are essentially folklore of love and passion and are written in Punjabi.

(G) Ragasagar

- Ragasagar consists of different parts of musical passages in different ragas as one song composition.
- These compositions have 8 to 12 different ragas and the lyrics indicate the change of the ragas.
- The peculiarity of this style depends on how smoothly the musical passages change along with the change of ragas.

(H) Tarana

- Tarana is a style consisting of peculiar syllables woven into rhythmical patterns as a song.
- It is usually sung in faster tempo.

(I) Chaturang

- Chaturang denotes four colours or a composition of a song in four parts:
- Four parts are: Fast Khayal, Tarana, Sargam and a "Paran" of Tabla or Pakhwaj.

(J) Ghazal

- The ghazal is mainly a poetic form than a musical form, but it is more song-like than the thumri.
- The ghazal is described as the "pride of Urdu poetry". The ghazal originated in Iran in the 10th Century AD.
- The ghazal never exceeds 12 shers (couplets) and on an average, ghazals usually have about 7 shers.
- The ghazal found an opportunity to grow and develop in India around 12th Century AD when the Mughal influences came to India, and Persian gave way to Urdu as the language of poetry and literature.
- It developed and evolved in the courts of Golconda and Bijapur under the patronage of Muslim rulers.

The 18th and 419th centuries are regarded as the golden period of the ghazal with Delhi and Lucknow being its main centres.

Personalities of Hindustani Music

Bhimsen Joshi	He was on Indian vocalist in the Hindustani classical tradition. He was the member of the Kirana Gharana. He is famous for Khyal form of singing. He enriched the kirana gharana by adding his own distinctive style and adopting characteristics from other gharanas.He was the recipient of s evera l prestigi ous awards including Padma Shri , Padma Bhushan and Padma Vibhushan. Bhimsen Joshi is renowned for his unique style and mastery over ragas.
Mallikarj un Mansur	He was an Indian Hindustani classical singer of the Khyal style in the Jaipur- Atrauligharana. He had received many awards including Padmabhushan, Kalidas Summan etc.
Pandit Jasraj	He is the exponent of the Mewati Gharana of Hindustani classical music. Pandit Jasraj's greatest contribution to Indian music is his conception of an unique and novel jugalbandhi based on the ancient system of moorchanas, between a male and a female vocalist, each singing in their respective scales and different ragas at the same time. Pandit Jasraj is the recipient of several honors and awards.
Begum Parveen Sultana	She is a Assamese Hindustani classical singer of the Patiala Gharana. She is among the foremost classical vocalist in India. She is known as Queen of Classical Vocal. She was confer red the Padmashri in 1976.

Kumar Gandharva	He was a Hindustani classical singer, famous for his unique vocal style. He did not follow any kind of Gharana. He experimented out his own styles. He was awarded the Padma Vibhushan in 1990.
Siddheswari Devi	She was a Hindustani singer from Varanasi. She sang Khyal, Thumri and short classical forms as dadra, chaiti, Kajri etc. Siddheswar's music had all the salient features of the Banaras style such as simple charm, intensity of feeling and effective expression of emotions.
Girija Devi	She was an Hindustani classical singer of the Banaras gharana. She sings different general of Hindustani vocal music like Khyal, Thumri, Dadra, Chaiti and Kajri. But her forte lies in singing the poorab and Thumri. So she is called the Queen of Thumri.
Gangubai Hanga	He was an Indian Hindustani musical singer of the Khyal genre. She belonged to the Kirana Gharana. She was famous for her deep and powerful voice.

Musical Instruments and its Exponents Indian Music

Musical Instruments	Exponents
Mridangam	Palakkad Mani Iyer, T.R. Murthy, Guruvayoor Doraiswami, Karaikudi R.Mani, Umayalpuram Shivaraman, Velloor A. Ramabhadran, Mavelikara Krishnan Kutty Nair.
Sitar	Pt. Ravi Shankar, Mushtaq Ali Khan, Vilayat Khan, Uma Shankar Mishra, Nikhil Banerjee,Raiz Khan, Harashankar Bhattacharya , Budhaditya Mukherjee, Abdul Halim Jaffer Khan.
Sarod	AmjadAli Khan, Ali Akbar Khan, Rajiv, Taranath
Violin	V.G. Jog, Lalgudi Jayaraman, T.N. Krishnan, Yehudi Mennuhin, M.S.Gopala krishnan,Kunnukkudi Vaidyana than, Kalyana Krishna Bhaga vatar , L.Subr amaniam, Chandayya, Kantha Devi, Gajannan Rao Joshi (Hindustani), Zubin Mehta (Western).
Santoor	Shiv Kumar Sharma , Tarun Bhattacharya, Bhajan Sopperi.
Flute	N.Ramani, Hariprasad Chaurasia, T.R. Mahalingam, Pannalal Ghosh, T. S. Shankaran, Sikkil Sisters
Mandolin	U. Srinivas, S.Balamurali Krishna.
Piano	Surojeet Chatterji, Kaikhoshha purji , Sorabjee.
Shehnai	Bismillah Khan , Bagheshwari Gamar, Bade Gulam Ali.
Tabla	Al la Rakha , Zakir Hussian, Shankar Ghosh, Aba d Mistry, Rimba Shiva , Santha Prasad, Sheikh Dawood, Sharafat Ahmed Khan, Kishan Maharaj , Ahmed, Tirkuva, Pt. Samta Prasad.
Veena	Chitti Babu, Mysore Doraiswami Iyankar, Azad Ali Khan (Hindustani), Badik Ali Khan, Kumara Swami Iyer (Carnatic), Kalpakkom Swaminathan, Ka lya na K ris hna Bhaga vata r, S. Balachander.
Sarangi	Pandit Ram Narayan, Sultan Khan, Sabri Khan.
Clarnet	Sheikh Mohammed Arif.

Carnatic Music

- The Tamil classic of the 2nd century A.D. titled the Silappadhikaram contains a vivid description of the music of that period. The Tolkappiyam, Kalladam and the contributions of the Saivite and Vaishnavite saints of the 7th and 8th centuries A.D. also serve as resource material for studying musical history.

- It is said, that South Indian Music, as known today, flourished in Deogiri the capital city of the Yadavas in the middle ages, and that after the invasion and plunder of the city by the Muslims, the entire cultural life of the city took shelter in the Carnatic Empire of Vijayanagar under the reign of Krishnadevaraya. Thereafter, the music of South India came to be known as Carnatic Music.

- In the field of practical music, South India had a succession of brilliant and prolific composers who enriched the art with thousands of compositions. After Purandaradasa, Tallapakam Annamacharya Narayana Tirtha, Bhadra-chalam Ramdasa and Kshetranja made contributions to the wealth of compositions

- The birth of the Musical Trinity - Tyagaraja, Muthuswami Dikshitar and Syama Sastri - at Tiruvarur between the years 1750 to 1850 A.D. ushered in an era of dynamic development in Carnatic music.

- Outstanding feature of Carnatic music is its raga system & highly developed and intricate tala system. Though clear cut demarcations in the style of musical presentation, similar to the gharanas of Hindustani music are not seen in Carnatic music, yet, we do come across different styles in rendering compositions.

- The ancient musical forms like Prabandhas, etc. gradually gave away to the different musicals forms that are in use in present day music, though the basic elements of the ancient Prabandhas are still retained in the modern forms. The following musical forms offer interesting study:

Gitam : Gitam is the simplest type of composition. Taught to beginners of music, the gitam is very simple in construction, with an easy and melodious flow of music.

Suladi : Very much like the gitam in musical structure and arrangement, the Suladis are of a higher standard than the gitam.

Varnam : The Varnam is a beautiful creation of musical craftsmanship of a high order, combining in itself all the characteristic features of the raga in which it is composed. Practice in Varnam singing helps a musician to attain mastery in presentation and command over raga, tala and bhava.

Svarajati : This is learnt after a course in gitams. More complicated than the gitas, the Svarajati paves the way for the learning of the Varnams. The theme is either devotional, heroic or amorous.

Jatisvaram : Very similar to the svarajati in musical structure, this form- Jatisvaram-has no sahitya or words. The piece is sung with solfa syllables only.

Kirtanam : The Kirtanam had its birth about the latter half of the 14th century. It is valued for the devotional content of the sahitya. Clothed in simple music, the kirtanam abounds in Bhakti bhava. It is suited for congregational singing as well as individual presentation.

Kriti : The Kriti is a development from the Kirtana. It is an highly evolved musical form. The highest limit of aesthetic excellence is reached in the Kriti composition. The raga bhava is brought out in all the rich and varied colours in this form.

PADA : Padas are scholarly compositions in Telegu and Tamil. Though they are composed mainly as dance forms, they are also sung in concerts, on account of their musical excellence and aesthetic appeal. The music is slow-moving and dignified.

Javali :A javali is a composition belonging to the sphere of light classical music. Sung both in concert programmes and dance concerts, the javalis are popular because of the attractive melodies in which they are composed. In contrast to the padas which portray divine love, javalis are songs which are sensuous in concept and spirit.

Tillana : The Tillana, corresponding to the Tarana of Hindustani music, is a short and crisp form. It is mainly a dance form, but on account of its brisk and attractive music, it sometimes finds a place in music concerts as a conclusion piece.

Pallavi: This is the most important branch of creative music. It is in this branch of manodharma sangeeta, that the musician has ample opportunities of displaying his or her creative talents, imaginative skill, and musical intelligence.

Tanam : This is a branch of raga alapana. It is raga alapana in Madhyamakala or medium speed. There is perceptible rhythm in this. The rhythmical flow of music, flowing in fascinating patterns, makes tanam singing the most captivating part of raga exposition.

INDIAN VOCALISTS

Carnatic	M .S. Subbu lakshmi , Balamurali Krishna ,Chembai Vaidya natha Bhagavathar, Semmangudi SinivasaIyer, M.L.Vasantha Kumari, M.D. Ramanathan, G.N. Balasubramaniam, Ariyakudi Ramaniya Iyyengar.
Hindustani	Bhimsen Joshy, Mallikarjun Mansur, Pandit Jasraj, Parveen Sul- tana, Naina Devi, Siddheswari, Girija Devi, Kumar Gandharva.

Devotional Music Of India

- India is a land of diverse faiths and beliefs and is bound by a common thread of music. Indian earlier classical music 'Prabandh Sangeet' and 'Dhruvapada' were all devotional in character.
- Later other forms of devotional music like 'bhajans', 'kirtans', 'shabads' and 'qawalis' came into being.

Bhajan

- Bhajans belong to the Bhakti Movement, it is a popular form of devotional singing prevalent in north India. Stories and episodes from the 'Ramayana' and 'Mahabharata' are popular themes for bhajans.
- Bhajan singing is usually accompanied by musical instruments like 'jhanj', 'manjira', 'daphli', 'dholak' and 'chimta'.
- Meera Bai, Kabir, Surdass, Tulsidas, guru Nanak and Narsi Mehta are some of the most significant names in bhajan singing.

Shabad

- *Shabads* are devotional songs of the Sikhs originated as a musical composition around the 17th century AD.
- Guru Nanak and his disciple Mardana are credited with the development and popularity of *shabad*.
- Besides the shabads, these are twenty two 'vars' or ballads, which are mentioned in the Guru Granth Sahib.

Qawwali

- Quawwali is a devotional form of music, prevalent among the sufis. The lyrics are in praise of Allah.

- It is written in Persian, Urdu and Hindi is composed in a specific 'raga'. Originally it was sung to the beat of the 'daff'.
- Amir Khusro (1254–1325 AD) is believed to have incorporated meaningful words into the 'qaul'. Which over a period of time developed into qawwali.

Kirtan

- *Kirtan* is an ancient folk tradition of musical meditation was transformed into song and dance congregations by Chaitanya Mahaprabhu.
- Kirtans are of two types *'Nama-Kirtana'* and *'Lila-Kirtana'*.

Abhangs

- These are also referred as *'Vittala'* and 'Vittoba' in Maharashtra. These are devotional songs sung in praise of Lord Krishna.
  These were popularised by renowned saints like Gnaneshwar, Eknath and Tukaram.

Bhatiyali

- These songs are sung mainly by the East Bengal boatmen while boating on the rivers.

Tevaram

- These are the devotional hymns sung by Oduyars and others in South India.

Gharanas Of Hindustani Music

The *Gharana* or family is a school of a particular style of singing or playing instruments. The following are the important Gharanas of Hindustani vocal music.

Gharana's Name	Founders	Exponents
Agra Gharana	Haji Sujan Khan, Ustad Ghagge Khuda Bakhsh	Faiyyaz Khan, Latafat Hussain Khan
Benaras Gharana	Pandit Gopal Mishra	Rajan Mishra and Sajan Mishra
Bhendi Baza Gharana	Ustad Chajju Khan	Aman Ali Khan Shashikala Koratkar
Delhi Gharana	Ustad Mamman Khan	Chand Khan, Nasir Ahmed Khan
Gwalior Gharana	Ustad Hassu Khan, Ustad Haddu Khan	Balakrishna Bura Ichalkaranjikar, Vinayakrao Patwardhan
Indore Gharana	Ustad Amir Khan	
Jaipur Atrauli Gharana	Ustad alladiya Khan	Kesarbai Kerkar, Mogubai Kurdikar
Patiala Gharana	Ustad Fatch Ali Khan Ustad Ali Bakhsh	Bade Ghulam Ali Khan, Munawar Ali Khan

Indian dance

An Introduction

- In India dance is considered to be divine in origin. Shiva's cosmic dance. *Tandava*, is belived to encompass creation, preservation and destruction.
- The common root of all classical dance forms can be traced to Bharata's *Natyashastra*,. According to the *Natyashastra*, Brahma, the creator and the first of the Hindu Triad, was asked to create a part time by the gods.
- For creating drama, Brahma took pathya (words) from the Rigveda, *abhinaya* (gesture) from the Yajurveda, *geet* (music and chant) from Samaveda and *rasa* (sentiments and emotions) from Atharvaveda to form the fifth Veda, Natyaveda.
- Indian dance is divided into *nritta* – the rhythmic elements, *nritya* – the combination of rhythm with expression and *natya* – the dramatic element.
- Nritya is usually expressed through the eyes, hands and facial movements. Nritya combined with *Nritta* makes up the usual dance programmes.
- There are four strong elements of the classical dance *form:shastra* sculpture, folk tradition and ancient literature.

Indian Classical Dances

India has thousands of year old tradition of fine arts and classical and folk music and dances. Some of the world-famous dance forms that originated and evolved in India are Bharatnatyam, Kathak, Kathakali, Kuchipudi, Manipuri, Mohiniattam and Odissi. All these dance forms use basically the same 'mudras' or signs of hand as a common language of expression and were originally performed in the temples to entertain various Gods and Goddesses.

Indian Folk and Tribal Dances

India is a land of varied cultures and traditions. Indian folk and tribal dances are product of different socio-economic set up and traditions. Indian folk and tribal dances are simple and are performed to express joy. In India we have festivals and celebrations virtually every day. This has added to the richness of Indian culture.

Various dance forms

Dance Forms	Origin	Lagends
Odissi (Odisha)	Odissi is believed to be the oldest form of Indian dance from the state of Odisha, It is considered a dance of love, joy and intense passion, pure, divine and human. It divides the body into three parts, head, bust and torso	Kelucharan Mohapatra Sonal Mansingh Mayadhar Raut, Jhelum Paranjape, KumKum Mohanty, Madhumita Raut, Aloka Kanungo, Ileana Citaristi
Bharat Natyam (Tamil Nadu)	Bharatnatyam is more popular in South Indian states. This dance is almost 2,000 years old. This dance flourished in the Hindu temples of South India.	Alarmel Valli, Yamini Krishnamurthy, Rukmini Devi, Padma Subramanyam, Yamini Krishnamurthy, Mrinalini Sarabhai, Meenakshi Sundaram Pillai, Padma Subramanyam, Balasarswati
Kuchipudi (Andhra Pradesh)	It presents scenes from Hindu Epics and mythological tales through dance-dramas combining music, dance and acting.	Bhavana Reddy, Yamini Reddy, Raja & Radha Reddy, Kaushalya Reddy
Kathak (North India (Lucknow-Banaras-Jaipur))	This north Indian dance form is inextricably bound with classical Hindustani music, and the rhythmic nimbleness of the feet is accompanied by the tabla or pakhawaj	Pandit Birju Maharaj, Kumudini Lakhiya, Sitara Devi, Shovana Narayan, Malabika Mitra, Kumudini Lakhiya, Kartik Ram - Kalyan Das, Manisha Gulyani
Kathakali (Kerala)	It literally means story play and is an elaborate dance depicting the victory of truth over false-hood	Kalamandalam Krishna Prasad, Kavungal Chathunni Panicker, Kavungal Chathunni Panicker, Kalamandalam Ramankutty Nair, Kalamandalam Kesavan Namboodir, Kottakkal Sivaraman, Kalamandalam Gopi
Mohiniyattam (Kerala)	It is a very graceful dance meant to be performed as a solo recital by women.	Smitha Rajan, Sunanda Nai, Jayaprabha Menon, Pallavi Krishnan, Gopika Varma, Vijayalakshmi
Manipuri (Manipur)	The most striking part of Manipur dance is its colorful decoration, lightness of dancing foot, delicacy of abhinaya (drama), lilting music and poetic charm	Poushali Chatterjee, Rajkumar Singhajit Singh, Sohini Ray, Guru Nileswar Mukharjee, Guru Bipin Singha
Yakshagana	It is a classical dance drama popular in the state of Karnataka. This theater art involves music, song, dance, acting, dialogue, story and unique costumes.	

States and their Folk Dances

Jharkhand	Chhau, Sarahul, Jat-Jatin, Karma, Danga, Didesia, Sohrai, Paika, Bheja
Uttarakhand	Gadhwali, Kumayuni, Kajari, Jhora, Raslila, Chappeli, Bhotia
Chhattisgarh	Goudi, Karma, Jhumar, Pali, Tapali, Navrani, Diwari, Mundari.
Andhra Pradesh	Kuchipudi (classical), Ghantamardala, Otttam Thedal, Mohiniattam, Kummi, Siddhi Madhuri, Chhadi.

Arunachal Pradesh	Mask dance (Mukhauta Nritya), War dance.
Himachal Pradesh	Jhora, Jhali, Charhi, Dhaman, Chhapeli, Mahasu, Nati, Dangi, Chamba, Thali, Jhainta, Daf, Stick dance etc.
Goa	Mandi, Jhagor, Khol, Dakni etc.
Assam	Bihu, Bichua, Natpuja, Maharas, Kaligopal, Bagurumba, Naga dance, Khel Gopal, Tabal Chongli, Canoe, Jhumura Hobjanai Pojapali etc.
West Bengal	Kathi, Gambhira, Dhali, Jatra, Baul, Marasia, Mahal, Keertan etc.
Kerala	Kathakali (Classical), Ottam Thulal, Mohiniattam, Kaikottikali, Tapptikali, Kali Auttam.
Meghalaya	Laho, Baagla etc.
Manipur	Manipuri (Classical), Rakhal, NatRash, MahaRash, Raukhat etc.
Nagaland	Chong, Khaiva, Lim Nuralim etc.
Orissa	Odissi (Classical), Savari, Ghumara, Painka, Munari, Chhau, Chadya Dandanata etc.
Maharashtra	Lavani, Nakata, Koli, Lezim, Gafa, Dahikala Dasavtar or Bohada, Tamasha, Mauni, Powara, Gouricha etc.
Karnataka	Yakshagan, Huttari, Suggi, Kunitha, Karga, Lambi
Gujarat	Garba, Dandiya Ras, Tippani Juriun, Bhavai.
Punjab	Bhangra, Giddha, Do, Dhaman etc.
Rajasthan	Ghumar, Chakri, Ganagor, Jhulan Leela, Jhuma, Surisini, Ghapal, Panihari, Ginad etc.
Jammu & Kashmir	Rauf, Hikat, Mandjas, Kud Dandi nach, Damali.
Tamil Nadu	Bharatnatyam, Kumi, Kolattam, Kavadi
Uttar Pradesh	Nautanki, Raslila, Kajri, Jhora, Chappeli, Jaita.
Bihar	Jata-Jatin, Bakho-Bakhain, Panwariya, Sama-Chakwa, Bidesia, Jatra etc.
Haryana	Jhumar, Phag Dance, Daph, Dhamal, Loor, Gugga, Khor, Gagor etc.

Theatres and Films

Theatre in India

- India has a longest richest tradition in theatre going back to at least 5000 years.
- Bharata's Natya Shastra (2000 BC to 4th century AD) was the earliest and most elaborate treatise in dramaturgy written anywhere in the world.
- In Natya Shastra, Bharata Muni described ten classifications of drama.
- Hindu theorists from the earliest days conceived of plays in terms of two types of production : lokadharmi (realistic), which involved the reproduction of human behaviour on the stage and the natural presentation of objects and natydharmi (Conventional), which is the presentation of a play through the use of stylized gestures and symbolism and was considered more artistic and realistic.

Sanskrit Theatre

- It is difficult to determine the precise origins of the Sanskrit drama. The earliest phase of Sanskrit. Theatre was based almost entirely on the rules, regulations and modifications laid down in the Natya Shastra.
- One of the earliest plays written was sariputra prakarana by Asvaghosa.
- Shudraka, Harsha, Visakhadatta, Bhasa, Kalidasa and Bhava bhuti were the six outstanding Sanskrit playwrights who have contributed in a great measure.
- There are ten types of Sanskrit plays : *Nataka Prakarma, Anka, Vyayoga, Bhana, Samvakara, Vithi, Prahasana, Dima*, and *Ithamgra*.

Koodiyattam or Koothiyattam

- It is considered to have been introduced in India by Aryans. It is derived from the sanskrit word kurd meaning to "to play".
- It is widely believed that Kulasekhara Varma cheraman Perumal, an ancient king of Kerala, was the creator of Koodiyattam in the present form.
- Traditionally, Koodiyattam is presented by Chakyars, a temple caste of Kerala, and Nangiars, the woman of Nambiar caste.
- Koodiyattam was traditionally a part of the temple rituals, performed as a kind of visual sacrifice to the deity and is normally performed in koothambalams or temple theatres.
- All the main characters in Koodiyattam enact *Nirvahana*, a recollection of past events in the story.

Puppetry in India

- Puppet Theatre is found in all parts of the world, it is a form of entertainment. In India, the roots of the puppet theatre lie in a dancer's mask.
- There are four kinds of puppets–glove, string, rod and shadow. The glove puppet in Orissa is called *Kundhei Nacha*. and *Pava koothu* in Kerala.
- String puppets are found in Andhra Pradesh, Rajasthan, Orissa, Tamil Nadu and Karnataka.

State	–	*Puppet Show Name*
Rajasthan	–	Kataputali
Orissa	–	Sakhi Kundhei
Assam	–	Putla Nach
Maharashtra	–	Malasutri Bhaulya
Tamil Nadu	–	Bommalattam
Karnataka	–	Gombeyatta

Post–Independence Theatre in India

- Indian theatre and drama got a new footing, when Sangeet Natak Akademi was started in January 1953.

- Lather, the National School of Drama under the directorship of Ebrahim Alkazi promoted much modern Indian theatre.

- The year 1972 turned out to be a landmark for the Indian theatre when Vijay Tendulkar's Marathi play 'Ghashiram Kotwal' produced waves by its brilliant use of traditional folk forms in modern contemporary theatre.

- Munjula Padmanabhan was the first Indian to earn international acclaim with her play '*Bitter Harvest*'.

Some of the Important Theatres of Modern India

Name	Founder	Year and Place of Establishment	People Associated with it
National School of Drama (Deemed University)	Ministry of Culture, Government of India.	1959, New Delhi	Naseeruddin Shah, Irrfan Khan, Anupam Kher, Nawazuddin Siddiqui, Pankaj Kapur, Himani Shivpuri and many more
Bhartendu Academy of Dramatic Arts	Padma Shri Raj Bisaria.	1975, Lucknow,	Rajiv Jain, Raajpal Yadav, Anupam Shyam
Theatre Arts Workshop (TAW)	Raj Bisaria	1966, Lucknow	

Hindi Films

Bollywood is the Hindi Language film industry which is based in Mumbai, Maharashtra. They are one of the largest film producers in India and one of the largest centres of film production in the world. Raja Harishchandra (1913), by Dadasaheb Phalke, is known as the first silent feature film made in India. The first Indian sound film, Ardeshir Irani's Ara (1931), was a major commercial success. In 1937, Ardeshir Irani, of Alam ara fame, made the first colour film in Hindi, Kisan Kanya.

Festivals of India

India, 'A Land of Festivals' is a Multi religious and multi-lingual country. It is but natural to find festival of all major religions in the world being celebrated in India.

Religious Festivals of India

Hindu Festivals of India

Diwali, Durga Puja, Dussehra, Ganesh Chaturthi, Holi, Janmashthami, Karwa Chauth, Navaratri, Ram Navami, Skanda Shashthi, Vasant Panchami.

Buddhist Festivals of India

- Buddha Purnima, Losar, Tseschu Festival.

Christian Festivals of India

Christmas, Easter, Good friday, St. Francis Xavier's Day, The Goa Carnival.

Jain Festivals of India

Mahavir Jayanti, Paryushana, Maha mastak Abhishek.

Jewish Festivals of India

Feast of Passover, Purim or festivals of Lots.

Muslim Festivals of India

Eidal-Fitr, Eidal–Adha, Miladun-Nabi, Muharram, Shab-e-Barat.

Parsi Festivals of India

Jamshed Novroz, Zarthost No Deeso, Khordad Sal.

Sikh Festivals of India

Gurupurabs, Holla Mohalla.

Sindhi Festivals of India

Cheti Chand, Teejri, Thadri Utraan.

Cultural Festivals of India

- Gadwad Festival.
- Ladakh Festival.
- Thyagaraja Festival.
- Khajuraho Festival of Dances.
- Vijaynagra Hampi Festival.

Languages In India

- There are 418 languages listed for India. Of those, 407 are living languages and 11 are extinct.
- Now, India has 22 officially recognised languages which are mentioned in the Eight Schedule of the Constitution.
- Hindi in the Devanagari script is the official language of the Union of India.
- English is the second official language and is also the authoritative, legislative and judicial language.
- Broadly the Indian languages can be put into six groups : (1) Indo-Aryan, (2) Dravidian, (3) Sino-Tibetan, (4) Negroid, (5) Austric and (6) Others.
- The VIII Schedule originally contained 15 languages. By the 71st Amendment of the constitution, Konkani, Manipuri and Nepali have been added to the Schedule in 1992.

Tourism

India has become a popular tourist destination with thousands of people visiting different parts of India each year. It has much to offer to travelers and tourists. It is a land of hills, rivers, plateaus, plains, beaches, deltas and deserts. Some of the major tourist destinations in India are the Himalayas, Agra, Jaipur, Goa, Kerala, Delhi, Odisha and Maharshtra.

Famous Tourist Destination in India

Akshardham Temple

The 108 feet tall temple was built on 2nd, November 1992 in memory of Pramukh Swami in Gandhinagar district of Gujarat.

Ajmer Sharif

It is sufi shrine dedicated to the sufi saint Moinuddin Chishti. It is situated Ajmer, Rajasthan. The Dargah attracts people from different faith who come and worship here.

Amarnath Cave

It is situated in Jammu and Kashmir and is one of the ancient pilgrimages in India. It is famous for the Linga which is created naturally by ice every year. The Amarnath Yatra is an annual event taken up by Hindu pilgrims who reach the temple after a rigorous trek to the cave temple.

Ajanta and Ellora Caves

They contain a cluster of Hindu and Jain temples along with cave monuments. Ajanta along with Ellora caves are one of the major tourist attraction of Maharastra, Primariy for their cave paintings.

Beaches of Goa

Goa is famous for its beautiful beaches, wonderful churches, wildlife sanctuary, goan cuisine, water sports and most happening night life. The well-known beaches of Goa are Baga Beach, Aguada Beach, Arambol Beach, Palolem Beach, Calangute Beach, Butterfly Beach, Colva Beach etc and the magnificent churches are Basilica of Bom Jesus, Rachol Seminary and Church, St. Alex Church, Church of St Francis of Assisi, Immaculate Conception Church, Se Cathedral.

Bandipur Wildlife Sanctuary

Established in 1947 Bandipur Wildlife sanctuary is well known for its tiger reserve. The entire area constitute the vast Nilgiri Biosphere Reserve which comprises the tracts of protected forest.

Badrinath

It is located in the Chamoli district in Uttarakhand. It is the most important of the four sites in India's Char Dham pilgrimage. It is also gateway to several mountaineering expeditions headed to mountains like Nilkantha.

Bodhgaya

It is one of the most important and sacred Buddhist pilgrimage center in the world situated in Gaya district in Bihar. It is famous as the place where Gautama Buddha is said to have obtained Enlightenment under the Bodhi Tree.

Dwarkadhish Temple

The temple is situated on the bank of river Gomti and dedicated to lard Krishna, The temple is constructed of limestone which is still in immaculate condition.

Dal Lake, Ladakh

The enchanting lake of Jammu and Kasmir bordered by ice covered mountains from three sides is famous for its gardens, shikara rides and house boat stay.

Golden Temple

A symbol of brotherhood and equality the Harmandir Sahib Gurudwara, is commonly called as Golden Temple is located in Amritsar is famous for its sanctity and is the main pilgrimage of sikh community but it welcomes a large no. of tourists every years despite of their religion caste and creed.

Gateway of India

It is a crude jetty made by British People in the year 1914 in Mumbai which is a basalt arc and having a height of 26 feet.

Haji Ali Dargah

The very famous dargah (tomb) is located on an islet of the coast of Worli in the Southern part of Mumbai built in 1431 in the memory of a wealthy merchant Sayyed Peer Haji Ali Shah Bukhari, who gave up all his worldly possessions before making a pilgrimage to Mecca.

Hemkund Sahib

It is a Sikh place of worship situated in Chamoli district, Uttarakhand, India, devoted to Guru Gobind Singh Ji, the tenth Sikh Guru. The scenic beauty of the place is astounding as this shrine is located amidst lofty hills that are covered with snow.

Haridwar

It is one of the most ancient cities located on the banks of river Ganga in the state of Uttarakhand. The Kumbha Mela which happens once in every 12 years attracts millions to the city with devotees thronging the place all year round.

Jagannath Temple, Puri

It is a sacred Hindu temple dedicated to Lord Jagannath situated in Odisha and is one of the char dham pilgrimages that every Hindu intends to visit.

Jama Masjid

It is situated in Delhi and is one of the largest mosques in India. It was built by Shah Jahan between 1644 and 1656.

Kerala Backwaters

A chain of brackish water lagoons lying parallel to the Malabar Coast of Kerala in southern part of India which is a large web of water bodies i.e. five large lake interconnected natural and manmade canals and fed by 38 rivers.

Kanyakumari

The southernmost part of Tamilnadu which was formerly known as Cape Comorin and famous for place of tourist interests like Vivekananda Rock Memorial, Thiruvalluvar Statue, Our Lady of Ransom Church, Tsunami Memorial Park.

Kaziranga National Park

This national park was established in the year 1904 in Golaghat and Nagaon districts of the state of Assam are famous for the heavy population of one-horned rhinoceros. Among the other specialties of this national park tall elephant grass, marshland, and dense tropical moist broadleaf forests, river crisscross of four major rivers, including the Brahmaputra, and the park includes numerous small bodies of water are well-known.

Khajuraho Group of Monuments

It is a group of Hindu and Jain temples situated in Madhya Pradesh. The temples are famous for the nagara style architecture and erotic sculptures.

Konark Sun Temple

It is situated in Odisha. The iconic temple is in the form of a gigantic chariot, built in the 13th century. It also features on the list of seven wonders of India.

Lotus Temple

It is located in New Delhi, is a Bahai House of Worship constructed in 1986.

Mahabaleshwar

It is a vast magnificent plateau located at a distance of 120 km south west of Pune with an average height of 1353 meters. It is bound by valley from all sides and having some beautiful high rise peaks. The highest peak is known as Wilson or Sunset Point.

Mathura

It is known as the birthplace of Lord Krishna located 50 km North of Agra in Uttar Pradesh. The Krishna Janbhoomi temple is visited by a large number of devotees throughout the year. During Janmashtami the town becomes overcrowded with devotees from all over India.

Rishikesh

It is the starting point of the chardham pilgrimage situated in the Uttarakhand. The city is regarded as one of the holiest places to Hindus and also referred as the Yoga Capital of the World. It has innumerable Hindu temples and the heavy settlement of yoga centers.

The Great Rann of Kutch

It is a seasonal salt marsh is spread over an area of 7,505.22 square kilometers (2,897.78 sq mi) in Thar Desert. It is the land of various well known sanctuaries such as Wild Ass Sanctuary, bird-rich Nawa Talao lake, Nalsarovar Bird Sanctuary.

Somnath Mahadev Temple

Adding to the beauty of western ghat the famous Somnath Mahadev Temple of Prabhas Patan is believed to be the first among twelve Jyotirling of Shivas. The age old temple was initially built in the 11th century by Solanky rajput . but it was rebuilt in 1951.

Siddhivinayak Temple

It is one of the richest Hindu temple built in the heart of Mumbai city on 19 November, 1801 built by Laxman Vithu and Debubai Patil.

Taj Mahal

It is a white marble mausoleum located on the southern bank of the Yamuna river is Agra, Uttar Pradesh. It was built by Shah Jahan in 1632 in the memory of his loving wife Mumtaz Mahal.

Tirumala Venkateswara Temple

It is an iconic vaishnavite temple located in Tirumala at Tirupati in Chittoor district of Andhra Pradesh. It is one of the most visited Hindu temples in India with a footfall of 60,000 pilgrims each day.

Valley of flowers

A national park situated in West Himalayas and renowned for its meadows of endemic alpine flowers and the variety of flora.

Vaishno Devi Temple, Jammu Kashmir

The temple is recognized as one of the "Shakti Peeths" of goddess Durga. The holy shrine is situated in the folds of mighty 'Tirkuta' Hills' which attracts lakhs of devotees from all parts of India and abroad.

Varanasi

It is one of the most popular pilgrimages for the Hindus. It houses one the Shakti Peethas and one of the twelve Jyotir Linga sites in India. The Ganga Arti performed ritualistically every morning and evening at the Ganga ghats which enhances its divinity.

Top Ten States/UTs of India in Number of foreign Tourist Visits in 2016

Rank	State/UT	Foreign Tourist Visits in 2016	
		Number	Percentage (% Share
1	Tamil Nadu	4721978	19.1
2	Maharashtra*	4670048	18.9
3	Uttar Pradesh	3156812	12.8
4	Delhi#	2520083	10.2
5	West Bengal	1528700	6.2
6	Rajasthan	1513729	6.1
7	Kerala	1038419	4.2
8	Bihar	1010531	4.1
9	Goa	680683	2.8
10	Punjab	659736	2.7
	Total of Top 10	21500719	87.0
	Others	3207012	13.0
	Total	24707732	100.0

Source: State/UT Tourism Departments.
 * Estimated using All India Growth Rate
 # Estimating using Growth Rate of FTAs of Delhi Airport

Arts & Crafts of India

- India has the widest variety of crafts anywhere in the world. Handicraft items that were patronized by the Mughal royalty show a remarkable refinement of workmanship.
- Historically speaking the discovery of the Indian arts and crafts by the officers of the East India company and the British Raj and their subsequent display at the Indian Museum in East India House around the first half of the 19th century was a remarkable event.

Clay Crafts

- Clay pottery is an ancient art form in India dating back to well over 10,000 years.
- The clay objects are found at the excavation sites of the Indus Valley Civilisation.
- Jhuker Pottery was related with the people of the Harappa and the Red ware was the most popular type of pottery during the late vedic period.
- Terracotta is a porous and brittle material formed by the low heat of a traditional Indian kiln.

Textiles

- In the 13th century, Indian silk was used as baster for spice from the western countries:
- In the end of the 17th century, the British East India company had begun export of the famous fine Muslin cloth of Bengal, Bihar and Orissa.
- Before the introduction of mechanized means of spinning in the early 19th century, Indian cottons and silks were hand spun and hand woven.
- Kanchipuram, Ahmedabad, Aurangabad, Varanasi, Jaipur, Chanderi, Paithan, Gadhwal, and Kashmir were important centres of textiles from ancient times.
- In the 19th century, Benaras silk manufacturers used vegetable and animal forms which were derivations of the Mughal tradition.
- The Paithani Saris, produced in Paithan near Aurangabad, are made of silk in rich, vivid colours with gold embroidery.
- The finest textures of northern parts of the country are the *Maheshwari* and *Chanderi saris* of Madhya Pradesh and Jamdani of Tanda and Benaras in Uttar Pradesh.
- **List of different fabrics related to their states is given below :–**

Fabric	Related states/Places
Tangail cotton	West Bengal
Tusar silk	Bihar
Sambalpuri and Vichitrapuri Saris	Orissa
Kasavumundu and Karalkuda	Kerala
Kancheepuram Silk	Tamil Nadu
Telia Kummals	Andhra Pradesh
Irkali Saris	Bijapur
Paithani Saris	Paithan near Aurangabad
Himroo Shawls	Aurangabad

- Sanganer, near Jaipur, is famous for the finest hand – black printing and design, dyeing and Ornamentation.
- Bagru prints are famous for floral designs.
- Barmer prints are famous for floral designs.
- Barmer prints called 'ajrakh' are known for their bold geometric patterns.
- Shawl wearing flourished in Kashmir under the patronage of the Mughals. The pashmina and shahtoosh shawls of Kashmir are woven out of the fleece of the Tibetan Goat.

Ivory Works

- According to history, king Soloman acquired Indian Ivory in 10th Century B.C. *Brahmins* used *Khadaon* or the sandals made of ivory in India.
- India is known for craft on tusks of elephants. The Ivory carvers produce objects such as the *ambari hathi* or processional elephant, models of bullock, carts, palanquins and frames for the European market.

Glass Work

- In the epic *Mahabharata* literary evidences point towards the existence of glass in India from ancient times.
- Hyderabad is renowned for the Sonabai bangles and the *churi ka jodas*.
- Varanasi specializes a type of very thin glass called *tikuli*.
- Saharanpur is an important centre for making beautiful toys filled with Coloured liquid called *Panchkora*.

Leather Work

- Leather tanning as an art form reached its zenith in India by 3000 BC.
- India's extremely comfortable and fashionable *kolhapuri chappals* are made in Maharashtra.
- *Mojadi* or *Jutti* is an attractive footwear items of Rajasthan.
- Kupi, a bottle made of camel hide to keep oil or 'attar' (perfume), is a speciality of Bikaner.
- In the *Manoti art*, articles like lamps and lampshades are made out of camel hides.

Metal Work

- Copper and tin were the earliest non– ferrous metals, later were mixed to form an alloy called *bronze*. The Matsyapurana describes various methods of casting bronze images.
- Tamil Nadu is one of the famous bronze producing regions where the artisans or '*stapathis*' produce stylish images of Pallava, Chola and Nayaka periods.
- The statues of Shiva's *tandava* dance described as the *gaja tandava* is the production of Kerala.
- Orissa is known for its Dhocra casting and Silver filigree work.
- Hyderabad is famous for silver objects like *paandaan*, *ugaldaan* and *itardaan*.
- Marwar in Rajasthan is famous for it zinc-pots called *badla*.
- Moradabad has become famous for *khudai* or metal engraving work done in nakashi style. The *kammalas* of Thanjavur in Tamil Nadu are famous for metal encrusting work.
- *Koftagiri* mostly practised in Alwar and Jaipur is a technique of inlaying a light metal on a dark one.
- Delhi and Jaipur are known for *meenakari* In *bidri* work, practised in Bidar in Karnataka, silver inlay work is done against dark metal backgrounds.
- *Mohras*, a unique metal craft of Himachal represents a deity.

Indian Jewellery

- Ornaments made of gold, silver and copper have been discovered in civilizations as ancient as the Harappa and Mohenjodaro.
- Traditional Indian literature records sixteen nodes of female adornment described as the Solah Shringaar .
- Jaipur is the centre for gold *kundan* work and diamond and emerald cutting.
- The Thewa jewellery of Rajasthan is an extremely fine work in gold leaf depicting scenes from *rasalila* episodes.
- Orissa is famous for its silver anklets called *painri* and *paijam* and silver knitted ornaments called gunchi.
- The *thali*, an essential component of the marriage ceremony of many communities, is a gold necklace consisting of numerous emblems, usually a phallic symbol, which hangs in the centre.

Wood Work

- The Kashmiri wooden architecture, made from walnut and deodar wood, has flourished from the 11th century AD.
- The elegant *tharavad* homes of Kerala, corresponding to the *havelis* of Gujarat, are brilliant pieces of architecture in deep brown teakwood.
- *Raktachandan*, a red sandalwood of Andhra Pradesh, is traditionally being used to Carve figure of deities and dolls.
- The wood carving of he Northeastern tribes are executed in wood, which is generally known as *kumisyng*.
- Assam is noted for its special styles and object like the *namghar* or *kirtanghar* (a wooden house), hukkas, sandals and book-rests.
- Wood *lacquer* work is popular in Rajasthan, Kashmir, Karnataka and Maharastra.

Stone Work

- A major tradition of stone carving seems to be focused around temples in India.
- The glory of stonework is truly revealed in sculptures of the Mauryan period, Buddhist carvings at Bharhut and Sanchi and the rock – cut caves of Ajanta and Ellora and Khajuraho.
- Agra is famous for its Marble work. The white Makrana marble (*sange malmal*) of Rajasthan has a great demand as a building and decorative stone.

India has got international acclamation in terms of its beautiful and creative handicrafts. Given below are the states with diversified crafts.

State	Handicrafts
Odisha	Weaving craft, palm leaf writing, patachitra-the chitrakar's foray, applique, stone carving, metal craft,
Delhi	Zardozi, lacquer work, clay and paper made dolls
Maharastra	Paithani saris, sawantwadi crafts, warli paintings, kolhapuri chappals, narayan peth
West Bengal	Artistic leather craft, brass & bell metal, pottery, mat making, dhokra metal casting, cane & bamboo, fine arts, clay dolls, horn work, jute products, shell & conch shell, sholapith, famous handloom sarees like dhakai jamdani, tangail etc
Gujrat	Bead-work, jewellery, inlay work, embroidery, wood carving, cloth printing, dyeing, patola fabric, zari work
Rajasthan	Tie-and-dye textiles, hand block printing, quilting, jewellery, gems and stones, blue pottery, leather craft, woodcarving
Himachal Pradesh	Jewelry, leather craft, woodcarving, architecture, kangra paintings
Goa	Pottery & Terracotta, Brass metal ware, Crochet & Embroidery, Bamboo Craft, Fiber Craft, Jute Macrame Craft, Coconut Mask carving, sea shell craft
Andhra Pradesh	Priceless Pearls
Karnataka	Woodcarving, Ivory carving
Jharkhand	Wood craft, paitkar paintings, metal work, stone carving, ornaments, toy making
Manipur	Wood carving, textile weaving, stone-carving, block printing, kauna (water reed) mat, hand-embroidery
Jammu & Kashmir	Carpets, basket weaving, namdas, pashmina shawls, papier-mchie, leather and fur, wood carvings

Fashion in India

- In Indian History the kinds of costumes and accessories worn can be seen to fulfill two criteria : simplicity and opulence.
- Amarakosha and the Brihat–kalpa–sutra ancient works mention a range of subjects including textiles and garments.
- Several terms for the female upper garment were used in Sanskrit and Prakrit literature including uttarasanga, uttariyavasan uttariyavasa, udaramsbuka, samvyana, stanam sbuka and Stanottariya.
- The lower garment worn by women were also described by a variety of names like ambara, amsbuka, antariya, jaghanamsbuka, nivasana, paridbana, vasana, vastram, vasas and sauli.
- First Indian first fashion show was held in 1958. Jeannie Naoroji wins credit for initiating the first wave of fashion shows in India.
- Several institutes like National Institute of Fashion Technology (NIFT), Indian Institute of Fashion Technology (11FT) and other fashion academis have been established where the students are taught to translate their creativity into dresses and fabric designs.
- Today the fashion designers from India have created a lasting impression on the world market. Ravi Bajaj, Ritu Beri, Gitanjali Kashyap, Rohit. Bal have designed various fashion lines.

Exercise -1

1. Rabindranath Tagore's 'Jana Gana Mana' has been adopted as India's National Anthem. How many stanzas of the said song were adopted?

   (a) Only the first stanza

   (b) The whole song

   (c) Third and Fourth stanza

   (d) First and Second stanza

2. Amrita Pritam's work "A Revenue Stamp" is –

   (a) A book of stories   (b) A novel

   (c) A biography   (d) An autobiography

3. 'Natya - Shastra' the main source of India's classical dances was written by –

   (a) Nara Muni   (b) Bharat Muni

   (c) Abhinav Gupt   (d) Tandu Muni

4. Who authored the 'Gitanjali', an anthology of poems?

   (a) Sumitranandan Pant   (b) Makhanlal Chaturvedi

   (c) Rabindranath Tagore   (d) Maithili Sharan Gupt

5. 'Dandia' is a popular dance of

   (a) Punjab   (b) Gujarat

   (c) Tamil Nadu   (d) Maharashtra

6. 'Kathakali' is a folk dance prevalent in which state?

   (a) Karnataka   (b) Odisha

   (c) Kerala   (d) Manipur

7. Who amonst the following is the author of the book 'Freedom from Fear'?

   (a) Nelson Mandela   (b) Aung San Suukyi

   (c) Taslima Nasreen   (d) Benazir Bhutto

8. Which of the following dances is a solo dance?

   (a) Ottan Thullal   (b) Kuchipudi

   (c) Yakshagana   (d) Odissi

9. 'Ethics for the New Millennium' is a book written by:

   (a) Dalai Lama   (b) Tiger Woods

   (c) Hillary Clinton   (d) Andrew Miller

10. Thillana is a format of –

    (a) Kuchipudi   (b) Odissi

    (c) Baharatanatyam   (d) Kathak

11. 'Madhubani', a style of folk paintings, is popular in which of the following states in India?

    (a) Uttar Pradesh   (b) Rajasthan

    (c) Madhya Pradesh   (d) Bihar

12. Which of the following is the author of play/book 'Yashodhara':

    (a) Maithili Sharan Gupt

    (b) Khushwant Singh

    (c) Bankimchandra Chatterjee

    (d) Sarojini Naidu

13. In which of the following festivals are boat races a special feature?

    (a) Onam   (b) Ranali Bihu

    (c) Navratri   (d) Pongal

14. Which of the following places is famous for Chikankari work, which is a traditional art of embroidery?

    (a) Lucknow   (b) Hyderabad

    (c) Jaipur   (d) Mysore

15. 'Kathakali' is a folk dance prevalent in which state?

    (a) Karnataka   (b) Odisha

    (c) Kerala   (d) Manipur

16. Central Board of Film Certification comes under which of the following Ministries of the Government of India?

    (a) Ministry of Tourism and Culture

    (b) Ministry of Human Resources Development

    (c) Ministry of Information and Broadcasting

    (d) Ministry of Youth Affairs and Sports

17. The UNESCO (United Nations Educational Scientific and Cultural Organization) has inscribed three Indian performing art forms in the Representative List of the Intangible Cultural Heritage of Humanity. What are these?

    (a) Mudiyettu, Chhau and Kathak

    (b) Chhau, Mudiyettu and Kalbeli

    (c) Chhau, kalbeli and Goti Pua

    (d) Mudiyettu, Goti Pua and Kathak

18. Which one of the following is not a form of Carnatic music?

    (a) Kriti   (b) Thillana

    (c) Slokem   (d) Tappa

19. Yakshagana is a folk dance-drama of:

    (a) Maharashtra   (b) Karnataka

    (c) Gujarat   (d) W. Bengal

20. Onam is the regional festival of:

    (a) Gujarat   (b) Kerala

    (c) Assam   (d) Tamil Nadu

21. Which one of the following pairs is correctly matched?

   (a) Naqqual–Bihar   (b) Tamasha–Orissa

   (c) Ankia Nat– Assam   (d) Baha–Punjab

22. Which one of the following dances involves solo performance?

   (a) Bharatanatyam   (b) Kuchipudi

   (c) Mohiniattam   (d) Odissi

23. The Raga which is sung early in the morning is:

   (a) Todi   (b) Darbari

   (c) Bhopali   (d) Bhimpalasi

24. Which one of the following is not correctly matched?
    Prominent Indian Writer Language

   (a) Raja Rao   : Telugu

   (b) Gobind Trimbuk Desnpande : Marathi

   (c) Subramaniyam Bharati   : Tamil

   (d) Tara Shankar Joshi   : Gujarati

25. Among the following, who are the Agaria community?

   (a) A traditional toddy tappers community of Andhra Pradesh

   (b) A traditional fishing community of Maharashtra

   (c) A traditional silk- weaving community of Karnataka

   (d) A traditional salt pan workers community of Gujarat

26. Peking is the sacred place of

   (a) Confucianism   (b) Judaism

   (c) Taoism   (d) Shintoism

27. Papeti is the festival of:

   (a) Sikhs   (b) Jains

   (c) Buddhists   (d) Parsis

28. Khordad sal is the festival of

   (a) Jains   (b) Parsis

   (c) Sikhs   (d) Buddhists

29. Jaubani is a dance form traditionally performed in North-Eastern India by the

   (a) Dimasas   (b) Mizos

   (c) Khasis   (d) Bodos

30. Who among the following cultures were the first to paint their pottery?

   (a) Mesolithic   (b) Chalcolithic

   (c) Neolithic   (d) Iron-age

31. Which one of the following is not correctly matched ?

   (a) Pandit Krishna Maharaj : Tabla

   (b) Pandit Birju Maharaj   : Sarod

   (c) Ustad Bismillah Khan   : Shehnai

   (d) Ustad Vilayat Khan   : Sitar

32. Who among the following is an accomplished Veena player?

   (a) K.R. Kumaraswamy Iyer

   (b) Hari Prasad Chaurasia

   (c) Pannalal Ghose

   (d) Baluswamy Dikshitar

33. A Hindustani classical musician, Ali Akbar Khan, often referred to as Khansahib or by the title Ustad (master) belongs to:

   (a) Maihar Gharana   (b) Gwalior Gharana

   (c) Agra Gharana   (d) Patiala Gharana

34. Which of the following statements is correct with regard to classical dancer Mallika Sarabhai?

   (a) She is a noted Kuchipudi and Bharatnatyam dancer.

   (b) She is a leading exponent and torch-bearer of the Kalka-Bindadin Gharana of Lucknow.

   (c) She is a Kathak maestro.

   (d) It is believed that she had declined the chair of the President of India, once offered by Morarji Desai, the then Prime Minister of India.

35. How is Shobhana Chandrakumar well known as ?

   (a) Dancer

   (b) Environmentalist

   (c) Educationist and a member of the National knowledge Commission

   (d) Sportsperson

36. Navroze is a festival celebrated in India by the

   (a) Hindus   (b) Muslims

   (c) Parsis   (d) Christians

37. The Patola weave was traditionally done in

   (a) Pochampally and Kanchipuram

   (b) Surat and Patan

   (c) Dacca and Benares

   (d) Benares and Paithan

38. How is Kishori Amonkar well known as?

   (a) Classical dancer   (b) Classical singer

   (c) Poet   (d) Theatre personality

39. With reference to India's culture and tradition, what is 'Kalaripayattu'?

   (a) It is an ancient Bhakti cult of Shaivism still prevalent in some parts of South India

   (b) It is an ancient style bronze and brasswork still found in southern part of Coromandel area

   (c) It is an ancient form of dance-drama and a living tradition in the northern part of Malabar

   (d) It is an ancient martial art and a living tradition in some parts of South India

40. Teejan Bai, a recipient of the M. S. Subbulakshmi Centenary Award, 2016, is an exponent in

    (a) Kannada classical vocal

    (b) Kajari dance

    (c) Bihu dance

    (d) Pandavani, a traditional performing art

41. Consider the following pairs:

    Traditions- Communities

    1. Chaliha Sahib Festival- Sindhis

    2. Nanda Raj JaatYatra- Gonds

    3. Wari-Warkari-Santhals

Which of the pairs given above is/are correctly matched ?

(a) 1 only

(b) 2 and 3 only

(c) 1 and 3 only

(d) None of the above

42. With reference to Manipuri Sankirtana, consider the following statements:

    1. It is a song and dance performance.

    2. Cymbals are the only musical instruments used in the performance.

    3. It is performed to narrate the life and deeds of Lord Krishna.

Which of the statements given above is/are correct?

(a) 1, 2 and 3.

(b) 1 and 3 only

(c) 2 and 3 only

(d) 1 only

Exercise -2

Statement Based MCQ

1. Consider the following famous historical persons:
   1. Ashvaghosha   2. Bhavabhuti
   3. Nagarjuna   4. Naga sena

   Who of the above are Buddhist scholars?
   (a) 1 and 3 only   (b) 2, 3 and 4
   (c) 1, 3, and 4   (d) 1, 2 and 4

2. Consider the following statements regarding the Chakiarkoothu form of dance:
   1. It is performed by Chakiar caste
   2. It cannot be traditionally witnessed by the higher caster Hindus
   3. Mizhavu is the accompanying instrument
   4. Its theatre form is called Koothambalam

   Which of these statements are correct?
   (a) 1, 3 and 4   (b) 1, 2 and 3
   (c) 2, 3 and 4   (d) 1, 2 and 4

3. Consider the following statements:
   1. The National School of Drama was set up by Sangeet Natak Akademi in 1959.
   2. The highest honour conferred by the Sahitya Akademi on a writer is by electing him its Fellow.

   Which of the statements given above is/are correct?
   (a) 1 only   (b) 2 only
   (c) Both 1 and 2   (d) Neither 1 nor 2

4. Consider the following pairs:

Tradition		*State*
1. Gatka, a traditional martial art	:	Kerala
2. Madhubani, a traditional painting	:	Bihar
3. Singhey Khababs Sindhu Darshan Festival	:	Jammu & Kashmir

   Which of the pairs given above is/are correctly matched?
   (a) 1 and 2 only   (b) 3 only
   (c) 2 and 3 only   (d) 1, 2 and 3

5. Consider the following famous names:
   1. Amrita Sher-Gil   2. Bikash Bhattacharjee
   3. N.S. Bendre   4. Subodh Gupta

   Who of the above is/are well known as artist(s)?
   (a) 1 only   (b) 1 and 4 only
   (c) 2, 3 and 4 only   (d) 1, 2, 3 and 4

6. At which of the following places, Kumbh Mela is held?
   1. Nasik   2. Haridwar
   3. Prayag   4. Ujjain
   (a) 1 and 2   (b) 2, 3 and 4
   (c) 2 and 4   (d) 1, 2, 3 and 4

7. Consider the following statements in respect of protection of copyright in India.
   1. Copyright is a legal right given to creators of literacy, dramatic, musical and artistic works and produces of cinematograph films and sound recordings.
   2. Copyrights protects only the expression and not the ideas. There is no copyright of in idea.

   Which of the statement given above is/are correct.
   (a) 1 only   (b) 2 only
   (c) Both 1 and 2   (d) Neither 1 nor 2

8. Consider the following statements
   1. An Inconvenient Truth is a documentary film about global warming directed by AI Gore.
   2. The film focuses on AI Gore and his travels in support of his efforts to educate the public about the severity of the climate crisis.

   Which of the statements given above is/are correct?
   (a) 1 only   (b) 2 only
   (c) Both 1 and 2   (d) Neither 1 nor 2

9. Which of the following is/are correct:
   1. Bhimsen Joshi was the leading exponent of the Khayal Form of Singing.
   2. Bhimsen Joshi was awarded Bharat Ratna in 2007.
   3. M.F. Hussain won the Golden Bear Award" for his painting Mahabharata.
   (a) 1 only   (b) 2 only
   (c) 3 only   (d) 1 and 2

10. Which of the following statements are correct with regard to the Bharatanatyam?
    1. It is a dance of Tamil Nadu in southern India.
    2. It traces its origins back to the Natyashastra, an ancient treatise on theatre written by the mythic priest Bharata.
    3. The dance movements are characterized by bent legs, while feet keep rhythm.
    4. Hands may be used in a series of mudras, or symbolic hand gestures, to tell a story.

    Select the answer from the codes given below:
    (a) 1, 2, and 3   (b) 2, 3, and 4
    (c) 1, 3, and 4   (d) 1, 2, 3 and 4

11. Consider the following statements:
    1. Kathakali is the classical dance form of Kerala.
    2. Kathakali is a religious dance. It draws inspiration from the Ramayana and stories from Shaiva traditions.
    3. In Kathakali, costumes and makeup are especially elaborate, with faces made to look like painted masks and enormous headdresses.
    4. Kathakali is traditionally performed by women.

    Select the answer from the codes given below:
    (a) 1, 2, and 3   (b) 2, 3, and 4
    (c) 1, 3, and 4   (d) 1, 2, 3 and 4

12. Which of the following statements are correct with regard to the Manipuri classical dance?
    1. It is characterized by smooth and graceful movements.
    2. Female roles are especially fluid in the arms and hands, while male roles tend to have more forceful movements.
    3. The dance may be accompanied by narrative chanting and choral singing.
    4. A striking part of Manipur dance is its colourful decoration, lightness of dancing foot, delicacy of Abhinaya (drama), lilting music and poetic charm.

    Select the answer from the codes given below:
    (a) 1, 2 and 3
    (b) 2, 3 and 4
    (c) 1, 3 and 4
    (d) 1, 2, 3 and 4

13. Which of the following statements are correct with regard to the Kuchipudi classical dance?
    1. Kuchipudi derives its name from the Kuchipudi village of Andhra Pradesh.
    2. It needs talent in both dancing and singing.
    3. This dance, from the state of Andhra Pradesh in southeastern India, is highly ritualized.
    4. A formalized song-and-dance introduction, sprinkling of holy water, and burning of incense, along with invocations of goddesses is part of this dance.

    Select the answer from the codes given below:
    (a) 1, 2, and 3
    (b) 2, 3, and 4
    (c) 1, 3, and 4
    (d) 1, 2, 3 and 4

14. Which of the following statements are correct with regard to the Odissi classical dance?
    1. It is predominantly a dance for women, with postures that replicate those found in temple sculptures.
    2. Based on archaeological findings, Odissi is believed to be the oldest of the surviving Indian classical dances.
    3. It is a very complex and expressive dance, with over fifty mudras (symbolic hand gestures) commonly used.

    Select the answer from the codes given below:
    (a) 1 and 2
    (b) 2 and 3
    (c) 1 and 3
    (d) 1, 2 and 3

15. Which of the following statements are correct with regard to the movie 'Raja Harishchandra' ?
    1. It is a 1913 Indian talking film.
    2. It was directed and produced by Indian icon director Dhundiraj Govind Phalke (Dadasaheb Phalke).
    3. It is the first full-length Indian feature film.
    4. The complete film is no longer available.

    Select the answer from the codes given below:
    (a) 1, 2, and 3
    (b) 2, 3, and 4
    (c) 1, 3, and 4
    (d) 1, 2, 3 and 4

16. With reference to the famous Sattriya dance, consider the following statements : [CSAT 2014 - I]
    1. Sattriya is a combination of music, dance and drama.
    2. It is a centuries-old living tradition of Vaishnavites of Assam.
    3. It is based on classical Ragas and Talas of devotional songs composed by Tulsidas, Kabir and Mirabai.

    Which of the statements given above is/ are correct?
    (a) 1 only
    (b) 1 and 2 only
    (c) 2 and 3 only
    (d) 1, 2 and 3

17. Consider the following pairs : [CSAT 2014 - I]
    1. Garba — Gujarat
    2. Mohiniattam — Odisha
    3. Yakshagana — Karnataka

    Which of the pairs given above is/are correctly matched?
    (a) 1 only
    (b) 2 and 3 only
    (c) 1 and 3 only
    (d) 1, 2 and 3

Matching Based MCQ

DIRECTIONS (Qs. 18 to 28) : Match List-I with List-II and select the correct answer using the codes given below the lists.

18.

List I (Book)		List II (Author)	
(A)	In custody	(1)	Amartya Sen
(B)	Sea of Poppies	(2)	Amitav Ghosh
(C)	The Argumentative Indian	(3)	Anita Desai
(D)	Unaccustomed Earth	(4)	Jhumpa Lahiri

    (a) A – 4; B – 1; C – 2; D – 3
    (b) A – 4; B – 2; C – 1; D – 3
    (c) A – 3; B – 2; C – 1; D – 4
    (d) A – 3; B – 1; C – 2; D – 4

19.

List-I (States)		List-II (Festivals)	
(A)	Tamil Nadu	(1)	Bhageli Bihu
(B)	West Bengal	(2)	Onam
(C)	Kerala	(3)	Sarhul
(D)	Assam	(4)	Pongal
		(5)	Dol Purnima

    (a) A – 3; B – 4; C – 5; D – 2
    (b) A – 4; B – 2; C – 2; D – 1
    (c) A – 3; B – 2; C – 5; D – 4
    (d) A – 4; B – 5; C – 2; D – 1

20.

List I (Author)		List II (Book)	
(A)	Amartya Sen	(1)	An Ordinary Person's Guide to Empire
(B)	Bimal Jalan	(2)	The Argumentative Indian
(C)	Arundhati Roy	(3)	The Future of India
(D)	Mani Shankar Aiyar	(4)	Confession of a Secular Fundamentalist

    (a) A – 3; B – 2; C – 1; D – 4
    (b) A – 2; B – 3; C – 1; D – 4
    (c) A – 3; B – 2; C – 4; D – 1
    (d) A – 2; B – 3; C – 4; D – 1

21.

List I (Person)		List II (Known As)
(A) Bhajan Sopori	(1)	Bharatnatyam dancer
(B) Birju Maharaj	(2)	Exponent of Santoor
(C) Priyadarsini Govind	(3)	Mridangam maestro
(D) T.V. Gopalakrishnan	(4)	Kathak dancer

(a) A – 2; B – 1; C – 4; D – 3
(b) A – 3; B – 1; C – 4; D – 2
(c) A – 2; B – 4; C – 1; D – 3
(d) A – 3; B – 4; C – 1; D – 2

22.

List-I (Folk Dance-Dramas)		List-II (States)
(A) Yakshagana	(1)	Uttar Pradesh
(B) Tamasha	(2)	Gujarat
(C) Nautanki	(3)	Maharashtra
(D) Bhavi	(4)	Karnataka
	(5)	Madhya Pradesh

(a) A – 3; B – 4; C – 2; D – 1
(b) A – 4; B – 3; C – 1; D – 2
(c) A – 4; B – 5; C – 3; D – 2
(d) A – 3; B – 2; C – 4; D – 5

23.

List-I (Person)		List-II (Form of Music)
(A) Pandit Vishnu Digambar Paluskar	(1)	Introduced the scheme of Raga classification of Indian music
(B) Venkatamahi	(2)	Proponent of Carnatic music
(C) Shyama Shastri	(3)	Proponent of the Khayal form of Hindustani music
(D) Amir Khusrau	(4)	Wrote the music for the song 'Vande Mataram'

(a) A – 4; B – 1; C – 3; D – 2
(b) A – 4; B – 1; C – 2; D – 3
(c) A – 1; B – 4; C – 3; D – 2
(d) A – 1; B – 4; C – 2; D – 3

24.

List-I (Artist)		List-II (Medium of music delivery)
(A) Balamurali Krishna	(1)	Hindustani vocal
(B) Mita Pandit	(2)	Ghatam
(C) Kanyakumari	(3)	Sitar
(D) Nikhil Bannerjee	(4)	Violin
	(5)	Carnatic Vocal

(a) A – 5; B – 1; C – 2; D – 3
(b) A – 4; B – 3; C – 1; D – 5
(c) A – 3; B – 1; C – 5; D – 2
(d) A – 5; B – 4; C – 1; D – 3

25.

List-I (Festival)		List-II (State)
(A) Ugadi	(1)	West Bengal
(B) Nababarsha	(2)	Gujarat
(C) Bhadra Purnima	(3)	Maharashtra
(D) Gudi Padwa	(4)	Andhra Pradesh

(a) A - 4; B - 1; C - 2; D - 3
(b) A - 4; B - 2; C - 1; D - 3
(c) A - 3; B - 2; C - 1; D - 4
(d) A - 3; B - 1; C - 2; D - 4

Hints and Explanations

EXERCISE-1

1. (a) 2. (d) 3. (b) 4. (c) 5. (b) 6. (c)
7. (b) 8. (a) 9. (a) 10. (c) 11. (d) 12. (a)
13. (a) 14. (a) 15. (c) 16. (c) 17. (b) 18. (d)
19. (b) 20. (b) 21. (c)

22. (a) Bharatnatyam is the dance of Tamil Nadu. The dance involves solo performances by devadasis or the temple dancer.

23. (a) Raga Todi which was invented by Mian Tansen is sung early in the morning.

24. (a) 25. (d) 26. (a) 27. (d) 28. (b) 29. (a)
30. (c) 31. (b)

32. (a) Kumaraswamy Iyer took active part in the restoration of Swati Tirunal's compositions with the support of the Travancore royalty. Among his other contributions to the music world was his setting the tunes for rare compositions of Saint Achyuta Dasa and Kamakoti Sastrigal.

33. (a) The Maihar Gharana is a Gharana or school of Hindustani or North Indian classical music formed principally by the sarod maestro Ustad Allaudin Khan in Maihar in the Madhya Pradesh state of India.

34. (a) Mallika Sarabhai is a noted Kuchipudi and Bharatnatyam dancer from Ahmadabad, Gujarat. Born to famous dancer Mrinalini Sarabhai and the well-known space scientist Vikram Sarabhai.

35. (a)

36. (c) Parsis

37. (b) Patola saris are a double ikat woven sari, usually made from silk, made inPatan, Gujarat, India. Velvet patola styles are also made in Surat. Patola-weaving is a closely guarded family tradition.

38. (b) Kishori Amonkar, an Indian classical vocalist, recognized as one of the foremost singers in the Hindustani tradition is an innovative exponent of the Jaipur gharana.

39. (d) Kalaripayattu is an ancient martial art and a living tradition in some parts of Kerala/ South India.

40. (d) Teejan Bai is an exponent of Pandavani, a traditional performing art form, from Chhattisgarh, in which she enacts tales from the Mahabharata, with musical accompaniments.

41. (a) 1. Chaliha Sahib: Sindhi festival regarding Jhulelal. So first pair is right.

2. Nanda Raj JaatYatra: Nanda Devi related festival in Uttarakhand. Gonds are not native to this state, so 2 is wrong.

3. Wari-Warkari: Wari is a pilgrimage for the Warkari sect related to Pandharpur god Vithobain Maharashtra, and it's part of Bhakti movement rather than festival of a particular tribal group. Besides, Santhals are not native to this state, So #3 is wrong.

Accordingly, answer "A": 1 only.

42. (b) In Manipuri Sankirtana, two drummers and ten singer dancers are usually present. Meaning either cymbals are not the only instrument OR they're using drums instead of cymbals. In either interpretation- statement 2 is wrong. Hence answer "B" 1 and 3 only. Ccrtindia.gov.in says Males dancers play Pung and Kartal during Manipuri Sankirtana.] in either case,#2 is wrong so answer remains "B".

EXERCISE-2

1. (c)

2. (d) Chakiarkoothu is the famous folk dance of Kerala regarding which statement 1, 2 and 4 are correct.

3. (c) 4. (c)
5. (d) 6. (d)

7. (d) Copyright is a legal concept, enacted by most government, giving the creator of an original work executive right to it, usually for a lifetime. Generally it is "the right to copy" but also gives the copyright holder the right to be credited for the work. It's area not only include cinema or artistic world but it covers anything whichever is thought to be copied.

8. (c) An Inconvenient Truth is a 2006 documentary film directed by Davis Guggenheim about former United States Vice President Al Gore's campaign to educate citizens about global warming. The documentary was great a success and box-office hit, got 2 Academy Awards.

9. (a)

10. (d) Originally, a temple dance for women, Bharatanatyam often is used to express Hindu religious stories and devotions. It was not commonly seen on the public stage until the 20th century.

11. (a) Kathakali is traditionally performed by boys and men, even for female roles. The word Kathakali literally means "Story-Play". Kathakali is known for its heavy, elaborate makeup and costumes. In fact, the colourful and fascinating costumes of Kathakali have become the most recognized icon of Kerala. Kathakali is considered as one of the most magnificent theatres of imagination and creativity.

12. (d) Manipuri comes from Manipur in northeastern India. It has its roots in that Manipur's folk traditions and rituals, and often depicts scenes from the life of the god Krishna.

13. (d) Kuchipudi derives its name from the Kuchipudi village of Andhra Pradesh. Traditionally, the dance was performed by men, even the female roles, although now it is predominantly performed by women.

14. (d) Odissi is a highly inspired, passionate, ecstatic and sensuous form of dance. Like most of the South Indian classical dances of India, Odissi too had its origin in the Devadasi tradition. The state of Orissa has a great cultural history.

15. (b) First screened on April 21, 1913 it is a silent film. The film revolves around the noble and righteous king, Harishchandra, who first sacrifices his kingdom, followed by his wife and eventually his children to honour his promise to the sage Vishwamitra. Though, in the end, pleased by his high morals, the Gods are pleased and restore his former glory, and further bestow him with divine blessings.

16. (d) Sattriya dance form was introduced in the 15th century A.D by the great Vaishnava saint and reformer of Assam, Mahapurusha Sankaradeva as a powerful medium for propagation of the Vaishnava faith. It is a neo-Vaishnava treasure of Assamese music,dance and drama. Music of Sattriya dance comprises of classical ragas (melodies), talas (rhythms) and traditional songs. Tulsidas, Kabir and Mira were Vaishnavite.

17. (c) Yakshgana is a theatre form of Karnataka. Mohiniattam is from Kerala and Garba is a dance form from Gujarat.

18. (c) 19 (d) 20. (b) 21. (c) 22. (b)

23. (d) Pandit Vishnu Digambar Paluskar introduced the scheme of Raga classification of Indian music, Venkatamahi wrote the music of the song 'Vande Matram', Shyama Shastri was a proponent of Karnatic music and Amir Khusrau was the proponent of Khyal form of Hindustani music.

24. (a) Balamurali Krishna is famous carnatic vocalist, Mita Pandit is famous Hindustani vocalist, Kanyakumari is famous for Ghatam from of singing and Nikhil Banerjee is famous sitar player.

25. (a)

SPORTS : AT A GLANCE

Trophies Associated with Sports

National

Name of the Trophy	Related game
Aga Khan Cup	Hockey
Barna Belleck Cup	Table Tennis
Beighton Cup	Hockey
Bombay Gold Cup	Hockey
Burdwan Trophy	Weight Lifting
D.C.M. Trophy	Football
Dhyan chand Trophy	Hockey
Dr. B.C. Roy Trophy	Football
Duleep Trophy	Cricket
Durand Cup	Football
Ezra Cup	Polo
I.F.A Shield	Football
Lady Ratan Tata Trophy	Hockey
Moin ud daula Gold Cup	Cricket
Rangaswami Cup	Hockey
Ranji Trophy	Cricket
Santosh Trophy	Football
Scindia Gold Cup	Hockey
Subroto Mukherjee Cup	Football (Inter-School)
Wellington Trophy	Rowing

International

Name of the Trophy	Related game
American Cup	Yatch Racing
Ashes Cup	Cricket (Australia-England)
Azlan Shah	Hockey
US Masters	Golf
Hopman Cup	Lawn Tennis
Colombo Cup Trophy	Football
Davis Cup	Lawn Tennis
Kings Cup Race	Air Races (England)
Merdeka Cup	Football (Asia)
Swaythling Cup	World Table Tennis
Thomas Cup	World Badminton (Men)
Uber Cup	World Badminton (women)
US Open	Lawn Tennis
French Open	Lawn Tennis
Australian Open	Lawn Tennis
Wimbledon	Lawn Tennis
Masters Champions Trophy	Hockey
British Open	Golf
Malaysian Open	Badminton
Tata Open	Lawn Tennis

Number of Players on each side

Games	No. of Players	Games	No of Players
Badminton	1 or 2	Polo	4
Baseball	9	Rugby Football	15
Basketball	5	Tennis and Table tennis	1 or 2
Cricket	11	Water Polo	7
Football	11	Volleyball	6
Hockey	11	Kabaddi	7
Chess	1		

Places Associated with Sports and Games

Cricket: Melbourne Cricket Ground (Melbourne, Australia); Old Trafford Cricket Ground (Manchester, England); Lord's Cricket Ground (London, England); Headingley Stadium (Leeds, England); The Oval Cricket Ground (Kennington, England); Trent Bridge Ground (Nottingham, England);

Adelaide Oval (Australia); Gaddafi Stadium (Lahore, Pakistan); Sydney Cricket Ground (Australia); Brisbane Cricket Ground (Australia); Western Australian Cricket Association Ground (Perth, Australia); Barabati Stadium (Cuttack, Odisha); Feroz Shah Kotla Ground (New Delhi); M. Chinnaswamy Stadium (Bangalore); Sawai Mansingh Stadium (Jaipur, Rajasthan); Sharjah Cricket Stadium (United Arab Emirates); Eden Gardens (Kolkata, West Bengal); M. A. Chidambaram Stadium (Tamil Nadu); DY Patil Stadium (Mumbai); Wanderers Stadium (Johannesburg, South Africa); Wankhede Stadium (Mumbai); JSCA International Cricket Stadium (Ranchi).

Football: Rungnado May Day Stadium (Pyongyang); Wembley Stadium (London); Azadi Stadium (Tehran, Iran); Santiago Bernabéu (Madrid, Spain); Salt Lake Stadium (Kolkata); Jawaharlal Nehru Stadium (New Delhi); Camp Nou (Barcelona); Stade de France (France); Signal Iduna Park (Dortmund, Germany); Estadio Azteca (Mexico City, Mexico).

Hockey: Patliputra Sports Complex (Patna); Kalinga Stadium (Bhubaneswar); Shivaji Hockey Stadium (New Delhi); National Hockey Stadium (Lahore, Pakistan); Merdeka Stadium (Kuala Lumpur); Sawai Man Singh Stadium (Jaipur); Lal Bahadur Shastri Stadium (Hyderabad); Nehru Stadium (Delhi).

Tennis: Arthur Ashe Stadium (United States); O2 Arena (United Kingdom); Wimbledon Centre Court (United Kingdom); Rod Laver Arena (Australia); Ahoy Rotterdam (Netherlands); SDAT Tennis Stadium (Chennai).

Horse Racing: Tokyo Racecourse (Tokyo); Flemington Racecourse (Melbourne); Epsom Downs (United Kingdom); Churchill Downs (United States); Sha Tin Racecourse (Hong Kong, China).

National Sports of Various Countries

Afghanistan	Buzkashi
Australia	Cricket
Barbados	Cricket
Bermuda	Cricket
Bhutan	Archery
Bangladesh	Kabaddi
Brazil	Football
Canada	Lacrosse (summer), Ice hockey (winter)
Cuba	Baseball
Chile	Chilean rodeo
China	Table Tennis
England	Cricket
Czech Republic	Ice hockey
Japan	Sumo
India	No game
Pakistan	Field hockey
Puerto Rico	Baseball
Russia	Bandy
Scotland	Golf
Spain	Football
Sri Lanka	Volleyball
United States	Baseball
Venezuela	Baseball

Terms used in Games and Sports

Badminton	Deuce, Double, Drop, Fault, Game, Let, love, Smash, Rally, Kill, Back Alley.
Baseball	Bunting, Diamond, Home, Pitcher, Put out, Strike, Error, On-Deck.
Billiards	Break, Cannons, Cue, In off, Jigger, Scratch,
Boat Race	Cox, stroke
Boxing	Hook, Jab, Knock-out, Punch, upper cut.
Bridge	Diamonds, Dummy, Grand slam, Little slam, Revoke, Ruff, Tricks, Trump.
Chess	Check, Checkmate, Gambit, Stalemate
Cricket	Bowling, Bouncer, Crease, Cover point, Drive, Duck, Follow on, Googly, Gulley, Hat Trick, Hit wicket, L.B.W. (Leg Before Wicket), Leg Break, Leg spinner, Leg bye Maiden over, No ball, Pitch, Run, silly point, Stumped, Wicket keeper.
Football	Dribble, Drop Kick, Foul, Hattrick, Off-side, Penalty, Throw in, Touch Down.
Golf	Bogey, Caddie, Hole, Links, Put, Putting the green, Stymie, Tee.
Hockey	Bull, Carry, Centre Forward, Carried, Dribble, Goal, Hat trick, Penalty corner, Scoop, Short corner, Sticks, Striking circle, Under cutting.
Horse Racing	Jockey, Place, Protest, Punter, Win.
Lawn Tennis	Back-hand-drive, Service, Smash, Volley, Deuce, Game, Set, Love.
Polo	Bunder, Chuckker, Mallet.
Rifle Shooting	Bull's eye.
Rugby	Drop kick, Screen.
Swimming	Stroke.
Volley ball	Booster, Deuce, Love, Service, Spikers.
Wrestling	Half Nelson, Heave.

Measurements of Sports Fields

Badminton	Court : 13.40 m × 5.18 m Net : 1.524 m high Shuttle : 4.75 to 5.50 gms
Cricket	Pitch : 22 yards (20 m) Bat : 97 cm length and 10.8 cm width Ball : 155.9 to 163 gms
Derby Course	Route length : 2400 metres or 1½ miles
Football	Field : 100 × 64 m to 110 × 75 m
Hockey	Field : 91.4 by 55.0 m Ball : 5.50 ounces to 5.75 ounces
Kabaddi	Field : 10 m × 13 m
Kho kho	Field : 29 m × 16 m
Lawn Tennis	Court : 23.77 × 8.23 metres Ball : 56.0 − 59.4g (weight) : 65.41–68.58mm diameter
Marathon Race	Route Length : 42,195 m (42.195 kms)
Table Tennis	Table : 274 cm × 152.5 cm, 76 cm above the ground (floor) Ball : 40mm (diameter); 2.7 gms (mass)
Volleyball	Court : 18 m × 9 m

Sports Grounds

Games	Grounds	Games	Grounds
Athletics	Track	Handball	Court
Badminton	Court	Hockey	Field
Baseball	Diamond	Ice Hockey	Ring
Boxing	Ring	Lawn Tennis	Court
Cricket	Pitch (Field)	Skating	Ring
Football	Field	Wrestling	Ring, Arena
Golf	Course		

Major Sport Disciplines

Acrobatic Gymnastics

Also known as sport acrobatics, the sports is a competitive gymnastic discipline in which gymnasts work together and perform figures which include acrobatic moves, dance and tumbling, according to music. There are various types of routines such as a 'balance' routine where the prime focus is on strength, poise and flexibility; secondly 'dynamic' routine which includes throws, somersaults and catches, and lastly a 'combined' routine which consists of elements from both balance and dynamic. International Federation of Gymnastics, the governing body of the sports has categorised the competition based on age groups; 11-16, 12-18, 13-19 and 15+ (Senior).

Baseball

The game is played between two teams with nine players each who take turns to bat and field. It started in the US in the mid 1800s, but got worldwide recognition in the 19th century. People of North America, South America, and East Asia mostly play baseball and baseball has been declared as the national pastime of the US keeping in mind the time spent by a lot of people in playing or watching baseball games.

World Baseball Softball Confederation (WBSC)

Is the world governing body for the sports of baseball and softball. It was established in 2013 and is headquartered in Lausanne, Switzerland.

Canoeing and Kayaking

These are boat related sports where the person has to paddle to move forward in the race. Both the sports have featured as competition sports in the Summer Olympic Games since the 1936 Games in Berlin, although they were demonstration sports at the 1924 games in Paris. The categories of canoeing in Olympic competition are slalom and sprint.

Boxing

It is a man to man combat sports which involves throwing of punches at each other for knocking out the opponent. Amateur boxing features in both Olympic and Commonwealth games although it also has its own World Championships. The origin of boxing can be traced back as an organized sport by the ancient Greeks as an Olympic game in BC 688. In the modern era it evolved during 16th and 18th century prize fights, mainly in Great Britain and later became a worldwide sport.

Billiards

Also known as cue sports, the game is played with a cue stick which is used to strike billiard balls. It is played on cloth covered billiard table with rounded corners and bounded by rubber cushions. The modern version of the sports was finally developed in 1800. The major categories with the sports include Carom billiards, Pool and Snooker. Carom billiards is played on a pocketless table with balkline and straight rail, cushion caroms, three-cushion billiards, artistic billiards and four-ball. Pool also known as pocket billiards is played on a pool table having six pockets along the rails, into which balls are deposited as the main goal of play and eight-ball and nine-ball are most popular versions. Snooker is played on a covered table with pockets at each of the four corners and in the middle of each of the long side cushions.

Basketball

The game was supposedly invented in December 1891 by a Canadian Dr. James Naismith, a physical education professor and instructor at the International Young Men's Christian Association Training School (YMCA). With the passage of time basketball has become one of the world's most popular and widely viewed sports. **National Basketball Association (NBA)** is the most popular and highest level of professional basketball in the world. The International Basketball Federation, also known as FIBA governs all the international competition in basketball. The game was demonstrated in the 1904 and 1924 Summer Olympics. It has been part of the Summer Olympic program since 1936.

Cricket

The game of cricket was probably first played in the 16th century in England and with the passage of time the sports was declared as the National sport of England in the 18th century. The first official Test match was played on 15th March 1877, between England and Australia at the Melbourne Cricket Ground (MCG). The first international Twenty20 match was played at Eden Park in Auckland on 17th February 2005 in between Australia and New Zealand. The first Limited Overs International was played in 1971. International Cricket Council (ICC) is the international governing body of cricket.

Football

The sport is assumed to be first played in China during the third and second centuries BC. The modern form of football came into being in 1863 after the formation of The Football Association in London, England which is the oldest football association in the world. **FIFA** (Fédération Internationale de Football Association) was founded in Paris on 21st May 1904 with **Robert Guérin** as the first president. The founding members of the associations are Belgium, Denmark, France, the Netherlands, Spain, Sweden and Switzerland. **"For the Game. For the World"** is the motto of FIFA.

Kabaddi

The contact sport originated in Ancient India. It is also known by various regional names, such as hadudu in Bangladesh, baibalaa in Maldives, chedugudu in Andhra Pradesh, sadugudu in Tamil Nadu and hututu in Maharashtra. Kabaddi is the national game of Bangladesh. The Indian Kabaddi team has dominated the world stage by winning all the world cups held till date. **Pro Kabaddi League (PKL)** is a professional kabaddi league in India which was first held in 2014.

Hockey

The advent of the sport dates back to the Middle Ages in England, Scotland and the Netherlands. The governing body of hockey is the International Hockey Federation (IHF). It is headquartered in Lausanne, Switzerland. "Fair Play Friendship Forever" is the motto of the federation. It is responsible for organising the Hockey Rules Board and developing the rules for the sport. It is the national sport of Pakistan, and is sometimes assumed to be India's national sport as well, although officially India does not have a national sport.

Archery

Archery is a skill-based sport which involves shooting arrows from a bow in an effort to score the most points by hitting the centre of a target. The sport first appeared in the Olympic Games in 1900, was contested again in 1904, 1908 and 1920, then again, after an absence of 52 years, from 1972 to the present. The only discipline competed at the Olympics is Recurve archery. The World Archery Federation is the governing body of the sport of archery. Its headquarter is located in Lausanne, Switzerland.

Athletics

The term Athletics is derived from Greek word **'athlos'** which means contest. The contest was made more specific in the 19th century by defining the events involved such as competitive running, walking, jumping and throwing. Athletics was included in the first modern Olympic Games in 1896 and with the 1928 Olympics women's events were introduced in the athletics programme. It has been the part of the Paralympic Games since the inaugural Games in 1960.

The International Association of Athletics Federations (IAAF)

Founded on 17th July 1912 is the international governing body for the sport of athletics. It has been headquartered in Monaco since October 1993. Sebastian Coe of the United Kingdom is the current president of IAAF.

Chess

The game of chess is assumed to be originated in India. Modern chess tournament play began in the mid 19th century and the first World Chess Championship was held in 1886. The first generally recognized World Chess Champion, Wilhelm Steinitz, claimed his title in 1886. **World Chess Federation** or FIDE is the international organization that acts as the governing body of international chess competition. FIDE was founded in Paris, France, on July 20, 1924. Its motto is "Gens una sumus" which is Latin for "We are one people".

Formula 1 Ace

The Formula 1 racing traces its roots to the European Grand Prix championships of the 1920s and 1930s. The foundation of Formula One was laid in 1946 with the Fédération Internationale de l'Automobile's (FIA's) standardisation of rules. The F1 season consists of a series of races, known as Grands Prix, held throughout the world on purpose-built F1 circuits and public roads.

Indian Grand Prix was a Formula One race of the FIA Formula One World Championship, which was held at the Buddh International Circuit in Greater Noida near New Delhi. The inaugural season took place on 30th October 2011, as the 17th race of the 2011 Formula One season. The inaugural race was won by Germany's Sebastian Vettel. Vettel won the subsequent Indian Grand Prix in the year 2012 and 2013.

Golf

The origin of the modern game is usually traced to Scotland in the 15th century. The game did not find international popularity until the late 19th century, when it spread into the rest of the United Kingdom and then to the British Empire and the United States. The rules of golf are internationally standardised and are jointly governed by The R&A, spun off in 2004 from The Royal and Ancient Golf Club of St Andrews (founded 1754), and the United States Golf Association (USGA). The major championships are: The Masters, the U.S. Open, The Open Championship and the PGA Championship.

Tennis

The place of origin of the sport is debated but most historians believe that tennis originated in the monastic cloisters in northern France in the 12th century. However, the modern game of tennis originated in Birmingham (England) in the late 19th century as "lawn tennis". The Wimbledon Championships, the world's oldest tennis tournament was first played in London in 1877. Wimbledon, the US Open, the French Open, and the Australian Open are the most prestigious events in tennis. The International Tennis Federation (ITF) is the governing body of world tennis is headquartered in London, England.

Volleyball

William G. Morgan is credited with the creation of the game of volleyball. It has been a part of the Summer Olympic Games since 1964. It is a team sport comprising of two teams of six players each who are separated by a net. The Fédération Internationale de Volleyball (or International Volleyball Federation) is the international governing body for the sports of indoor, beach and grass volleyball. Its headquarters are located in Lausanne, Switzerland.

Table Tennis

Also known as ping pong, the sport is played by two or four players who hit a lightweight ball back and forth across a table using a small, round bat. Table tennis is governed by the worldwide organization International Table Tennis Federation, founded in 1926. Table tennis has been an Olympic sport since 1988.

Kho Kho

It is a tag sport played by teams of twelve players, of which nine enter the field, who try to avoid being touched by members of the opposing team. The rules were first standardized in the early 1900s. A committee was formed at Gymkhana Poona in 1914 for framing the Kho-Kho rules and the first ever book of Kho-Kho rules was published from Gymkhana Baroda, in 1924. Kho kho is one of the two most popular traditional tag games of the Indian subcontinent, the other being kabbadi. The sport is also played in South Africa.

Shooting

Shooting as a sport was introduced in the inaugural 1896 Olympic Games. The International Shooting Sport Federation, also known with the acronym ISSF, is the governing body of the Olympic Shooting events in Rifle, Pistol and Shotgun disciplines, and of several non-Olympic Shooting sport events. The ISSF headquarters is based in Munich, Germany.

Swimming

Competitive swimming became popular in the 19th century. Men's swimming was included in the first modern Olympic Games in 1896 in Athens whereas women's swimming was introduced into the Olympics in 1912. The international governing body for competitive swimming is the Fédération Internationale de Natation or International Swimming Federation which is commonly known as FINA. It is based in Lausanne, Switzerland. Julio Maglione of Uruguay is the current FINA President. The four main strokes in swimming are: Butterfly, Backstroke, Breaststroke and Freestyle.

Weightlifting

It was developed as an international sport primarily in the 19th century. Weightlifting featured at the first modern Olympic Games in Athens in 1896. The two competition lifts in order are the snatch and the clean and jerk. The sport is governed by the International Weightlifting Federation (IWF) which is based in Budapest. It was founded in 1905.

Wrestling

Professional wrestling began in France around 1830. The first organized national wrestling tournament took place in New York City in 1888. Greco-Roman wrestling became an event at the first modern Olympic Games, in Athens in 1896. Since 1908, the event has been in every Summer Olympics. Freestyle wrestling became an Olympic event, in 1904. Women's freestyle wrestling was added to the Summer Olympics in 2004. United World Wrestling (UWW) is the international governing body for the wrestling and its duties include overseeing wrestling at the Olympics. UWW is based in Corsier-sur-Vevey, outside of Lausanne, Switzerland.

Badminton

The game is said to have been played in China in the 2nd millennium BC. However, The origin of modern badminton is attributed to Britain and its development took place in India, it was evolved in 1870 by some British officers serving in India and it was then called 'Poona Game' because of its popularity in Pune in 1876. The International Badminton Federation (IBF) was formed in 1934 when the rules of the game were standardized. Badminton was introduced in the Asian Games in 1962 at Jakarta (Indonesia) and made its debut in the Olympic Games at Barcelona in 1992. The First World Cup (Alba World Cup) was won by Prakash Padukone in 1981 and the first Asian Championship was won by Dinesh Khanna in 1965 (Farmen) and Sarojini Apte and Meena Shah (for women).

The game is played in three ways:

(i)　Single (one player on each side)

(ii)　Double (two players on each side)

(iii)　Mixed Double (one male and one female player on each side)

ASIAN GAMES

The idea of the Asian Games was first conceived by Prof. G.D. Sondhi. The suggestion for holding the Asian Games was first made in a conference of Asian countries held in New Delhi in 1947 and Jawaharlal Nehru suggested that it be called 'Asian Games'. The first Asian Games were held at New Delhi in March 1951. Since then Asian Games are held after every four years.

Asian Games since 1951

Games Serial	Year	Places	Number of Countries	Number of Sports	Number of Players
1	1951	New Delhi(India)	11	6	491
2	1954	Manila(Philippines)	18	8	1021
3	1958	Tokyo(Japan)	20	13	1422
4	1962	Jakarta(Indonesia)	16	13	1545
5	1966	Bangkok(Thailand)	18	14	1945
6	1970	Bangkok(Thailand)	18	13	1752
7	1974	Tehran(Iran)	25	16	2869
8	1978	Bangkok(Thailand)	25	19	3000

9	1982	New Delhi(India)	33	21	3447
10	1986	Seoul(S.Korea)	27	25	3883
11	1990	Beijing(China)	37	27	4500
12	1994	Hiroshima(Japan)	42	34	7300
13	1998	Bangkok(Thailand)	41	38	7000
14	2002	Busan(S.Korea)	44	38	7711
15	2006	Doha(Qatar)	45	39	9524
16	2010	Guangzhou(China)	45	42	9704
17	2014	Incheon(South Korea)	45	36	9501
18	2018	Jakarta (Indonesia)	46	40	13000
19	2022	Hangzhou, China		Future event	

Asian Games 2018

Rank	Countries	Gold	Silver	Bronze	Total
1	China	132	92	65	289
2	Japan	75	56	74	205
3	Republic of Korea	49	58	70	177
4	Indonesia	31	24	43	98
5	Uzbekistan	21	24	25	70
6	IR Iran	20	20	22	62
7	Chinese Taipei	17	19	31	67
8	India	15	24	30	69
9	Kazakhstan	15	17	44	76
10	DPR Korea	12	12	13	37

Medals of India in Asian Games 2018

Sports	Gold Medal	Silver Medal	Bronze Medal	Total
Athletics	7	10	2	19
Shooting	2	4	3	9
Wrestling	2	0	1	3
Bridge	1	0	2	3
Rowing	1	0	2	3
Tennis	1	0	2	3
Boxing	1	0	1	2
Archery	0	2	0	2
Equestrian	0	2	0	2
Squash	0	1	4	5
Sailing	0	1	2	3
Badminton	0	1	1	2
Hockey	0	1	1	2
Kabaddi	0	1	1	2
Kurash	0	1	1	2
Wushu	0	0	4	4
Table Tennis	0	0	2	2
Sepaktakraw	0	0	1	1

HOCKEY WORLD CUP

The concept for an international hockey competition at the world level originated in a joint proposal made by India and Pakistan at an international Hockey Federation FIH council meeting on March 30, 1969. The first world cup was held in Barcelona (Spain) in 1971. From 1978 onwards, the tournament has been held once in four years. India has won the tournament only once in 1975.

MEN'S HOCKEY WORLD CUP

Year	Host	Winner	Runner-up
1971	Spain	Pakistan	Spain
1973	The Netherlands	The Netherlands	India
1975	Malaysia	India	Pakistan
1978	Argentina	Pakistan	The Netherlands
1982	India	Pakistan	West Germany
1986	England	Australia	England
1990	Pakistan	The Netherlands	Pakistan
1994	Australia	Pakistan	The Netherlands
1998	The Netherlands	The Netherlands	Spain
2002	Malaysia	Germany	Australia
2006	Germany	Germany	Australia
2010	India	Australia	Germany
2014	The Netherlands	Australia	Netherlands
2018	India	–	–

WOMEN'S HOCKEY WORLD CUP

Name	Year	Host Country	Winner
Hockey World Cup London 2018 (W)	2018	London (ENG)	Netherlands
Rabobank Hockey World Cup The Hague 2014 (W)	2014	The Hague, Netherlands	Netherlands
BDO FIH World Cup (Women)	2010	Rosario, Argentina	Argentina
Hockey World Cup Madrid 2006	2006	Madrid, Spain	Netherlands
Hockey World Cup Perth 2002	2002	Perth, Australia	Argentina

Hockey World Cup Utrecht 1998	1998	Utrecht, Netherlands	Australia
Hockey World Cup Dublin 1994	1994	Dublin, Ireland	Australia
Hockey World Cup Sydney 1990	1990	Sydney, Australia	Netherlands
Hockey World Cup Amstelveen 1986	1986	Amstelveen, Netherlands	Netherlands
Hockey World Cup Kuala Lumpur 1983	1983	Kuala Lumpur, Malaysia	Netherlands
Hockey World Cup Buenos Aires 1981	1981	Buenos Aires, Argentina	West Germany
Hockey World Cup Madrid 1978	1978	Madrid, Spain	Netherlands
Hockey World Cup West Berlin 1976	1976	West Berlin, West Germany	West Germany
Hockey World Cup Mandelieu 1974	1974	Mandelieu, France	Netherlands

COMMONWEALTH GAMES

The Commonwealth Games are a festival of sports of the commonwealth countries. The games are held once in four years but only in between the Olympic years. When the games first began in 1930, only 11 countries participated. The Game s were originally known as the British Empire Games. These have undergone a change of name and expanded into a major multiracial and cultural event.

Commonwealth Games since 1930

Year	Places	Participant Countries	First Place	India's Medal
1930	Hamilton(Canada)	11	England	Not participated
1934	London(England)	16	England	1 Bronze Medal
1938	Sydney(Australia)	15	Australia	No medal
1950	Auckland(New Zealand)	12	Australia	Not Participated
1954	Vancouver(Canada)	24	England	No medal
1958	Cardiff (Wales)	35	England	Gold-2, Silver-1
1962	Perth (Australia)	35	Australia	Not Participated
1966	Kingston(Jamica)	34	England	Gold-3,Silver-4,Bronze-5
1970	Edinburgh (Scotland)	42	Australia	Gold-5,Silver-3
1974	Christchurch(New Zealand)	38	Australia	Gold-4,Silver-8,Bronze-3
1978	Edmonton(Canada)	48	Canada	Gold-5,Silver-4,Bronze-6
1982	Brisbane (Australia)	47	Australia	Gold-5,Silver-5,Bronze-3
1986	Edinburgh (Scotland)	26	England	Not Participated
1990	Auckland(New Zealand)	55	Australia	Gold-13,Silver-8,Bronze-7
1994	Victoria(Canada)	64	Australia	Gold-6,Silver-11,Bronze-10
1998	Kuala Lumpur (Malaysia)	70	Australia	Gold-07,Silver-10,Bronze-8
2002	Manchester(England)	72	Australia	Gold-32,Silver-21,Bronze-19 (Third Position)
2006	Melbourne (Australia)	71	Australia	Gold-22,Silver-17,Bronze-11 (Fourth Position)
2010	Delhi (India)	71	Australia	Gold-74,Silver-55,Bronze-48 (Second Position)
2014	Glasgow(Scotland)	71	England	Gold-15,Silver-30,Bronze-19 (Fiveth Position)
2018	Gold Coast (Australia)	71	Australia	Gold-26, Silver-20, Bronze-20
2022	Birmingham	–		

SAF GAMES

The SAF or South Asian Games was first held in 1984 at Kathmandu, Nepal. The seven participating countries are India, Pakistan, Sri Lanka, Bangladesh, Nepal, Bhutan and Maldives. The motto of SAF games is "Peace, Prosperity and Progress". The games year 1986 edition was not staged as it was a year of Commonwealth and Asian Games.

Year	Venue	Ranking Ist/IInd/IIIrd
1984	Kathmandu(Nepal)	India/Sri Lanka/Pakistan
1984	Dhaka (Bangladesh)	India/Pakistan/Bangladesh
1989	Islamabad (Pakistan)	India/Pakistan/Sri Lanka
1991	Colombo (Sri Lanka)	India/Sri Lanka/Pakistan
1993	Dhaka (Bangladesh)	India/Pakistan/Sri Lanka
1995	Chennai (India)	India/Sri Lanka/Pakistan
1999	Kathmandu (Nepal)	India/Nepal/Sri Lanka
2004	Islamabad	India/Pakistan/Sri Lanka
2006	Colombo (Sri Lanka)	India/Pakistan/Sri Lanka
2010	Dhaka (Bangladesh)	India/Bangladesh
2013	New Delhi (India)	India/Bangladesh
2014	Kathmandu (Nepal)	India/Bangladesh
2016	Hambantota (Sri Lanka)	India/Srilanka/Pakistan
2019	Kathmandu (Nepal)	—

OLYMPIC GAMES

Olympic Games are an international sporting event which is organised in the form of summer and winter sports. The Summer Olympic Games were first held in 1896. The Winter Olympic Games were created after the huge success of the Summer Olympics. Baron Pierre de Coubertin founded the International Olympic Committee (IOC) in 1894. The Olympic Games are held after every four years, with the Summer and Winter Games alternatively occurring every four years but two years apart from each other.

The Olympics games originated in the city of Olympia, an ancient city of Greece. These games were held at Mount Olympia. India officially participated in the Olympics for the first time in the year 1920, in the 6th edition of the games at Antwerp, Belgium.

The Olympic flag is made up of white silk and contains five intertwined rings as the Olympics emblem.

The colour of rings represents different continents as given below:

Blue	Europe
Yellow	Asia
Black	Africa
Red	America
Green	Australia and Ocenia

Winter Olympic Games

Winter Olympic games were started in the year A.D. 1924. The first game, were held at chamonix (France). The winter games are numbered in rotation as they are held. The programme at the winter games includes ice hockey, figure skating, speed skating, alpine skiing, skiting, etc. Like the summer games, the winter games are also awarded gold silver and bronze medals.

Year	Venue	Year	Venue
1924	Chamonix, France	1980	Lake placid, New York
1928	St. Moritz, Switzerland	1984	Sarajevo, Yugoslavia
1932	Lake Placid, New York	1988	Calgary, Canada
1936	Garmisch – Parten/ Kirchen, Germany	1992	Albertville, France
1948	St. Mortiz, Switzerland	1994	Lillehammer, Norway
1952	Oslo, Norway	1998	Nagano, Japan
1956	Cortina d' Ampezz, Italy	2002	Salt Lake City, USA
1960	Squaw Valley, United States	2006	Turin, Italy,
1964	Innbruck, Austria	2010	Vancouver, Canada
1968	Grenoble, France	2014	Sochi, Russia
1972	Sapporo, Japan	2018	Pyeongchang, South Korea
1976	Innsbruck, Austria	2022	Beijing, China

Summer Olympics

Year	Host	Opened by	Nations
1896	Athens, Greece	King George I	14
1900	Paris, France	–	24
1904	St. Louis, United States	Governor David R. Francis	12
1908	London, United Kingdom	King Edward VII	22
1912	Stockholm, Sweden	King Gustaf V	28
1920	Antwerp, Belgium	King Albert I	29
1924	Paris, France	President Gaston Doumergue	44
1928	Amsterdam, Netherlands	Prince Hendrik of the Netherlands	46
1932	Los Angeles, United States	Vice President Charles Curtis	37
1936	Berlin, Germany	Chancellor Adolf Hitler	49
1948	London, United Kingdom	King George VI	59
1952	Helsinki, Finland	President Juho Kusti Paasikivi	69
1956	Melbourne, Australia	Prince Philip, Duke of Edinburgh	72

Year	Host	Opened by	No.
1960	Rome, Italy	President Giovanni Gronchi	83
1964	Tokyo, Japan	Emperor Hirohito	93
1968	Mexico City, Mexico	President Gustavo Díaz Ordaz	112
1972	Munich, West Germany	President Gustav Heinemann	121
1976	Montreal, Canada	Queen Elizabeth II	92
1980	Moscow, Soviet Union	Chairman Leonid Brezhnev	80
1984	Los Angeles, United States	President Ronald Reagan	140
1988	Seoul, South Korea	President Roh Tae-woo	159
1992	Barcelona, Spain	King Juan Carlos I	169
1996	Atlanta, United States	President Bill Clinton	197
2000	Sydney, Australia	Governor-General Sir William Deane	199
2004	Athens, Greece	President Konstantinos Stephanopoulos	201
2008	Beijing, China	President Hu Jintao	204
2012	London, United Kingdom	Queen Elizabeth II	204
2016	Rio de Janerio, Brazil	Vice President Michel Miguel Elias Temer hulia	207
2020	Tokyo	–	–
2024	Paris	–	–
2028	Los Angeles	–	–

PARALYMPIC GAMES

Back in 1948, Sir Ludwig Guttman, a neurologist who was working with World War II veterans with spinal injuries at Stoke Mandeville Hospital in Aylesbury, began using sport as part of the rehabilitation programmes of his patients. He set up a competition with other hospitals to coincide with the London Olympics in that year.

The Paralympics are elite sport events for athletes from six different disability groups. Athletes include those with mobility disabilities, intellectual disabilities, visual impairments, cerebral palsy and amputees.

This event focuses on the athletes' achievements rather than their disabilities. Paralympic sports include athletics, cycling, judo, rowing, swimming, and volleyball. The Paralympic Games are always held in the same year as the Olympic Games. The name comes from the fact that it runs parallel to the Olympic Games hence the name Paralympics.

The first Paralympic Games were held in Rome, Italy, in 1960 and involved 400 athletes from 23 countries. Originally, only wheelchair athletes were invited to compete.

The Paralympics are held in two seasons: summer and winter. Athletes with disabilities have been competing in the Winter Games since 1976. Sweden hosted the first Winter Games, which included 12 countries competing in Alpine and Cross-Country Skiing events.

International Paralympic Committee: (IPC) is the global governing body of the Paralympic Movement. The IPC organizes the Summer and Winter Paralympic Games, and serves as the International Federation for nine sports, for which it supervises and co-ordinates the World Championships and other competitions.

Winter Paralympic Games

1976 - Paralympics I - Örnsköldsvik - Sweden
1980 - Paralympics II - Geilo - Norway
1984 - Paralympics III - Innsbruck - Austria
1988 - Paralympics IV - Innsbruck - Austria
1992 - Paralympics V - Albertville - France
1994 - Paralympics VI - Lillehammer - Norway
1998 - Paralympics VII - Nagano - Japan
2002 - Paralympics VIII - Salt Lake City - United States
2006 - Paralympics IX - Turin - Italy
2010 - Paralympics X - Vancouver – Canada
2014 - Paralympics XI - Sochi - Russia
2018 - Paralympics XII - Pyongyang - South Korea
2022 - Paralympics - XIII - Beijing - China

Summer Paralympic Games

1960 - Paralympics I - Rome - Italy
1964 - Paralympics II - Tokyo - Japan
1968 - Paralympics III - Tel Aviv - Israel
1972 - Paralympics IV - Heidelberg - West Germany
1976 - Paralympics V - Toronto - Canada
1980 - Paralympics VI - Arnhem - Netherlands
1984 - Paralympics VII - Stoke Mandeville - UK, New York - US
1988 - Paralympics VIII - Seoul - South Korea
1992 - Paralympics IX - Barcelona - Spain
1996 - Paralympics X - Atlanta - United States
2000 - Paralympics XI - Sydney - Australia
2004 - Paralympics XII - Athens - Greece
2008 - Paralympics XIII - Beijing - China
2012 - Paralympics XIV - London - United Kingdom
2016 - Paralympics XV - Rio de Janeiro - Brazil
2020 - Paralympics XVI - Tokyo - Japan
2024 - Paralympics XVII - Paris - France
2028 - Paralympics XVIII - Los Angeles - (US)

Books by Sports Persons

Sachin Tendulkar	Playing it my way
Kapil Dev	By God's Decree
Sunil Gavaskar	Idol, Sunny Days
Ajith Wadekar	The making of a cricketer
David Beckham	My Side

Tiger Wood	How to play golf?
Allan Border	Beyond Ten thousand
PT Usha	Golden Girl
Major Dhyan Chand	Goal

Javed Miandad	The cutting edge
Vishvanathan Anand	My best game of Chess
Yuvraj Singh	The test of my life
Abhinav Bindra	A Shot at History
Allan Donald	White Lightening

India in the Summer Olympics

Games	Gold	Silver	Bronze	Total	Rank
1896 Athens			did not participate		
1900 Paris	0	2	0	2	17
1904 St. Louis			did not participate		
1908 London			did not participate		
1912 Stockholm			did not participate		
1920 Antwerp	0	0	0	0	-
1924 Paris	0	0	0	0	-
1928 Amsterdam	1	0	0	1	23
1932 Los Angeles	1	0	0	1	19
1936 Berlin	1	0	0	1	20
1948 London	1	0	0	1	22
1952 Helsinki	1	0	1	2	26
1956 Melboume	1	0	0	1	24
1960 Rome	0	1	0	1	32
1964 Tokyo	1	0	0	1	24
1968 Mexico City	0	0	1	1	42
1972 Munich	0	0	1	1	43
1976 Montreal	0	0	0	0	-
1980 Moscow	1	0	0	1	23
1984 Los Angeles	0	0	0	0	-
1988 Seoul	0	0	0	0	-
1992 Barcelona	0	0	0	0	-
1996 Atlanta	0	0	1	1	71
2000 Sydney	0	0	1	1	71
2004 Athens	0	1	0	1	65
2008 Beijing	1	0	2	3	50
2012 London	0	2	4	6	55
2016 Rio de janeiro	0	1	1	2	67
Total	9	7	12	28	37

World Anti-Doping Agency (WADA)

The World Anti-Doping Agency (WADA) was established on 10th November 1999. Its primary aim is to promote and coordinate the fight against doping in sport internationally. The organization's headquarters is located in Montreal, Quebec, Canada. WADA was set up as a foundation under the initiative of the IOC with the support and participation of intergovernmental organizations, governments, public authorities, and other public and private bodies fighting doping in sport. WADA is accountable for the World Anti-Doping Code, adopted by more than 600 sports organizations, including international sports federations, national anti-doping organizations, the IOC, and the International Paralympics Committee. Sir Craig Reedie is the current president of the agency.

National Anti Doping Agency

National Anti Doping Agency is responsible for conducting for dope free sports in India. The primary objectives are to implement anti-doping rules as per WADA code, regulate dope control programme, to promote education and research and creating awareness about doping and its ill effects. India is among one of the nation who signed the Copenhagen Declaration on Anti Doping in December 2004.

Exercise -1

1. In which sports it is illegal to play left-handed?
   - (a) Discus Throw
   - (b) Polo
   - (c) Lacrosse
   - (d) Chess
2. Who is the first Indian batsman to score a triple century in Test Cricket?
   - (a) V. V. S. Laxman
   - (b) Rahul Dravid
   - (c) Sachin Tendulkar
   - (d) Virendra Sehwag
3. Merdeka Cup is associated with
   - (a) Hockey
   - (b) Football
   - (c) Basketball
   - (d) Badminton
4. With which game is 'Bully' associated ?
   - (a) Cricket
   - (b) Football
   - (c) Golf
   - (d) Hockey
5. Thomas Cup is associated with
   - (a) Table Tennis
   - (b) Golf
   - (c) Football
   - (d) Badminton
6. The three core values of the Commonwealth Games movement are
   - (a) Equality, Brotherhood and Unity
   - (b) Humanity, Equality and Destiny
   - (c) Humanity, Equality and Brotherhood
   - (d) Unity, Humanity and Equality
7. Dola Banerjee is related with which of the following games?
   - (a) Badminton
   - (b) Archery
   - (c) Tennis
   - (d) Table Tennis
8. In order to win the Grand Slam in Tennis, a player must win which one of the followings groups of tournaments?
   - (a) Australian Open, U.S. Open, Wimbledon, French Open
   - (b) Wimbledon, French Open, U.S. Open
   - (c) Wimbledon, French Open, Paegas Czech Open, U.S. Open
   - (d) Davis Cup, Wimbledon, French Open
9. Starting with the Australian Open Lawn Tennis Tournament, which one of the following is the correct chronological order of the other three major Lawn Tennis Tournaments?
   - (a) French Open – US Open – Wimbledon
   - (b) French Open – Wimbledon – US Open
   - (c) Wimbledon – US Open – French Open
   - (d) Wimbledon – French Open – US Open
10. The host of the 2018 world cup football is :
    - (a) Japan
    - (b) Spain
    - (c) Brazil
    - (d) Russia
11. Which among the following sports is NOT a part of the London Olympics?
    - (a) Triathlon
    - (b) Taekwondo
    - (c) Table Tennis
    - (d) Baseball
12. Which of the following is a Manipuri version of Hockey?
    - (a) Khong Kangjei
    - (b) Hiyang Tanaba
    - (c) Yubi Lakpi
    - (d) Yubi-Lakpi
13. In which Indian state did the game of Polo originate?
    - (a) Meghalaya
    - (b) Rajasthan
    - (c) Manipur
    - (d) West Bengal
14. The 'Dronacharya Award' is given to...?
    - (a) Sportsmen
    - (b) Coaches
    - (c) Umpires
    - (d) Sports Editors
15. Which of the following is a pair names of the same game?
    - (a) Soccer - Football
    - (b) Golf - Polo
    - (c) Billiards - Carrom
    - (d) Volleyball – Squash
16. Tripping is associates with
    - (a) Snooker
    - (b) Volleyball
    - (c) Football
    - (d) Cricket
17. If you scored a cannon, which game would you be playing?
    - (a) football
    - (b) Billiards
    - (c) Cricket
    - (d) Hockey
18. Which of the following is correctly matched?
    - (a) Nehru Trophy - Table Tennis
    - (b) B.C. Roy Trophy - Lawn Tennis
    - (c) Holkar Trophy - Bridge
    - (d) Ruia Trophy - Kabbadi
19. The 'Agha Khan Cup' is associated with which game?
    - (a) Badminton
    - (b) Hockey
    - (c) Football
    - (d) Cricket
20. Which of the following games is **not** included in the Olympic Games?
    - (a) Skiing
    - (b) Cycling
    - (c) Cricket
    - (d) Archery
21. Which one of the following is not a football tournament?
    - (a) I-League
    - (b) Irani Trophy
    - (c) Bardoloi Trophy
    - (d) Durand Cup
22. With which sport the term' Caddie' is associated?
    - (a) Polo
    - (b) Golf
    - (c) Bridge
    - (d) Billiards
23. The Indian Football team made its first appearance at Olympics in
    - (a) 1940
    - (b) 1948
    - (c) 1950
    - (d) 1951
24. Who was the first ODI captain for India?
    - (a) Ajit Wadekar
    - (b) Bishan Singh Bedi
    - (c) Kapil Dev
    - (d) Vinoo Mankad
25. The term 'Gambit' is associated with
    - (a) Chess
    - (b) Tennis
    - (c) Basketball
    - (d) Baseball
26. 'Ashes' is the term associated with which of the following sports?
    - (a) Cricket
    - (b) Badminton
    - (c) Basketball
    - (d) Football
27. National Sports Day is observed on
    - (a) 29th Aug.
    - (b) 4th Dec.
    - (c) 14th Nov.
    - (d) 28th Oct.
28. The normal length of a football ground must be
    - (a) 110 – 120 m
    - (b) 100 – 110 m
    - (c) 90 – 100 m
    - (d) 120 – 130 m
29. The term 'bogey' is associated with
    - (a) Cricket
    - (b) Chess
    - (c) Golf
    - (d) Baseball

30. Who among the following women won the Wimbledon title successfully nine times?
    (a) Steffi Graf   (b) Martina Navratilova
    (c) Serena Williams   (d) Chris Evert
31. Who was the first Indian woman who won the gold medal in Asian Games?
    (a) PT Usha   (b) Sunita Rani
    (c) Shiny Abraham   (d) Kamaljeet Sandhu
32. In which Indian state did the game of 'Polo' originates?
    (a) Nagaland   (b) Manipur
    (c) Mizoram   (d) Kerala
33. Who was the first Indian to win an individual medal in Olympics?
    (a) PT Usha   (b) Karnam Malleshwari
    (c) Deepika Kumari   (d) Sania Nehwal
34. Gautam Budha circuit is the venue for which Grand Prix race?
    (a) Malaysian Grand Prix
    (b) Indian Grand Prix
    (c) British Grand Prix
    (d) Italian Grand Prix
35. When did the Wimbledon Grand Slam Tennis tournament start?
    (a) 1857   (b) 1877
    (c) 1897   (d) 1898
36. In which year, the Grand Master title of Chess started?
    (a) 1971   (b) 1972
    (c) 1973   (d) 1974
37. Which one of the following countries had hosted the first world Paralympic Games in 1960?
    (a) Rome, Italy   (b) Mumbai, India
    (c) Madrid, Spain   (d) Paris, France
38. Who founded the IOC to organise the Olympic Games in 1894?
    (a) J.H. Bacquerel   (b) Baron de Coubertin
    (c) Khalid Ali Ansari (d) None of the above
39. Which one of the following countries had hosted the first winter Paralympic Games?
    (a) Sweden   (b) France
    (c) Soviet Union   (d) China
40. Among the following which one is not a football club?
    (a) Arsenal   (b) Aston villa
    (c) Chelsea   (d) Monte Carlo
41. What is the National Game of Russia?
    (a) Chess   (b) Bandy
    (c) Table Tennis   (d) Baseball
42. In which Olympic Games, Hockey was introduced for the first time
    (a) London, 1908   (b) Stockholm, 1912
    (c) St. Louis, 1904 (d) Paris, 1900
43. The first World Cup Hockey was played in
    (a) Amsterdom, 1972 (b) Barcelona, 1971
    (c) Kualalumpur, 1975 (d) Mumbai, 1976
44. The great lawn tennis player Bjorn Borg is from which country?
    (a) Sweden   (b) Australia
    (c) USA   (d) Italy

45. In which one of the following Indian States is the game of polo said to have originated?
    (a) West Bengal   (b) Meghalaya
    (c) Manipur   (d) Sikkim
46. Which one of the following statements about WADA (World Anti-Doping Agency) code is not correct?
    (a) The code is the core document that provides the framework for harmonized anti-doping policies, rules and regulations within sport organisations and among public authorities.
    (b) The code entered into force from January 1, 2004.
    (c) Under the code, the use of any prohibited substance by an athlete for medical reasons is not possible.
    (d) Under the code, a sanction could be applied in cases where there is evidence that an anti-doping rule violation has occurred, but where there is no positive doping-control test.
47. The 'Thomas Cup is associated with
    (a) Table Tennis   (b) Lawn Tennis
    (c) Badminton   (d) Billiards
48. Who among the following was defeated by Chile to won the Copa America Football Championship, 2016?
    (a) Colombia   (b) Argentina
    (c) Ecuador   (d) Peru
49. Who among the following won a Gold medal for India in Men's Javelin Throw event at the 2016 Rio Paralympic Games?
    (a) Rinku Hooda   (b) Devendra Jhajharia
    (c) Sundar Singh Gurjar (d) Mariyappan Thangavelu
50. In which one of the following cities are the Summer Olympics, 2020 going to be held?
    (a) London   (b) Paris
    (c) Tokyo   (d) Moscow
51. Who among the following is the first Indian sportsperson to reach the finals in the world badminton Championship (Women) in 2015?
    (a) Jwala Gutta   (b) Saina Nehwal
    (c) P.V Sindhu   (d) Madhumita Bisht
52. Leander paes won the US Open Mixed Doubles Tennis Title (2015) Partnering with :
    (a) Kristina Mladenovic (b) Flavia Pennetta
    (c) Martina Hingis   (d) Sania Mirza
53. Which one of the following countries has failed to quality for the first time in 60 years for the FIFA World Cup to be held in Russia in the year 2018?
    (a) Mexico   (b) Iran
    (c) Saudi Arabia   (d) Italy
54. Which one of the following is the Official Mascot of the FIFA World Cup, 2018?
    (a) Fuleco   (b) Zakumi
    (c) Pille   (d) Zabivaka
55. The Headquarters of the proposed National Sports University (as per the National Sports University Ordinance, 2018) will be set up in
    (a) Chhattisgarh   (b) Manipur
    (c) Kerala   (d) West Bengal

Exercise -2

1. Consider the following statements about lawn tennis court
    1. Hard courts are faster than clay courts but not as fast as grass courts.
    2. The French Open is played on a hard court, but the US Open is played on a clay court.
    3. An approximate north/south orientation of the court is desirable during evening play.
    Which of the statements given above is/are correct?
    (a) 1 and 2   (b) 3 only
    (c) 1 and 3   (d) 1, 2 and 3

2. Consider the following statements
    1. The Walker Cup is associated with Golf.
    2. The event is contested biennially in odd numbered years.
    3. The teams contesting the trophy comprising the leading amateur golfers of the United Kingdom and Great Britain and Ireland.
    Which of the statements given above is/are correct?
    (a) 1, 2 and 3   (b) 1 only
    (c) 2 and 3   (d) 1 and 3

3. Which of the statements are correct regarding Uber Cup Tournament?
    1. It is the World Team Badminton Championships for men only.
    2. It was first held in 1956–57. It was held once in every three years but since 1984, the Cup is held bi-annually.
    3. China has won the cup for maximum number of times.
    Select the answer from the codes given below:
    (a) 1 and 2   (b) 1 and 3
    (c) 2 and 3   (d) 1, 2 and 3

4. Which of the statements are correct regarding Thomas Cup Tournament?
    1. It takes place every three years and it was the Badminton World Federation's (BWF) first major international tournament.
    2. The championships was first staged in 1948–49.
    3. China is the most successful team, having won the tournament thirteen times.
    Select the answer from the codes given below:
    (a) 1 and 2   (b) 1 and 3
    (c) 2 and 3   (d) 1, 2 and 3

5. Which of the following statements are correct regarding Official Olympic Flag?
    1. It was created by Pierre de Coubertin in 1914.
    2. The flag contains five interconnected rings on a white background.
    3. The five rings symbolize the five significant continents.

4. The Olympic flag was first flown during the 1940 Olympic Games.
    Select the answer from the codes given below:
    (a) 1, 2, and 3   (b) 2, 3, and 4
    (c) 1, 3, and 4   (d) 1, 2, 3 and 4

6. Which of the following statements are correct regarding Vijay Hazare Trophy?
    1. Vijay Hazare Trophy was started in 2002–03.
    2. It is the one-day version of the Ranji Trophy.
    3. It is a domestic competition among the states teams from the Ranji Trophy for limited over.
    4. Delhi won the trophy for maximum times (four times)
    Select the answer from the codes given below:
    (a) 1 and 2   (b) 2 and 3
    (c) 1, 2 and 3   (d) 1, 2, 3 and 4

7. Which of the following statements are correct regarding Fédération Internationale de Football Association (FIFA)?
    1. FIFA World Cup Men's championship is organized in every four years.
    2. An equivalent tournament for women's football, the FIFA Women's World Cup, was first held in 1991 in China.
    3. FIFA also organises international tournaments for youth football.
    4. The FIFA Confederations Cup is a tournament held every year.
    Select the answer from the codes given below:
    (a) 1, 2, and 3   (b) 2, 3, and 4
    (c) 1, 3, and 4   (d) 1, 2, 3 and 4

8. Consider the following statements :
    1. 'The Rajiv Gandhi Khel Ratna' is India's highest honour given for achievement in sports.
    2. It carries a medal, a scroll of honour and a substantial cash component.
    Which of the above is/are true?
    (a) 1 only   (b) 2 only
    (c) Both 1 and 2   (d) None of these

9. Consider the following statements :
    1. Dhyan Chand Award is India's highest award for lifetime achievement in sports and games.
    2. The award is named after the legendary Indian Hockey player Dhyan Chand.
    Which of the above is/are true?
    (a) 1 only   (b) 2 only
    (c) Both 1 and 2   (d) None of these

10. Consider the following statements :
    1. The term catch out is associated with Golf.
    2. Pierre de Coubertin is the father of modern olympic games.
    Which of the given above is/are true?
    (a) 1 only   (b) 2 only
    (c) Both 1 and 2   (d) None of these

11. Consider the following statements :
    Arrange the international tennis opens chronologically from the beginning of a year tournament schedule?
    1. Wimbledon   2. Australian open
    3. US open   4. French open
    (a) 2, 4, 1, 3   (b) 1, 2, 3, 4
    (c) 3, 1, 4, 2   (d) 4, 3, 2, 1
12. Consider the following statements :
    1. Hopman cup is the mixed team championship Lawn Tennis Cup.
    2. Hopman cup is the International Tennis Tournament held every three years.
    Which of the statements given above is/are correct?
    (a) 1 only   (b) 2 only
    (c) Both 1 and 2   (d) Neither 1 nor 2
13. Consider the following statements :
    1. Davis Cup is the premier international team even in men's tennis.
    2. Davis cup was begun in 1900 as a challenge between Britain and the United states.
    3. Davis cup is the premier international team event in women's tennis championship.
    Which of the statements given above is/are correct?
    (a) 1 only   (b) 2 only
    (c) 1, 2 and 3   (d) 1 and 2 only
14. A player wins Grand Slam in tennis when he wins in:
    1. Australian open   2. Wimbledon
    3. French open   4. Davis cup
    5. China cup   6. US open
    (a) 1, 2 and 4   (b) 4, 5, 6
    (c) all the above   (d) 1, 2, 3 and 6
15. Consider the following statements given below :
    1. The first commonwealth games were held in 1930 at Hamilton, Canada.
    2. India, for the first time, participated in the second commonwealth games held in London in 1934.
    Which of the statements given above is/are correct?
    (a) 1 only   (b) 2 only
    (c) Both 1 and 2   (d) None of these
16. Consider the following statements :
    1. The first SAF Games were held in Kathmandu in 1984.
    2. The Motto of SAF games is 'Peace, Prosperity and Progress'.
    3. The SAF games were held in India for the first time at Chennai 1995.
    Which of the statements given above is/are correct?
    (a) 1, 2 and 3   (b) 1 and 2
    (c) 2 and 3   (d) 1 and 3
17. Consider the following statements :
    1. The game basketball was invented by Dr. James Naismith of USA in 1891 at Springfield college.
    2. International Basketball Federation was set up in 1940.
    3. Basketball Federation of India was formed in 1950.

Which of the statements given above is/are correct?
(a) 1, 2 and 3   (b) 1 and 3
(c) 3 only   (d) None of these
18. Consider the following statements.
    To be eligible for the Arjuna Award, a sportsperson should
    1. Have good performance consistently for the previous three years at the international level with excellence for the year for which the Award is recommended.
    2. show qualities of leadership, sportsmanship and a sense of discipline.
    Which of the above is/are true?
    (a) 1 only   (b) 2 only
    (c) Both 1 and 2   (d) None of these
19. Consider the following statements about the World anti-Doping Agency (WADA).
    1. It was set up on November 10, 1999 in New York.
    2. The agency's key activities include scientific research, education, development of anti-doping capacities and monitoring of the World Anti-Doping Code.
    Which of the above is/are true?
    (a) 1 only   (b) 2 only
    (c) Both 1 and 2   (d) None of these
20. Consider the following statements.
    1. The Paralympic Games are where athletes with a physical disability compete.
    2. All Paralympic Games are governed by the International Paralympic Committee (IPC).
    Which of the above is/are true?
    (a) 1 only
    (b) 2 only
    (c) Both 1 and 2
    (d) None of these
21. Consider the following statements.
    1. The National Sports Day is observed on 29th August.
    2. Mardeka Cup is associated with the game of Football.
    Which of the above is/are true?
    (a) 1 only   (b) 2 only
    (c) Both 1 and 2   (d) None of these
22. Consider the following statements.
    1. Stanley Cup is associated with the hockey.
    2. Heisman Trophy is associated with the football.
    3. Wightman Cup is associated with the track and field.
    Which of the following is wrong?
    (a) 1 only   (b) 2 only
    (c) 3 only   (d) None of these
23. Consider the following statements
    1. The Walker Cup is associated with Golf.
    2. The event is contested biennially in odd numbered years.
    3. The teams contesting the trophy comprising the leading amateur golfers of the United Kingdom and Great Britain and Ireland.
    Which of the statements given above is/are correct?
    (a) 1, 2 and 3
    (b) Only
    (c) 2 and 3
    (d) 1 and 3

Matching Based MCQ

DIRECTIONS (Qs. 24 to 31) : Match List-I with List-II and select the correct answer using the codes given below the lists.

24.

List-I (Country)	List-II (National game)
A. India	1. Hockey
B. Spain	2. Bull Fighting
C. Japan	3. Table Tennis
D. China	4. Judo

Codes:

	A	B	C	D		A	B	C	D
(a)	1	2	4	3	(b)	2	1	4	3
(c)	4	3	2	1	(d)	1	4	3	2

25.

List-I (Grand slam tournament)	List-II (Surface)
A. Wimbledon	1. Grass
B. US open	2. Hard (Turf)
C. French open	3. Clay
D. Australian open	4. Hard (Plexicushion)

	A	B	C	D		A	B	C	D
(a)	1	2	3	4	(b)	4	3	2	1
(c)	3	4	1	2	(d)	2	1	4	3

26.

List-I (Game)	List-II (Terminology)
A. Butterfly	1. Baseball
B. Upper cut	2. Swimming
C. Diamond	3. Golf
D. Bunker	4. Boxing

Codes:

	A	B	C	D		A	B	C	D
(a)	1	2	3	4	(b)	2	4	1	3
(c)	4	3	2	1	(d)	3	4	2	1

27.

List-I (Country)	List-II (National Game)
A. Russia	1. Football
B. Spain	2. Bull Fighting
C. Japan	3. Table Tennis
D. China	4. Judo

Codes:

	A	B	C	D		A	B	C	D
(a)	1	2	3	4	(b)	2	1	4	3
(c)	3	2	4	1	(d)	1	2	4	3

28.

List-I (Trophy)	List-II (Game)
A. Aga Khan Cup	1. Bridge
B. Durand Cup	2. Hockey
C. Irani Trophy	3. Football
D. Holker Trophy	4. Cricket

Codes:

	A	B	C	D		A	B	C	D
(a)	1	2	3	4	(b)	2	3	4	1
(c)	3	2	4	1	(d)	3	4	1	2

29.

List-I	List-II
A. Bull's Eye	1. Cricket
B. Caddy	2. Tennis
C. Deuce	3. Shooting
D. Googly	4. Golf

Codes:

	A	B	C	D		A	B	C	D
(a)	1	2	3	4	(b)	2	1	3	4
(c)	4	2	3	1	(d)	3	4	2	1

30. Match the following   [2009-II]

List-I (Name)	List-II (Game)
A. Dola Banerjee	1. Badminton
B. Aparna Popat	2. Snooker
C AnujaThakur	3. Chess
D. Panmarjan Negi	4. Archery

Codes :

	A	B	C	D		A	B	C	D
(a)	2	3	1	4	(b)	4	1	2	3
(c)	2	1	3	4	(d)	4	1	3	2

31. Match the following   [2009-II]

List-I	List-II
A. Jeev Milkha Singh	1. Archery
B. Jayanta Talukdar	2. Cricket
C. N Kunjarani Devi	3. Power lifting
D. Jhulan Goswami	4. Golf

Codes

	A	B	C	D		A	B	C	D
(a)	4	1	3	2	(b)	4	3	1	2
(c)	2	3	1	4	(d)	2	1	3	4

Hints and Explanations

1. (b)   2. (d)   3. (b)   4. (d)
5. (d)   6. (b)   7. (b)
8. (a) There are four grand slam tournaments in Tennis–Australian Open, U.S. Open, Wimbledon and French Open. So a player has to win any of them to win grand slam and if he wins all four its called "Golden Grand Slam".
9. (b)   10. (d)   11. (d)   12. (a)   13. (c)   14. (b)
15. (a)   16. (c)   17. (b)
18. (c) Nehru Trophy - Boat race B.C. Roy Trophy - FIFA Holkar Trophy - Bridge Ruia Trophy - Bridge
19. (b)   20. (c)
21. (b) The Irani cup (also called Irani Trophy) tournament was conceived during the 1959-60 season to mark the completion of 25 years of the Ranji Trophy and was named after the late ZR Irani. It is associated with Indian Cricket.
22. (b) In golf, a caddy or caddie is the person who handles a golf player's bag and clubs, and gives also some insightful advice and moral support to him.
23. (b) India's first major football international tournament was in 1948 London Olympics, where a predominately barefooted Indian team lost 2–1 to France.
24. (a) India had played her first ODI in 1974 under the captaincy of Ajit Wadekar.
25. (a) A Gambit is a term associated with the game of Chess. Gambit is a chess opening in which a player sacrifices material, usually a pawn, with the hope of achieving a resulting advantageous position.
26. (a) The term 'ashes' is associated with cricket.
27. (a) National Sports Day is celebrated on 29th August in the memory of the great hockey player Major Dhyan Chand.
28. (b) The average length of the football field is 100 – 110m (110 – 120 yards) with width is in the range of 64 to 75 m (70–80 yd).
29. (c) A bogey is a score of 1-over par on any individual hole on a golf course. Golf holes are typically rated as par 3, par 4 or par 5.
30. (b) Martina Navratilova is a retired Czech American tennis player and coach. She is the greatest singles, doubles and mixed doubles player. She reached the Wimbledon singles final 12 times, including nine consecutive years from 1982 through 1990, and won the women's singles title at Wimbledon a record nine times.
31. (d) Kamaljeet Sandhu is a former woman Indian athlete who won gold medal at 1970 Asian Games in 400 m race. She was the first woman to win Gold in any Asian games.
32. (b) The modern game of polo, though was formalised and popularised by the British, is actually derived from Manipur, India, where the game was known as 'Sagol Kangjei', 'Kanjai-bazee', or 'Pulu'.
33. (b) Karnam Malleshwari is an Indian weightlifter. She is the first Indian to win an individual medal in Olympics.

racing circuit in Greater Noida, Uttar Pradesh. The circuit is best known as the venue for the annual Formula One Indian Grand Prix, which was first hosted on 30 October 2011.
35. (b)   36. (b)
37. (a) The 1960 Summer Paralympics, originally known as the 9th Annual International Stoke Mandeville Games were the first international Para Olympic Games held in Rome, Italy from September 18 to 25, 1960.
38. (b) The International Olympic Committee (IOC) is a Swiss non-profit, non-governmental organisation based in Lausanne, Switzerland, created by Pierre, Baron de Coubertin, on 23 June 1894 with Demetrios Vikelas as its first president.
39. (a) The winter Olympics were first held in 1976 in Örnsköldsvik Sweden.
40. (d) Arsenal Football Club is an English Premier League football club based in Holloway, London. Chelsea Football Club is an English football club based in Fulham, London. Aston Villa Football Club is an English professional association football club based in Witton, Birmingham. Monte Carlo is not any football club.
41. (b)
42. (a) Hockey (as field hockey) was introduced in Olympics for the first time in Summer Olympics London in 1908.
43. (b) The first world cup Hockey was played in Barcelona in 1971 whose final winner was Pakistan.
44. (a) Bjorn Borg is a former world No. 1 tennis player from Sweden.
45. (c) The origins of the game in Manipur are traced to early precursors of Sagol Kangjei. This was one of three forms of hockey in Manipur, the other ones being field hockey (called Khong Kangjei) and wrestling-hockey (called Mukna Kangjei). In Manipur, polo is traditionally played with seven players to a side.
46. (c)
47. (c) Thomas Cup is associated with Badminton.
48. (b) Argentina was defeated by Chile in the final of Copa America Football Championship, 2016.
49. (b) Devendra Jhajharia won a Gold medal for India in the Men's Javelin Throw event at 2016 Rio Paralympic Games in Rio de Janeiro, Brazil. His javelin throw was 62.25 meters. His fellow Indians were Rinku Hooda, at fifth-place, and Sundar Singh Gurjar, who did not start the event. Mariyappan Thangavelu won Gold medal in high jump.
50. (c) The 2020 Summer Olympics (Games of the XXXII Olympiad) will be held in Tokyo, Japan, which will feature 207 participating nations, more than 12,000 athletes, and 324 in 33 sports. The opening and closing ceremony will be held on July 24 and 9 August respectively.

51. (b) Saina Nehwal became the first Indian women's player to be World No. 1 in Badminton. She is presently ranked two in the world.
52. (c) Leander Paes and Martina Hingis win US open Mixed Doubles Tennis Title in year 2015.
53. (d) Qualify
54. (d) 55. (b)

EXERCISE-2

1. (c) Wimbeldon is the most famous grass court tournament. US Open and Australia Open are played on hard court. The French Open uses clay courts unlike the other three Grand Slam Tournaments. There are four Grand Slam played in a year.
2. (a) The Walker Cup is a golf trophy named after George Herbert Walker, who has president of United States Golf Association in 1920, when the series (Walker Cup) was initiated.
   The Cup contested biennially in odd numbered years between the leading amateur golfers of the United States, Great Britain and Ireland.
3. (c) It is the World Team Badminton Championships for women. It was named after a former British women badminton player, Betty Uber. She gave the idea of hosting a women's event similar to that of the men (Thomas Cup).
4. (a) Indonesia is the most successful team, having won the tournament thirteen times. China, which did not begin to compete until the 1982 series, follows Indonesia with nine titles, while Malaysia has won five titles.
5. (a) The rings, from left to right, are blue, yellow, black, green, and red. The colours were chosen because at least one of them appeared on the flag of every country in the world. The Olympic flag was first flown during the 1920 Olympic Games.
6. (c) Tamil Nadu won the trophy four times and Delhi won the trophy in 2012–13 only.
7. (a) The FIFA Confederations Cup is a tournament held one year before the World Cup at the World Cup host nation(s) as a dress rehearsal for the upcoming World Cup.
8. (c) The Rajiv Gandhi Khel Ratna is India's highest honour for achievement in sports awarded annually. It carries a medal, scroll of honour and cash component.
9. (c) Both A and R is correct. Dhyan chand award is highest award for lifetime achievement in sports and games. Dhyan chand was the greatest Indian player of Hockey.
10. (b) Catch out is associated with Cricket and Mr. Pierre de Coubertin is considered to be the father of Modern Olympic Games. Modern Olympic games were first held in 1896. The Olympic Games are considered the world's foremost sports competition with more than 200 nations participating. The Olympic Games are held every four years, with the Summer and Winter Games alternating by occurring every four years but two years apart. Their creation was inspired by the ancient Olympic Games, which were held in Olympia, Greece, from the 8th century BC to the 4th century AD.
11. (a) Australian open – French open – Wimbledon – US open.
12. (a) Hopman Cup is the mixed team championship Lawn Tennis Cup. It is the International Tennis Tournament held every year.
13. (d) Davis Cup is the premier international team event in men's tennis started between Britain and the United states in 1900. This championship is only for men.
14. (d) A player wins Grand Slam in tennis, if he competes in Australian open, French open, Wimbledon and American open title.
15. (c) The first commonwealth games were held in 1930 at Hamilton, Canada and India first time participated in London games in 1934.
16. (a) SAF Games means South Asian Federation Games. It is sport festival of South Asian countries. The South Asian sports Federation comprising India, Pakistan, Srilanka, Bangladesh, Nepal, Bhutan and Maldives was formed in New Delhi on November 26, 1982.
17. (b) International Basketball Federation was set up in 1932. This game was invented by Dr. James Naismith of USA in 1891.
18. (d) 19. (b) 20. (c) 21. (c) 22. (c)
23. (a) The Walker Cup is a golf trophy contested biennially in odd numbered years between teams comprising the leading amateur golfers of the United States and Great Britain and Ireland.
24. (a) Correctly matched :

Country	—	National game
India	—	Hockey
Spain	—	Bull Fighting
Japan	—	Judo
China	—	Table Tennis

25. (a) Correctly matched :

Wimbledon	—	Grass
US open	—	Hard (Turf)
French open	—	Clay
Australian open	—	Hard (Plexicushion)

26. (b) Correctly matched :

Games	Terminology
Butterfly	Swimming
Upper cut	Boxing
Diamond	Baseball
Bunker	Golf

27. (d) 28. (b) 29. (d)
30. (b) Dola Banerjee- Archery
   Aparna Popat - Badminton
   Anuja Thakur- Snooker
   Parimarjan Negi- Chess
31. (a) Jeev Milkha Singh - Golf
   Jayanta Talukdar- Archery
   N Kunjarani- Power lifting
   Jhulan Goswami- Cricket

AWARDS AND HONOURS

Bharat Ratna

- Also known as the Jewel of India, it is the highest civilian award in India.
- The award was instituted on 2nd January 1954 to honour people in recognition of their exceptional service of the highest order without any distinction of race, occupation, position, or sex.
- The award is conferred in any field of human endeavour including achievements in the field of arts, literature, science, and public services.
- The recommendations for the Bharat Ratna are commenced by the Prime Minister to the President, with a maximum of three nominees being awarded per year.
- The recipients of the award receive a Sanad (certificate) signed by the President and a peepal-leaf–shaped medallion; there is no monetary grant associated with the award.
- C. Rajagopalachari, Sarvepalli Radhakrishnan, and C. V. Raman were the first recipients of the Bharat Ratna in 1954.
- The award to naturalised citizen, Mother Teresa is the only one till date whereas the two non-Indians to receive the award are Khan Abdul Ghaffar Khan (Pakistan) and former South African President Nelson Mandela.

Year	Awarders
1954	C. Rajagopalachari, Sarvepalli Radhakrishnan, C. V. Raman
1955	Bhagwan Das, M. Visvesvaraya, Jawaharlal Nehru
1957	Govind Ballabh Pant
1958	Dhondo Keshav Karve
1961	Bidhan Chandra Roy, Purushottam Das Tandon
1962	Rajendra Prasad
1963	Zakir Husain, Pandurang Vaman Kane
1966	Lal Bahadur Shastri
1971	Indira Gandhi
1975	V. V. Giri
1976	K. Kamaraj
1980	Mother Teresa
1983	Vinoba Bhave
1987	Khan Abdul Ghaffar Khan
1988	M. G. Ramachandran
1990	B. R. Ambedkar, Nelson Mandela
1991	Rajiv Gandhi, Morarji Desai, Vallabhbhai Patel
1992	Abul Kalam Azad, J. R. D. Tata, Satyajit Ray
1997	Gulzarilal Nanda, Aruna Asaf Ali, A. P. J. Abdul Kalam
1998	M. S. Subbulakshmi, Chidambaram Subramaniam
1999	Jayaprakash Narayan, Amartya Sen, Gopinath Bordoloi, Ravi Shankar
2001	Lata Mangeshkar, Bismillah Khan
2009	Bhimsen Joshi
2014	C. N. R. Rao, Sachin Tendulkar
2015	Madan Mohan Malaviya, Atal Bihari Vajpayee

Padma Awards

Padma Vibhushan

- It is the second highest civilian award in India after Bharat Ratna. It was established on 2nd January 1954.
- It is awarded to recognize a person's exceptional and distinguished service to the nation in any field, including government services without distinction of race, occupation, position, or sex.
- The first recipients of Padma Vibhushan were Satyendra Nath Bose, Nandalal Bose, Zakir Husain, Balasaheb Gangadhar Kher, V. K. Krishna Menon, and Jigme Dorji Wangchuk.

Padma Bhushan

- It is India's third highest civilian award after Bharat Ratna and Padma Vibhushan.

- The award was instituted on 2nd January 1954 by the President of India to recognize distinguished service of a high order to the nation, in any field.
- The award is announced on the occasion of Republic Day of India every year.
- It is conferred by the President of India at a function held at Rashtrapati Bhavan in March/ April.

Padma Shri

- It is the fourth highest civilian award in India, after the Bharat Ratna, the Padma Vibhushan and the Padma Bhushan.
- The award was instituted in 1954 in recognition of contribution in various spheres of activity including the Arts, Education, Industry, Literature, Science, Sports, Medicine, Social Service and Public Affairs.

Wartime Gallantry awards

Param Vir Chakra (PVC)

- The award is India's highest military decoration awarded for the highest degree of valour or self-sacrifice in the presence of the enemy.
- The award was instituted on 26th January 1950 by the President of India, with effect from 15th August 1947.
- The medal has been awarded 21 times, 14 of which were posthumous awards (20 are from the Indian Army and one from the Indian Air Force).
- Medal is a circular bronze disc 1.375 inches (3.49 cm) in diameter. The state emblem appears in the centre, on a raised circle. Surrounding this, four replicas of Vajra. The rear end of the medal features at the plain centre, are two legends separated by lotus flowers. The words Param Vir Chakra are written in Hindi and English.
- The Param Vir Chakra is held by a purple ribbon, 32 millimetres (1.3 in) in length.

Name of the recipients	Regiment
Major Somnath Sharma (1947)	4th Battalion, Kumaon Regiment
Naik Jadu Nath Singh (1948)	1st Battalion, Rajput Regiment
Second Lieutenant Rama Raghoba Rane (1948)	Bombay Sappers, Corps of Engineers
Company Havildar Major Piru Singh Shekhawat (1948)	6th Battalion, Rajputana Rifles
Lance Naik Karam Singh (1948)	1st Battalion, Sikh Regiment
Captain Gurbachan Singh Salaria (1961)	3rd Battalion, 1st Gurkha Rifles
Major Dhan Singh Thapa (1962)	1st Battalion, 8th Gurkha Rifles

Subedar Joginder Singh (1962)	1st Battalion, Sikh Regiment
Major Shaitan Singh (1962)	13th Battalion, Kumaon Regiment
Company Quartermaster Havildar Abdul Hamid (1965)	4th Battalion, The Grenadiers
Lieutenant-Colonel Ardeshir Burzorji Tarapore (1965)	17th Poona Horse
Lance Naik Albert Ekka (1971)	14th Battalion, Brigade of the Guards
Flying Officer Nirmal Jit Singh Sekhon (1971)	No. 18 Squadron
Second Lieutenant Arun Khetarpal (1971)	17th Poona Horse
Major Hoshiar Singh (1971)	3rd Battalion, The Grenadiers
Naib Subedar Bana Singh (1987)	8th Battalion, Jammu and Kashmir Light Infantry
Major Ramaswamy Parameshwaran (1987)	8th Battalion, Mahar Regiment
Captain Manoj Kumar Pandey (1999)	1st Battalion, 11th Gorkha Rifles
Grenadier Yogendra Singh Yadav (1999)	18th Battalion, The Grenadiers
Rifleman Sanjay Kumar (1999)	13th Battalion, Jammu & Kashmir Rifles
Captain Vikram Batra (1999)	13th Battalion, Jammu & Kashmir Rifles

Maha Vir Chakra (MVC)

- It is the second highest military decoration in India and is awarded for acts of conspicuous gallantry in the presence of the enemy, whether on land, at sea or in the air.
- The medal is made of standard silver and is circular in shape. Embossed on the obverse is a five pointed heraldic star with circular centre-piece bearing the gilded state emblem of India in the centre.
- The words "Mahavira Chakra" are imprinted in Devanagari and English on the reverse with two lotus flowers in the middle. The decoration is worn on the left chest with a half-white and half-orange ribbon about 3.2 cm in width, the orange being near the left shoulder.

Vir Chakra

- The Indian gallantry award is presented for acts of bravery in the battlefield.
- The award was established by the President of India on 26 January 1950 with effect from 15 August 1947.
- The medal is 1-3/8 inch circular silver medal. A five pointed star, with the chakra in the centre, and, on this, the domed gilded state emblem. The decoration is almost always named and dated on the edge. Around a plain

centre, two legends separated by lotus flowers; above Vir Chakra in Hindi and in English. The ribbon is 32 mm, half dark blue and half orange-saffron. Dark blue 16 mm, saffron 16 mm.

Peacetime Gallantry Awards

Ashoka Chakra

- It is India's highest peacetime military decoration awarded for valor, courageous action or self-sacrifice away from the battlefield.
- The medal was originally established on 4 January 1952 as the "Ashoka Chakra, Class I".
- The decoration can be awarded either to military or civilian personnel and may be awarded posthumously.
- It is the peace time equivalent of the Param Vir Chakra.

Kirti Chakra

- It is an Indian military decoration awarded for valour, courageous action or self-sacrifice away from the field of battle. It may be awarded to civilians as well as military personnel, including posthumous awards.
- It is second in order of precedence of peacetime gallantry awards and comes after Ashoka Chakra and before Shaurya Chakra.
- The award was established as the "Ashoka Chakra, Class II" by the President of India on 4th January 1952 with effect from 15 August 1947.

Shaurya Chakra

- It is an Indian military decoration awarded for valour, courageous action or self-sacrifice while not engaged in direct action with the enemy. It may be awarded to civilians as well as military personnel, sometimes posthumously.
- It is the peacetime equivalent of the Vir Chakra.
- It is third in order of precedence of peacetime gallantry awards and comes after the Ashoka Chakra and the Kirti Chakra.
- The award was established as the "Ashoka Chakra, Class III" by the President of India, 4th January 1952 with effect from 15th August 1947. The statutes were revised and the decoration renamed on 27th January 1967.

Film Awards

National Film Award

- It is the most prestigious film award ceremonies in India which was established in 1954 and was first awarded on 10th October 1954.
- Since 1973, the Indian Directorate of Film Festivals administers the ceremony along with other major film events in India annually.
- The awards are categorized in three sections; Feature Films, Non-Feature Films and Best Writing on Cinema.

Each section having its individual aims, Feature Film and Non-Feature Film sections aim at encouraging the production of films of aesthetic and technical excellence and social relevance.

- All the award winners are awarded with a Medallion, cash prize and a certificate of merit. The award ceremony is held in New Delhi, where the President of India presents the awards.

Filmfare Awards

- The Filmfare Awards are presented annually by The Times Group to honour both artistic and technical excellence of professionals in the Hindi language film industry of India. The Filmfare ceremony is one of the oldest film events in India.
- The awards were first introduced in 1954, the same year as the National Film Awards. They were initially referred to as the Clare Awards or The Clares after Clare Mendonca, the editor of The Times of India.
- It is often referred to as the Hindi film industry's equivalent to The Oscars.
- Do Bigha Zameen was the first movie to win the award for Best Film. The first winners for other four categories were: Bimal Roy for his direction of Do Bigha Zameen, Dilip Kumar for his performance in Daag, Meena Kumari for her performance in Baiju Bawra, and Naushad Ali for his music in Baiju Bawra.

Dadasaheb Phalke Award

- It is India's highest award in cinema presented annually at the National Film Awards ceremony by the Directorate of Film Festivals.
- The recipient is honoured for their outstanding contribution to the growth and development of Indian cinema and is selected by a committee consisting of eminent personalities from the Indian film industry.
- The award comprises of a Swarna Kamal, cash Prize of Rs. 10,00,000 and a shawl.
- The award was established to honour the Father of Indian Cinema, Dhundiraj Govind Phalke. He is the man who made the first Indian Feature film Raja Harishchandra in 1913.
- The Dadasaheb Phalke Award was introduced in 1969 by the government to recognise the contribution of film personalities towards the development of Indian Cinema. The first recipient of this award was Devika Rani.

Year	Recipient
1969	Devika Rani
1970	Birendranath Sircar
1971	Prithviraj Kapoor
1972	Pankaj Mullick
1973	Ruby Myers(Sulochana)
1974	Bommireddy Narasimha Reddy
1975	Dhirendra Nath Ganguly

1976	Kanan Devi
1977	Nitin Bose
1978	Raichand Boral
1979	Sohrab Modi
1980	Paidi Jairaj
1981	Naushad
1982	L. V. Prasad
1983	Durga Khote
1984	Satyajit Ray
1985	V. Shantaram
1986	B. Nagi Reddy
1987	Raj Kapoor
1988	Ashok Kumar
1989	Lata Mangeshkar
1990	Akkineni Nageswara Rao
1991	Bhalji Pendharkar
1992	Bhupen Hazarika
1993	Majrooh Sultanpuri
1994	Dilip Kumar
1995	Rajkumar
1996	Sivaji Ganesan
1997	Kavi Pradeep
1998	B. R. Chopra
1999	Hrishikesh Mukherjee
2000	Asha Bhosle
2001	Yash Chopra
2002	Dev Anand
2003	Mrinal Sen
2004	Adoor Gopalakrishnan
2005	Shyam Benegal
2006	Tapan Sinha
2007	Manna Dey
2008	V. K. Murthy
2009	D. Ramanaidu
2010	K. Balachander
2011	Soumitra Chatterjee
2012	Pran
2013	Gulzar
2014	Shashi Kapoor
2015	Manoj Kumar
2016	Kashinathuni Viswanath
2017	Vinod Khanna

Literary Awards

Sahitya Akademi Award

- This award is annually conferred on writers of the most outstanding books of literary merit in any of the major Indian languages recognised by the Sahitya Akademi, New Delhi.

- The award was established in 1954. It comprises of a plaque (designed by the Indian film-maker Satyajit Ray) and a cash prize of ₹ 100,000.
- The purpose of the award is to recognize and promote excellence in Indian writing and also acknowledge new trends which involve a 12 month selection process.
- 2015 Sahitya Akademi awards were awarded in 23 languages which include six books of short stories, six of poetry, four novels, two books each of essays, criticism and plays and a memoir. The winner in Bangla was to be announced later

The Winners

Kula Saikia (Assamese)	BK Brahma (Bodo);
Dhian Singh (Dogri)	Cyrus Mistry (English);
Rasik Shah (Gujarati)	Ramdarash Mishra (Hindi);
KV Tirumalesh (Kannada)	Bashir Bhadarwahi (Kashmiri);
Uday Bhembre (Konkani)	Man Mohan Jha (Maithili);
KR Meera (Malayalam)	Kshetri Rajen (Majipuri);
Gupta Pradhan (Nepali)	Bibhuti Pattanaik (Odia);
Jaswinder Singh (Punjabi)	Madhu Acharya;
Ashawadi (Rajasthani)	RS Awasthi (Sanskrit);
Rabilal Tudu (Santhali)	Maya Rahi (Sindhi);
A Madhavan (Tamil)	Volga (Teluge);
Shamim Tariq (Urdu)	Arun Khopkar (Marathi);

Jnanpith Award

- It is a literary award in India along with the Sahitya Akademi Fellowship is one of the two most prestigious literary honours in the country.
- The award was instituted in 1961 and a criterion to win the award requires that the Indian citizen writes in one of the 22 languages listed in Schedule Eight of the Indian constitution. The award is presented by the Bharatiya Jnanpith, a trust founded by the Sahu Jain family, the publishers of the newspaper The Times of India.
- It carries a cheque for ₹ 11 lakh, a citation plaque and a bronze replica of Saraswati.

Jnanpith Award recipients

Year	Name	Language
1965	G. Sankara Kurup	Malayalam
1966	Tarasankar Bandyopadhyay	Bengali
1967	Kuppali Venkatappa Puttappa	Kannada
	Umashankar Joshi	Gujarati
1968	Sumitranandan Pant	Hindi
1969	Firaq Gorakhpuri	Urdu
1970	Viswanatha Satyanarayana	Telugu
1971	Bishnu Dey	Bengali
1972	Ramdhari Singh Dinkar	Hindi
1973	Dattatreya Ramachandra Bendre	Kannada
	Gopinath Mohanty	Oriya

1974	Vishnu Sakharam Khandekar	Marathi
1975	P. V. Akilan	Tamil
1976	Ashapoorna Devi	Bengali
1977	K. Shivaram Karanth	Kannada
1978	Sachchidananda Vatsyayan	Hindi
1979	Birendra Kumar Bhattacharya	Assamese
1980	S. K. Pottekkatt	Malayalam
1981	Amrita Pritam	Punjabi
1982	Mahadevi Varma	Hindi
1983	Masti Venkatesha Iyengar	Kannada
1984	Thakazhi Sivasankara Pillai	Malayalam
1985	Pannalal Patel	Gujarati
1986	Sachidananda Routray	Oriya
1987	Vishnu Vaman Shirwadkar	Marathi
1988	C. Narayana Reddy	Telugu
1989	Qurratulain Hyder	Urdu
1990	Vinayaka Krishna Gokak	Kannada
1991	Subhas Mukhopadhyay	Bengali
1992	Naresh Mehta	Hindi
1993	Sitakant Mahapatra	Oriya
1994	U. R. Ananthamurthy	Kannada
1995	M. T. Vasudevan Nair	Malayalam
1996	Mahasweta Devi	Bengali
1997	Ali Sardar Jafri	Urdu
1998	Girish Karnad	Kannada
1999	Nirmal Verma	Hindi
	Gurdial Singh	Punjabi
2000	Indira Goswami	Assamese
2001	Rajendra Shah	Gujarati
2002	D. Jayakanthan	Tamil
2003	Vinda Karandikar	Marathi
2004	Rehman Rahi	Kashmiri
2005	Kunwar Narayan	Hindi
2006	Ravindra Kelekar	Konkani
	Satya Vrat Shastri	Sanskrit
2007	O. N. V. Kurup	Malayalam
2008	Akhlaq Mohammed Khan 'Shahryar'	Urdu
2009	Amar Kant	Hindi
	Lal Shukla	Hindi
2010	Chandrashekhara Kambara	Kannada
2011	Pratibha Ray	Oriya
2012	Ravuri Bharadhwaja	Telugu
2013	Kedarnath Singh	Hindi
2014	Bhalchandra Nemade	Marathi
2015	Raghuveer Chaudhari	Gujarati
2016	Shankha Ghosh	Bengali
2017	Krishna Sobti	Hindi

Sports Awards

Rajiv Gandhi Khel Ratna Award

- It is India's highest honour given for achievement in sports, given by the Ministry of Youth Affairs and Sports, Government of India.
- The award is named after the late Rajiv Gandhi, former Prime Minister of India.
- It carries a medal, a scroll of honour and a cash prize of ₹ 750,000.
- The award was instituted in the year 1991–92 to supply the lack of a supreme national accolade in the field of sports. The award is conferred for outstanding sporting performance, either by an individual or a team and includes all sporting disciplines in a given year.

Year	Name	Sport
1991–92	Viswanathan Anand	Chess
1992–93	Geet Sethi	Billiards
1994–95	Cdr. Homi D. Motivala, Lt. Cdr. P. K. Garg	Yachting (Team)
1995–96	Karnam Malleswari	Weightlifting
1996–97	Nameirakpam Kunjarani	Weightlifting
	Leander Paes	Tennis
1997–98	Sachin Tendulkar	Cricket
1998–99	Jyotirmoyee Sikdar	Athletics
1999–2000	Dhanraj Pillay	Hockey
2000–01	Pullela Gopichand	Badminton
2001–02	Abhinav Bindra	Shooting
2002–03	Anjali Bhagwat	Shooting
	K. M. Beenamol	Athletics
2003–04	Anju Bobby George	Athletics
2004–05	Lt. Col Rajyavardhan Singh Rathore	Shooting
2005–06	Pankaj Advani	Billiards and Snooker
2006–07	Manavjit Singh Sandhu	Shooting
2007–08	Mahendra Singh Dhoni	Cricket
2008–09	Mary Kom	Boxing
	Vijender Singh	Boxing
	Sushil Kumar	Wrestling
2009–10	Saina Nehwal	Badminton
2010–11	Gagan Narang	Shooting
2011–12	Vijay Kumar	Shooting
	Yogeshwar Dutt	Wrestling
2012–13	Ronjan Sodhi	Shooting
2014-15	Sania Mirza	Tennis
2016	P.V. Sindhu	Badminton

2016	Dipa Karmakar	Gymnastics
2016	Jitu Rai	Shooting
2016	Sakshi Malik	Wrestling
2017	Devendra Jhajharia	Para Athlete
2017	Sardara Singh	Hockey
2018	Virat Kohli	Cricket
2018	S. Mirabai Chanu	Weight Lifting

Arjuna Award

- The award is given by the Ministry of Youth Affairs and Sports, Government of India to recognize outstanding achievement in National sports.
- The award was instituted in 1961; and carries a cash prize of ₹ 500,000, a bronze statue of Arjuna and a scroll.
- Gurbachan Singh Randhawa (Athletics) was the first awardee in 1961. Stephie D'Souza was the first woman to win the Arjuna Award.
- The government has revised the rules of conferring the award from 2001 and now the award will be given in disciplines falling under the categories which include Olympic Games / Asian Games / Commonwealth Games / World Cup / World Championship Disciplines and Cricket; Indigenous Games or Sports for the Physically Challenged.

Arjuna Award 2018

S.No.	Name of the Sports person	Discipline
1	Shri Neeraj Chopra	Athletics
2.	Naib Subedar Jinson Johnson	Athletics
3.	Ms. Hima Das	Athletics
4.	Ms. Nelakurthi Sikki Reddy	Badminton
5.	Subedar Satish Kumar	Boxing
6.	Ms. Smriti Mandhana	Cricket
7.	Shri Shubhankar Sharma	Golf
8.	Shri Manpreet Singh	Hockey
9.	Ms. Savita	Hockey
10.	Col. Ravi Rathore	Polo
11.	Ms. Rahi Sarnobat	Shooting
12.	Shri Ankur Mittal	Shooting
13.	Ms. Shreyasi Singh	Shooting
14.	Ms. Manika Batra	Table Tennis
15.	Shri G. Sathiyan	Table Tennis
16.	Shri Rohan Bopanna	Tennis
17.	Shri Sumit	Wrestling
18.	Ms. Pooja Kadian	Wushu
19.	Shri Ankur Dhama	Para-Athletics
20.	Shri Manoj Sarkar	Para-Badminton

Dronacharya Award

- The Dronacharya Award is given to honour eminent coaches who have successfully trained sportspersons or teams and enabled them to achieve outstanding results in international competitions.
- The award comprises a bronze statuette of Dronacharya, a scroll of honour and a cash component of ₹ 500,000. It was instituted in 1985.
- B.I. Fernandez is the first foreign coach to be awarded Dronacharya Award.

Dronacharya Award 2018

S.No.	Name of the Coach	Discipline
1.	Subedar Chenanda Achaiah Kuttappa	Boxing
2.	Shri Vijay Sharma	Weightlifting
3.	Shri A. Srinivasa Rao	Table Tennis
4.	Shri Sukhdev Singh Pannu	Athletics
5.	Shri Clarance Lobo	Hockey (Life Time)
6.	Shri Tarak Sinha	Cricket (Life Time)
7.	Shri Jiwan Kumar Sharma	Judo (Life Time)
8.	Shri V.R. Beedu	Athletics (Life Time)

Dhyanchand Award

- It is award for Lifetime Achievements in Sports and Games given to honour those sportspersons who have contributed to sports by their performance and continue to contribute to the promotion of sports even after their retirement from active sporting career. The award was instituted in the 2002.
- The award carries a cash prize of ₹ 500,000, a plaque and a scroll of honour.
- The first awardees in the year 2002 were Aparna Ghosh (Basketball), Ashok Diwan (Hockey) and Shahuraj Birajdar (Boxing).

Dhyan Chand Award 2018

S.No.	Name of the Sports Person	Discipline
1.	Shri Satyadev Prasad	Archery
2.	Shri Bharat Kumar Chetri	Hockey
3.	Ms. Bobby Aloysius	Athletics
4.	Shri Chougale Dadu Dattatray	Wrestling

Rashtriya Khel Protsahan Puruskar 2018		
S.No.	**Category**	**Name of the entity**
1.	Identification and Nurturing of Budding & Young Talent	Rashtriya Ispat Nigam Limited
2.	Encouragement to Sports through Corporate Social Responsibility	JSW Sports
3.	Sports for Development	Isha Outreach

Maulana Abul Kalam Azad (MAKA) Trophy 2017-18

Guru Nanak Dev University, Amristar

Exercise -1

1. Jnanpith Award is given for which field?
   - (a) Journalism
   - (b) Music
   - (c) Science
   - (d) Literature
2. Highest award given to civilian in India is
   - (a) Bharat Ratna
   - (b) Padma Vibhushan
   - (c) Sharam Award
   - (d) Padma Bhushan
3. Sports coaches receive which of the following awards?
   - (a) Rajiv Gandhi Khel Ratna Award
   - (b) Dronacharya Award
   - (c) Arjuna Award
   - (d) None of these
4. In which year National Film Awards were initiated?
   - (a) 1952
   - (b) 1953
   - (c) 1954
   - (d) 1955
5. Which of the following is different from the others?
   - (a) Kirti Chakra
   - (b) Ashok Chakra
   - (c) Vir Chakra
   - (d) Shaurya Chakra
6. Vyas Samman is awarded annually by
   - (a) Azim Premji Foundation
   - (b) Times Group
   - (c) KK Birla Foundation
   - (d) Ministry of Culture
7. Vishwakarma Rashtriya Puraskar is given by which ministry?
   - (a) Ministry of Culture
   - (b) Ministry of Labour
   - (c) Ministry of Minority
   - (d) Ministry of Rural Development
8. Saraswati Samman is given to which field?
   - (a) Culture
   - (b) Science
   - (c) Literature
   - (d) Social Harmony
9. Bharat Ratna, Padma Vibhushan and Padma Shree are given on the eve of
   - (a) Republic Day
   - (b) Independence Day
   - (c) Gandhi Jayanti
   - (d) Pravasi Bhartiya Divas
10. The award is given for extraordinary act of bravery in the field of Naval, Air and Army is
    - (a) Arjuna Award
    - (b) Paramvir Chakra
    - (c) Kalinga Award
    - (d) Ashok Chakra
11. The second highest Gallantry award is
    - (a) Mahavir Chakra
    - (b) Vir Chakra
    - (c) Arjuna Award
    - (d) Ashok Chakra
12. The award is given in the field of agriculture
    - (a) Bhatnagar Award
    - (b) Bourlog Award
    - (c) Dhanwantari Award
    - (d) Kaling Award
13. The award is conferred to journalists aims to providing financial assistance :
    - (a) Appan Menon Memorial Award
    - (b) Jnanpith Award
    - (c) Bhatnagar Award
    - (d) Kalinga Award
14. Vachaspati Samman is given in the field of
    - (a) Sanskrit Literature
    - (b) Medical Science
    - (c) Indian Philosophy
    - (d) Hindi Literature
15. Dhanwantari award is conferred in the field of :
    - (a) Medical Science
    - (b) Sports
    - (c) Indian Philosophy
    - (d) Agriculture
16. The National bravery award is also known as :
    - (a) Bharat Puraskar
    - (b) Hind Puraskar
    - (c) Bharati Puraskar
    - (d) Rashtriya Puraskar
17. Tansen Samman is conferred in the field of :
    - (a) Music
    - (b) Literature
    - (c) Science
    - (d) Journalism
18. Dhyanchand Puraskar conferred in the field of
    - (a) Music
    - (b) Sports
    - (c) Science
    - (d) Literature
19. 'Ashoka Chakra' is awarded for
    - (a) the most conspicuous bravery or self sacrifice on land, air or sea but not in the presence of the enemy
    - (b) acts of gallantry in the presence of enemy
    - (c) gallantry by children
    - (d) outstanding contribution to literature
20. Shanthi Swaroop Bhatnagar awards are given for
    - (a) exploring new dimensions in creative writing in Indian languages
    - (b) outstanding contribution to science
    - (c) creating mass awareness on environmental issues
    - (d) excellence in film direction
21. Manav Seva Award has been instituted in the memory of
    - (a) Rajiv Gandhi
    - (b) Dr. Rajendra Prasad
    - (c) Indira Gandhi
    - (d) Acharya
22. The prestigious Ramon Magsaysay Award was conferred upon Mr. Arvind Kejriwal in which of the following category?
    - (a) Emergent Leadership
    - (b) Literature
    - (c) Community Welfare
    - (d) Government Service

23. The Nobel prize was instituted by which country?
    - (a) USA
    - (b) UK
    - (c) Russia
    - (d) Sweden
24. When did the Nobel prize in the Economics Sciences launched?
    - (a) 1901
    - (b) 1942
    - (c) 1968
    - (d) 1975
25. The Academy award is also known as
    - (a) Oscar Award
    - (b) BAFTA Award
    - (c) Matthews Award
    - (d) Palm d'ore
26. Pulitzer prize was established in
    - (a) 1917
    - (b) 1918
    - (c) 1922
    - (d) 1928
27. BAFTA prize is distributed by
    - (a) UK
    - (b) Russia
    - (c) India
    - (d) USA
28. Golden Globe award is given by
    - (a) UK
    - (b) France
    - (c) USA
    - (d) China
29. 'Palme d'or prize is given by
    - (a) France
    - (b) USA
    - (c) UK
    - (d) Indonesia
30. Which of the following is an award instituted by UNESCO?
    - (a) Kalinga Award
    - (b) Pulitzer prize
    - (c) Stirling prize
    - (d) Pritzker prize
31. International Gandhi Peace prize is instituted in
    - (a) 1995
    - (b) 1996
    - (c) 1997
    - (d) 1998
32. The India Human Development award in association with UNDP instituted in
    - (a) 2010
    - (b) 2011
    - (c) 2012
    - (d) 2013
33. Which of the following award is given by World Economic Forum?
    - (a) Crystal Award
    - (b) Kalinga prize
    - (c) Pulitzer Award
    - (d) Abel prize
34. Right Livelihood award is instituted in
    - (a) 1980
    - (b) 1982
    - (c) 1984
    - (d) 1985
35. Which of the following prizes is also known as the Alternative Nobel prize?
    - (a) Pulitzer prize
    - (b) Magsaysay award
    - (c) Booker prize
    - (d) Right Livelihood award
36. Magsaysay award is given by
    - (a) USA
    - (b) UK
    - (c) Malaysia
    - (d) Philippines
37. The 'Cannes Award' is given for excellence in which field?
    - (a) Films
    - (b) Journalism
    - (c) Literature
    - (d) Environment
38. Pulitzer prize is awarded for outstanding work in the field of
    - (a) Science and Technology
    - (b) Environmental Studies
    - (c) Literature and Journalism
    - (d) International Understanding
39. Booker prize is given to the field of :
    - (a) Fiction
    - (b) Poetry
    - (c) Drama
    - (d) Essay
40. FiFi awards are given in_____industry:
    - (a) Film
    - (b) Home Appliances
    - (c) Perfumes
    - (d) Automobiles
41. Arrange the following countries in ascending order on the basis of the total medals earned by them in Rio Olympic 2016 :
    1. United States   2. China
    3. Great Britain   4. Russia
    Select the correct answer using the code given below :
    - (a) 1, 2, 3, 4
    - (b) 1, 3, 2, 4
    - (c) 4, 3, 2, 1
    - (d) 4, 3, 1, 2
42. Which one of the following is a Peacetime Gallantry Award?
    - (a) Shaurya Chakra
    - (b) Vir Chakra
    - (c) Yudh Seva Medal
    - (d) Pararn Vir Chakra
43. Who among the following is the recipient of the Jnanpith Award, 2016?
    - (a) Shankha Ghosh
    - (b) Raghuveer Chaudhari
    - (c) Pratibha Ray
    - (d) Rehman Rahi
44. Who among the following is the recipient of the Dadasaheb Phalke Award, 2016?
    - (a) Nana Patekar
    - (b) Manoj Kumar
    - (c) Javed Akhtar
    - (d) K. Viswanath

Exercise -2

Statement Based MCQ

1. Consider the following statements :
   1. The Saraswati Samman is the most prestigious award of the KK Birla Foundation.
   2. The Samman is given annually to an outstanding literary work published in Hindi only during the last 10 years.
   3. It was initiated in 1991.
   Which of the statements given above is/are correct?
   (a) 1, 2 and 3   (b) 1 and 2
   (c) 1 and 3   (d) 2 only

2. Consider the following statements :
   1. Bharat Ratna is not awarded to the dead persons like the Nobel Prize.
   2. The holders of the Bharat Ratna rank 7th in the Indian order of precedence.
   Which of the statements given above is/are correct?
   (a) 1 only   (b) 2 only
   (c) Both 1 and 2   (d) Neither 1 nor 2

3. Consider the following statements :
   1. Jnanpith Award is given to any of Indian citizens who writes in the eight scheduled languages of India.
   2. Jnanpith Award was awarded for the first time in 1961.
   Which of the statements given above is/are correct?
   (a) 1 only   (b) 2 only
   (c) Both 1 and 2   (d) Neither 1 nor 2

4. Who presents the following mentioned awards to the winners?
   1. Swarna Kamal
   2. Rajat Kamal
   3. Dadasaheb Phalke Award
   (a) The President
   (b) Vice-President
   (c) The Prime Minister
   (d) Minister of Cultural activities

5. Consider the following statements :
   1. Padma Vibhushan is the second highest civilian award of India.
   2. Tagore Literature Awards are jointly instituted by the Sahitya Akademi and UNESCO.
   Which of the statements given above is/are correct?
   (a) 1 only   (b) 2 only
   (c) Both 1 and 2   (d) Neither 1 nor 2

6. Consider the following statements :
   1. Ashok Chakra is the country's highest peace time gallantry award equivalent to Param Vir Chakra.
   2. Kirti Chakra is awarded for conspicuous gallantry.
   3. Shaurya Chakra is awarded for an act of gallantry.
   Which of the statements given above is/are correct?
   (a) 1 and 2 only   (b) 2 and 3 only
   (c) 1 and 3 only   (d) 1, 2 and 3

7. Which of the following medals are awarded to personnel of all the three services?
   1. Param Vishisht Seva Medal (PVSM)
   2. Ati Vishisht Seva Medal (AVSM)
   3. Vishisht Seva Medal (VSM)
   Which of the statements given above is/are correct?
   (a) 1 and 2 only   (b) 2 and 3 only
   (c) 1 and 3 only   (d) 1, 2 and 3

8. Consider the following statements :
   1. Rajiv Gandhi Environment Award is given for outstanding contributions to neat technology and development.
   2. First Bharat Ratna Award initiated in 1954.
   3. The Indira Gandhi Award for National Integration consists of a citation and ` 5 lakh in cash.
   Which of the statements given above is/are correct?
   (a) 1 and 2 only   (b) 2 and 3 only
   (c) 1 and 3 only   (d) 1, 2 and 3

9. Consider the following statements :
   1. The Times of India Group founded the Bharatiya Jnanpith Trust.
   2. ICAR gives the Swamy Sahajanand Saraswati Award.
   Which of the statements given above is/are correct?
   (a) 1 and 2   (b) 1 only
   (c) 2 only   (d) Neither 1 nor 2

10. Consider the following statements :
    1. Tagore Awards have been instituted as part of Hope Project, a corporate social responsibility initiative.
    2. Under this award literary works in 24 Indian languages are eligible.
    Which of the statements given above is/are correct?
    (a) 1 only   (b) 2 only
    (c) 1 and 2   (d) Neither 1 nor 2

11. Consider the following statements :
    1. Sahitya Akademi Award, the highest literary prize given by the government of India.
    2. Indira Gandhi Paryavaran Puraskar is an environmental prize.
    Which of the statements given above is/are correct?
    (a) 1 only   (b) 2 only
    (c) Both 1 and 2   (d) Neither 1 nor 2

12. Consider the following statements:
    1. Devika Rani was the first Indian to win Dadasaheb Phalke Award.
    2. Bhanu Athaiya was the first Indian Oscar Winner.
    3. Arundhati Roy is the first Indian to win Booker Prize.

Which of the statements given above is/are correct?
(a) 1, 2 and 3   (b) 1 and 2
(c) 2 and 3   (d) 2 Only

13. Consider the following statements
1. Rajiv Gandhi Khel Ratna Award was instituted in the year 1991-92 to national accolade in the field of sports.
2. Viswanathan Anand was the first recipient of th Rajiv Gandhi Khel Ratna Award.
Which of the statements given above is/are correct?
(a) 1 only   (b) 2 only
(c) Both 1 and 2   (d) Neither 1 nor 2

14. Consider the following statements
1. Dadasaheb Phalke Award is India's highest award in cinema given annually by the government of India for lifetime contribution to Indian cinema.
2. Prithviraj Kapoor was the first recipient of the Dadasaheb Phalke Award.
Which of the statements given above is/are correct?
(a) 1 only   (b) 2 only
(c) Both 1 and 2   (d) Neither 1 nor 2

15. National Urban Water Awards is instituted by Ministry of Urban Development for excellence in
1. Services to the Poor
2. Citizen Services and Governance
3. Urban Sanitation
4. Communication Strategy and Awareness Generation
(a) 1, 2, 3 and 4   (b) 1 and 3 only
(c) 2 and 4 only   (d) 3 only

16. Which of the following statements is/are correct?
1. Tagore Literature Awards are jointly instituted by the Sahitya Akademi and Nokia.
2. The Awards are given to the best of literary contributions by writers in 8 Indian languages.
3. Literary works in 24 Indian languages are eligible for consideration under the Scheme.
4. Awards have been instituted as part of Hope Project, a corporate social responsibility initiative.
Select correct answer form the codes given below
(a) 1, 2 and 3 only   (b) 1, 2 and 4 only
(c) 3 and 4   (d) 1, 2, 3 and 4

17. Consider the following fields
1. Biology   2. Physics
3. Medicine   4. Mathematics
Which of the fields given above is/are awarded in the Shanti Swarup Bhatnagar Prize?
(a) 1, 2, 3 and 4   (b) 1, 2 and 3 only
(c) 2 and 3 only   (d) 3 and 4 only

18. Consider the following statements
1. The first recipient of the Bharat Ratna was politician C. Rajagopalachariwho was honoured in 1960.
2. In 1966, former Prime Minister Lal Bahadur Shastri became the first individual to be honoured posthumously.
Which of the statements given above is/are correct?
(a) 1 only   (b) 2 only
(c) Both 1 and 2   (d) Neither of these

19. Consider the following statements
1. The Lady Tata Memorial Trust was established by Sir Dorabji Tata in April 1932 in memory of his wife, Lady Meherbai.
2. Awards are restricted to studies of leukaemogenic agents, and the epidemiology, pathogenesis, immunology and genetic basis of leukaemia and related diseases.
Which of the statements given above is/are correct?
(a) 1 only   (b) 2 only
(c) Both 1 and 2   (d) Neither of these

20. Consider the following statements:
1. Jawaharlal Nehru Award for International Understanding was founded in 1965.
2. Mother Teresa was the first person to get the Jawaharlal Nehru Award for International Understanding.
Which of the statements given above is/are correct?
(a) 1 only   (b) 2 only
(c) Both 1 and 2   (d) Neither 1 nor 2

21. Consider the following statements:
1. Indira Gandhi Prize for Peace, Disarmament and Development is awarded only to Indians.
2. UNICEF is the only agency of the United Nations to get the Indira Gandhi Prize for Peace, Disarmament and Development.
Which of the statements given above is/are correct?
(a) 1 only   (b) 2 only
(c) Both 1 and 2   (d) Neither 1 nor 2

22. Consider the following statements:
1. Nobel Prize is sometimes given to the outstanding persons in the related fields posthumously.
2. The Nobel Prizes in Physics, Chemistry, Physiology or Medicine, Literature and peace were first awarded in 1901.
Which of the statements given above is/are correct?
(a) 1 only   (b) 2 only
(c) Both 1 and 2   (d) Neither 1 nor 2

23. Consider the following statements:
1. The Miss World pageant is the oldest surviving major international beauty pageant. It was created in the United Kingdom.
2. Miss Universe is an annual international beauty contest that is run by the Miss Universe organization. The contest was founded in 1953 by California.
Which of the statements given above is/are correct?
(a) 1 only   (b) 2 only
(c) Both 1 and 2   (d) Neither 1 nor 2

24. Consider the following statements:
1. The Kalinga Prize is an award given by UNESCO for exceptional skill in presenting scientific ideas to lay people.

2. World Economic Forum gives the 'Crystal Award'.
3. Laureates award is related to sports.
Which of the statements given above is/are correct?
Codes:
(a) 1 and 2 only (b) 2 only
(c) 2 and 3 only (d) All of the above

25. Consider the following statements:
1. BAFTA award is presented in Britain.
2. Golden Globe Award is presented in USA.
3. Palm D'or Award is presented in France.
Which of the statements given above is/are correct?
(a) 1 only (b) 2 only
(c) 1 and 2 only (d) All of the above

26. Consider the following statements:
1. International Gandhi Peace Prize is awarded biannually by the Government of India.
2. The Government of India launched the International Gandhi Peace Prize in 1995.
3. It was started on the occasion of the 125th Birth Anniversary of Mahatma Gandhi.
Which of the statements given above is/are correct?
(a) 1 only (b) 2 only
(c) 1 and 2 only (d) All of the above

27. The correct fields in which Ramen Magsaysay Award is given:
1. Government Services
2. Public Services
3. Journalism, Literature and Creative communication Arts
4. Emergent Leadership
Codes:
(a) 1, 2 and 3 (b) 1 and 2
(c) 2, 3 and 4 (d) All of the above

28. Consider the following statements:
1. International Children's Peace Prize is conferred by the Kids Right Foundation of Netherland.
2. Man Booker International Prize is conferred for the eminent writing skill.
3. Pritzer Award is presented in the field of Architecture.
4. Abel Prize is conferred to the Mathematics.
Which of the statements given above is/are correct?
(a) 1 and 2 only (b) 2 and 3 only
(c) 3 and 4 only (d) All of the above

29. Consider about BAFTA Awards
1. It is the British Counterpart of the Academy Awards (Oscars).
2. It was first awarded in 1939.
3. It honours the best national and foreign films.
Select the correct answer from the codes given below
Codes:

(a) 1 and 2 (b) 1 and 4
(c) 1 and 3 (d) All of the above

30. Consider the following statements
1. The Pulitzer Prize was established in 1917 by provisions in the will of American (Hungarian-born) publisher Joseph Pulitzer, and is administered by Columbia University in New York City.
2. In twenty of the categories, each winner receives a certificate and a US$10,000 cash award.
Which of the statements given above is/are correct?
(a) 1 only (b) 2 only
(c) Both 1 and 2 (d) Neither of these

31. Consider the following statements
1. Golden Peacock Awards have given boost to the Industry worldwide.
2. Award winners cannot use the Golden Peacock Awards Logo on all promotional literatures.
Which of the statements given above is/are correct?
(a) 1 only (b) 2 only
(c) Both 1 and 2 (d) Neither of these

32. Consider the following statements
1. The Man Booker International Prize is an international literary award given every two years to a living author of any nationality for a body of work published in English or generally available in English translation.
2. The inaugural winner was Albanian writer Ismail Kadare.
Which of the statements given above is/are correct?
(a) 1 only (b) 2 only
(c) 1 and 2 only (d) Neither of these

33. Consider the following statements:
1. Nobel Peace Prize is presented annually in Oslo by the King of Norway.
2. The Nobel laureate receives three things- a diploma, a medal and a document confirming the prize amount.
Which of the statements given above is / are correct?
(a) 1 only (b) 2 only
(c) Both 1 and 2 (d) neither 1 nor 2

34. Consider the following statements:
1. Nobel Prize award in Economics has been awarded since 1969.
2. Arjuna Award was introduced in 1965.
Which of the statements given above is / are correct?
(a) 1 only (b) only
(c) both 1 and 2 (d) neither 1 nor 2

Matching Based MCQ

35. Match List-I with List-II and select the correct answer from the codes given below :

List-I	List-II
A. Padma Vibhushan	1. For distinguished service in any field.
B. Padma Bhushan	2. For distinguished service of high order.
C. Padma Shri	3. For exceptional and distinguished service

Codes:

	A	B	C		A	B	C
(a)	3	2	1	(b)	1	2	3
(c)	2	1	3	(d)	2	3	1

36. Arrange the following awards in the correct chronological order :
   1. Rajiv Gandhi Khel Ratna Award
   2. Arjuna Award
   3. Dhyanchand Award
   4. Dronacharya Award

   Select the correct answer from the codes :

   Codes:
   (a) 3, 2, 4, 1   (b) 2, 3, 4, 1
   (c) 2, 4, 1, 3   (d) 3, 2, 1, 4

37. Match List-I with List-II and select the correct answer from the codes given below :

List-I	List-II
A. Saraswati Samman	1. Science
B. Kabir Award	2. Sports
C. Arjuna Award	3. Social solidarity
D. Bhatnagar Award	4. Literature

Codes:

	A	B	C	D		A	B	C	D
(a)	4	3	2	1	(b)	2	1	4	3
(c)	3	2	1	4	(d)	3	4	1	2

38. Match List-I with List-II and select the correct answer from the codes given below :

List-I	List-II
A. Jnanpith Award	1. Literature (1961)
B. Saraswati Award	2. Literature (1991)
C. Vachaspati Samman	3. Sanskrit (1992)
D. Shankar Award	4. Indian philosophy

Codes:

	A	B	C	D		A	B	C	D
(a)	1	2	3	4	(b)	1	4	3	2
(c)	2	3	1	4	(d)	2	4	1	3

39. Match List-I with List-II and select the correct answer from the codes given below :

List-I	List-II
A. Param Vir Chakra	1. Highest gallantry award
B. Mahavir Chakra	2. Second highest gallantry award
C. Vir Chakra	3. Third highest gallantry award

Codes:

	A	B	C		A	B	C
(a)	1	2	3	(b)	3	2	1
(c)	3	1	2	(d)	1	3	2

40. Match List-I with List-II and select the correct answer from the codes given below:

List-I	List-II
A. Grammy Award	1. Music
B. Ramon Magsaysay Award	2. International understanding
C. Pulitzer Award	3. Agriculture
D. Borlaug Award	4. Journalism

Codes:

	A	B	C	D		A	B	C	D
(a)	1	2	3	4	(b)	1	2	4	3
(c)	4	3	2	1	(d)	4	2	3	1

Hints and Explanations

EXERCISE-1

1. (d) The Jnanpith award is a literary award which along with the Sahitya Akademi Fellowship is one of the two most prestigious literary honours in the country. The award was instituted in 1961. Any Indian citizen who writes in any of the official languages of India is eligible for the honour.

2. (a) Bharat Ratna is India's highest civilian award. The official criteria for awarding the Bharat Ratna stipulated it is to be conferred "for the highest degrees of national service which includes artistic, literary, and scientific achievements, as well as "recognition of public service of the highest order". The last recipient of the award is the cricketer Sachin Tendulkar for the year 2014.

3. (b) Dronacharya award is an award presented by the government of India for excellence in sports coaching. The award comprises bronze statue of Dronacharya, a scroll of honour and a cash component of ₹ 500,000. The award was instituted in 1985. The last recipient of the award is Raj Singh for wrestling in the year 2014.

4. (c) The National Film awards, one of the most prominent film awards in India, were established in 1954. Every year, a national panel appointed by the government selects the winning entry, and the award ceremony is held in New Delhi where the President of India presents the awards.

5. (c) Vir Chakra is an Indian gallantry award presented for acts of bravery in the battlefield while the Ashok Chakra, Kirti Chakra and Shaurya Chakra in addition for separate acts of gallantry are awarded for valour, courageous action or self-sacrifice away from the battlefield.

6. (c) The Vyas Samman is a literary award which was first awarded in 1991. It is awarded annually by the K.K. Birla Foundation. To be eligible for the award, the literary work must be in the Hindi language and has been published in the past 10 years.

7. (b) The Vishvakarma Rashtriya puraskar and National Safety awards scheme was launched in 1965 by ministry of labour to motivate the brilliant workers and industrial units who deliver their best to curb mishaps and increase in the industrial (occupational) safety measures and work for the promotion of the interests of both the management and labour.

8. (c) The Saraswati Samman is an annual award for outstanding prose or poetry literary works in any Indian language. It was instituted in 1991 by the K. K. Birla Foundation. The award contains ₹ 15 lakh, a citation and a plaque. Candidates are selected from literary works published in the previous ten years by a panel that includes scholars and former award winners.

9. (a)

10. (b) The Param Vir Chakra is India's highest military decoration awarded for the highest degree of valour or self-sacrifice in the presence of the enemy. It can be awarded to officers or enlisted personnel from all branches of the Indian military and can be, and often has been, awarded posthumously.

11. (a) The Maha Vir Chakra is the second military decoration in India and is awarded for acts of conspicuous gallantry in the presence of the enemy, whether on land, at sea or in the air. The medal may be awarded posthumously.

12. (b) In order to recognize a scientist, who provides a breakthrough for agriculture through a new insight that has created high potential value for the future, the Norman Borlaug Award has been constituted. The nominations for the awards are for a scientist(s) of any discipline of agricultural and allied sciences. The award would be of ₹ 10 lakh in cash.

13. (a) The Appan Menon Memorial Award consisting of a grant of ₹ 1 lakh is given each year to a professional journalist working in the area of world affairs or development news with an Indian perspective.

14. (a)

15. (a) The prestigious Dhanwantari award, which recognizes contribution in medical science is awarded annually since 1972. The recipients include M.K. Mani, pioneer in nephrology in the country and Chief Nephrologist at Apollo Hospital, Chennai who has been honoured with the 40th Dhanvantari Award.

16. (a) National Bravery award also known as Bharat Puraskar for Indian Children is given each year by Government of India and Indian Council for Child Welfare (ICCW) to Indian children for meritorious acts of bravery against all odds. The award is given to around 24 children below the age of 16.

17. (a) Tansen Samman is conferred in the field of music which carries a cash prize of ` 2 lakh and a citation.

18. (b) Dhyan Chand award is India's highest award for lifetime achievement in sports and games. The award is named after the legendary Indian hockey player Dhyan Chand and was initiated in 2002. The award carries a cash prize of ` 5 lakh, a plaque and a scroll of honour.

19. (a)

20. (b) The Shanti Swarup Bhatnagar award for Science and Technology (SSB) is an award in India given annually by the CSIR. It is named after the founder Director of the CSIR and carries an award money of ₹ 5 lakh each.

21. (a)

22. (a) In 2006, Kejriwal was awarded the Ramon Magsaysay Award for Emergent Leadership

recognising his involvement in a grassroots movement Parivartan using right-to-information legislation in a campaign against corruption. The same year, after resigning from the IRS, he donated his Magsaysay award money as a corpus fund to found the Public Cause Research Foundation, a non-governmental organisation (NGO).

23. (d) The Nobel prize is a set of an international awards bestowed in a number of categories which is given annually to the winners by Swedish and Norwegian Committees in recognition of cultural and/or scientific advances. It was the will of the Swedish inventor Alfred Nobel that established the Nobel prizes in 1895 in Sweden.

24. (c) The Nobel prize in Economics or Economic sciences was established in 1968 and endowed by Sweden's central bank, the Sveriges Riksbank, on the occasion of the bank's 300th anniversary. While the Nobel Prize in particular was established in 1895.

25. (a) The Academy award is also known as the Oscar award which is presented for various categories in the Film industry. It was first given in 1929.

26. (a) The Pulitzer Prize is a U.S. award for achievements in newspaper and online journalism, literature, and musical composition. It was established in 1917 and administered by Columbia University in New York City by provisions in the will of American publisher Joseph Pulitzer.

27. (a) The British Academy Film awards are presented in an annual award show hosted by the British Academy of Film and Television Arts (BAFTA). It is given by UK and is considered to be the counter awards for Oscars.

28. (c) Golden Globe award is given in the field of film and television by Hollywood Foreign Press Association in United States of America.

29. (a) The Palme d'Or is the highest prize awarded at the Cannes Film Festival and is presented to the director of the best feature film of the official competition. It is presented by Festival International du film de, France.

30. (a) The Kalinga Prize for popularization of Science is an international distinction instituted by UNESCO. It was started in 1951 by donation from Mr Bijoyanand Patnaik, founder and president of the Kalinga Foundation Trust in India.

31. (a) International Gandhi Peace prize is given annually by Government of India to those individuals and organizations which contribute towards changes in the political, social or economic reforms via non-violence. It was instituted in 1995.

32. (c) The Manav Vikas India Human Development awards, instituted by the Planning Commission and UNDP was first given out in 2012.

33. (a) The World Economic Forum gives Crystal award to those artists who have improved the state of the world through their art.

34. (a) The prize was established in 1980 by German-Swedish philanthropist Jakob von Uexkull. This ispresented annually in early December.

35. (d) Right Livelihood prize is considered to be the alternative to Nobel prize. This is also an annual prize which is given to individuals who have done something exemplary to solve some of the most pressing issues in the world.

36. (d) Ramon Magsaysay award is given annually to those Asian people who have contributed extraordinary service in their respective fields. This award is given by Philippine in the memoir of Philippine President Ramon Magsaysay. He is considered to be one of the great examples of integrity, courage, and idealistic democrat.

37. (a) 38. (c) 39. (a) 40. (c)
41. (b)
42. (a) Peacetime Gallantry Awards recognize courage or self-sacrifice away from battlefield and include Ashok Chakra, Kirti Chakra and Shaurya Chakra. Param Vir Chakra and Vir Chakra are Wartime Gallantry Awards and recognizes self-sacrifice at battlefield. Yudh Seva Medal is military decorations for service during wartime.

43. (a)
44. (d) Dadasaheb Phalke Award is one of the highest and most prestigious awards that is given for the great contribution in the field of cinema.

EXERCISE-2

1. (c) The Saraswati Samman was instituted in 1991 by the K. K. Birla Foundation. The Saraswati Samman is an annual award for outstanding prose or poetry literary works in any Indian language .

2. (c) Both the statements are correct. The holders of the Bharat Ratna rank 7th in the Indian order of precedence and it has also been awarded posthumously to various persons.

3. (c) Both the statements are correct. Any Indian citizen who writes in any of the eighth scheduled languages of India is eligible for the honour. The award was instituted in 1961.

4. (a)
5. (a) Only statement 1 is correct. The Padma Vibhushan is the second highest civilian award in the Republic of India and is instituted by Samsung Electronics and the Sahitya Akademi and not by UNESCO.

6. (d)
7. (d) All the three medals are awarded to recognize "distinguished service of an exceptional order" to all ranks of the Indian armed forces.

8. (d) 9. (a)
10. (c) Tagore Literature Awards have been instituted as part of Samsung Hope Project and recognize the best literary contributions in 24 Indian languages.

11. (b) Only statement 2 is correct. Sahitya Akademy Award is the second-best award in literature.

12. (a) 13. (c) 14. (a) 15. (a) 16. (c) 17. (a)

18. (b) The first recipient of the Bharat Ratna was politician C. Rajagopalachari who was honoured in 1954.

19. (c) The Lady Tata Memorial Trust was established by Sir Dorabji Tata in April 1932 in memory of his wife, Lady Meherbai, who was struck with leukaemia in 1930 at the age of 50, and succumbed to the disease a year later in Wales, and passed away on 18th June 1931.

    The Trust offers one-fifth of its income to scholars doing scientific investigations in Indian Universities and Institutes into diseases of the blood, with special references to leukaemia, and for scientific research towards alleviation of human suffering from disease.

20. (a) Jawaharlal Nehru Award for International Understanding was founded in 1965. It is administered by the Indian Council for Cultural Relations (ICCR) to people "for their outstanding contribution to the promotion of international understanding, goodwill and friendship among people of the world". The money constituent of this award is 2.5 million rupees.

21. (d) Neither of the given statements are correct.

22. (b) The Nobel prize except the Economics first awarded in 1901.

23. (d)

    The Miss World pageant is the oldest surviving major international beauty pageant. It was created in the United Kingdom by Eric Morley in 1951. Since his death in 2000, Morley's wife, Julia Morley, co-chairs the pageant.

    Miss Universe is an annual international beauty contest that is run by the Miss Universe Organization. The contest was founded in 1952 by the California clothing company Pacific Mills. The pageant became part of Kayser-Roth, and then Gulf Western Industries, before being acquired by Donald Trump in 1996.

24. (a) Laureates Awards is associated with aerospace, aviation and defense arenes and Laureus awards is associated with sports.

25. (d)

26. (b) The government of India laurelled the International Gandhi peace prize in 1995. This is an annual award given to individuals and institutions for their contributions towards social, economic and political transformation through non-violence and other Gandhian methods. The award carries ` 10 million in cash, convertible in any currency in the world, a plaque and a citation. It is open to all persons regardless of nationality, race, creed or sex.

27. (d)

28. (d) International Childrens - Kids Rights Foundation - peace prize. The Kids Rights Foundation is an international children's aid and advocacy organisation based in Amsterdam, the Netherlands. Founded in 2003, Kids Rights raises funds for independent local aid projects in a number of countries around the world, including Zimbabwe, Ukraine and Haiti. The organisation's mission is to support and empower vulnerable children around the world, by raising funds for small-scale local projects, and by raising awareness for children's rights through the international media.

    Man Booker International Prize — Authors. The Man Booker International Prize is an international literary award given every two years to a living author of any nationality for a body of work published in English or generally available in English translation. The introduction of the International Prize was announced in June 2004. The award, sponsored by the Man Group, complements the Man Booker Prize and rewards an author's "continued creativity, development and overall contribution to fiction on the world stage."

    Pritzker Award — Architecture. The Pritzker Architecture Prize is awarded annually to "honour a living architect whose built work demonstrates a combination of those qualities of talent, vision and commitment, which has produced consistent and significant contributions to humanity and the built environment through the art of architecture."

    Abel prize — Mathematics. The Abel Prize is an international prize presented by the King of Norway to one or more outstanding mathematicians. Named after Norwegian mathematician Niels Henrik Abel (1802–1829), the award was established in 2001 by the Government of Norway and complements the Holberg Prize in the humanities, social sciences, law and theology. The Abel Prize has often been described as the "mathematician's Nobel prize". It comes with a monetary award of 6 million Norwegian kroner (NOK) (approximately US$1 million), to be used to fund future research.

29. (c)

30. (a) The Pulitzer Prize is an award for achievements in newspaper and online journalism, literature, and musical composition in the United States. It was established in 1917 by provisions in the will of American (Hungarian-born) publisher Joseph Pulitzer, and is administered by Columbia University in New York City. Prizes are awarded yearly in twenty-one categories. In twenty of the categories, each winner receives a certificate and a US$15,000 (raised from $10,000 in 2017) cash award. The winner in the public service category of the journalism competition is awarded a gold medal.

31. (a) Award winners are eligible to use the Golden Peacock Awards Logo on all promotional literatures.

32. (c) Ten writers are on the judges' list of finalists under serious consideration for the sixth Man Booker International Prize, the £60,000 award which recognises one writer for his or her achievement in fiction.

33. (a) In Oslo the Nobel Peace Prize is presented by the Chairman of the Norwegian Nobel Committee in the presence of Their Majesties the King and Queen of Norway, the Government, Storting representatives and an invited audience.

34. (a) Arjuna Award was introduced in 1961

35. (a) Padma Vibhushan is awarded to recognize exceptional and distinguished service to the nation in any field, including government service. It is awarded to recognize distinguished service of a high order to the nation in any field while Padma Shri is awarded to citizens of India to recognize their distinguished contribution in various spheres of activities including the Arts, Education, Industry, Literature, Science, Sports, Medicine, Social Service and Public Affairs.

36. (c) Arjuna Awards was instituted in 1961, Drona Charya award was instituted in 1985 while Rajiv Gandhi Khel Ratna award was commenced in the year 1991–92 and Dhyan chand award was initiated in 2002.

37. (a) Saraswati Samman is meant for outstanding literary work in any Indian language. Kabir Award is given for promotion of communal harmony. Arjuna Award is meant for sports and Bhatnagar Award is conferred in the field of Science.

38. (a) Jnanpith award is a literary award in India. The Saraswati Samman is also a literary award for outstanding prose or poetry literary works in any Indian language. Vachaspati Samman is given in Sanskrit literature while Shankar award is for Indian Philosophy.

39. (a) The Param Vir Chakra is India's highest military decoration award. The Maha Vir Chakra is the second highest military decoration while veer chakra is third in precedence in the war time gallantry awards.

40. (b) Grammy Award — Music. A Grammy Award (originally called Gramophone Award) – or Grammy – is an accolade by the National Academy of Recording Arts and Sciences of the United States to recognize outstanding achievement in the music industry. The first Grammy Awards ceremony was held on May 4, 1959 to honour the musical accomplishments by performers for the year 1958. Following the 2011 ceremony, NARAS overhauled many Grammy Award categories for 2012. The 56th Grammy Awards were held on January 26, 2014, at the Staples Center in Los Angeles, California.

Ramon Magsaysay Award — International understanding. The Ramon Magsaysay Award is an annual award established to perpetuate former Philippine President Ramon Magsaysay's example of integrity in government, courageous service to the people, and pragmatic idealism within a democratic society. The Ramon Magsaysay Award is often considered to be Asia's Nobel Prize. The prize was established in April 1957 by the trustees of the Rockefeller Brothers Fund based in New York City with the concurrence of the Philippine government.

Pulitzer Award — Journalism.

Borlaug Award — Agriculture.